THE REFLECTIVE TURN

Case Studies In and On Educational Practice

D0169049

THE REFLECTIVE TURN

Case Studies In and On Educational Practice

Edited by
Donald A. Schön

TEACHERS COLLEGE PRESS

Teachers College, Columbia University
New York and London

Published by Teachers College Press, 1234 Amsterdam Avenue
New York, NY 10027

Library of Congress Cataloging-in-Publication Data
The Reflective turn: case studies in and on educational practice /
  edited by Donald A. Schön.
       p.   cm.
    Includes bibliographical references and index.
    ISBN 0-8077-3046-7 (alk. paper).—ISBN 0-8077-3045-9 (alk. paper
: pbk.)
    1. Teaching—Case studies.   2. Self-knowledge, Theory of—Case
studies.   I. Schön, Donald. A.
    LB1025.2.R443   1991
    371.1'02—dc20   90-42909

ISBN 0-8077-3046-7
ISBN 0-8077-3045-9 (pbk.)

Printed on acid-free paper
Manufactured in the United States of America
98 97 96 95 94 93 92 91   8 7 6 5 4 3 2 1

Contents

THE REFLECTIVE TURN

Case Studies In and On Educational Practice

Introduction

DONALD A. SCHÖN

A COUPLE OF YEARS AGO, the sudden popularity in educational circles of the terms *reflection* and *reflective practice,* some of it induced by my own recent work (Schön, 1983, 1987), led me to think that it would be a good idea to produce a book of examples of reflection in and on practice—cases that would illustrate a variety of theoretical frameworks and methods for doing this sort of research, suggest the kinds of issues critical to it, and provide opportunities to explore what it means to do it well.

I invited a group of people who seemed to me well equipped to produce good studies of practice, representing a variety of theoretical persuasions, methodological approaches, and points of view, to join in the work of preparing this book. Seventeen people answered my call. Over the last year they have prepared and revised their cases, and most of them were able to join in a 3-day workshop to discuss and criticize one another's work. I will draw on some of these discussions in my concluding comments.

THE AUTHORS AND THEIR CASES

The 14 cases in this book can be grouped in several ways, according to the practice settings chosen by the authors; their ways of defining and bounding what they consider as "practice"; the intellectual and practical issues of greatest concern to them; their choice of units for observation, description, and analysis; and the particular sense in which their work constitutes a case study.

In so far as one type of practice setting predominates among these cases, it is the school. The studies by Bamberger, Erickson and MacKinnon, Clandinin and Connelly, Newberg, and Russell and Munby all have to do with primary or secondary schools. The other authors concern themselves with a wide variety of occupations and institutions. Parlett studies counselors to hearing-impaired children in the United Kingdom; Mattingly, occupational therapists in a teaching hospital in Boston. Baum's case has to do with a planner in a public agency; Forester explores a city planner's interaction with real estate developers and city officials. Hirschhorn writes about managers and professional staff in a not-for-profit organization; Greenwood studies managers and workers at Fagor, a large industrial cooperative group in Mondragón in the Basque region of Spain. Lanzara's study is about the development of a new educational computing system at MIT. Putnam describes his long-term tutorial relationship with an organizational development consultant in an industrial firm. Bar-On reflects on his interviews with children of Nazi perpetrators of crimes during the Third Reich.

Across these very diverse practice settings, the cases reveal different conceptions of a practice as an object of study and different ways of setting the terms of reference for a "case." These differences are rooted in the researchers' backgrounds, interests, and purposes. For example, Davydd Greenwood, Cheryl Mattingly, and Malcolm Parlett share an ethnographic orientation to social research. Mattingly's study of occupational therapists in a teaching hospital, Parlett's study of counselors in the British system of services to the hearing-impaired, and Greenwood's study of workers and managers at Fagor all deal with groups of individuals and seek to discover the common challenges and predicaments they face and the various understandings, strategies, and feelings that inform their responses. Mattingly's and Parlett's studies reveal a great deal about *professions*, of occupational therapist and counselor to the hearing-impaired, respectively, and suggest how these professions are shaped and constrained by their institutional settings. Similarly, Greenwood's study considers the practice of managers and workers in terms of the evolving culture of the cooperative.

Dan Bar-On, a psychotherapist and social psychologist, probes deeply into practice in the broadest sense of the term: the practice of living. His subjects are adults who share versions of a common cultural-political-family predicament and who try, ambiguously and falteringly, to come to terms with it.

The several researchers who deal with schools have chosen different ways of "cutting"—that is, selecting, bounding, and grouping—the practice of teachers, children, or administrators, and their "cuts" makes sense in the light of their different concerns with families of practice issues.

The case written by Gaalen Erickson and Allan MacKinnon, science educators, draws on a 5-year collaboration with three high school science teachers. It focuses on a lesson about batteries and bulbs taught by one of these teachers, Colin, to three students, and Colin's dialogue about the lesson with Rosie, an apprentice teacher. Jeanne Bamberger, a musician, cognitive psychologist, and educator, draws on her 4-year collaboration with teachers at the Graham and Parks elementary school in Cambridge, Massachusetts, where she and they have developed the Laboratory for Making Things—an environment in which teachers and children work with objects, such as gears, blocks, and mobiles, and write computer programs in the LOGO language. Moving back and forth between material objects and the computer, between "hand knowledge" and "symbolic knowledge," children "build structures that work and make sense." Bamberger's case explores a dialogue with a group of teachers who are doing and reflecting on experiments like the ones the kids carry out in the Laboratory. In both of these cases, the authors focus on how kids or teachers actually tackle substantive problems and try to make sense of them, and how someone (Colin, in the first case; Bamberger, in the second) helps them to reflect on their evolving substantive understandings.

In the cases prepared by Tom Russell and Hugh Munby, educators concerned mainly with teacher education, and by Jean Clandinin and Michael Connelly, educational philosophers, the focus is on individual practitioners—two teachers, in the first case; a school principal, in the second—whose behavior in a classroom or school occupies center stage over a relatively long period of time. Russell and Munby are interested in how teachers may come to see their teaching in new ways, to "reframe it," over time. Their study resembles Robert Putnam's, which focuses on a single organizational development consultant, Paul, who works with Putnam over several years in order to improve his ability to live out a "Model II" approach to consulting practice. Clandinin and Connelly are mainly interested in how Phil, a school principal at the Bay Street School in Toronto, attempts to realize his image of a community school. Their work with Phil is part of an 8-year study at Bay Street in which they have worked with teachers to construct mutual accounts of ways in which teachers know their practice. They trace the experiential roots of Phil's knowing-in-practice to his earlier experiences, as child and adult, in community and school. Their case resembles Howell Baum's study of a planner in a public agency, an attempt on Baum's part to trace the inner development of an organizational career.

John Forester—like Baum, a professor of planning—also deals with a city planner, but he focuses on a single event: the planner's meeting with a developer, the developer's architect, and city officials to discuss the future of a proposed real estate project. Forester tries, by examining what the planner does in this episode, to discover what his "work" consists of and what kinds of knowledge he calls upon in order to play his role effectively.

Norman Newberg, an educator with a background in sociotechnical systems theory, takes as his starting point the massive dropout rates that afflict public schools in Philadelphia. His unit of study is a "feeder subsystem" in one school district, and he describes a multiyear project in which he worked with teachers, parents, and administrators to diagnose and address the causes of the dropout problem.

Giovan Francesco Lanzara, finally, chooses as his unit of analysis a "self-study" in which he worked over a period of years with Bamberger, her computer programmer, and other members of the MIT music section to trace the development and attempted dissemination of Music LOGO, a computer environment for conducting and reflecting on experiments in musical understanding. Lanzara, a systems analyst and social reseacher, concentrates on the philosophical predicament of an inquirer who seeks, in the face of his own and participants' multiple, shifting stories, to tell the truth about what happened.

These several ways of bounding practice are closely linked to the different issues and theoretical frameworks with which the case writers are mainly concerned. The writers give privileged status to different kinds of phenomena and favor different theories. In their cases, they do not put their theoretical frameworks to the test; they use them, rather, to generate more specific, local hypotheses. In Hirschhorn's case, for example, the framework is an "object relations" variant of psychoanalytic theory. In Baum's, it is Erik Erikson's developmental theory of personal identity. For Bar-On, a critical idea is that of "working-through"—in his case, the ways in which his interviewees struggle with working through the threatening, sometimes horrifying, experiences of their early years. Greenwood centers on the idea of culture, and more specifically, the relationships among such key notions as democracy, equality, and participation in the culture of the industrial cooperatives of Mondragón. Newberg brings a version of systems theory to his participatory action research in the schools. Mattingly, and Clandinin and Connelly, work from versions of contemporary theories of narrative, narrative reasoning, and hermeneutic analysis.

Each case illustrates a close connection between the authors' chosen theoretical frameworks, the kinds of phenomena and knowledge they treat as privileged—the things and relations they take as centrally important to reflect *on*—and the modes of reflective activity they adopt. These clusterings of theory, phenomena, and reflective activity help to set the conditions that determine in each case what it means to do a good study of practice.

THE REFLECTIVE TURN

The differences outlined above are substantial—substantial enough, perhaps, to make the reader ask why I think these cases belong in the same book.

My answer is that in spite of the authors' very different theoretical frameworks and definitions of practice, they share a critically important perspective: They have taken a reflective turn. Paraphrasing Jeanne Bamberger and Eleanor Duckworth (Bamberger & Duckworth, 1982), I can say that they all attempt to "give practitioners reason": In different ways and to varying degrees, they observe, describe, and try to illuminate the things practitioners actually say and do, by exploring the understandings revealed by the patterns of spontaneous activity that make up their practice. Whenever these patterns appear strange or puzzling, the authors assume that there is an underlying *sense* to be discovered and that it is their business as researchers to discover it. As a consequence, they are sometimes led to reflect on their own understandings of their subjects' understandings; in order to discover the sense in someone else's practice, they question their own.

What the authors of these cases do *not* do is to regard practice mainly as a field of applications. They do not try to subsume practitioners' decisions under a research-based theory or model—decision theory or microeconomics, for example. When they bring an explicit theoretical framework to their studies, they use it to guide observation, description, or analysis of what practitioners already know or how they already learn in the context of their own practice.

The reflective turn is, as I put it in *Educating the Reflective Practitioner* (1987), a kind of revolution. It turns on its head the problem of constructing an epistemology of practice. It offers, as a first-order answer to the question, What do practitioners need to know?, reflection on the understandings already built into the skillful actions of everyday practice. Even when the author wants to help practitioners acquire a new set of skills or insights—helping teachers learn to work in new ways with kids, computers, and materials, in Jeanne Bamberger's case; or, in Robert Putnam's, helping an organizational development professional learn to use a Model II theory of action—his or her primary concern is to discover and help practitioners discover what they already understand and know how to do.

It is important to emphasize, on the other hand, that just as the authors of our cases take different cuts at practice and adopt different boundaries and units of analysis, depending on the issues with which they are mainly concerned, so they also differ in the kinds of reflective activity through which they give people reason. There is nothing in the reflective turn that requires a uniform approach to reflection; on the contrary, researchers who have taken the reflective turn are likely to feel an obligation to give *one another* reason. As one of the authors of these studies put it, "Our discussions did not try to reduce one [person's] perspective to another's. . . . We could understand each other, criticize and improve each other's work, and yet we could go our own ways."

Perhaps the major difference among the studies, in this respect, is in the degree to which the researchers distance themselves from their subjects, sticking to the role of observer or interviewer, or, on the contrary, try to engage their subjects as collaborative inquirers. On this continuum, we can organize our cases into three groups. Forester, Baum, and Parlett are clearly at the first pole; Newberg, Greenwood, Putnam, Bamberger, Mattingly, Lanzara, Clandinin and Connelly, and Erickson and MacKinnon are clearly at the second; and Bar-On, Russell and Munby, and Hirschhorn fall somewhere in between the two.

Researchers in the first group treat practitioners as subjects, in keeping with prevailing traditions of social research. Nevertheless, through interviews or observation, they try to discover the intelligence that guides what their subjects actually say and do. Their bias is clearly toward a belief that patterns of practice would make sense if one could only discover that sense. Forester's close observation of the city planner's nonverbal behavior leads him, for example, to formulate a view of the planner's anticipatory intelligence. Baum's interviews with a planner in a public agency lead him first to puzzle over the planner's paradoxical organizational career and then to propose a novel solution: He suggests that the planner really lives out two practices, a manifest practice of professional work in the agency and a hidden practice consisting in the work of personal development through which the planner first builds confidence in his professional identity and only then takes advantage of an opportunity to join the organization's inner club. Parlett's interviews with counselors to hearing-impaired children center on the sources of the counselors' advice and on the stereotypes that implicitly shape their judgments. The sense Parlett attributes to his counselors provokes on his part a criticism of their injustice toward children they have labeled as abnormal.

At the other pole of the continuum, researchers give reason to participants not only by inquiring into the understandings implicit in their everyday behavior but also by involving them as co-researchers. But they do this in very different ways. Newberg and Greenwood carry out versions of participatory action research. Newberg's project is a sustained exploration of the dropout problem, in which he helps participants acquire a systems view of that problem and involves teachers, parents, kids, and administrators from many different locations in the "feeder subsystem" in a series of boundary-crossing explorations. Newberg wants them to shift from blaming to understanding one another; he wants them to discover how the problem actually looks to individuals elsewhere in the system. More fundamentally, he wants "the system" to take cognizance of itself.

Greenwood begins at Fagor with the aim of educating a group of personnel managers in the methods of anthropological fieldwork, taking their own institution as the field site. Following David Penney (1984), Greenwood believes that "every literate person can do good fieldwork," sometimes more sophisticated than that of professional anthropologists. He leads his group through a survey of workers' beliefs and attitudes, and then a series of roundtable discussions with them, focusing on the topics of equality, democracy, and participation—all central to the founding ideology of Mondragón. As the investigators come closer to workers' actual thinking, their initial diagnosis of "member apathy" gives way to an emphasis on the dynamic pluralism inherent in the Mondragón culture.

Mattingly, who begins her study of occupational therapists with an ethnographic study of the practice setting, soon involves her subjects in collective discussions of videotapes of their work with patients—engaging them in reflection on the strategies and understandings built into their practice. The "engine" of her study is not a presenting organizational problem—such as the school dropout rate or apathy among the members of the cooperative—but the therapists' growing enthusiasm as they explore how they live out certain key stories with their patients, how they draw on repertoires of know-how, how they occasionally get stuck and, in order to extricate themselves, make on-line revisions of their guiding stories.

Clandinin and Connelly, as participant-observers at the Bay Street School, join Phil in his work and in constructing interpretations of the stories he lives out as he tries to build a community school. As they give these interpretations back to Phil, they help him see how his present stories are relivings of stories of his earlier experiences. Reflecting on missed opportunities for other possible retellings, Clandinin and Connelly illustrate how stories of practice are never finally closed by the conclusion of a case study.

Lanzara, acting at first as participant-observer, adopts a strategy unusual among social researchers: He writes accounts of events he takes to be critical and then iteratively submits these to participants, listens to their "backtalk," revises the stories and resubmits them. It is through this form of collaboration with his subjects that he becomes a historiographer of stories that shift over time and discovers the central theme of his research: the predicament inherent in the effort to achieve valid historical knowledge.

In Erickson and MacKinnon's case study, Colin, the experienced science teacher, joins Rosie, an apprentice teacher, in observing and discussing videotapes of classes each of them has taught. The authors analyze what they describe as Colin's "reflective teaching," as they observe him trying to get in touch with and influence his students' evolving understandings of batteries-and-bulbs experiments. They present a dialogue in which Colin tries to help Rosie see and reflect on the differences between his way of teaching and hers. Bamberger, in her case, leads a group of teachers through an inquiry into the meanings they are giving to objects and relations in LOGO programming, generating a process of "conceptual chaining" through which the participants move from the LOGO materials to more general ideas, such as "rotation and revolution" and the meaning of a "variable." In her work with the teachers, a Hall of Mirrors develops in which the teachers' reflection on their own substantive learning, and their experience of her efforts to help them pursue it, become a prototype for the inquiries they will carry out with their students in the Laboratory for Making Things.

It is worth noting that these variants of collaborative reflection on practice are profoundly *educative* in intent, and sometimes in outcome, whether or not they have to do with schools; and that, in order to become effective at this sort of research, as Kurt Lewin pointed out long ago, researchers must become educators—practitioners who reflect in and on their own inquiry and draw on their reflections to design educational experiences for others.

Another group of studies falls between the polar extremes described above. Russell and Munby involve themselves in joint reflection with the two teachers described in their case, as they explore how each of these has begun to reframe teaching practice. Bar-On, who began his study of children of Nazi perpetrators in the role of a distanced social researcher, moves steadily toward a position somewhere between the clinical stance of a psychotherapist and the empathic stance of an engaged human being who gradually becomes aware that "under some circumstances most of us can become mass-murderers."

And Hirschhorn, who treats organizational consulting as a method of research, writes about a consulting project in an organization where he makes on-line diagnoses of the dynamics of relationships between boss and subordinates, and intervenes on the basis of his diagnoses—in some measure involving his clients in considering and testing the theories he has constructed.

CENTRAL THEMES

The reflective turn is consequential. It makes research into a reflective practice in its own right, posing a set of questions—in some instances, dilemmas—that researchers avoid at their own peril. Among these questions are the following:

1. What is it appropriate to reflect *on*? All contexts of practice are complex, "full" in the sense of being overwhelmingly rich in data. There is no end of things and relations to which one might pay attention, no end of patterns and possibilities one might bring to the practitioner's attention. How should the researcher choose a strategy of attention? What kinds of phenomena, what levels of phenomena, determine the legitimate scope of study? When is it appropriate to say that one has included too much, or has not studied fully enough? How should one choose units of description and analysis? Under what circumstances, and by what criteria, for example, does it make sense to study a 20-minute episode of interaction, or an individual's 15-year life in an organization? An individual's thought and action, a group's evolution, an organizational system, the "culture" shared by a family of organizations?

2. What is an appropriate *way* of observing and reflecting on practice? In what sort of activity does reflection consist—or ought it to consist? These are questions that pertain both to media and to strategies of representation and description. Do we "reflect," for example, only when we talk about things we say and do, or may gesture, drawing, artifact, or action itself constitute a reflection on action? How ought we to represent, in words or other symbols, our discoveries about practice and practice knowledge? By telling stories—and, if so, what kinds of stories? By means of procedural descriptions? Explanatory models? The construction of "theories" implicit in patterns of action? And, on the assumption that different strategies of representation may be appropriate for different purposes, how shall we assess the consequences of

our choices? Are some modes of description better suited than others to particular objectives?

3. When we have taken the reflective turn, what constitutes *appropriate rigor?* To observe and study practice, in order to discover the understandings already embedded in it, is to forgo a particular conception of rigorous research—the kind of rigor inherent in technical rationality, that is, the view of professional knowledge as practical, instrumental knowledge made rigorous through the application of science-based theory. As I have argued elsewhere (Schön, 1983), the choice of technical rationality as an exclusive epistemology of practice leads to a dilemma of rigor or relevance: It forces us to choose between the "rigor" contained in technically rational analysis of relatively unimportant problems—say, the application of operations research models to the design of an inventory control system—and the "relevance" of inquiry into messy problematic situations of manifest inportance where, however, we are unable to be rigorous in our studies in any way we know how to define. When we take the reflective turn, we avoid this dilemma because we do not give priority to technical rationality as a privileged source of rigorous knowledge. On the other hand, we take on an obligation to make clear what we mean by rigor appropriate to the reflective study of practice. When we fail to take this obligation seriously, "reflection" becomes an *open sesame* to woolly-headedness, a never-never land where anything goes.

Appropriate rigor in the reflective study of practice has to do with two closely coupled criteria: validity and utility. First of all, what shall we take as evidence for the truth of our assertions? How do we know what we claim to know? On the basis of what sorts of data, for example, would we be prepared to give up or revise our claims to truth? How much evidence, of what kinds, will be "enough" for us? Is it enough to tell a plausible story that accounts for the data we have chosen to provide, or ought we also to consider other plausible stories, thereby generating a requirement for discrimination among alternates, revision, or synthesis of our stories? In any case, however, "truth" is not enough. The reflective turn carries with it an intention to make the study of practice useful to practitioners: We intend them to learn, directly or indirectly, from our studies of or with them. What, then, counts as a "useful" study of practice? What are the tests of utility? And what follows from a commitment to make our studies more or less immediately useful to practitioners—that is, to help practitioners learn in the present from our research rather than see ourselves as contributing to a gradually accumulating body of knowledge from which, eventually, they may be able to derive useful applications? And how are the distinct demands of validity and utility interrelated? How should we think differently about appropriately rigorous testing of our claims to truth *because* we also aim at the production of immediately useful knowledge?

4. Finally, what does the reflective turn imply for the researcher's *stance* toward his enterprise—toward his "subjects," his research activity, and himself? This is a matter of ethics as well as attitude, method, and epistemology. In what sense, for example, should the researcher "give reason" to the practitioner he or she studies? Does giving reason stop with the attempt to discover how the practitioner's patterns of action make sense and reveal tacit understandings, or should the researcher treat the practitioner as a researcher in his own right, an actual or potential collaborator in the process of reflection on practice? And depending on this choice, what follows for the practice of research? To what extent and in what ways does a collaborative stance commit the reseacher to make herself vulnerable to reflection on her own practice as a reseacher? In what ways may it affect her pursuit of meaning, truth, and utility? How may the rules of the game and the demands on research artistry shift when the researcher becomes, in Geoffrey Vickers's (1980) terms, an agent-experient rather than a spectator-manipulator? How much of the researcher's subjectivity should enter into the researcher's conduct of research and account of research results? To oversimplify it, to what extent should the researcher adopt the "objective" voice of a distanced, neutral spectator, or to what extent should she speak in the first person and describe her research and its results in terms of her own experience? And what are the different ethical demands placed on the researcher as a result of such a choice of role and stance? What kinds of promises—of confidentiality, confrontability, accountability, for example—should she make and try to keep?

These questions are central, in greater or lesser degree, to all of the authors of the cases presented in this book. They are also the main themes around which the book is organized. The cases suggest different ways of posing these questions and different ways of answering them; they should be read with these questions in mind.

The book is divided into seven parts, each consisting of two cases, according to the following topics:

I. Exploring Children's and Teachers' Understandings
   Erickson and MacKinnon, Bamberger

REFERENCES

Bamberger, J., & Duckworth, E., with J. Gray & M. Lampert. (1982). *Analysis of data from an experiment in teacher development.* Mimeo, Massachusetts Institute of Technology, Cambridge, MA.

Penney, D. (1984). *Hints for research workers in the social sciences.* Ithaca, NY: Center for International Studies.

Schön, D. (1983). *The reflective practitioner: How professionals think in action.* NY: Basic Books.

Schön, D. (1987). *Educating the reflective practitioner: Toward a new design for teaching and learning in the professions.* San Francisco: Jossey-Bass.

Vickers, G. (1980). *Responsibility—Its sources and limits.* Seaside, CA: Intersystems, Systems Inquiry Series.

Part I

EXPLORING CHILDREN'S AND TEACHERS' UNDERSTANDINGS

1

Seeing Classrooms in New Ways: On Becoming a Science Teacher

GAALEN L. ERICKSON and
ALLAN M. MacKINNON

THE PURPOSE OF THIS CHAPTER is to discuss a number of issues that we think are central to the problem of nurturing and enhancing professional growth in the practice of teaching. We approach this problem by using a specific example of an experienced teacher working with a novice teacher in a practicum setting. The experienced teacher is one member of a group of classroom teachers and university personnel who have created a collaborative research team for the purpose of developing a systematic approach for teaching science using a "constructivist perspective" (Driver & Oldham, 1986; White, 1988). Although our work has been limited to science teaching, we think that the methods we have employed and the findings we have reported from this project may also be applicable to learning the underlying knowledge and dispositions that lead to competent performance in many areas of professional practice.

As a backdrop to our case story, we begin our discussion by looking at the practical and theoretical contexts of our research program. The subsequent case material that we present is taken almost exclusively from a single supervisory conference. The primary purpose of this conference was to discuss a set of teaching moves used by the experienced teacher to find out more about the thinking of a small group of students working on a laboratory exercise. The case is framed around the problems associated with introducing a novice teacher to thinking about and acting in classroom situations in ways that are often very different from those exemplified by her previous classroom experiences, which were primarily as a student. Briefly stated, this alternative way of *seeing* class-rooms follows from a perspective that portrays learners as being pur-poseful sense-makers—constantly engaged in the task of *constructing* ideas to make sense out of the situations they encounter.

The analysis of the case material yields a number of conjectures con-cerning the role played by an experienced teacher both in modeling par-ticular teaching moves and in explaining these to a novice teacher. In analyzing these moves, we propose a number of pedagogical principles. This case is oriented around two overarching questions: What is the nature of a constructivist approach to science teaching? How can we best communicate that approach to a novice science teacher?

CONTEXT AND RATIONALE OF THE RESEARCH PROGRAM

The material for this chapter comes from a collaborative project in-volving university educators and classroom science teachers. This re-search team has been working to develop teaching strategies and ma-terials that address the critical role played by the knowledge that students have already constructed prior to entering the classroom. (See Erickson, 1986, 1988, for an extended description of this project.) This constructivist perspective has gained increasing acceptance in the re-search literature on the teaching of subject-matter knowledge, particu-larly in science and mathematics.

The early work of this project was aimed at translating this general perspective on learning into a set of practical activities for classroom use. At the outset we were faced with two problems. First, much of the literature on the nature of students' intuitive knowledge is based on clinical interviews and hence has limited direct application to the con-text of a classroom. Second, the theoretical frames and analytic schemes used to structure and represent students' knowledge vary widely (Driver & Erickson, 1983; Driver, Tiberghien, & Guesne, 1985; West & Pines, 1985). The task of our group was to try to distill from this diverse literature a general orienting frame that would help teachers develop a functional repertoire of materials and strategies for working in class-rooms with 30–35 students. A further consideration in the development of this frame was the need to generate a type of "working language" that would enable us not only to interpret and analyze the characteristic features we associate with constructivist science teaching, but also would permit us to communicate that understanding to others. This chapter, then, represents one such endeavor.

Constructing a Frame for Analyzing Practice

After numerous meetings and discussions over a period of a year, an orienting frame for analyzing practice gradually emerged. The origins of this frame can be traced back to our many deliberations about the practical classroom problems encountered by the teachers in our project group. As the year progressed, these problems became framed more frequently in terms of the insights and language drawn from selected articles that were read by the group members. These articles represented two distinct bodies of literature. The first group of articles on constructivist approaches outlined the nature of students' intuitions about science concepts and the pedagogical implications of this approach (e.g., Driver et al., 1985). A second group of articles focused on the nature and growth of professional knowledge, most notably Schön (1983,1987) and Shulman (1987).

Our work with other teachers has centered on two identifiable groups—experienced science teachers currently in the field and novice teachers in preservice preparation programs. We have found the preservice preparation program (in particular the practicum) especially productive, and it is our work in this latter setting that forms the basis for the case material presented below.

In summary, then, our project is committed to the development and translation of a particular perspective on teaching. We think this perspective will contribute to a better appreciation of the nature of student learning in the design and delivery of instruction. A second aim in our work is to encourage teachers to become more reflective about their practice. We argue that both of these outcomes will lead to an improvement in science teaching, since they respect the personal and intellectual integrity of both students and teachers as *learners* in search of understanding. Further elaboration of our conceptual and empirical work can be found in a series of project papers (Erickson, 1987, 1988; Gurney, 1988; Kuhn & Aguirre, 1987; MacKinnon, 1987, 1988; Sieben, 1987).

Communicating the Frame to Teachers

As many commentators have acknowledged, the task of communicating characteristic features of a complex practice is neither easy nor straightforward. The stance we have adopted is that we should endeavor to reconstruct practice settings so as to optimize the possibilities for teachers "to see" that practice situation from the interpretive frame we are trying to communicate. This notion of "seeing" is taken from a philosophical literature often traced to Wittgenstein's (1953/1963) writings on ordinary language analysis and subsequently elaborated upon by writers such as Goodman (1978, 1984), Kuhn (1970), and Schön (1983). In this literature, seeing and perceiving are viewed as cognitively intertwined: They argue that "seeing" is largely determined by the inteptretive, cognitive frame available to us. The interesting and significant pedagogical question then becomes: How do we go about constructing new, conceptual frames that will allow us to see the world in different ways?

We have found some of the strategies and models outlined by Schön (1987) for bringing about this sort of conceptual change to be fruitful. Specifically, his insights concerning the role of modeling in learning a new interpretive frame and his analysis of the structure of modeling in terms of the two complementary processes of "telling" and "showing" have served as the basis for much of our work with preservice teachers. The case study that follows is an example of how one of the teachers in the project attempted to provide a reconstruction of some classroom events for the purpose of both "telling" and "showing" a student teacher how one might begin "to see" a typical classroom task from the point of view of a constructivist teacher. We argue that it requires many such encounters—or "reflective conversations," as Schön might call them—before one becomes adept at "seeing" *and* acting on the basis of those perceptions.

The Practicum as a Forum of Practical Knowledge

Given that one of the primary concerns of our project is the construction (or reconstruction) of practical knowledge in an action setting, we have focused much of our attention in the preservice program around the practicum setting. We have found this to be a useful strategy for several reasons. First, we think that much of the kind of knowledge we wish to convey to novices can most effectively be communicated by the mutually interactive processes of "showing and telling" the novice teacher the sorts of teaching moves we think are useful in becoming a competent practitioner. A second, and somewhat unexpected reason, is that the experienced teachers in our group actually found it easier to unpack their own knowledge and understanding in the context of working with a novice teacher. This situation often required them to make explicit both the procedures and actions that they engaged in (which were often routine and tacit in nature) as well as the rationale for doing them. This act of making one's knowledge explicit and providing reasons for one's behavior rarely occurs in the normal activities and routines engaged in by a teacher.

THE CASE STUDY

The tenth-grade class, which provides the general setting for this case, consisted of 27 students studying the topic of static electricity and electric current. The unit was jointly introduced by Rosie, the student teacher, and her supervising teacher, Colin. Rosie, who had just completed her first week in this practicum, was enrolled in a post-degree teacher education program. At 26 years of age, she had completed a bachelor of engineering science degree and had worked as an engineer for 2 years prior to entering the program. Colin was an 18-year veteran of physics teaching, well known and respected among his colleagues in the province for producing excellent physics students. He holds a master of arts degree in science education and has been involved with our project since its inception.

During the first 3 weeks of the unit, the focus was on static electricity. The unit included activities relating to the following topics: various historical models of the atom and how they explain static charge, charge by conduction, the electrostatic series, factors determining the size and direction of forces between charged objects, and charge by induction. The latter half of the unit dealt with electric current, the topic area of the lesson we will examine in more detail.

The Principles of Constructivist Teaching

In the first 3 weeks Colin worked closely with Rosie, assisting her in the planning of lessons and explicitly modeling a number of features that he felt characterized good science instruction. During this time Colin identified several aspects of Rosie's teaching performance that became a subject of discussion during their daily supervisory conferences. One such aspect was the classic problem that is evident in the performance of most novice teachers: "extended teacher elaboration." Early in their teaching experience novices often feel more secure and in control of the class by doing most of the talking during the lesson. Colin framed this particular issue in terms of a principle that he articulated as "giving over more responsibility for learning to the students." An example of how he introduced this principle to Rosie is contained in the following dialogue, taken from a supervisory conference in which they were jointly viewing a videotape of one of Rosie's lessons.

COLIN: One of the things that I've noticed is that you take on a lot of the responsibility for what is happening in the class. And by that I mean, you see it as your role to always explain things.
ROSIE: To make sure they have their thoughts straight.

Later in the dialogue, after examining more of the video of Rosie's teaching, Colin returns to this topic.

COLIN: You're doing a lot of the explaining. Do you see what I mean?
ROSIE: Well, isn't that what teachers do? Like, that's a part of it, isn't it?
COLIN: Well, I think that your explanations are good. But the way I see it, the objective here is to gradually, as much as possible, give over the responsibility for learning to the kids. And they will. . . . I think they're quite willing to take that on, but they have to learn what you mean by that. But if you're always seen in the explaining role, well, that's the role that you will be cast in.

In this particular exchange Colin used a "telling" move to alert Rosie to an issue that they would work on together. During the next several weeks of the practicum, Colin shifted over more to a series of "showing" moves, modeling for Rosie, in a variety of lesson contexts, how a teacher might relinquish some of the usual control mechanisms found in classroom organization and hence give more responsibility to the students for their own learning.

Once Rosie seemed a bit more comfortable with this notion of giving more responsibility to the students, Colin moved to a second principle of the teaching perspective he was attempting to communicate. Colin phrased this principle in terms of the importance of "validating student's ideas." This second principle could be considered as more basic than the first, since it would appear to be an important, if not necessary, condition for achieving the ideal of increased student responsibility.

In the dialogue below, Colin was attempting to communicate to Rosie an example of how he tries to validate student thinking in his class. This discussion occurred while they were viewing a videotape of Colin reviewing with the class several previous lessons on the phenomena of charging an object by conduction and induction. He selected an instance in which the student's response to his question was certainly different from what he had expected—and no doubt would be considered by many to be simply "wrong."

COLIN: Now, can I tell you what was going through my mind here now? There are, in my view, there are two ways to looking at a student response. One is to say, "Well what is wrong with it?" The other is to say, "What's right about it?" But this is the part [from the lesson] that I remember: "Okay, you rub two things together. There's a word to describe that." So he [a student] said, "Yes, positive and negative." Now, that was not the correct response in my mind, at least what I meant by the question.

ROSIE: Yeah, you wanted conduction and induction.

COLIN: Right, I wanted conduction and induction. Now I could say, "No, that's not what I'm looking for. You're wrong." Now, what I did was realize that conduction and induction were two different things—there were two different charges—so I tried to validate his response by saying, "Those are two types of charge." In other words, I was trying to explain why that person said that.

ROSIE: And then still bring it back around to get conduction.

COLIN: Right, I didn't stay there. "One way was mentioned. Okay, rubbing two things together." Now, that's a pattern that I do quite deliberately. And that's what I mean by validating the students' ideas. That is, try to give some sense to the students' responses. Because, well, one of the things, if you don't do that

ROSIE: They'll stop responding

COLIN: Yeah

ROSIE: Because they think that, "Well, if I don't have the right answer, then I'll shut up because I'll just get put down" or whatever.

COLIN: And instead of saying, "Is that the right answer?" in my mind, I just kind of think consciously, or almost unconsciously now, "What is right about that answer?" Or "What can I make of that answer?"

Because we are lacking the context and detail provided by the videotape, it is somewhat difficult to follow the specific details of this example. What is apparent, however, is Colin's position on how teachers should approach student ideas. This view is succinctly summarized in his concern to "look for what is right in an answer as well as what is wrong." We would argue that this expression, although it could be likened to a trade homily or rule of thumb, is actually a type of *practical principle*. That is, it prescribes a course of conduct in the practice setting that is guided by a more general pedagogical principle, in this instance "the validation of student knowledge."

In returning to the above example, Colin was trying to "show" Rosie how one can begin to make sense out of a student's response by actively looking for what might be *right* about that response. He conjectured that the student knew that there were two different methods of charging an object and that the student had confused the *names* of the charges (positive and negative) with the *methods* for charging an object (conduction and induction). Hence Colin initiated a teaching move that was designed to *open up* rather than *close* an opportunity for that student to think through his response to the question. A further byproduct of this approach, as Rosie correctly intuited, is that it encourages continuing student participation in class discussions.

These sets of dialogue also illustrate some of the difficulties of communication. While the excerpts are very brief, the reader may be able to obtain a sense of the difficulty Rosie was having in understanding Colin in the earlier excerpt. Her quizzical comments—such as "Well, isn't that what teachers do?" and "Is that what most teachers are like?"—portray something of this mystery. In the second excerpt, only a week and a half later, we see a somewhat more confident Rosie taking part in the dialogue, occasionally even completing Colin's sentences for him. Yet the principles of constructivist teaching that were the focus of these excerpts do not come easily to novice teachers. Hence much of the remainder of the practicum was devoted to modeling, discussing, and practicing particular strategies that exemplified these principles.

A Lesson on Electrical Circuits

The primary data for this case study come from excerpts from a lesson occurring during the third week of the unit. This particular lesson began with Rosie setting up a laboratory-type activity for the students to complete. She put three problems on the board:

1. Use one battery to light a bulb.
2. Use two batteries to light a bulb.
3. Use two batteries to light a bulb so it shines just as brightly as it did in #1.

Students were instructed to work together in groups of two or three, with each group being given a bulb (in a holder), two cells (batteries), and some wires. Throughout the lesson Rosie and Colin circulated among the students as they worked on the problems. One of us (AM) was also in the room with a videocamera and taped several of the groups of students working. During the supervisory conference after school, Colin suggested viewing the tape of a group of three female students who were attempting to clarify for Colin their initial response to problem #3.

Prior to examining the data from this conference, a few preliminary remarks on the instructional context for this case may be helpful. The intent of this laboratory activity was to encourage the students to explore the nature of different types of simple circuits and to see whether they could spontaneously construct the "series" and "parallel" connections required by questions #2 and #3 respectively. The brief instructional encounter dealt with in this case warrants attention, in part, because it illustrates both of the principles of constructivist science teaching discussed above. Rather than discourage the unorthodox approach to the problem taken by this group of students, Colin took their ideas seriously and encouraged them to take the responsibility of "thinking through" their interpretations and results. In the process he was able to discern that some of the conceptual difficulties they were experiencing could be attributed to their commitment to a common, but scientifically naive, conception of an electric circuit.

In brief, these students thought that positive charges are generated at one terminal of a cell and negative charges are generated at the other terminal. These charges then flow through the wire and meet at the bulb, where the charges are consumed. In this view, each terminal acts as a separate "reservoir" of electrical charge and there is no movement of charge *through* the battery. (See Shipstone, 1985, for an expanded description of students' intuitive beliefs about electrical circuits.) This is a quite different view from the current scientific model of the way in which a cell "works" in an electrical circuit. In simple terms, a chemical reaction within the cell results in an accumulation of negative charges at one terminal and positive charges at the other terminal, creating a difference in electrical potential energy between the terminals. When a conducting pathway—such as wires and a properly connected bulb—is attached to both terminals, there is a flow of charge through this pathway until the two terminals are at the same electrical potential (that is, the cell becomes "discharged"). The important difference between the naive conception held by the students and the contemporary scientific conception is that the cell is an integral part of the circuit of moving charges, not simply two isolated sources of charge. Colin's understanding of these different conceptions played a pivotal role in shaping his responses during this brief teaching episode.

There are two primary sources of data from the supervisory confer-

ence under consideration—one from the videotape of the classroom lesson sequence and the other from the supervisory dialogue. Each excerpt
of transcript data will be identified by a subheading. (The transition
between lesson and supervisory dialogue occurred when either Colin
or Rosie stopped the playback deck.) As with any case study, we have
only used selected excerpts of supervisory and lesson dialogue to illustrate what we consider to be germane to this case.

Colin began the conversation by explaining to Rosie why he became
engaged with this group of students.

Supervision Dialogue

> COLIN: And this group here, for example, the one on the tape, I
>   thought they understood it. And I looked at their diagram and
>   I thought, "Oh, the diagram doesn't look quite right because
>   the negatives and positives were marked wrong." The reason I
>   had them do it for me was I was not sure whether they knew
>   what they were doing because of their diagram. Otherwise I
>   thought that they knew . . . Did you think that that was a use-
>   ful stage? Do you think it was useful to spend time on having
>   them do that sort of a broad problem [referring to the whole
>   laboratory exercise]?
> ROSIE: Yeah, I think so. Like I think that I'd do it again.
> COLIN: Because what we've done is, I mean I think this is the crux
>   of what we mean by constructive and transmission. I could
>   have said, "The way you connect a parallel circuit is you con-
>   nect the like poles together and then you connect and so on."
> ROSIE: Well, some of them still did that. It was because they read
>   the battery. But it's a little bit different because it's, uh,
> COLIN: But do you see what the transmissive mode means here?
>   Now what we have done is we've given this to them as a prob-
>   lem. We say, "We want you to construct a solution to this." The
>   idea, I think, here is that now they've had a bit of playtime
>   and figuring the problem. What we're trying to claim, I think,
>   is that when they go to the next stage now they're ready to
>   have this problem solved because it was a real problem for
>   them. They haven't been able to solve it. They struggled in a
>   number of ways. Some of them have worked their way
>   through. But now we build it up to the . . .
> ROSIE: "This is what you did."
> COLIN: Yeah, and the idea is that the raw experience, well, just
>   like we were discussing about how the "What Happens" sec-

tion fits into the "Debriefing" [terms used to describe some of the components of Colin's unit plans]. The raw experience first. Well, were they generally involved with the problem, do you think?

ROSIE: Yeah.

COLIN: I wonder why.

ROSIE: Well, they were really interested in it. The materials were simple. I don't know. I guess, too, that a lot of them don't really have any experience with electrical stuff.

Here we again see Colin trying to reinforce some of the principles that inform his approach to teaching. The task of articulating the differences between what he means by a "transmission approach" and a "constructive approach" is not easy, however, and it is not clear whether Rosie was able to appreciate Colin's explanation at this point in the conversation. Colin continued to try to reduce the complexity of the distinction by referring to some earlier discussions regarding the importance of "the raw experience first." But "telling" alone is not sufficient to communicate the complexity of a teaching practice. As this case will illustrate, these telling moves had to be accompanied by "showing" Rosie the importance of attending to students' ideas through the use of such techniques as the "on-the-spot experiment" (Schön, 1983).

Colin was prompted to initiate such an experiment after sensing that the students' diagram "doesn't look quite right" and hence decided to inquire further into these students' understanding of electrical circuits. This on-the-spot experiment consisted of a series of instructional moves in which he asked these students to show him their solution to the problem and explain to him their ideas about the circuits they had constructed. We begin the lesson dialogue with the three students explaining to Colin how they attached the two cells together to solve question #3 of their laboratory exercise. Diagrams of the cell arrangements are included to illustrate the connections they were making.

Lesson Dialogue

SUE: Okay, first we attach the negatives, and then you tip it over and touch the positives and the negatives together and they work . . . And then you can do it to the other side and it works again. And if you use both of them, it doesn't work. (*See Figure 1.1.*)

COLIN: You know the third problem was to use both of them [the cells]

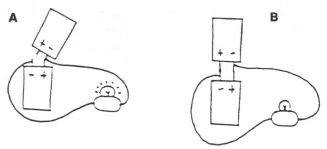

Figure 1.1

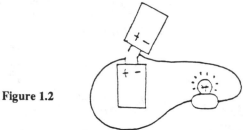

Figure 1.2

ANN: To make it as bright . . .

COLIN: To make it just as bright as #1. Did you do that?

SUE: We did, that's *(points to arrangement in Figure 1.1a)...*

ANN: That's as bright as #1.

COLIN: Have you tried all the possibilities that are there?

(The students proceed to try several other possibilities by switching the wires to the terminals.)

SUE: Just a sec . . . *(she tries the circuit shown in Figure 1.2; bulb lights)* Well, these are two negatives *(surprised)*. This is bizarre. So I guess it isn't that the opposites are working, as long as one doesn't have a wire attached to it, it's going to work . . . So it would be like positives and negatives, that's what would be doing it, but . . .

JAN: Well, it still must be that way, because this is positive *(she places the cells down on the table and traces "the path taken by the electricity" with her fingers)*. What am I thinking of here? . . . No, because this is positive, no, this is negative and so it's going to the bulb . . . and this is going from the bulb to the positive *(laughs)* I don't know . . .

Supervision Dialogue

> COLIN: Do you know what she's saying there? I've seen this before. That if this is attached to the negative and that's attached to the positive, it should work. You go from positive to bulb to negative, and you don't have to form a complete path. And she says, "I don't understand why that doesn't work."

In this dialogue we see Colin alerting Rosie to several important features of the students' work with the materials. Colin took a noninterventionist stance by encouraging them to consider whether they had tried all of the possible options and so provides an opportunity to learn more about how they were thinking about the problem. When Sue's "theory" of needing a positive and a negative emerged, Colin indicated to Rosie that because he had seen that type of idea before, he could understand why Jan and Sue seemed so puzzled when it worked after they connected the two negative terminals. He also pointed out to Rosie that they did not yet seem to have grasped the notion of a "complete path." While it is not yet apparent in the dialogue, Colin's sense that they were lacking this notion was the basis for his encouraging the girls in further experimentation with the materials.

After trying several more different arrangements, the girls were still clearly puzzled. When one of their trials produced a much brighter light than their earlier trials, Colin once again intervened by encouraging them to analyze this arrangement a bit more closely than they had done previously.

Lesson Dialogue

> COLIN: When you had it connected the way you did just a minute ago, can you describe the order in which it was connected. (*See Figure 1.3a.*)
>
> SUE: Okay (*puts the cell down*). This is the negative (*points to the wire on the negative terminal*).
>
> COLIN: And where does it go from there?
>
> SUE: Negative goes into there (*follows wire to bulb—see Figure 1.3b*). And this is positive (*points to wire on other cell*) and it goes into there (*follows wire to the bulb*).
>
> JAN: So it's connected (*with much excitement in her voice*). It's just making a circuit. It's like when you put these together, it's like that other cable that we had joining these two. [She is referring to an earlier arrangement where they used other wires (or cables) to connect the cells and bulb instead of touching the cells directly.]

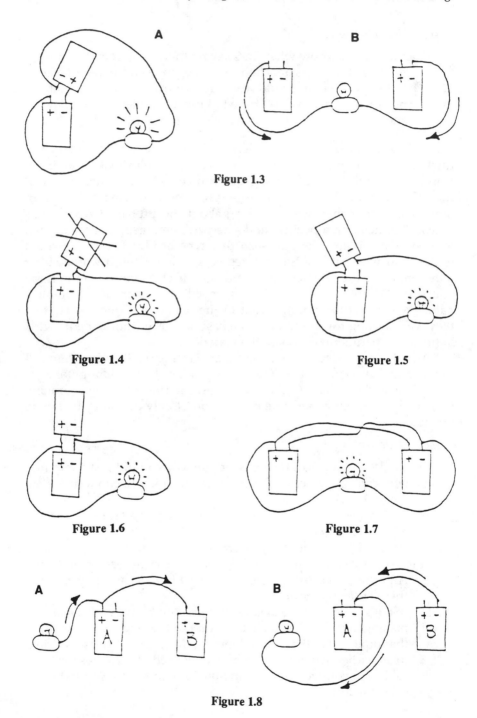

Figure 1.3

Figure 1.4   Figure 1.5

Figure 1.6   Figure 1.7

Figure 1.8

Supervision Dialogue

> COLIN: You see, there's the "Ah ha!" Right there. Did you see that? That is the first "Ah ha!" You know, I just thought that was such a terrific event. She just sees it like that. (*Colin displays as much excitement in his voice as did Jan when she realized that touching the terminals directly was the equivalent of using wires.*)

Lesson Dialogue

> JAN: It goes there (*pointing to bulb*) and comes out there (*pointing back to the same cell*).
>
> SUE: Yeah, so it goes in and out, right? (*She traces a path through both cells.*) It goes all the way around.
>
> JAN: It's not using this battery when it does that (*indicating arrangement shown in Figure 1.4*). That's what it's doing because you're making the wire connect there (*points to negative terminal with no wire*).
>
> COLIN: Okay, now make it the same brightness as with one.
>
> JAN: The same brightness as with one cell?
>
> SUE: I thought we had done that (*constructs arrangement shown in Figure 1.5*).
>
> COLIN: Does that solve the problem? Are you using both cells?
>
> JAN: Oh, I see what you are saying.

Supervision Dialogue

> COLIN: This is another "Ah ha!" right here.

Lesson Dialogue

> SUE: Negative to negative . . .
>
> JAN: There . . . I'm touching both (*constructs arrangement shown in Figure 1.6*).
>
> SUE: Are you touching both?
>
> ANN: Why does that work?
>
> SUE: You are touching both. I don't know, why is it working now?
>
> JAN: Because the circuit is using both batteries.
>
> COLIN: If you get some more wires, could you connect something that did the same as that, as what you just did?
>
> ALL IN UNISON: Yeah.

Supervision Dialogue

> COLIN: What I was trying to do here, they had the solution, but I wanted to pull it apart.

Figure 1.9

ROSIE: Yeah, it's really hard to see it.

Lesson Dialogue

(*After several trials of attaching wires to both batteries and the bulb in various combinations, they arrive at the arrangement illustrated in Figure 1.7.*)

JAN: Wait a minute, what did we do here?

ANN: That doesn't make sense.

JAN: That doesn't make sense. Okay, look . . . negative to negative (*points to wires between the cells*), positive to positive, positive to bulb, and negative to bulb.

COLIN: How many circuits do you have here? Let's try to keep it straight.

SUE: One, two, three, four (*counting the wires*).

JAN: I think it's all one circuit, you know.

SUE: But we have four wires.

ANN: Two. It's two because these aren't connected. It goes from here to here (*constructing arrangement shown in Figure 1.8a*). But then it splits and goes from there to there (*constructing arrangement shown in Figure 1.8b*).

COLIN: What do you mean that it splits?

ANN: Well you have two . . .

JAN: But it goes through the battery (*uses hand to connect the terminals; see Figure 1.9*).

Supervision Dialogue

> COLIN: Did you see what happened there? Up to now they've
> been treating the inside of the cell as not being part of the cir-
> cuit. The positive pole is an origin of something, the negative
> pole is an origin of something, but they haven't got the idea
> that it's complete right through the inside of the cell. So they're
> missing that idea of a circuit. You have separate supplies.
> When she puts her hand across there, that's really an insight.
> ROSIE: To signify that it's part of the circuit.

In this short excerpt Colin was trying to show Rosie how important
this insight was to Jan. He suggested that this lack of awareness about
the cell's being an integral part of the circuit was a factor in the students'
general difficulties in developing an adequate explanatory model of
electrical circuits. With this insight about the cell, Jan was then able to
make more sense of their earlier trials. She realized that in many of their
previous arrangements they were really using only one cell, not two, as
they thought.

For Colin to make the above conjectures about these students' ideas
he clearly requires considerable understanding of both the subject matter itself and possible student interpretations of this content. It is this
understanding, a type of "pedagogical content knowledge" (Shulman,
1987), that formed the basis for many of the judgments Colin made even
during this short instructional episode. In viewing the lesson videotape,
one can see numerous places where Colin had to make decisions about
whether to intervene in the students' explorations—decisions that we
think were based upon his extensive experience of students' intuitive
ideas about electricity. The experiment was ended when Colin was satisfied that the students appeared to grasp the fundamental notion of a
circuit *and* that the cell itself was a part of this circuit. In the dialogue
cited, Jan seems to have grasped this point. In a further sequence, lasting several minutes (only partially described above), Colin was able to
test his conjecture about the other two students' understanding when
he asked them to use wires to construct the circuit instead of directly
touching the terminals of the cells. Their ability to solve this problem
and to show him the two parallel circuits they had made convinced him
that Sue and Ann shared Jan's understanding, and so the "experiment"
was terminated.

The kind of understanding that underlies these judgments cannot
be directly taught to novice teachers, in part because of the complex,

contextual factors involved. For example, in the present case it was very difficult for Rosie to identify the ideas held by these students because of the unusual arrangement of the cells they used and their often confused and ambiguous description of what they were attempting to do.

In the following supervisory dialogue, Colin summarized some of the features of this teaching episode and his own personal feelings about teaching in this manner.

Supervision Dialogue

> COLIN: I like that. There's so many things that are there. One of the things is that it takes a bit of practice to pick up things like that.
>
> ROSIE: It's sort of a matter of listening for it.
>
> COLIN: Yeah. Well, I remember when I first started dealing with things that kids were coming up with that had never occurred to me. And after a while you begin to recognize patterns. For example, there were a lot of new things in that video. The new things were this idea that they're not thinking of a circuit, really. They don't have a clear idea that the cell is part of the closed path. Actually, that is something new in my mind. I hadn't quite dealt with that before, so I was learning something. But in a way, because I was involved with these kids for 15 minutes, I knew what they were trying, I got a very clear idea of where they were going and why they were failing. But there was tremendous satisfaction in being able to intervene. You can't do that for every kid all the time. But if I could do that once with this group, if they have a sense of that once, they begin to take ownership and they begin to do that themselves. I mean, did you see the puzzlement, and then at the end, the satisfaction? In my view at least, I thought there was such great achievement there.
>
> ROSIE: And then tomorrow when I go up there it'll be, "Oh yeah, that makes sense, that makes sense." Not, "Okay, we draw it like this."
>
> COLIN: If you've just drawn something, it's not a real problem for them. If they say, "Gee, I'm stuck on this and I can't figure out why this damn thing doesn't work." Well then it's a real problem. I think this is the question of becoming reflective in one's teaching. That is, that you know, you just don't recognize it at first. You begin to recognize it here and there and you develop a repertoire of particular instances, but also a pattern.

In discussing his own understanding of the sense that the students were constructing from this instructional encounter and his reflections on his own actions, Colin attempted to locate this understanding in a longer-term developmental perspective. His reference to the role of "practice" and to the importance of "becoming reflective in one's teaching" provides an indication of how Colin views professional growth. One of Colin's intents in this discussion may have been to reassure Rosie that she should not expect to be able to do the same "sense-making" of complex classroom situations as he does, since it takes time to "develop a repertoire of particular instances [and subsequently] a pattern." We think Colin was also attempting to provide further credibility, through a type of "mirroring strategy" (Schön, 1987), for his constructivist stance on learning by claiming that teachers, like students, construct knowledge that allows them to see classroom phenomena as instances of more general patterns.

In this final dialogue Colin also displayed some of his personal commitments in teaching. For example, his excitement and enjoyment at seeing his students move from a state of puzzlement to understanding was most apparent. Such enjoyment and commitment to fostering this kind of student learning, which was evident throughout the video of the lesson and supervisory dialogues, would seem to be important in sustaining the sort of reflective inquiry that Colin perceives to be central to his own teaching practice.

Before leaving this discussion of the lesson and supervisory excerpts, we want to comment on a feature of the supervisory dialogue that may have created a sense of uneasiness in some readers—the appearance of Colin as monopolizing the conversation. We refer to this as an "appearance" for the following reasons. First, as indicated earlier, we have used only selected excerpts from a much larger body of transcript data. In this selection we tended to focus more on the "telling" moves than the "showing" moves because the latter are not easy to capture in prose. Second, we structured the data presentation so as to focus on Colin's reflections on his actions and on those of the students during the lesson so that we could provide an overt explanation and rationale for the modeling actions that were occurring in the lesson. Finally, since this lesson was less than half-way through Rosie's practicum, Colin was still engaged in the process of explaining to her many of the relevant features and characteristics of his teaching approach. The data which we have *not* presented here, but which would have been useful for seeing the larger story of Rosie's practicum experiences, is that of Rosie reflecting upon her own teaching encounters and interpreting them in terms of her own growing understanding both of what it means to teach *and* of Colin's teaching perspective. That, however, is another story.

SOME CONCLUDING THOUGHTS

The events related in this chapter demonstrate something of the difficulties in learning a complex practice such as teaching. Although we directed most of our attention to how a novice teacher might learn "to see" a classroom through the conceptual lenses supplied by an experienced teacher who subscribed to a constructivist approach to teaching, some of the lessons and principles we drew from this case certainly could be applied to other teachers who are seeking to *reconstruct* their understanding of their current teaching practice.

What we have had to omit from our story is any discussion of the many constraints we expect to face as we begin to work with other teachers. These constraints, which may lead to considerable resistance to change, can be roughly grouped into two categories: those emanating from personal sources and those deriving from situational or institutional factors. In this regard, we think that a major obstacle can be found in some of the dominant metaphors of teaching and learning in the educational community. In our experience, many practitioners and commentators view teaching as the *transmission of knowledge* as encapsulated in the metaphors of the "learner as a sponge" or the "learner as an empty vessel." While these are rather clichéd characterizations of teaching and learning, which incidentally were the subject of attack by earlier critics of our educational system (Holt, 1964; Illich, 1971; Reimer, 1971), we must unfortunately report that these metaphors are still alive and well in the thinking of preservice teachers (Aguirre & Haggerty, in press); and a functionally similar metaphor, "the school as a factory," dominates much contemporary writing in educational policy documents (Clarke, 1989).

Accomplishing any type of significant shift in our personal and institutional perspective on education will require individuals who are prepared to take personal and professional risks. It will also require appropriate *enabling conditions* from our institutional structures to encourage the kind of inquiry-oriented practice that we see modeled by Colin in the above case story.

While the obstacles to implementing a constructivist perspective on teaching and learning are many, we nonetheless are encouraged by the results we have obtained in our limited work in practicum settings and by the response we have received from other experienced teachers who have been exposed to our project through more informal professional development activities. This has been a sufficient incentive for us to continue to develop the structures and strategies that we think will lead to a more mature and fruitful view of professional knowledge in teaching and how it is constructed and communicated to other teachers.

ACKNOWLEDGMENTS

The authors would like to acknowledge the financial assistance from the Social Sciences and Humanities Research Council of Canada. We also wish to acknowledge the dedication and insights provided by Ken Kuhn, a teacher who has worked closely with us on this project.

REFERENCES

Aguirre, J., & Haggerty, S. (in press). Student teachers' conceptions about science teaching and learning: A case study in pre-service teacher education. *International Journal of Science Education*.

Clarke, P. (1989). *A metaphor-examining approach to the practice of problem setting in policy research: The case of schools*. Doctoral dissertation in preparation at the University of British Columbia, Vancouver.

Driver, R., & Erickson, G. (1983). Theories-in-action: Some theoretical and empirical issues in the study of students' conceptual frameworks in science. *Studies in Science Education, 10*, 37–60.

Driver, R., & Oldham, V. (1986). A constructivist approach to curriculum development in science. *Studies in Science Education, 13*, 105–122.

Driver, R., Tiberghien, A., & Guesne, E. (Eds.). (1985). *Children's ideas in science*. Milton Keynes, England: Open University Press.

Erickson, G. (1986). *Development of an instructional approach based upon a cognitive perspective* (Final report on research project 410-85-0611, submitted to Social Sciences and Humanities Research Council of Canada).

Erickson, G. (1987, April). *Constructivist epistemology and the professional development of teachers*. Paper presented at the annual meeting of the American Educational Research Association, Washington, DC.

Erickson, G. (1988, June). *Processes and products from the (SI)² Project: Anatomy of a collaborative approach*. Paper presented at the annual meeting of the Canadian Society for the Study of Education, Windsor, Ontario.

Glasersfeld, E. von (1987). Constructivism. *The international encyclopedia of education*. London: Pergamon.

Goodman, N. (1978). *Ways of worldmaking*. Hassocks, England: Harvester Press.

Goodman, N. (1984). *Of mind and other matters*. Cambridge, MA: Harvard University Press.

Gurney, B. (1988, June). *Conceptual change through negotiation*. Paper presented at the annual meeting of the Canadian Society for the Study of Education, Windsor, Ontario.

Holt, J. (1964). *How children fail*. New York: Pitman.

Illich, I. (1971). *Deschooling society*. New York: Harper & Row.

Kuhn, K., & Aguirre, J. (1987). A case study of the "journal method": A method designed to enable the implementation of constructivist teaching in the classroom. In J. Novak (Ed.), *Proceedings of the 2nd International Seminar on Misconceptions and Educational Strategies in Science and Mathematics*. Ithaca, NY: Cornell University.

Kuhn, T. (1970). *The structure of scientific revolutions* (2nd ed.). Chicago: University of Chicago Press.

MacKinnon, A. (1987). Toward a conceptualization of a reflective teaching practicum in science teaching. In J. Novak (Ed.), *Proceedings of the 2nd International Seminar on Misconceptions and Educational Strategies in Science and Mathematics*. Ithaca, NY: Cornell University.

MacKinnon, A. (1988, June). *Conceptualizing a science teaching practicum: "The hall of mirrors"*. Paper presented at the annual meeting of the Canadian Society for the Study of Education, Windsor, Ontario.

Magoon, A. J. (1977). Constructivist approaches in educational research. *Review of Educational Research, 47*, 651–693.

Pepper, S. (1942). *World hypotheses: A study in evidence*. Berkeley: University of California Press.

Reimer, E. (1971). *School is dead*. Garden City, NY: Doubleday.

Schön, D. (1983). *The reflective practitioner: How professionals think in action*. New York: Basic Books.

Schön, D. (1987). *Educating the reflective practitioner*. San Francisco: Jossey-Bass.

Shipstone, D. (1985). Electricity in simple circuits. In R. Driver, E. Guesne, & A. Tiberghien (Eds.), *Children's ideas in science*. Milton Keynes, England: Open University Press.

Shulman, L. (1987). Knowledge and teaching: Foundations of the new reform. *Harvard Educational Review, 57*, 1–22.

Sieben, G. (1987). Introducing concept mapping in the day to day science curriculum. In J. Novak (Ed.) *Proceedings of the 2nd International Seminar on Misconceptions and Educational Strategies in Science and Mathematics*. Ithaca, NY: Cornell University.

West, L. H. T., & Pines, A. L. (Eds.). (1985). *Cognitive structure and conceptual change*. London: Academic.

White, R. (1988). *Learning science*. Oxford, England: Blackwell.

Wittgenstein, L. (1963). *Philosophical investigations* (G. Anscombe, Trans.). Oxford, England: Blackwell. (Original work published 1953)

2

The Laboratory for Making Things: Developing Multiple Representations of Knowledge

JEANNE BAMBERGER

Reflections are *made* by the reflecting surface.
Even mirrors are only rarely passive;
They transform images—enlarging, diminishing, dimming,
    reversing, bending, twisting—
In implausible, unpredictable ways . . .
Until you learn to follow the (sometimes circuitous) but always
Orderly course the reflector takes
In reflecting back the sending beam.

WRITING IN THE CONTEXT of a book on "reflective practice" encourages reflection on reflection itself, and this, in turn, suggests a paradox: In actual practice, "reflecting" is at best an on-the-spot action, a knowing response to an immediate situation; but more often than not, the knowing along with the moment of reflecting disappear, transparent to and absorbed into their effective result. How, then, do we learn to recognize, even to *see*, "reflective practice"? And if we do, how do we learn to reflect *on* these moments that have disappeared without introducing the distortions of hindsight and "historical revisionism"? These questions, or versions of them, will form a continuing and puzzling theme through all that follows.

THE LABORATORY FOR MAKING THINGS

The context for our work is a project and a place called the Laboratory for Making Things. The place is a large room in the Graham and Parks Alternative Public School in Cambridge, Massachusetts. The project involves a consortium of people and institutions: faculty and students from MIT, consultants from the "real world" (a sculptor, an architect, a musician), and 12 teachers from within the school who, over the 4 years of its existence, have brought their respective classes to the Lab—in all, about 250 children between the ages of 6 and 14.

Background

The Lab was created in an effort to address a poorly understood but well-recognized phenomenon: Children who are most successful, even virtuosos, at using their hands to build and fix complicated things in the everyday world around them (bicycles, plumbing, car motors, musical instruments, games and gadgets, or a clubhouse out of junk from the local construction site) are often the same children who are having the most difficulties learning in school. These children are frequently identified as having trouble in working with common symbolic expressions—numbers, graphs, music notation, written language—the "privileged languages" that form the core of schooling. With the emphasis in schooling on symbolic knowledge, it is not surprising that attention focuses on what these children *cannot* do, and it is also not surprising that the school world sees them not as virtuosos but as "failing to perform."

Starting from a different assumption, namely that "hand knowledge" and "symbolic knowledge" constitute equally powerful but different and not equally appreciated ways of organizing worldly phenomena, I asked first: How can we gain insight into the kinds of knowledge and especially the *ways of learning* that children bring with them from the world outside of school? And second, if we could better understand the kind of knowledge children bring to what they do so well, could we also help them use this knowledge not as a *deterrent* but rather as a *source* for achieving success in the kind of learning and understanding that is expected of them in the classroom?

My earlier work on musical development suggested some directions for seeking answers. For instance, I found that the musical entities and relations to which musical notation refer are quite different in kind from the inner mental representations that guide the sequence of continuous actions in singing a song or playing a piece "by ear" on an instrument. And the research also showed that a critical aspect in the development of musical intelligence is the ability to *notice* these differences, to selectively shift focus among varied and possible musical relations so as to make multiple "hearings" of even the same moment (Bamberger, 1981, 1986, in press).

Drawing on these findings, I speculated, for example, that children who use their "smart hands" to work effectively with everyday objects might also be focusing on kinds of entities and relations that are quite different from those to which conventional symbolic expressions typically refer. Moreover, perhaps some children were failing in school not because they were "unmotivated" but because the functional entities that they can "put their hands on" are left unnamed and unrecognized in the school world. If so, this might help to explain why the knowledge that works so well outside school can only maintain a covert existence inside the classroom and, conversely, why the kind of learning that is expected of children inside school often fails to travel outside its doors. And finally, I postulated that, as I had found in the development of musical intelligence, it was important for children to learn to *notice* these differences, to learn to selectively shift focus among varied and possible ways of seeing objects and relations. In short, we needed to help children *confront* these differences and through these confrontations to help them develop multiple representations of the world around them.

The Laboratory for Making Things was designed as an environment in which to play out these speculative proposals. The Lab is a large room "furnished" with a wealth of materials for designing and building structures that work—gears and pulleys, Lego blocks, pattern blocks and large building blocks, Cuisenaire rods, batteries and buzzers for building simple circuitry, foamcore, wood and glue for model house construction, as well as drums and keyboards for making music. There are also 15 Apple IIe and several Macintosh computers in the Lab, and they serve as another medium for building structures that work and that make sense—what we have come to call "working systems."

Our task, as I initially saw it, was to learn how to help children move back and forth between making things with the materials of the real world and making things with the computer, as well as to encourage them to actively *confront* differences and similarities that emerged as they moved across materials, sensory modalities, and kinds of descriptions. For example, in moving between hand-made and computer-made structures, the relations between action and description are interestingly reversed: With computer-made objects, one begins by making *descriptions* within the constraints of a computer language, and the descriptions result in actions; with hand-made objects, one begins with *actions* and only after-the-fact and after-the-act (if then) are these actions "held still" by descriptions. Moreover, the results of computer commands are often surprising, and these moments of surprise, if confronted, can help reveal entities that otherwise remain hidden in our all-at-once actions and perceptions. At the same time, such confrontations can illuminate the hidden assumptions built-in to the conventional symbol systems associated with a domain. In this way, the computer functions as a kind of mediator, a "transitional object" between sensory/action know-how and symbolic know-how.

But there is also important potential for insight in the unexpected *similarities* that emerge between one "working system" and another, between one description and another. For example, there are moments in which we may spontaneously see a resemblance between the workings of a familiar "working system" and one that is still new, but not yet be able to say what that similarity is. But in trying to make the similarity criteria explicit, there is the potential for "liberating" a *principle* that is embodied by both "working systems," one that they both share—a principle that might otherwise have remained hidden in the single instance of the prototype (see also, Kuhn, 1977, pp. 305–308).

In seeing similarities between two "working systems," it is almost as if one were *reflecting* the other, even imitating the other—like an infant's natural and quite remarkable ability to imitate another's actions, such as someone sticking out their tongue or blinking their eyes (see Piaget, 1962), or an older child imitating another's walk or how he throws a ball. Perhaps our bodily capacities to imitate the actions of others is a kind of basic, primitive version, a procedural model, for our abilities to see how the actions of one structure "imitate" the actions of another. But just as with an infant's imitation, there is not only reflection but also *selection:* The infant does not imitate all the actions of the other, but only those that his or her momentary attention selects. And it is this cognitive and reflective act of selection that makes the difference: In seeing a resemblance, a particular configuration of relations is singled out as shared; and it is these selected relations that can take us beyond what we know already to general principles, albeit seen vaguely. But then turning back, we also resee the two structures in new ways, thus liberating new features in both prototype and new working system.

There is, then, *generative value* in asking children and teachers to move back and forth between actions and descriptions, among various media for designing and building, as well as among various modes and media for making descriptions. While each of these kinds of activities embodies, or holds implicit within itself, different kinds of features and relations, the potential immanent in their active confrontation might result in those critical transformations that could help children both enhance their "smart hands" and come to make sense of the sense intended by symbolic expressions.

Moving In

These ideas were to take shape in a public school in a working-class neighborhood where classes included neighborhood kids peppered with children whose parents were academics or left-over 1960s types attracted to the "alternative" part of school's name. But what would the *teachers* make of these ideas born and bred in the academic ivory tower? I had to assume that these adults (who happen to be teachers), as well as the children in their classes, were used to keeping neatly separate the symbolic knowledge they were taught in school and the practical knowledge they used to make sense of and to navigate the everyday world outside school. But that being so, to *tell* them that, or even to give them curriculum units or lesson plans, was not going to help. They were going to have to confront head-on these inner and outer representations that were often at odds with one another. And I was going to have to do that right along with them. In what follows I focus on the teachers' learning because, as I had suspected, *their* learning was not only critical; it was what they learned and, most of all, *how* they learned it that was later going to be mirrored in the children's learning in the Lab.

We started work in October 1985. Eight teachers joined the group in response to a short, quite vague letter we had put in all mailboxes and a 10-minute description at the start of a regular staff meeting earlier in the school year. We offered to pay participants ($300 for the year) as "consultants" to the project.

Work began with weekly meetings of what came to be known as the "teacher group." Susan Jo Russell (my co-director during the first year) and I met with the teachers in the Lab each Monday after school for about 2 hours. The group included six regular classroom teachers, who, among them, taught grades K–8 (classes in the school are grouped in pairs—grades 1–2, 3–4, 5–6, 7–8). Together with the "adjunct teacher" (who would later assist all the others in working with kids in the Lab) and the special education teacher, there were eight in all. At the beginning of our work together we talked hardly at all about teaching, about children, or about curriculum projects. Instead, we spent the time making things together and probing our varied understandings of how we did that. We made experiments with circuitry, built structures with Lego blocks and tunes with Montessori bells, struggled to understand how gears worked, and in all of this looked closely at the differences in our strategies for both making and describing what we had made. The teachers also learned LOGO to greater or lesser degrees, using it to make graphic designs as well as melodies and rhythms.

While we had anticipated that after 2 or 3 months the focus of our discussions would move to planning projects for children, it was only in March of that first year, 6 months after we had begun our work together, that teachers felt "comfortable enough" with *their* learning to begin work on the design of activities for their students. And it was only in late April or May that all of the participants were finally bringing children to the Lab.

Going On

I have tried to find a way to tell the reader about the evolution of the teachers' learning without cleaning it up or making it read like a "method" that went neatly forward toward preplanned goals and objectives. As I had anticipated, I couldn't *tell* the teacher-participants, either; they had to take time to make of it, individually and collectively, what they could—meanings changing as their experience changed the context in which these ideas lived. Their learning has been organic and slow, often lost in the flow of time.

This sense of lost learning became vividly clear toward the end of the second year, when we devoted our Monday meeting to a discussion of how we could help new teachers who wanted to join the group. The discussion centered around very practical questions: How can we tell teachers what the project is all about? How can we tell them what we have been doing, and how can we help them know what to do in working with their classes in the Lab? The discussion was revealing in its pervasive sense of elusiveness; and yet for most, this was interestingly coupled with a strong sense of what "the project" was *not*. One teacher, whom I will call David, put it like this:

> We could pass any of this stuff (curriculum projects invented by the group) on to someone else and it would not have the same impetus. But the *situation*, if we could only describe the situation and the elements of the situation, that's what we need to pass on. . . . Forget the content, it doesn't matter. It's the situation that's powerful.

What was this "situation," and what made it so "powerful"? How had the current group of teachers learned to recognize it, to create it, while still being unable to *describe* it? What had they learned how to do, how they had changed, what had contributed to these changes, and why was it so difficult to *say?*

The difficulties the teachers had in making an accounting of their learning (and I shared this with them) lie partly in looking for an accounting that matches the conventions, the privileged descriptions, of what such an accounting is supposed to be—one that is consistent with the idealized modes of learning that we are taught to teach. The teachers' learning, which was later mirrored in the children's learning in the Lab, has been more like learning that occurs in everyday life: *How* you have learned happens over time, and that is lost when *what* you have learned is embodied only in the *present* actions of doing it.

For example, to build a gate that works, you feel the surfaces, the shapes of the "stuff" in your hands; and this seeing/feeling of the materials as they change under your hands through time "tells" you how the materials work, what they can do, what you can do with them. Practicing a sequence of actions on materials—improvising, detecting, and correcting as you go along—you find a sequence of actions that works. And once found, this interlocked chain of actions, each one triggered by the one before, becomes a familiar path that you can follow again, like following a familiar walk through the woods—next–next–next. Similarly, as you practice moving about on a musical instrument, the feel of the instrument's geography becomes a familiar terrain, and a practiced sequence of actions that plays a particular composition becomes a familiar "felt path"—your most intimate "knowledge" of how the piece *goes*. But in building a gate or playing a piece, your actions and the "shapings" of the materials *do not stop*—the past disappears, giving way only to the present situation. So this *going-on* makes it difficult to take apart actions, to isolate events and look *at* the separate features of objects that, in doing it, *happen all-at-once*; and this going-on also makes it difficult to compare actions, events, and objects that happened at different times or in different spaces. How, then, do we ever come to "know" and to account for what we have learned to do?

If we are to make an accounting of such learning, and, indeed, if we are to help it along, we need to develop strategies for capturing these happenings on-the-wing—albeit risking the potential for distortion that comes from *stopping* what is always going on. Consider a brief moment in the life of the teacher group—a moment that illustrates the learning that has been going on there.

During a Monday session one of the teachers, Mary, told a puzzling story about 8-year-old Jeff, who, in the process of making a mobile, was trying to balance two different objects on a stick suspended from its middle. As she watched, Mary noticed that he immediately "knew" which way to push the object that was tipping the stick. Fascinated, she asked Jeff how he did that. Not surprisingly, he answered that he "just knew"; and asked again, he said, "I had a feeling of it, like on a teeter-totter." In telling the story to the teacher group, Mary asked: What is it that Jeff "knows" in being able to do that, how did he learn it, and what did he mean by his comment about the teeter-totter?

Intrigued, the teachers themselves became involved in working on the problem of balancing. Like Jeff, they found they could "intuitively" push objects in the right direction to make them balance. But that led them to ask of themselves what *they* knew how to do when they did so. As they stepped off the moving path of their own actions to look *at* them, they found themselves facing confusion. Unlike Jeff, they had, of course, learned the formula about "weight times distance," but what they had been taught and what they had learned to *say* seemed disconnected from what they could directly see and feel. As Mary put it in trying to make sense of what she could see:

> The trouble is, I don't know where to look. What is "the balance"—the stick, the string, the weights, the distance, or the whole thing? And anyhow, what does weight have to do with distance; they seem like totally different kinds of things. This is making me very uncomfortable.

This brief moment illustrates my hunch that these adults, like most, were used to keeping neatly separate their school knowledge and their everyday knowledge. But it also holds in it the teachers' growing abilities to recognize and to dare to confront the incongruences between these ways of knowing—on one hand, the know-how, the "hand knowledge," that worked "by the feel of it" and, on the other, the meanings implicit in learned formalisms. Moreover, they had learned how to ask questions that probed these incongruences even when that made them "very uncomfortable." And most of all they had learned that to get from feelings and actions to the meanings implicit in a formalism, they first had to come to grips with a situation in which they didn't "know where to look." For it is only when you have recognized that as "the trouble" that you can begin to look for and find those objects, features, and relations that until then have been hidden from view, transparent to the outcomes of your own actions that you know how to do already.

But how have they learned to do *that?* I have tried to trace that process by looking back over transcripts of some of the teacher sessions. What I have found is a process much like learning to build a gate: In the teachers' work together and the conversations about this work, knowledge gained in their hands-on experiments in building structures, along with questions and unresolved confusions raised along the way, became shared experiences, the makings of a common culture. And within this common culture, these collective experiences, like the materials in building a gate, functioned as the base to which they always returned. As they moved from one project to another, questions, confusions, and insights gained along the way were used and reused in new situations. And through this process, more general ideas evolved, ideas that always returned again to the particulars of a specific experience now seen differently. These "reflecting transformations"—the sense (image) of one person's description, view, insight transforming as it bounced off the meanings held by another—were more like the transforming reflections of shapes in moving water. I have dubbed this going-on of ideas evolving through time "conceptual chaining." And the learning that occurs through this group process of conceptual chaining is, I think, much like the interlocked chain of actions that characterizes learning to build a gate or to play a piece on a musical instrument. It was this way of learning—elusive because *how* you have learned is embodied by (exists only in) *what* you know how to do in the present—that made it so difficult for the teachers to describe; it is also, I believe, the quality that David could only point to as "the situation."

What has been my role in this learning process? At the time the discussions in the teacher group were occurring, it was always my sense that I was simply a participant in exploring ideas, asking questions that interested me about the structures we were making and to which, along with the others, we were together quite genuinely seeking possible answers. It was only as I reread transcripts of our sessions (many of which we taped) and through them relived our discussions, that I realized with some surprise that I had been doing much more: I was, in fact, *stopping* the going-on; and I was doing so by catching on-the-wing those moments in the midst of a conversation or a confusion that held the potential for acting out those underlying ideas that I could not otherwise *tell*. And once I saw such moments, the rumble of my underlying ideas helped me to generate questions, suggestions, probes, prods, and selective confirmations: a question, for example, that pulled out the potential for seeing one working system as another, or that prodded a moment in which the same structure might be seen different ways, or that elicited a new description that might lead us to take a new view of the situation. In this way I was guiding the course of our mutual reflections, our conceptual chaining, and also the kind of learning that occurred along the way. And in doing so, I was also playing out *with* the teachers what they were later able to do with kids in the Lab—learning that has clearly spilled over into their classrooms as well. To give the reader a feel for this process of learning as it unfolded in real time, I record here excerpts from a conversation that occurred during one of the teacher sessions.

THE SITUATION: LEARNING AS REFLECTING CONVERSATIONS

The conversation occurred early in the project (December 1985) during the course of a regular Monday afternoon session of the teacher group. In addition to Susan Jo Russell and myself, five teachers participate in the conversation. I have called them Ida, Lucy, Nina, Sam, and Mary. In tracing the ideas that emerge and the learning they hold, the reader will notice that at any one moment there are several interleaved strands of conversation going on. And as strands gradually make their way to the surface, each develops its own trajectory. Indeed, the dynamic of the discussion and the insights that evolve are often the result of what might be seen—and is by some participants—as "conversational drift." But it is exactly this "drift" that generated that aspect of the group's learning that I have called "conceptual chaining," the process by which one participant's comments reflect off and are reflected by another's.

In following the conversation, the reader will also observe that, with the help of my interventions, the group's learning played out many of the ideas that initially motivated the project. For example:

Seeing resemblances among working systems without being able to say with respect to what; and in making the resemblance criterion explicit, liberating a *principle* that working systems share

A computer program functioning as a "transitional object," putting assumptions into question and also revealing previously hidden aspects of hands-on construction

Multiple views and multiple modes and media of description that trigger both insight and confusion

My role in the conversation: Catching moments on-the-wing, I question, provoke, and prod, helping to guide the conceptual chaining as it unfolds

Setting the Scene

Earlier in the same session, before the present discussion begins, the teachers had been making experiments with simple circuitry. Working in pairs, they had first built a simple closed circuit that included a battery, wires, and a lightbulb. Each group then invented their own experiments. For instance, some wanted to see what happened if they changed the size or number of batteries, while others experimented with substituting a buzzer or a bell for the lightbulb, and so forth. These experiments formed the shared background for the conversation that followed.

The conversation began at what was intended to be a short break in the session on circuitry. During this break, while the group chatted and relaxed with some refreshments, one of the teachers, Sam, showed the others a LOGO computer procedure he had made while working on his computer at home. After the participants had admiringly watched the results of Sam's procedure evolving as graphics on the screen, they asked Sam to explain to them how he had devised it. Sam obliges with a rather full description of what he had done. But instead of returning to the experiments with circuitry as we had intended, Sam's procedure, and the puzzles it generates, turns out to be a jumping off place for a rather intense and wide-ranging conversation that goes on for about an hour. I shall only include here excerpts from the first part of this conversation, punctuating it with running commentary at critical moments. Sam begins, in response to the teachers' questions, with a description of his computer procedures. The LOGO commands he uses are FD, which tells the "turtle" (i.e., the screen cursor) to move forward the specified number of spaces, and RT, which tells the "turtle" to make a right turn of the specified number of degrees.

> SAM: First I wrote a procedure for CIRCLE and I put it in the editor (*Sam shows his procedure and runs it; see Figure 2.1*):
>
> ```
> TO CIRCLE
>    REPEAT 36 [FD 5 RT 10]
>    END
> ```
>
> SAM: Then I asked it [the computer] to repeat CIRCLE 40 times, and I added on, RT 10. I asked it to repeat CIRCLE and RT 10, 40 times. I called that procedure CIRCLES. (*Sam shows his CIRCLES procedure*):
>
> ```
> TO CIRCLES
>    REPEAT 40 [CIRCLE RT 10]
>    END
> ```
>
> SAM: So every time it made a circle, the turtle would just angle to the right 10 degrees and make another circle. (*Sam starts his CIRCLES procedure, then stops it to show the group what he means by "angled to the right 10 degrees"; see Figure 2.2.*)

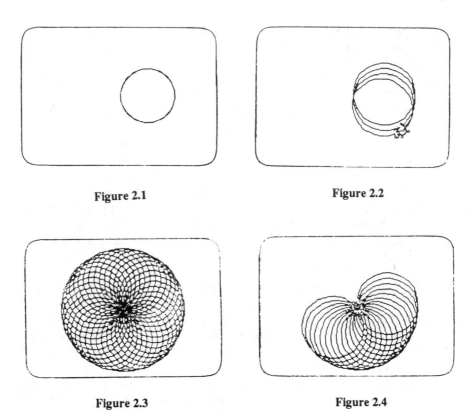

Figure 2.1   Figure 2.2

Figure 2.3   Figure 2.4

SAM: So here is my whole CIRCLES procedure. (*Sam runs his* CIRCLES *procedure; see Figure 2.3.*)

JEANNE: Now why did you ask it to go around *40* times instead of 36?

SAM: Well, I just estimated. The first time I did it, it was for 16 times. I think I found that it made it around about halfway (*see Figure 2.4*), so I asked it to go 32 times and then it didn't go quite all the way . . . .

MARY: So, yes, it was two circles. One is the individual *unit* [the circle], and then you repeat that unit 40 times to make another circle—40 circles within a large circle.

JEANNE: And the question is, when will it get back to the original circle?

LUCY: We found [in working with circles] that with a RT of 10, it comes back again after 36 repetitions. But if he got 40, why did it come out perfect?

MARY: I think it's an overlap.

Already in these first few moments of the conversation, we see multiple views and multiple descriptions developing. As comments are "handed-off" among the participants, each participant is both reflecting and transforming the comments of another. I step in first. My attention is attracted to Sam's use of "40"—the number of times he "asked" the computer to repeat his CIRCLE and RT 10 procedure. My question is interrogating the meaning he is giving to "40" and implicitly his understanding of how his own procedures work. Sam's answer tells us more about how he arrived at the end result: More like making hands-on constructions, he "estimated" in response to the results he saw on the screen.

Mary, working from her own sense of what Sam has told us, reflects back what she sees. And in doing so, she transforms Sam's procedural description into objects moving in nested actions—circles circling ("40 circles within a large circle"). Mary's redescribing is a first small instance of a "reflecting transformation" that will lead to others.

Lucy's focus, meanwhile, stays put on my questions, which she addresses by looking back at her own experience in making circle procedures with LOGO. And from this view, Lucy sees a mismatch between what she "found" earlier and what Sam tells her he has done. In the light of the comparison, she raises a new question: "Why did [40] come out perfect?" Mary, focusing now on Lucy's question, answers it but again puts her answer in terms of objects and actions rather than numbers: "I think it's an overlap."

Both participants are, of course, quite right; what is striking is the differences in their respective views. Lucy, thinking in terms of the numeric values in Sam's procedure, is pointing out that if the turtle turns 10 degrees on each of its repetitions, it will complete the circle ("come back again") after 36 repetitions. Mary's more action and visually oriented view is implicitly saying that with Sam's 40 repetitions, the extra 4 simply go over ("overlap") the first 4. And since we can't *see* that, the result only seems to "come out perfect."

At this point I make an abrupt shift in direction that initiates the next portion of the conversation.

Two Trajectories

> JEANNE: So it's like the earth going around, and then it's like the whole thing going around in the whole year. It's going around itself and then . . .
>
> IDA: It's like day and night and the seasons. Revolution and rotation. It's beautiful.
>
> MARY: But I don't think that that's what we were doing in making our butterfly procedure. Because those were larger and larger

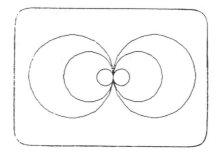

Figure 2.5

circles (*see Figure 2.5*). Yours sort of were all the same size. *Our variable was the size, his variable was position.* The size of the circle always changed.[1]

My abrupt shift in direction is only an apparent one; I am actually reflecting off of Mary's redescription—that is, her objects moving in nested action. Letting my initial questions go, I glimpse, *through* Mary's circles circling, a *resemblance* between Sam's procedures and "the earth going around." But without knowing with respect to what! Ida, following the trajectory of my reflection, elaborates on it: "It's like day and night and the seasons." And then, pursuing the new trajectory even further, Ida makes our *resemblance criterion explicit:* Sam's procedure, reviewed by Mary as circles circling, which I see as the earth turning, all enact the same complementary principles: "revolution and rotation."

So, in quick chaining, our mutual reflecting results in reseeing, seeing one working system as another, seeing a resemblance embodied by but still hidden in the materials, until *principles* finally precipitate out. And as the principles emerge in the context of our immediate and shared experience, principles and shared experience take on new meaning.

But meanwhile Mary, seemingly inattentive to this new trajectory and still puzzling over my initial questions, turns back on her own experience in making circle procedures. As for Lucy, Sam's procedure reminds her of a procedure she had made previously—her "butterfly" procedure. Comparing hers with Sam's, Mary sees similarities between them and thus liberates the features that made their *differences:* "Our variable was the *size;* his variable was *position.*" And while accounting for the strikingly different results of the two procedures, Mary, almost in passing, also articulates the *formal property* they both share: The procedures depend on different uses of the same powerful function—*variable!*

That is, while both Sam and Mary began with a circle procedure,

Figure 2.6: "...two trajectories, each of which spawns a new view...."

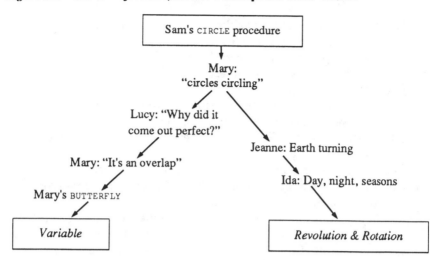

Sam's use of RT 10 changed the *position* of his circle on each repetition. In contrast, Mary's use of a changing value for FD (FD :F + 2) in her "butterfly" procedure changed the *size* of the circle on each repetition.

So our conceptual chaining, moved along by our mutual reflecting, leaves a linked trail that diverges into two trajectories, each of which spawns new views of the material through the emergence of more general ideas (see Figure 2.6). That is, while each of these trajectories begins with specific questions grounded in personal experiences with materials—Sam's procedures, along with Lucy's and Mary's—through reflecting off of them, seeing similarities and differences among these working systems, our conversation winds up and out of them to more general principles—first, *revolution and rotation*, then *variable*.

Finally, notice my participation in this chaining process. I could have pursued my initial questions in the service of *teaching* Sam and the others what they *did not* know—certain basic geometric principles and how they are played out in LOGO geometry. But instead, by letting it go, my initial questions become a jumping off place from which all of us are reflecting *back*, reflecting *on*, and building *from* what we *do* know. So as the conversation unfolds, I am playing a double role: mutual participant, freely joining in with the others in making my spontaneous associations and views known; and also watchful listener, looking for moments to grab on-the-wing so as to provoke, probe, prod, and reinforce germinating ideas. And, in going on with the conversation, I focus especially on those moments that might encourage the participants to see another familiar working system in a new way.

Shifting Meanings

JEANNE: Are there any variables, here, in your circuits?

MARY: Are there any variables in. . . .

JEANNE: In what you were just doing?

SAM: Yeah, there were variables.

JEANNE: Like what?

SAM: Like making one bell ring, making the other bell ring, trying to make both bells ring simultaneously.

SUSAN JO: Those are *differences*—different things that are happening, but I don't . . .

SAM: Oh, so like using circuits to do different things.

JEANNE: Yes. Each one of these—bell, buzzer, lightbulb—you could think of as a variable *in* the circuit.

SUSAN JO: That doesn't necessarily mean the same thing to me. Like in Sam's circle, the variable he uses—the number of repetitions as 16, 32, then 40—is . . . it's doing the *same things* but the number of *times* it does it changes. That's a *kind* of thing that stays the same, but the *amount* is varied.

IDA: A variable could be the *amount* of batteries.

JEANNE: So you vary the amount of *power*. Well, what if you just substituted the bell for the buzzer? That is, everything is the same except . . . would that be a variable?

NINA: Well, that's changing more than . . . if you're using a battery . . . you're increasing the light, or increasing the battery. Whereas if you switch—you use a bell or a buzzer—you're changing the whole . . . you're changing more, aren't you?

IDA: Sometimes you use a bell and sometimes a buzzer. But then the variable is *what is doing the work* . . .

SUSAN JO: So the *type* of work that's being done varies.

SAM: Yes, it would be. It would be the same thing; you're just working in a different *medium*.

JEANNE: So the lightbulb was one medium and the buzzer another? *But the circuit stays the same.*

IDA: This is just *substituting* . . . substituting something different.

MARY: So we're saying if *shape* . . . if visually it's a totally different form, that doesn't feel like a variable anymore. 'Cause that's really . . . *functionally*, the bell and the buzzer are pretty similar. It's just . . . they look like they're different species somehow . . .

IDA: In the computer we're using variables to change *quantities* of things. But with the color . . . shape . . . those are *qualities* . . . attributes . . .

JEANNE: But if you start with the *circuit as the basic thing*, then changing bell/buzzer doesn't make very much difference. But if you *look just at the bell and the buzzer*, they're very different things.

SUSAN JO: Well the *structure* stays the same, but the *function* . . .

JEANNE: *It depends on what you're looking at.*

Catching Mary's use of the term *variable* as it passes on-the-wing, I pluck it out and use it as a foil to prod the participants' understanding of the term. I do so by asking them to posit a function for *variable* within the circuitry materials that are still lying about on the table: "Are there any variables, here, in your circuitry?" At the same time I am using *variable* as a foil to help the group experiment with the possibilities for seeing one familiar working system as another. The ploy turns out to be a pivotal one. The participants find themselves following a "thought experiment": What will happen to the meaning they are giving to *variable* as a function embedded in LOGO computer procedures if they carry *variable* across and imagine it as potentially a function embedded in the circuitry with which they have just been working?

The experiment immediately exposes the term for scrutiny. At the same time, features and relations come to the surface that were previously hidden, transparent to the goals of all-at-once actions. And in carrying out this experiment, the computer is playing the role of "transitional object." With LOGO procedures as one of the two working systems through which we are interrogating the meaning of *variable*, the thought experiment helps to bridge the gap between meanings implicit in symbolic expressions and meanings embodied by materials and actions on them. Unlikely as it would have been if we had planned a "unit on variable," *variable* becomes the focus of the group's animated discussion.

Sam's initial response, followed by the quiet confrontation between Susan Jo and me, the leaders of the group, opens up the field and sets the terms for argument, speculation, and side-taking. The arguments hinge on what each person takes as a *kind* of thing that can change, along with a kind of thing that stays the same. For Sam, what changes are concrete objects and actions: "Like making one bell ring, making another bell ring." Susan Jo (who is also our math specialist) disagrees: "Those are *differences*—different things are happening." I elaborate on the object-meaning Sam is implicitly giving to variable, suggesting also a concrete object that might be staying the same: ". . . bell, buzzer, lightbulb you could think of as a variable *in* the circuit." Moving in, Susan Jo makes her view more clear. Arguing for its formal and canonical meaning as used in Sam's procedures, a variable is not a "variable" object but rather "a *kind* of thing (for example, REPEAT) that stays the same but the *amount* (16, 32, 40) varies."

It is important to notice that our conversation—along with the emerging meaning of this quite abstract notion, *variable*—is always *grounded* in specific materials that we are all looking at and trying to make sense of. As we continually go back to these materials in our conceptual chaining—seeing now one aspect, now another—the materials and their relations serve as the vehicles through which the participants carry themselves beyond what they know already to a new view. Searching for one another's meanings, each participant is at the same time informing his or her own. It is interesting to notice, too, that differences among the participants are made more friendly, less confrontational by attributing them to "feelings" rather than reasoned thought or conviction: Mary: ". . . that feels like a variable"; Ida: ". . . those things don't feel like variables . . . it would feel like a variable if . . ."

And as the conversation moves back and forth, each person actively reflecting the other, participants' comments continue to spiral between concrete examples and generalization. For example, Ida makes a general comment as she puts her finger on the "difference criterion" underlying our disagreements—quantities versus qualities: "In the computer we're using variables to change *quantities* of things. But with the color . . . shape . . . those are *qualities*, attributes." Her more general comment depends on, reflects *on* the specific examples that others have used in making their arguments. For instance, some people talk about the *amount* of batteries or of power, and the *number* of circuits or power sources; while others refer to *qualities* they can see, such as color, shape, medium: ". . . if visually it's a totally different form, that doesn't feel like a variable anymore." Indeed, the distinction implicit in our disagreements, which Ida makes explicit—quantities versus qualities—points to a general distinction that is often seen as critical in distinguishing between working in the virtual world of the computer and working in the real time/space world of hands-on materials.

Picking up on Ida's distinction, reflectively transforming it, turning it around, I propose another view: ". . . if you start with the circuit as the basic thing, then changing bell/buzzer doesn't make much difference. But if you look just at the bell and the buzzer, they're very different things." And pushing the level of generalization a little higher, the rumble of my covert ideas (multiple representations, multiple seeings) bubbles to the surface: "It depends on what you're looking at." But notice that "higher" is in no sense "better." For it is exactly the waves up and down (from materials to generalizations and back) and the resulting reciprocity among these moves that gives both the materials and the generalizations credibility and meaning. And through our conceptual chaining, these moves, with their shifting meanings, are also carrying the potential for learning.

Two Insights

But *what* was being learned? Surely, people were learning different things differently. Jumping ahead to the end of the conversation (which continued on for some time), we find that Mary and Susan Jo have each made discoveries, but they are of very different sorts.

Mary's insight seems to come from following the winding path of our conversation, and at the same time her comments embody in them the very processes that have given rise to this winding path—reflecting transformations, seeing in multiple ways, moves up and down between materials and generalizations. Mary's comments come in response to a question from Susan Jo, who at this point has become restless with our "conversational drift":

SUSAN JO: I have a question. What's in this about seeing variables in different places, that we can use, or would we use in teaching? Is this a notion that would be valuable to kids?

MARY: It's critical in understanding where a kid is at. Because you're teaching this, and the kid is giving these cockamamie answers. And then if you can, like go over there, I mean *over where the kid is looking from*, and you look out from there, *that's exactly what he ought to be seeing*. And then what the kid was saying makes perfect sense. So I don't think you can *teach* the kid about the variable, but you can try to find a path into what the kid is *seeing*. . . . And we can't just react . . .

The links in our conceptual chaining have helped Mary and others see what I could not have *told* them. And this is so because while Mary's insight follows the emerging path of our conversation, she has (as we do with materials in making a gate) reflectively transformed the materials and ideas that carried it along: Her insight is importantly grounded in the "materials" she knows best—events that happen with children in the real world of school. And with this grounding, those vague, inaccessible, rumbling ideas, such as the importance of paying attention to different ways of seeing, describing, and making sense of the world, become her own—practical, relevant, everyday events that the teachers, along with Mary, can recognize and feel.

For Susan Jo, in contrast to Mary, the conversation has all along been about the meaning of the term *variable*. Her insight, which seems to have been slowly germinating (the path of the conversation serving as nutritive medium), carries the conversation back to the initial controversies generated by Sam's computer procedure. Her own previous work, now reflected in the multiple mirrors of the group's discussion, helps Susan Jo see what she knew already in a new way:

> I'm still trying to figure out whether I think substituting the bulb for the bell is a variable. But it just struck me that when I did this sort of stuff with my kids—you know, varying the battery and the bulb gets brighter—but the constantness of the circuit itself is something that . . . that the thing you stick in there doesn't matter, never struck me before because we never had anything but bulbs so it wasn't in fact a variable. And yet it's so important . . . *the constantness of that circuit is such a fundamental thing. But if you don't vary the function of the things it's operating with, you never get to that.*

And I, responding to Susan Jo, use her comment to wrap up the conversation by turning it back on itself:

> Yeah. It's like what just happened here. I mean, we started talking about the . . . the . . . the thing that Sam had done, and that made us start thinking about *this* stuff [circuitry]. But if we hadn't had *both* things—Sam's computer procedure and the circuitry stuff— we might not have gotten to the issue of . . . the business of a constant and a variable might not have *leaped out* if we had just been sticking with one thing, this circuitry.

FOLLOWING THE PATH INTO THE LAB

But I began the project and this chapter with ideas and hopes for children's learning. What, then, can be said about that? I have suggested several times that the teachers' work in our sessions has been mirrored in their work with children in the Lab. I see this most clearly in Mary's work with children. Mary, who is in fact Mary Briggs, is one of the learning disabilities teachers in the school. Over the past 3 years, Mary and I have together worked with four or five children whom she brings to the Lab after school for 2 hours each week. My conversations with her while actually working in the Lab with children have been a major factor in helping me see how ideas born in the ivory tower can be put to work in the real life of school. I will conclude this chapter with a few remarks and a short example of Mary's learning as it was reflected in her work with one child, whom I will call Ruth.

Ruth joined our group when she was 8 and having real troubles in her regular classroom work. She had severe difficulties learning to read; she often disturbed her teacher by responding to directions or explanations with, "I don't understand, really"; and, as we saw in the Lab as well, she had serious problems putting into words what she was thinking about. Typically, in trying to say what she was thinking, Ruth would start up, then stop, then say, "I forgot," or "I don't know," or "Oh, forget about it."

In the Lab it gradually emerged that these moments of inarticulateness were in fact critical moments in which Ruth was germinating an idea. As such, they became for Mary, and eventually for the other children as well, a signal to stop what we were doing in order to help Ruth find out what it was she was thinking about. Smiling and often with a knowing laugh, Mary would say, "I'm sure you haven't really forgotten. Take your time, dear, it's worth it." And with this encouragement, along with the other children's respectful patience, Ruth's ideas would haltingly emerge, often in a form that was difficult to understand at first. As time went on, it became clear that the issue was not just Ruth's difficulties with words, although these difficulties were real. As it turned out, Ruth's ideas were very complex, and often at an extraordinary level of abstraction: It seems that she, unlike felt-path gate builders and many of the rest of us, could stop the "going-on" of her actions and, indeed, the actions of those materials that she could directly see and feel, so as to "mentally feel" and coordinate the relations among relations that must account for the workings of structures we were making and trying to make sense of—rhythms, gears, pendulums. But to find words to express this feel for what she could only see in her mind's eye was understandably difficult (that is why the formalisms of science have their privileged status). And that Ruth's understanding was in a very real sense a "feel for" came through clearly in the expressive gestures that often accompanied her halting words.

Through Mary's encouraging probes, it also became clear that Ruth's behavior in the classroom was deceptive indeed: Her expressed inability to understand the teacher's explanations stemmed not from an intellectual deficiency but from her own intellectual *demands*—she needed to know more. Or as Mary often put it later, "Ruth needs to know the whole, the why, before she can begin to deal with the details, the parts."

How did Mary come to understand these qualities of Ruth's thinking? She did so, in part, by mirroring, in her own reflecting way, the *kind* of learning we were practicing in the teacher group and by following the paths that had led to her generative insights, which, interestingly, Mary also had her troubles articulating. Recall, for instance, her insightful but groping comments in response to Susan Jo during our earlier conversation about the value of discussing variables with kids: ". . . if you can, like go over there, I mean over where the kid is looking from, and you look out from there, that's exactly what he ought to be seeing. And then what the kid was saying makes perfect sense. So I don't think you can *teach* the kid about the variable, but you can try to *find a path into what the kid is seeing*. . . . And we can't just react . . ." I illustrate with one short instance:

During the second year of Ruth's work in the Lab, we were working with two huge meshing gears that children in another group had made out of cardboard. There was one smaller gear (8 teeth) and one larger gear (32 teeth). As Ruth and others were playing with the gears—turning them around, watching what was happening—the following conversation ensued:

MARY: Now, which of these gears do you think is going the fastest?

SEVERAL CHILDREN: The smaller one.

RUTH: No. Both of them are going at the same speed.

SID: But the smaller one is going fastest.

MARY (*to Sid*): You say it's going faster, huh?

JEANNE (*to Ruth*): You said same speed?

RUTH: Because look, you can't make this one (the smaller gear) go faster. Every time this is going. . . . Oh, you mean how fast it's going around?

MARY: Well, I don't know, what do you think?

RUTH: *What kind of fastest do you mean?*

MARY: What are the choices?

RUTH: Well there's one kind of fastest where you can say for each tooth . . .

MARY: Wait, one kind you can say . . .

RUTH: Like for one kind of fastest you could say—like you could go—you could say how—like how each teeth goes in like that, ya know what I mean? And one kind of fastest, you could say how long it takes for this one [the smaller one] to go around.

MARY: Hmmm. So if you say it's the kind of fastness with the teeth, then which one wins, which is the fastest?

SID: The smaller one.

RUTH: No, they both are going the same speed.
MARY: Okay. And what about if you say which goes *around* the
    fastest?
RUTH: The smallest one.

It is important to note here that Mary herself was not at all clear about
the workings of the gears and, indeed, had at first been hesitant about
the whole gear project. So, in asking her questions, Mary was not *testing*
Ruth to see if she had the right answer; Mary was *genuinely interested in
hearing what Ruth had to say*—maybe, in the process, even helping herself
to clarify and inform her own understanding. This attitude, this way of
listening to Ruth, was Mary's way of "finding a path into what the kid
is seeing"; and in following that path, she was also helping Ruth to find
words to *say* what she felt.

And what she "mentally feels" turns out, as was often the case with
Ruth, to be of a complexity that helps account for the difficulties she has
in putting her ideas into words. What Ruth has understood, albeit still
to some extent embodied in the materials and expressed in a way that
sounds quite different from canonical "privileged descriptions," is the
principle of linear velocity (". . . how each teeth goes in like that") functioning simultaneously with angular velocity (". . . how long it takes for
this one to go around"). And in order to account for the two kinds of
"fastness," she needed to get off the path of the gears' actions and her
own, so as to differentiate and mentally coordinate actions that she
could not, at any one moment, directly see and feel.

Looking Back

Looking back to my initial ideas, those that motivated the project in
the first place, I realize that Ruth's difficulties also involved a mismatch
between inner mental representation and outer descriptions of it, but in
ways that I could not have imagined before. My focus earlier had been
on the problems that children or adults with well-functioning "sensory-
smarts" might have in making sense of the formal, symbolic languages
spoken in schools. And this I considered to be an issue of incongruences
among the felt paths of gate-makers or performers on musical instruments, the inner mental representations guiding these linked actions,
and the features and relations to which symbolic expressions refer. But
Ruth's troubles suggest a different kind of mismatch. Hers was a mismatch between, on one hand, the relations of relations that she could
somehow feel in the materials but that could only be represented in her

mind's eye, and on the other, the words she had available to say what she could mentally see.

The two kinds of problems converge in illuminating the special qualities of symbolic expressions—those qualities that probably explain why, through the long history of science, they have come to be: Symbolic expressions allow their users to say, to describe, just those relations of relations that we are able to find only when we are able to step off the singular felt path of our actions, stop their going-on. Reflecting *on* what we have seen, we can, but only in imagination, hear or see, for example, two simultaneous motions (angular and linear). And rather than leaving them undifferentiated so that they merge into a single stream of motion, we pull them apart, look at each one separately, and then coordinate them in a single higher-level structure. And that complex structure, still without collapsing the two streams of motions into one, encompasses them both. And it is these higher-level structures that can best, perhaps only, be expressed in the formalisms, albeit static in themselves, that have become the privileged languages of science.

It would seem, then, that the differences between the problems of gate-makers and the problems I have come to see in watching Mary and Ruth, are these: Gate-makers have yet to acquire inner mental representations that might make accessible to them the kinds of structures to which formalisms refer; others, like Ruth, can glimpse the kind of structures to which formalisms refer but have not yet learned to see *in* these formal expressions what they have already glimpsed in the phenomenon itself.

And to continue this conceptual chaining, it was Ruth's explanation, which still stayed close to the materials, nurtured by Mary's patient questioning, that later did indeed help Mary to understand the principles underlying what Ruth had discovered. And without saying more about it, I suspect, too, that seeing resemblances between one working system and another (Sam's procedure, the earth turning) and then making the resemblance criteria explicit so as to precipitate out a more abstract principle that they both share, is in some important way practicing the very same kind of intellectual activity that is involved in abstracting out two motions from the single perceived motion of gears, rhythms, or pendulums and constructing a further complex structure that is neither of them but accounts for them both.

Ruth will be in sixth grade next year. She is reading well, and while still shy and sometimes a little "dreamy," there is no longer any doubt about her abilities. I end this accounting with what I will call Ruth's "testimonial." At the last meeting of Ruth's third year in the Lab, Mary asked each of the children to say "one thing" they had learned during their time in the Lab. Ruth was eager to speak, and what she said creates another link in the chain of reflecting transformations. It is particularly interesting that for Ruth, who still has difficulties *saying* what she is thinking, the time she spent "talking about something" is a very important part of *what* she has learned, *how* she did that, and even *why* it was worth doing. Reflecting back and reflecting on her experience in the Lab, Ruth's response to Mary's question tells us, perhaps better than any of us could, what "the project" is all about and what "reflecting" is all about, too.

> RUTH: You have to do a lot of thinking. I like it that everyone does
> it kinda on their own. And it's so funny to compare ways
> 'cause you think you've got the *right answer,* but you don't
> have, you've just got *one* answer. And talking about some-
> thing. When you talk about it, you learn more from yourself.
> Like you know *why* but you can't explain it. 'Cause when you
> talk about something, you have to think about what you're
> thinking about or what you have in your mind. And you *know*
> you have a right answer or whatever, but when you say it . . .
> when you say it out loud you kind of think of it yourself in
> different ways—of what you did even when you were in first
> grade. Even the next time I go do that (*points to pendulums*), I
> might think about it in a different way. And explaining it, you
> feel good . . . you get what I mean?
> MARY: Ruth, I get you so well!

ACKNOWLEDGMENTS

The work reported here was funded by the Ford Foundation, the Spencer Foundation, the Jessie B. Cox Charitable Trust, and the Apple Foundation's "Wheels for the Mind."

NOTE

1. The procedures for BUTTERFLY were these:

```
TO WING1 :F              TO WING2 :F              TO BUTTERFLY
  IF :F > 4 [STOP]         IF :F > 4 [STOP]         WING1 1
  REPEAT 72 [FD :F RT 5]   REPEAT 72 [FD :F LT 5]   WING2 1
  WING1 :F + 2            WING2 :F + 2             END
END                      END
```

Note: :F is the "variable." The WING procedures begin by giving :F a value of 1 (e.g., WING1 1), which makes the smallest circle. They then add 2 to that value (:F+2) giving :F a value of 3 to make the next largest circle, and once more add 2, giving :F a value of 5 to make the largest circle.

REFERENCES

Bamberger, J. (1981). Revisiting children's descriptions of simple rhythms. In S. Strauss (Ed.), *U-shaped behavioral growth*. New York: Academic.

Bamberger, J. (1986). Cognitive issues in the development of musically gifted children. In R. J. Sternberg & J. E. Davis (Eds.), *Conceptions of giftedness*. Cambridge, England: Cambridge University Press.

Bamberger, J. (in press). *The mind behind the musical ear*. Cambridge, MA: Harvard University Press.

Kuhn, T. (1977). *The essential tension: Selected studies in scientific tradition and change*. Chicago: University of Chicago Press.

Piaget, J. (1962). *Play, dreams, and imitation*. New York: Norton.

Part II

PARTICIPATORY ACTION RESEARCH

3

Bridging the Gap: An Organizational Inquiry Into an Urban School System

NORMAN A. NEWBERG

EDUCATORS TALK ABOUT articulation between school units as students pass from a lower school to a higher one. Seldom, however, is this transition accomplished in a manner that addresses the complex needs of students who must adjust to the transition. Too often in this transition the social, emotional, and academic needs of students moving from fifth to sixth and from eighth to ninth grade are handled in bureaucratic ways. Records are passed; a counselor or roster specialist from the receiving school advises the sending school on how to select programs or courses; sometimes a brief orientation is held at the receiving school. While each of these activities offers some help, they are insufficient. For students, the transition is abrupt and awkward, and many will never make it across.

In middle-income communities students enter the next level with family support, a record of academic accomplishment, and schools attuned to their concerns. But for students from low-income families these transition points are hazardous, because their previous academic deficits compound in the new and more complex setting, making their failure predictable. It is this population that is often at risk of dropping out of high school as the possibility of graduation becomes increasingly unattainable.

Teachers working in urban schools sense the gap in their ability to cope with students as they enter middle and senior high school. Receiving school faculties, for example, often question the adequacy of the preparation students received from their previous school; they may also question the validity of grades or ability group placements that sending school faculties assigned to students. They may even question their ability to teach the kinds of students they are receiving or the students' ability to learn.

In this chapter, I will examine the problem of bridging the gap between elementary, middle, and high schools. I will also show how educators can use these transition points to evaluate the strengths and weaknesses of student achievement. This reflected knowledge becomes the basis for recommending a change process in which school levels act as an interconnected system that is more accountable for sustained student progress.

Bridging the Gap has been a research and intervention project designed to increase articulation and direct interaction between feeder subsystems within District 1 of the School District of Philadelphia. The project started in February 1987 with three schools: Yates Elementary, Radcliffe Middle, and Manning Senior High School. (All names of particular schools are fictitious.) In the fall of 1988 two elementary and one middle school were added. And in the fall of 1989 the feeder cluster was completed by adding five elementary schools and the remaining middle school. The material reported on in this chapter was derived from work with the original three schools. The high school and those middle/junior high and elementary schools that send significant percentages of their students to it formed the basic organizational structure for this project. Schools selected for intervention derived 40% of their student populations from low-income families.

The method used in Bridging the Gap was tailored to the multiple needs of the problem situation under investigation. The method incorporated several approaches derived from these streams of thought: action research, reflective practice, processes for intervention, and planned change. An opportunity existed to bring these together in a joint process of learning and action. What do we mean by learning and action? Within an organizational context, the recurrent needs are to act, reflect on the appropriateness of that action, and choose to act the same or differently based on that derived knowledge. Also, all practitioners inside organizations need to become diagnosticians of their past and present behavior so that they can effectively design for a desirable future.

However, seldom do organizations sustain their capacity to function as learning systems. Built into the structure of organizational life are roles and human processes that limit the organization's capacity to respond to changes in either the immediate or external environment. Defensive behavior shields the organization from considering alternative structural options, procedures, or behaviors (Argyris, 1985). When organizations are locked into defensive routines they may need the services of an outside agent, or consultant, whose job is to teach the organization how to learn and to reflect. Through intervention, action researchers build the capacity within the organization to be more conscious of itself, to use the relevant information to form a diagnosis, to analyze problems, and to gain freedom to act in more original ways.

The process of organizational inquiry was facilitated by establishing several interactive forums where problems could be raised and solutions invented and recommended for implementation. The basic unit for these discussions was the transition team that each participating school organized. Consisting of administrators, teachers, counselors, and parents, the transition teams examined how transitions were managed within and across grade school levels. Transition teams met weekly or biweekly; a team member chaired the meeting. As action researchers, Burton Cohen, a researcher from the University of Pennsylvania's School of Social Work, and I were available to consult with the teams. We were most active in the beginning sessions. Once the teams agreed on an agenda and showed evidence of being able to work toward project goals, they became more independent of the researchers.

Teachers and administrators tend to see the gap as a function of conditions external to their influence, such as the drug problem; single-parent, female-headed households; and students who enter first grade without the benefit of a preschool or kindergarten experience. Much of what the researchers did initially was to move the participants closer to the problem they were trying to solve by getting them more intimately involved in understanding why students succeed or fail. Educators claim to know why students fail. But often they understand the situation in ways that perpetuate the status quo. At the first meeting of all the teams representing the three school levels, we made two interventions designed to help participants break their perceptual set. First we asked them to think of two students at risk—one who seemed to show significant improvements as a result of the teacher's efforts, and a second student who remained at risk. They presented these cases to each other and discussed the similarities and differences these students displayed. The information they shared included anecdotal statements, test performance, and the particular instructional strategies tried.

We found that teachers had little difficulty sharing this kind of information. But we sensed that they did not see the connection between these individual cases and the population that aggregates to become problematic at the next school level. Therefore, our second intervention was to ask participants to look more closely at data and, in particular, to notice the cumulative impact of failure longitudinally. We encouraged the Bridging the Gap teams to examine school-based records and to ask teachers who work at a different level about the nature of the gap at the major transition points. Team members generally agreed that by the end of the fifth grade students were 1 to 2 years behind in reading, while eighth-graders entering high school were 2 to 3 years behind. This perception was confirmed by the high school testing coordinator, who noted that the reading levels of incoming ninth-graders averaged 6 years, 2 months. At Manning High School an average of 50% were retained in ninth grade, and over 4 years of high school 44% drop out. Ferreting out this data and confronting it directly helped participants to see the consequences of failure.

Through our interventions we wanted participants to be able to read the early warning signs in elementary school and continue to sustain intensive support for those students who are at risk of failure throughout secondary school so that dropout prevention might become an attainable objective. But it may also be necessary to rethink the way these three units understand their separate roles in educating students as well as their relationship to one another. At the first Bridging the Gap meeting in February 1987, we asked the participating schools to think of a metaphor that best characterized their relationship to students. The progression they described was revealing. The elementary school said "a family" and the middle school, "a rented apartment." The high school said: "We're the bill collectors. We show them the street."

These metaphors suggest that teachers believe students need to be dependent and require nurturing in elementary school. In middle school they are expected to assume more independent living in a temporary home—a rented apartment. By high school, students are expected to be independent. The supports are withdrawn, and they must face the consequences of their failure. But failure may be inevitable given the assumptions educators make about the maturity of students and the level of their academic accomplishments.

The high school, however, can take little comfort in failing large numbers of students if the result is massive numbers of dropouts. This progressive distancing of school professionals from students' continuing need for nurturance and dependence may contribute to the gap that needs to be bridged. When we suggested the need to change the way students are supported, participants expressed concern that we were advocating a reversion to social promotion and a watering down of standards. The opposite was the case. We consistently said that standards needed to be upheld, but that it was also possible to rethink how instruction is delivered and how school is organized so that those at risk could be more successful.

Again, if the evidence proved that urban students were thriving as a result of the assumptions attached to each school level and the functions each performed, change would not be necessary. But that is not the case. High school teachers cannot assume that students are secure emotionally and socially. In the first few months the researchers questioned the myths and assumptions that formed the operating framework for each level in order to reframe the problem in a more complete manner. We invited participants to research the field with us by examining statistical data as well as by interviewing students, parents, and teachers. We used imagery, such as the metaphors mentioned above, to locate a feeling for current operations. We also invited participants to imagine a very different set of conditions in which it was possible for these students they taught to succeed.

In order to give the administrators a role in setting the pace and direction of activities and to facilitate an intimate forum for dialogue among a group of professionals who previously had had little interaction, we scheduled a monthly meeting of the principals at one of their schools. Principals reported on progress to date and shared problems and possible solutions. At these meetings the researchers built an agenda for a monthly meeting of all the transition teams.

This chapter documents how educators become more aware of both the ways in which students are progressively at risk of failure and the need for interventions that increase at-risk students' chances for success. The research typical of Bridging the Gap has been homegrown, experimental research on practice. As transition teams from the three school levels became interested in finding answers to various questions, they designed specific activities in order to seek them out. Through this process, teams not only learned more about their initial area of inquiry but also discovered new issues and ideas for other activities. This promoted continued action. While the teams often initially constructed activities in isolation from the others, through the mechanisms of monthly joint team meetings and principals' meetings, activities became a matter of public knowledge, and activities on one level informed related activities at another. Sets of activities based on common themes, therefore, occurred at overlapping points of time (Chevalier, 1968; Pava, 1984).

A DEVELOPMENTAL PROCESS FOR INTRODUCING CHANGE IN URBAN SCHOOLS

At one level, this project has been concerned with "bridging the gap," that is, how schools can better manage the transitions that students experience when they move from one level in the school system to the next. At a more general level, the research agenda for this project has also been concerned with how changes in awareness and practice can be introduced into the public schools. Large urban school systems are often seen as "resistant to change." In Schön's (1971) terms, they are "dynamically conservative," that is, they fight hard and expend energy in order to stay the same. When change occurs, it is often through a mandated set of procedures and practices that are introduced throughout the entire system at once. Our approach to introducing change, therefore, has largely relied on the belief that a group of teachers, administrators, and parents in each school can be made aware of the problem and can invent and carry out interventions that make sense in their own situation. Furthermore, they can learn how to negotiate with other levels or parts of the system once they learn to see them as resources rather than impediments.

Based on our involvement with Bridging the Gap, we see a developmental process that has taken place. The phases of this process, which will each be described in more detail, are the following:

1. Confronting blaming cycles by increasing contact and interaction (between teachers, administrators, and parents at all levels in feeder school subsystems)
2. Developing a larger awareness (among teachers and administrators of how large percentages of students become progressively more at risk of failure)
3. Redesign of strategic or leading parts of the system

In the following section, for each phase in the process we will state the kind of problem evoked and the nature of the intervention employed to address the problem.

Confronting Blaming Cycles by Increasing Contact and Interaction

At the beginning of the project, distrust and a tendency to blame the school level above or the one below for problems seemed to be a defensive routine (Argyris, 1985). The elementary school blamed parents for placing students (30% of them) in first grade "right off the street, without preschool or kindergarten." They blamed the high school for housing an alternative high school program in their elementary building, thus forcing them to offer only a half-day kindergarten. The lack of space, they claimed, made full-day kindergarten impractical.

The elementary school principal had not made these concerns known to either the high school principal or his immediate supervisor.

The high school blamed the elementary and middle schools. The high school team handed them a list of questions dealing with the appropriate certification to teach certain subjects and promotional standards for students. The questions challenged the competence levels of teachers and administration.

At one meeting when all teams met, the high school implied that the middle school was practicing social promotion by passing students who had not mastered grade-level work. The middle school principal countered that it was school district policy to allow retaining once between grades K–4 and once more between grades 5–8 and then to require passing on the basis of social promotion. Realizing that limitations exist at all levels, given the policy, the teams began to share the implications of the problem and stopped blaming one another.

Gradually a climate of trust was created by encouraging educators to state their understanding of how students become at risk and what each party was willing to do to assist. Facilitators labeled blaming as defensive behavior that promotes both bickering and isolation and stops the flow of reliable information about the performance of students, parents, and teachers in their roles. These blaming strategies were exposed as dysfunctional and divisive, while problem solving based on a shared appreciation of the problem setting was shown to make blaming less necessary or desirable.

School units are isolated from their feeder systems. That insularity may contribute to the need some educators feel to blame those with whom they have little or no contact. Principals and teachers in a feeder cluster do not know how teachers at another level teach, what is actually learned, or how school is managed at different buildings. To reduce blaming and increase genuine inquiry, we encouraged frequent faculty and administration visits to each level of the feeder system. Attitudes among teachers and administrators changed over time through increased contact with various school levels; and as activities necessitated collaboration, barriers that may have existed gave way to more trust and communication. School visitations were integral to the process. What follows is a sample of the comments high school teachers made after their visits.

An English teacher reported that a middle school teacher felt that they get "no information from the elementary school about where kids are when they enter middle school. Very little has been done to bridge the gap."

Several teachers visited the elementary school; they were appreciative that elementary teachers had made teaching and learning a high priority. One of the high school teachers observed third- and fourth-grade reading classes. She was impressed that students were attentive and motivated. However, she was concerned that some teachers were not sure of the policies for promotion. These elementary school teachers informed her that "they noticed that at the third- and fifth-grade levels students with D's who were passing reading courses may be 2 years behind." The high school teacher warned her colleagues of the consequences of this phenomenon: "This [the gap] starts back there—you won't have all at grade level. It has to be compensated for with reading material."

The across-school visitations seemed to sharpen teachers' perceptions of how problems started and deepen their appreciation for the quality of teaching. These perceptions are especially valuable for high school teachers, who may regard themselves as having depth knowledge in subject matter. Elementary and middle school teachers often resent the feelings of superiority they sense from high school teachers. But if the visitations revealed the professional competence of their lower school colleagues, they also unearthed some problems. Some children were passed on even though they had serious deficits. The problem was blamed on an inadequate understanding of the promotion policy. However, what became clear to the high school teachers was that it is an illusion to think that students entering ninth grade will be on grade level. Therefore high school teachers have to be prepared to teach these students at their level.

The teacher visitations raised awareness among all parties as to how school is conducted longitudinally. These activities began to weave together the purpose of school and how it changes at each level, revealing both weaknesses and strengths. And, most importantly, they produced concrete, direct ways for teachers to experience continuity in caring for the progress of students.

Developing a Larger Awareness

Educators tend to see such vexing problems as the persistent failure of students from low-income families through a single perspective. An important intervention of Bridging the Gap has been to reframe the problem as a pervasive one that requires systems thinking. This shift enables all the key stakeholders from each level to pose problems of common concern and search jointly for appropriate solutions. At some point, after sufficient interactions, visitations, and opportunities to see parts of the school system through the eyes of another, transition team members began to see the problem of increasing numbers of students becoming progressively at risk as more of a systemic phenomenon with multiple causes and multiple points of intervention. This is a fundamental shift that goes beyond seeing more and more of the pieces until one can observe the whole. Rather, it involves a "reframing" of the problem—an ability to accept a definition of the problem that is fundamentally different from the one originally held—that can incorporate elements and values from both one's own and others' definitions. The problem of students being at risk for failing ceases to be one that can be addressed by very targeted interventions aimed at a specific group of students, teachers, or administrators (while everyone else continues to behave as usual); instead, it becomes one that requires a rethinking of the basic things that go on in the classroom.

How does this shift in awareness occur, and can it be helped along? In some cases it will occur naturally as participants gain experience, ask tougher questions of themselves and others, and begin to produce real data about system performance. For instance, at some point the high school administrators realized that a majority of the students were failing at least one subject, that only 12% of the ninth-graders passed all their subjects, and that some students might even regress in math or reading after beginning high school. While these data were alarming to administrators, they seemed distant from teachers' concerns. The researchers believed that a macro understanding of broad patterns of student failure alone could not motivate change in teacher behavior toward students at risk. Teachers, we hypothesized, needed a grainier, up-close look at the life histories of a small group of students to appreciate how they experienced school over time. Once teachers had a direct appreciation of the problem, they might begin to link micro and macro analyses in a way that would affect how they taught. Analyzing the cumulative records of several students over a period of 11 years offered a good starting point.

Manning High made the first step at collecting a sample of school life histories. Manning selected 21 students who at the time of the study were in eleventh grade and had been former students at Yates and Radcliffe. The results were disturbing: Of the 21, only three had never been retained in a grade; six had been retained in a grade once; six had been retained twice; and five had been retained three or more times. Seventeen of the 21 students with available test scores from the previous 3 years fell below the median in reading, in math, or in both; ten students were below in both areas. As the high school team members studied these records and interviewed the students, they began to see them not as exceptions but as indicative of a larger population.

The news of this study made personnel at the other two school levels curious, and defensive only at first, as to patterns existing among their past or present students. The elementary school asked the middle school to randomly choose ten of their former students who were ready to leave middle school and to conduct a study similar to the one the high school had done. The results showed that six of the ten had been retained in middle school, and only one scored over the 50th percentile in citywide reading and math tests from the previous year. In addition, seven of the students were labeled at-risk by their teachers, based on criteria such as previous retentions, failure in two or more subjects, and poor behavior and attendance. When the elementary team was presented with these results, they were in disbelief. Doubting the randomness of the sample, they requested that the middle school "do ten more." Ten more were done, this time with the elementary team making a blind selection. The results were similar. These data prompted Yates to look more closely at how it supported some of its weaker students before they left the school.

Yates started its within-school inquiry by identifying ten sixth-grade students who would graduate to the next level but whose performance indicated they might be at risk for failure in middle school. The transition team organized a number of activities to strengthen their students' academic skills and their readiness for middle school. The counselor met with students individually and in small groups to discuss goal-setting and time-management strategies. The reading specialist reviewed each student's progress and reinforced areas that needed improvement. The students' parents met with the elementary school principal and the principal of the receiving school. Even though their children had not failed, they were advised to send them to summer school so that they would not lose the skills they had attained.

Six months after the start of the next school year, the elementary school team asked to visit their former pupils at the middle school. Students were interviewed individually, using a common set of questions devised by the team. Regarding the activities the teachers had designed to assist them in making a more successful transition, the students felt that most of the things helped. When asked what Yates teachers could have done the previous year that they did not do, the answers were revealing. All the students wanted more science and more experiments. One student put it this way: "At Yates for science you memorize definitions; at Radcliffe you do science." The teachers from Yates concurred that they were weak in the teaching of science. They noted that they did not have a science teacher on staff and that, while they did have some science equipment, they felt inadequately prepared to use it. They asked their principal for more staff development. The following year a science teacher was assigned to the school. And the transition team arranged for the sixth grade to visit the middle school to experience a science lesson taught by a middle school teacher. The trial lesson was so successful that additional science classes were scheduled for the elementary students.

The second observation the Yates ten made was that they felt inadequate in their ability to take notes and make outlines. This comment surprised the transition team. When they discussed this criticism back at their school, teachers said those skills were taught several times in fourth, fifth, and sixth grades. The skills were taught, but the students had not internalized them. As they reflected on this puzzle, they wondered if this problem was symptomatic of a larger issue. Their students, from first grade on, answered a lot of prepared worksheets on which they were required to circle correct answers or fill in blanks. They had little expertise in taking an experience, digesting it, organizing it in their own words, and writing a response that would be recognizable to the teacher. Notetaking and outlining were often taught as abstract skills, unrelated to the skill's purpose. The transition team resolved to bring a writing specialist to their faculty meeting. The specialist offered to conduct a couple of sessions on notetaking and outlining, connecting those skills in a holistic approach to writing. She followed these sessions with individual conferences with teachers who wanted more particular help.

The events described took place over a period of a year and a half, from the identification of the students at risk to the interventions designed to make course corrections in instruction so that subsequent students might benefit. Schools, except small private schools, seldom see it as their responsibility to find out how their students are progressing at the next level. Further, they do not see that the success or failure of these graduating students may have some implication for how they should teach in the future. Too often teachers teach in the vacuum of their own classroom cell, protected by the walls of their building. What is unusual about these teachers is that they had the courage to inquire. And they learned from the inquiry, so that some errors could be corrected. Note, too, that while the initial inquiry was about a small group of students considered at risk, the solutions needed had implications for all students at the elementary school.

But what of the Yates ten? How did they actually perform? After interviewing the students, the teachers examined their performance on their final report cards. The results were humbling. Two students had left the area; therefore their records were unavailable. Of the eight remaining students, four passed and four were retained. Teachers were clearly disappointed with the results. They explained the retentions this way:

> "These kids have rough, unstable home lives."
> "I taught summer school last year. It was so disorganized that it probably didn't help."
> "For some of these kids school isn't for them. They need a job or vocational training."
> "A couple of these kids did much worse than I expected."
> "These kids were shaky to begin with."
> "We gave them too little, too late."

Based on these results, the team decided to pick a new group of students for special attention. "These students are stronger," team members reported. "They will need a lot of help, but they can make it." They also made several changes in how they worked with them. Instead of identifying the students at risk in May, they made the selection in January so that they had more time to work with them. In addition to the activities they first used, they added mentoring and tutoring components.

Boundary spanning, reaching up to the next level, had made it possible for the Yates transition team to see their own shortcomings. The larger context had freed them to gain a new perspective, one that allowed them to become more reflective within their school. Interactions between and among these three levels contributed to creating a less defensive, more open climate that allowed Yates to change. At first they could not accept that so many of their students did so poorly in middle school. They distrusted the sample the middle school pulled; they thought it was not typical of their students. The second sample, which they controlled, produced similar information. Then they began to look more closely at how the Yates ten actually performed. Conversations with their former students disclosed important information about how they taught science, notetaking, and outlining. These learnings moved them to design interventions that addressed the improvement of how they taught.

It is not clear at this juncture in the project how the Yates case will unfold. At some point the school may decide that an incremental approach to change may be less effective than major restructuring. If so, the issue will no longer be managing transitions within and across school boundaries to reduce the number of students at risk of failure. Rather it will become how an elementary school can be organized so that the majority of the school's population enters middle school on grade level in reading and math. Restructuring from the bottom up holds out the hope that the cumulative course of failure can be interrupted and redirected. But teachers are reluctant to redesign even one grade, let alone an entire level of schooling. They are suspicious of optimal plans in a world that requires constant compromise. They also have limited energy for changing their teaching routines.

Redesign of Strategic or Leading Parts of the System

The elementary school was not ready for redesign. It was, however, ready for serious inquiry, which gave teachers a more complex awareness of how their work affected subsequent student performance. They were prepared to make discrete, limited changes. Redesign should be tried late in the process, after participants can see the nature of the problem with fresh insight and can generate a range of alternative solutions. The following section describes how the Manning Freshman Academy moved slowly toward redesign.

In 1975, a Freshman Academy was set up in a facility physically distant from Manning High School's main building. There the education of the ninth-grade students focused on basic skill development, which was thought to be best achieved in a tightly controlled atmosphere of "law and order." Since that time, few changes have been made at the Freshman Academy. As part of the Bridging the Gap activity at the high school, a major emphasis has been on the redesign of the Freshman Academy. A series of faculty meetings were held at the Academy to address this issue during the last 3 months of the 1986–1987 school year and were resumed in fall 1987. Through a self-examination process of the Freshman Academy by the principal, vice-principal, Bridging the Gap transition team members, and Freshman Academy faculty, a number of concrete changes have taken place while many others have been proposed. The process that led to these changes becomes evident by reviewing activity from the meetings.

During the first two meetings the faculty began to examine the problems at the Freshman Academy. Group discussion centered on the principal's question, "If you had the power to change something here, what would you do?" Suggestions included increasing parental involvement, enforcing uniform rules and procedures in the classroom, and addressing the issues of poor attendance and lateness. In addition, the faculty voiced interest in visiting the other two schools involved in the Bridging the Gap project. At the second meeting, faculty were invited to discuss their ideas about what could be done to change the at-risk factors of students. One teacher commented: "The problem is that we think of only negative things and we don't think of anything for the kids that do attend school. We need more positives."

At the third meeting, the faculty reported their observations from the visitations to other school levels and were informed about a high school redesign in Boston; both activities served as additional resources to prompt a more critical look at their own situation and the possibilities of change. Twelve teachers reported in detail about their visits, commenting on such areas as school and classroom atmosphere, class size, teacher instruction, and student participation and behavior. Complementing teacher observations, the principal researcher of Bridging the Gap reported the success of the redesign of ten Boston public high schools. The Boston program reorganizes the ninth grades into clusters with five teachers teamed with 120 students and provides career awareness activities, remediation, and student incentives. Many of the aspects of this program were incorporated into the Freshman Academy redesign, even though the faculty and administration did not initially move to restructure completely.

From September 1987 to May 1988, teachers worked at changing the climate at the Freshman Academy. The vice-principal assigned by the principal to this project monitored student progress carefully. She presented the faculty with updates on student performance. At these times she raised questions about how failing students could be redirected so that better progress could be attained. She was willing to regroup students and reassign staff so that a new solution might have a chance of success. At an end-of-the-year meeting, the researcher asked the faculty to evaluate each intervention on two dimensions—degree of implementation and degree of effectiveness. The faculty decided to continue those interventions that had demonstrated positive results. The meeting shifted to plans for the next year. The researcher framed the question this way: "Last year you claimed that you wanted to find many more positives to do for those kids who do come to school. The ideas you implemented speak to that point. What additional ideas could make a difference?" The faculty produced three ideas:

Divert overage students into the main building program
Invent effective teaching strategies that enliven learning for students
Invent ways to know about and connect with students on a more personal level (e.g., house plans, family groups, monitoring devices).

When the faculty ranked these three suggestions, it was almost unanimous that overage students be diverted from the Academy's program;

the house plan ranked second and new teacher strategies, third. Diverting the overage students became plausible because of an agreement struck among the three school levels to identify these students before sending them to middle school or high school. The high school took the initiative to gain a similar agreement with the two additional middle schools that feed it. Because the agreement was shared among all the relevant parts of the system, a preferred form of programming could be designed for age-appropriate students at the Freshman Academy and for overage students at the main high school building.

The decision to restructure into two house plans proved to be a highly demanding venture for the faculty and administration. The primary focus for these houses was to break down the anonymity and bureaucratic nature of the Freshman Academy. Two houses were established in September 1988, each with approximately 135 students and a team of teachers who work exclusively with them. Each house has a team leader, a peer, who calls weekly house meetings to discuss individual students and house projects as well as to develop future directions. After a year's work, teachers feel these houses produced a superior learning environment for students, as the comments below reflect:

> "A lot of kids are trying to get their work done. They ask to do make-ups . . . in the past, they didn't care."
> "We can't get the kids to leave. They come early. They don't leave. I ask them, I say, 'Won't you leave?' This is a new problem; we've never had this problem before."

Of course the redesign of the Freshman Academy into two houses has not alleviated all problems. Some students still fail; their skill levels cannot be brought up to standard. As one teacher put it, "In reading, some are on the sixth-grade level, so by this time they give up. I'm trying as hard as I can, then they put their heads down. Others are willing to do the work, but it isn't enough." On balance, however, the positives outweigh the negatives. And the gains in student attendance and achievement are impressive. In the 1986–1987 academic year, with an enrollment of 265 students, the average monthly attendance was 77.5%. In 1987–1988, with 418 enrolled, 76.1% was the average monthly attendance. But in 1988–1989, with 269 students enrolled, the attendance was 84.4%—a 9% gain over the previous year. Teachers rightly correlate the potential to achieve with regular attendance. Spotty attendance produces gaps in knowledge that make it increasingly difficult for the student to catch up. In the Freshman Academy case, the rise in attendance did correlate with an increase in the number of students promoted to tenth grade.

Before the start of Bridging the Gap, from 1983 to 1987, an average of 50% of the students were promoted. In contrast, 64% in 1988 and 82% in 1989 were promoted. The 14% gain in 1988 may be attributed to several changes recommended and implemented by teachers, including student recognition programs for achievement and/or attendance, initiation of a student government, a course in career guidance, emphasis on study skills, and intensive tutoring for students at risk of failure by the third report card. The major reason for the 18% increase (from 64% to 82%) in 1989 may be attributed to the reorganization of the school into two houses. It should also be noted that by agreement with the three middle schools that feed Manning, students who had been retained two or more times and were overage were diverted to a special program held at the main building. While the Freshman Academy is not selective, the most at-risk students are no longer included in its population. Academy teachers, however, reported that entering students continued to function between 1 and 2 years below grade level in basic skills. Therefore, the improvement in percentage promoted is at least in part a result of the interaction of these interventions: higher teacher expectations, improved student attendance, moderate experimentation with alternative instructional methods, careful and frequent monitoring of student progress, and increased teacher participation in decision making.

The Freshman Academy presented an opportunity for redesign after the researchers had worked with the faculty for a year and a half. This school was not instantly receptive to the notion of restructuring when it was presented as an alternative in the fifth month of consultation. The response, in fact, was apathy and noninterest. These faculty members needed some "small wins" (Weik, 1984) before they might be willing to tackle a major reshaping of their organization. The initial successes, which changed the climate of the school from one that felt like boot camp to one that was warmer and more nurturant of students, gave the faculty the courage to try bolder interventions. Equally important, their visitations to the middle and elementary levels gave them a broader perspective on how students become at risk and what they might specifically do at their level to arrest the tide of large-scale failure. Knowing that many teachers at lower levels were teaching responsibly prompted Academy teachers to reevaluate their own capacity to change.

From a researcher's vantage point, it seemed essential that one level try a major restructuring to provide an exemplar for the other levels of the kinds of changes required to produce significant outcomes in student achievement. But the Academy's change, while mostly a function of its own efforts, was abetted by a more interdependent relationship with its feeder schools. It is possible for any level within a system to restructure. But it is improbable that one could make significant improvements and sustain them without the cooperation of all of the other levels. A student's achievement is the sum total of the work done in previous grades. It represents a combination of the student's ability to achieve and the quality of instruction he or she experienced. Some changes in student achievement are made possible only by redesigning a major part of the system. While increased numbers of students promoted indicates that more students stand a chance of graduating from high school, it does not necessarily suggest an improvement in the quality of that achievement. At this stage in the development of Bridging the Gap, participating schools experience different degrees of inquiry and varying capacities to promote major change. Reductions in failure, retention, and dropout rates in urban schools are major problems, massive in scale and depth. If interventionists demand redesign at all levels, it is likely to induce paralysis. It is important to have an exemplar as a beacon. But it is equally important not to discount "small wins" as a means of moving step by step toward a larger, more elusive goal.

CONCLUDING COMMENTS

When we started this project, as action researchers we wanted to get a fresh perspective on the cumulative effects of student failure at the major school-level transitions. A guiding assumption was that blaming cycles among educators within a level and across levels had to be interrupted and transformed into productive, collective inquiry so that more effective solutions could be considered. It was important that they inquire collectively, because the different levels constitute different parts of an interconnected system. Focusing on transitions, those undefined times for which no one takes responsibility, offered a space for conversation about students, teachers, administrators, and parents. Because transitions remain unclaimed by the bureaucracy, they allow diverse actors to join the discussion. They also require a systems approach, so that a more complex sense of the multiple reasons for the problem can be appreciated. In a system that makes explicit demarcations for content mastery and even methods of instruction within a grade and a school level, or in how one must carry out a professional role, transitions can become teachable moments.

Transitions mark points of great instability in going from one structure to another (elementary to middle, middle to high school), from one biological and social age to another (child to prepubescent to adolescent); from one level of cognitive processing to the next (from concrete operations to formal operations [Piaget, 1968]). For school-age children, transitions can be exciting and challenging if they feel realistically self-assured that they can master the new situation or material. Or the transition can be a danger signal that intensifies feelings of incompetence and low self-esteem as the student predicts that he or she will not make the grade and is thus condemned to a larger sense of failure and despair.

The nature of school transitions as experienced by students is not well understood by educators. Some teachers may think about transitions, but it is mainly from a developmentalist perspective, such as that of preschool and kindergarten teachers or reading and math specialists. Regular teachers often see the transitions in terms of scope and sequence of curricula, evaluating what other teachers before them have or have not accomplished with their present students. Teachers and principals also perceive transitions, but these are mostly related to biological or life-cycle changes. Their work as an elementary or secondary school teacher or principal locks them into a single-setting view of the schooling process. Students move from grade to grade, level to level, school to school. Educators, generally speaking, do not experience a rapid succession of transitions. They teach fourth grade or secondary math in the same building for several years, sometimes for an entire career. For professional educators the work setting provides an efficient "steady state," even though the environment is constantly changing.

Collective inquiry across grades and levels that focuses on how students fail and how more can succeed might make dropout prevention programs for ninth- and tenth-grade students irrelevant. This more inclusive type of thinking views students as part of a process, one in which teachers could identify students at risk and make interventions at necessary points during their school years. Systems thinking also entails designing ways of involving the numerous stakeholders—seeing, for instance, how stressed single parents can realistically become involved.

Finally, one of the most interesting findings of this study relates to the organic way the research and interventions have produced new potential for decentralization and school-to-school accountability. While it is necessary for large school districts to mandate certain policies centrally, issues of articulation are more appropriately addressed by schools that have a stake in what happens to their students as they move to the next level. Thus the feeder subsystem becomes an appropriate unit of analysis and intervention for reducing failure and for sustaining improved student performance. By working with the feeder subsystem in the ways we have described, teachers and principals begin to see it as in their mutual self-interest to monitor progress across school boundaries; as a natural expression of responsibility to colleagues they know and respect; and as an acknowledgment that their involvement with students is not transitory, but sustained for the students' entire school career.

ACKNOWLEDGMENT

I want to thank Burton Cohen and Donald Schön for their suggestions in revising this paper. I also wish to thank Julie Spiegel, the research assistant who transcribed field notes for the Bridging the Gap meetings. Her help was more as a co-investigator than as an assistant. Funding for this project was made possible by grants received for the Metropolitan Life Foundation and the Pew Charitable Trusts.

REFERENCES

Argyris, C. (1985). *Strategy, change and defensive routines.* Boston: Pitman.

Chevalier, M. (1968). A strategy of interest-based planning. Unpublished doctoral dissertation, University of Pennsylvania.

Fine, M. (1987). Why urban adolescents drop into and out of public high school. In G. Natriello (Ed.), *School dropouts: Patterns and policies* (pp. 89–105). New York: Teachers College Press.

Lipsitz, J. (1984). *Successful schools for young adolescents.* New Brunswick, NJ: Transaction.

Pava, C. (1984). Towards a concept of non-synoptic systems change (Working Paper). Cambridge, MA: Harvard Business School.

Piaget, J. (1968). *Six psychological studies.* New York: Vintage.

Schön, D. A. (1971). *Beyond the stable state.* New York: Random House.

Schön, D. A. (1983). *The reflective practitioner.* New York: Basic Books.

Weik, K. E. (1984). Small wins: Redefining the scale of social problems. *American Psychologist, 39* (1), 40–49.

4

Collective Reflective Practice Through Participatory Action Research: A Case Study from the Fagor Cooperatives of Mondragón

DAVYDD J. GREENWOOD

AN EVOCATION

THE LABOR-MANAGED INDUSTRIAL cooperatives of Mondragón in the Spanish Basque country are famous for their success. The largest such industrial cooperatives in the world, they have become a model discussed and emulated everywhere.

What follows are juxtaposed direct quotes from cooperative members made in the context of six roundtable discussions about the cooperatives. The roundtables were part of a 3-year participatory action research (PAR) project there. The themes of the roundtables were the value-added of being a member of a cooperative rather than an ordinary firm, the tension between hierarchy and equality in their system, and the response of the cooperatives to the European recession of 1979–1987. Members of the PAR team from the cooperatives selected these themes and ran the roundtables themselves. About 50 members from different cooperatives and from positions ranging from the workfloor to management participated.

I have organized the quotes to highlight the contrasting visions they embody.

Identification with the Cooperatives

Embodying cooperative values

- [In the cooperatives] there is greater identification with all of the objectives and efforts made at the management level, greater than in other places [i.e., ordinary firms].
- Beyond management, there are many more people [than in an ordinary firm] who are committed and who identify with our effort.
- The values [of the founders] have not been lost, they have been institutionalized.
- Freedom of thought here is supported by job security; we know that they are not going to throw us out in the street.
- If there had not been solidarity, this [the cooperatives] would not have worked.
- The membership is dealing with the economic problems, even though it demands personal sacrifices.
- In an ordinary firm, someone who does not work well is fired—with a larger or smaller severance check—but they get rid of him. Here he will be relocated, more or less well, but he keeps his job and pay. This is an advantage for the individual member but not for the business.
- At the moment of truth, most operators, technicians, and managers would not leave the cooperatives in significant numbers. . . . Only specific, very large personal offers would cause some people to leave.

Expressing concern over the cooperatives' operation and future

- We have to realize that we are not isolated, that we have competitors, and that either we are profitable or, in the long run, this system is not viable.
- In extreme situations, the membership responds well and the system functions. In ordinary daily life, there are many things that could and should be improved.
- What happens is that we are not capable of developing all the possibilities that the cooperatives offer.
- What matters to people is to have a job and get paid at the end of the month.
- No matter how little I work, I get paid the same.
- The cooperative is too much [for most members]. He wants to work his 8 hours, cover his basic needs, and not take on additional duties.

- The lack of trust among members is incredible.
- The people are burned out, tired. The moment has arrived to say "enough!"

The Quality of Participation in the Cooperatives

Embodying cooperative values

- I certainly believe that the members participate; the number of amendments [to the annual business plan] they present shows that people care and participate.
- Cooperatives are a much more public scene than other businesses. Here you have to convince everyone before making a decision. This proves that power is widely distributed.
- The cooperative goes much further than a corporation. We feel ourselves integrated into it from head to toe, for good or ill.
- The social bodies [of the cooperatives] have diminished labor problems. Now such problems do not even get to plenary sessions [of the cooperative]; they are resolved in the plant, and even progressively now at the section level.

Expressing concern over the cooperatives' operation and future

- We are slow in making decisions, with so many committees, discussion, council, and rules.
- There is an excess of bureaucracy and slowness in making decisions.
- Poor, too rapid decisions have been made.
- There is a lack of dialogue.
- The membership suffers from the results of decisions, but it does not identify with them.
- We provide a great deal of information, but the people cannot participate because they do not understand it.
- Decision making is becoming professionalized. One can participate less and less because you cannot understand everything.
- There is too much openness with information.
- The proper atmosphere for participation is missing.
- People are not so interested in participating in decisions. They want money.
- For many people, participation is reduced to participation as in any democracy. Every 4 years, you vote—period.
- In the general assembly, you participate through your vote, but it is managed. If you vote in favor, it is because you trust them.

> If you vote against, it is because you do not trust them, and thus [it's] you against them.

- You don't have a voice or a vote.
- I do not participate because I am disenchanted.

Equality in the Cooperatives

Embodying cooperative values

- We are not equal in everyday work, but we are in decision making.
- At voting time, we have the same rights as the general manager.
- In the cooperatives, no one feels him/herself less than anyone else, regardless of the job he/she does.
- We are equal, in that salaries are closer to each other.
- To manage here means to have to give explanations, to have the capacity to recognize errors and accept daily criticism and social control. And this is difficult in practice.
- I dislike the terms [those above and those below, *los de arriba y los de abajo*] because they make me feel separated from that with which I am perfectly united.
- The origin of "those above and those below" is not hierarchical, it is physical [i.e., the supervisors used to stand physically above the workfloor].
- In a cooperative as large as Ulgor, you have to create a hierarchical structure.

Expressing concern over the cooperatives' operation and future

- The enterprise is no longer everyone's. It belongs to those above.
- Here there is one head, the one who does everything and the rest of us [who] dance to his tune.
- The higher up the pyramid you go, the less equal we are.
- We are afraid to be equal.
- Those above [management] do whatever they want.

What are we to make of this contradictory information, emanating from the heart of one of the most egalitarian and participatory industrial systems as yet founded? This is both a key analytical and action decision. It must be remembered that the roundtables were purposely structured to bring together groups who were likely to have divergent views. We built them around themes designed to evoke strong personal feelings. The affirmative and skeptical statements all occurred together in the different roundtables in the form of argument and dialogue. Though I have selected more skeptical quotes, because of the often romanticized external image of the cooperatives, the affirmative and skeptical were reasonably balanced in the roundtable discussions.

Faced with these materials, there are many possible moves. We might question how we collected the data, including sampling, honesty of the respondents, formulation of the questions, and so forth. We might conclude that the cooperatives are in deep trouble because of disaffection within the ranks. We might argue that cooperativism is an impossibility, as these data demonstrate. During the study we conducted of the cooperatives, we explored each of these possibilities.

In the face of such information, analysts should not rush to judgment. Anthropologists, when faced with confusing and apparently contradictory information, are encouraged not to give in to negative judgments about the culture under study. We are disciplined to assume that possibly we do not understand what is going on and should collect more information. By mastering the immediate temptation to pass judgment, anthropologists have learned a great deal about other cultures.

Understood this way, anthropology's cultural relativism played a major role in how we came to understand the above data. After collecting a great deal of data and analyzing it, we concluded that this apparently contradictory picture is an accurate portrait of the diversity of experiences within the cooperatives. Further, we came to believe that the tensions between these views is the stuff of the success of these cooperatives. It may be that diversity of voices and experiences is an important characteristic of successful organizations and that organizational change agents must both learn from and respect that diversity.

This is one of the key contributions anthropology can make to the study of reflective practice and organizational learning. Anthropology has tried hard to diversify our view of human nature, contesting unilateral views of human nature and discouraging judgment of behavior and views unlike our own as inferior. Anthropologists have tried to persuade readers to seek understanding of the structure and causes of diversity rather than to judge different behavior as inferior or, worse, to destroy it.

There is more than one context for this lesson. Focusing on diversity inside of organizations is a very specific way of bringing this anthropological vision to bear on organizational behavior. The lesson that, within an organization, there is more than one valid view of what is going on is important. Managers and workers alike tend to treat each others' visions and experiences as defective or even duplicitous. The realization that there is room, and perhaps even an organizational requirement, for a diversity of views and experiences of an organization is an essential step in the direction of reflective practice and organizational learning.

THE CASE

The case presented is the result of 3 years of participatory action research (PAR) centering on the study of organizational culture. The process involved a team of more than 25 people who studied the Fagor Cooperative Group, 12 labor-managed, industrial cooperatives in the Mondragón complex in the Spanish Basque country. Because these cooperatives were created and structured to reflect specific democratic values, it is generally expected that they provide a paradigm case of reflective uniformity. Indeed, most explanations of the success of the cooperatives rely on notions about an underlying cultural homogeneity that makes cooperation possible.

We came to reject this kind of cultural explanation and have constructed a different view. Within the cooperatives, commitment to industrial democracy is high, and yet divergent and continually diversifying views of industrial democracy are an essential part of the system. Reflective debates are the stuff of which Mondragón is made.

The Setting

The town of Mondragón (population 30,000) is located in the province of Guipúzcoa in the Spanish Basque country. A small land area, the Basque country has about 2 million inhabitants (6% of Spain's population total) and a high population density. The area is historically known for its resistance to Franco's forces during the Civil War and to his regime thereafter, as well as for its industry. It is currently an area of continuing civil violence.

The Basque language is unique, unrelated to any of the present or historically known languages or language families in the world. Thus the Basque language stands entirely alone. Despite this unique cultural marker, which has become an important political resource, Basque culture is integrally European in its material culture, social organization, and systems of belief (Caro Baroja, 1971).

Because it has been the most highly industrialized region of Spain throughout this century, the area has received a good deal of migration from the rest of Spain. The identifiable non-Basque surname population is now about 24% of the total in the region. More recently, Basque industry has undergone the same decline affecting all smokestack industry in Europe, exacerbated by the recession that began in 1979. This occasioned major dislocations and bankruptcies, a comprehensive restructuring of Basque industry, and, now, a significant recovery. Nevertheless, over the past few years, unemployment has stayed above 27%.

It is hard to imagine a less promising location or historical moment for the development of labor-managed cooperatives than the Spanish Basque country in the mid-1950s, the depths of Franco's dictatorship. Yet it was here that the largest and most successful private group of industrial labor-managed cooperatives in the world developed. This challenges most views of both the economic and political determinants of democracy and, thus, has attracted a great deal of attention over the years (see Whyte & Whyte, 1988).

The Cooperatives of Mondragón

The industrial cooperative movement in Mondragón began in 1956, with five leaders and 16 colleagues, under the supervision of a Basque priest, Don José María Arizmendiarreta. Now the cooperatives employ more than 19,000 people, 7% of the total industrial labor force in the Basque country. There are 173 cooperatives spread around the Basque landscape, 94 in industrial production, 17 in construction, 9 in agriculture and food supply businesses, 6 service cooperatives, 45 educational institutions, a cooperative bank, and a consumer cooperative. Sales reached $1.4 billion in 1987. Despite the major recession, the cooperatives have not laid off members. They export about 30% of their production, although this percentage varies widely across their 193 product lines.

The cooperatives rest on the principles of worker ownership and participation in governance. New members pay an entry fee to join (an amount equivalent to a 1-year salary in the lowest-paying job). From this point on, the member receives a distribution of the profits (or losses) from the cooperative in the form of a salary and a payment to the member's capital account. The exact amount available for distribution depends on how the cooperative has done during the year, and the members vote on the actual distribution of profits each year.

The distribution follows a job classification scheme that ranks positions from 1 to 4.5. The lowest figure is calculated to match the starting pay for unskilled labor in private firms in the same business. This is one of the most egalitarian pay scales found anywhere in industry.

The structure and history of the cooperatives is fully described in William Foote Whyte and Kathleen King Whyte's book about Mondragón (Whyte & Whyte, 1988), and we advise the interested reader to turn to this source for details. Each cooperative has a general assembly in which all members have an equal vote on all major issues, including the annual business plan. A governing council is elected from this group by a general assembly vote. The general manager, a cooperative member, is appointed to the position by the governing council and can be removed at the pleasure of that council. The governing council oversees a management council that focuses specifically on business matters. Another group, the social council, is elected from the membership, voting from their work stations. It is charged with bringing all issues of concern to the membership to the governing council and general manager. Thus the cooperatives are both worker-owned and participatory in governance. The cooperatives are supported by "second-level cooperatives" that provide total health care, social security, financing of cooperative business development, and research and development capabilities.

Many of the Mondragón cooperatives are linked into one of the 14 cooperative groups. Of these, the Fagor Group is the largest and oldest, containing Ulgor, the founding cooperative of Mondragón. Within such groups there are centralized services and cross-subsidies that permit economies of scale and the buffering of business cycles in particular product areas.

Although the Mondragón area has long been a focus of industrial activity, there is nothing at all unique about this town that might explain the emergence of cooperatives there rather than elsewhere. In 1941, the town had a population of 8,000. At that time, Don José María Arizmendiarreta was sent to assist the parish priest. A secular priest who had been a Republican journalist during the Civil War, Don José María became responsible for youth-oriented programs in the parish. He decided to emphasize the development of technical and professional education programs and in 1943 opened a professional school, which later became the cooperative polytechnical school. From among its students came the first five founders of the cooperatives. After a number of experiences in private industry, they, with the support of Don José María, decided to found a cooperative business of their own, manufacturing an imitation of an existing product, a petroleum stove.

This cooperative rapidly grew. In the 1960s, their own hard work and good business sense also benefited from the astonishing level of industrial growth achieved in Spain. New cooperatives spun off, new products developed, and strategic investments were made. In 1964, they formed the Ularco Regional Group, now called the Fagor Cooperative Group. The late 1970s saw a dramatic decline in Europe's economic fortunes, coming closely on the heels of the democratization of the

Spanish political structure. By the 1980s, the area was reeling under the joint pressure of recession, industrial decline and reorganization, and redevelopment efforts. Now a significant upturn is evident and the co-operatives are once again growing.

The Fagor Group

While the name of Mondragón is famous, the Fagor Cooperative Group itself may not sound familiar. It is the largest and oldest group of cooperatives in the Mondragón system, with more than 6,000 members in 12 cooperatives located in and around Mondragón. Its sales account for a third of the sales volume for the whole Mondragón complex, and it employs roughly a third of the workforce. The central offices of Fagor link and support Fagor's marketing, technology development, and financial management activities.

The workforce averages 38 years of age, and 25% of them are women. About half the members were born in the Mondragón area; another 25% came from the nearby provinces, and the rest from elsewhere in Spain. Members have an average of 14 years of service in the cooperatives.

The Fagor Study

The 3-year PAR study of Fagor examined the social and cultural realities of cooperative life and developed a critical analysis aimed at producing improvements in linkage between democracy in governance and democracy on the workfloor. It was carried out by a team drawn from within the Fagor Group and from Cornell University (see Whyte, Greenwood, & Lazes, 1989). The Fagor members included staff from the central Fagor department of personnel, the directors of personnel from most of the Fagor Group cooperatives, and representatives of the social governance bodies and workers from the shopfloor. The main Cornell University members were myself and William Foote Whyte.

PAR is a research modality in which professional social researchers and members of the organization under study form a single research group that decides the subject of the research, learns about and selects appropriate techniques, collects and analyzes the data, and assists in the process of applying the results to the organization. The professional researcher in PAR is a combined consultant, teacher, researcher, and team member who must become committed to the team's goals.

This process tests standard techniques and models to the limit, because they must result in analyses that are convincing and informative

to members of the organization and lead to sensible action consequences. In PAR, social theories must be made operational by being
fitted to local contexts recognizable to those living in them. This can
create a useful dynamic in which social theories are winnowed down to
essential and important propositions and local views and analyses are
subjected to rigorous collective scrutiny. It also transcends the usual limits of data collection because insider team members are so knowledgeable about the organization in question and because commitment to
having a PAR team in the organization often means that data about the
organization are made available to the group.

For those team members from the organization under study, PAR
also has some unique value. It causes them to develop testable propositions about the organization, and, through this, it often provides them
unexpected results. It is also stressful, because insider members face the
dilemma of studying and attempting to change a system while being
part of it.

Finally, we came to describe a particular virtue of the PAR process
as its ability to "create organizational space." By this, we meant that PAR
created an arena within the organization where members could discuss
and debate fundamental issues that were hard to tap through ordinary
organizational processes. We communicated this phenomenon to ourselves by a variety of terms: the creation of "organizational space," the
creation of "space for reflection," and the like. This topographic language pointed to the development of a neutral turf within the system
where concepts could be tested and concerns expressed. While PAR is
not the only intervention method that can produce this result, the creation of organizational space for reflection is one of its most valuable
and likely outcomes.

The initial aim of the study, defined by Fagor, was pedagogical and
analytical: to improve the internal capability for social research within
Fagor and to study the "industrial anthropology" of the group. How
this aim was to be met and what it truly meant was for the team to
decide. Out of this broad and diffuse commitment to self-examination
and improvement grew a 3-year study that has resulted in a team-
written book on Fagor (Greenwood & González Santos et al., in press)
and a variety of changes in orientation within the cooperative group.

The History of the Project

The project came about as the result of a visit to Mondragón by
William Foote Whyte in 1983, where he was collecting data for his recent
book on Mondragón (Whyte & Whyte, 1988). At the end of his 3-week

stay, Whyte gave a seminar on his findings, including some criticism of the lack of symmetry between the cooperatives' sophisticated technical and economic development methods and their very limited social research capacity. In response, José Luis González, director of personnel of the Fagor Group, suggested that Whyte develop a proposal about how to help them improve.

When Whyte returned to Cornell, he and I joined forces and, together with González, wrote a proposal for funding that received support from the Joint Spain–United States Committee on Educational and Cultural Exchange. This grant was renewed for a second year, with myself and González as co-principal investigators. The Fagor Group itself funded a final year of my collaboration.

The research portion of the PAR began in earnest in the summer of 1985 with a month-long seminar on social research methods that resulted in a pilot study of key incidents in the history of the Ulgor Cooperative. In the following year we broadened the focus to the whole Fagor Group, and research moved from discussions in a large seminar room to the archives of the cooperatives, interviews, and roundtables with members. During the final year, a writing party developed the book, which describes the entire research project in detail.

We deal with the complexity and vagaries of this process in detail in the book. Here, it is only necessary to point out that the project was a confluence between anthropological and personnel interests in the context of a severe economic downturn in Europe that had a profound effect on Fagor. The guiding vision on the Fagor side was that the bad economic conditions created both a necessity and an opportunity for reflection and fundamental change, a good example of converting a problem into an opportunity.

Internal debates within the Mondragón cooperative system affected the study. Among cooperativists, there are two dominant visions of the character of cooperative history and the path toward the future. One group sees the cooperatives as invented through the brilliance of Don José María and the energy and idealism of the founders. As time has gone by, this initial vision has been obscured by growth, politics, and other forces of confusion. For them, the way to the future is to "get back to the basics" by studying Don José María's vision and bringing organizational structures back into concert with it.

Another group sees the cooperatives as an open experiment, requiring continual innovation in the face of little understood forces. While valuing the principles of the founders, this group sees innovation and fundamental change as the only way to keep the principles alive. They fear the entropy that robs systems of their flexibility and vitality, perceiving it as the greatest enemy of the cooperatives' future.

The PAR study was encouraged and carried out by a group that shared the second, experimental vision of the cooperatives. For them the PAR process offered an opportunity to develop a more explicit and systematic understanding of the forces of rigidity and entropy within the system. This, in turn, was to provide insight into ways to keep the system open and dynamic.

First phase. The PAR process was neither easy nor smooth. My task—teaching the industrial anthropology of Fagor—was so unclear that I had to enter the scene with no aim other than finding out what the Fagor member thought they meant by that. For the Fagor members, their previous experiences had been either with university professors who lectured or with consultants who generally had tightly organized programs. The first month was a negotiation around these divergent expectations and views. We ultimately concluded this negotiation successfully, and the month ended with the writing of a pilot study of Ulgor that excited all present about the possibilities for collaborative social research in Fagor.

Since mutual expectations were so unclear, the mechanism I used to move the discussion forward was to have the team read and respond collectively to some of the best-known writings about the cooperatives. By criticizing these works, the group members became aware of their own theories about the cooperatives. Once these theories were on the table, I was able to bring my anthropological knowledge of the culture and history of the Basque country to bear on issues of importance to the Fagor members, thereby accomplishing the desired linkage between anthropology and industry. In particular, I was able to link my own studies of the dynamic and changing character of Basque ethnic identity over the centuries to issues of identity and change in the cooperatives. This connection proved energizing to the PAR team.

While this was useful, in order for the project to continue, it was essential to show that PAR could bring useful perspectives to bear on problems of key practical importance to Fagor. For this reason, the team elected to conduct a pilot study of the Ulgor cooperative, the oldest cooperative in the Mondragón system, and to examine its two most difficult moments, the only strike in the history of the cooperatives and its response to the recession in Europe. These two subjects are very important to the cooperatives. The first ideologically represents the threat that internal conflict represents to the cooperative idea. The second embodies the question of whether or not cooperatives can really survive when having to deal with ordinary firms in a competitive economic arena.

At the end of this phase, we delivered our results to the management of the Fagor Group and asked them to decide whether or not the

PAR process should continue. We believed that the process should be open to modification or termination at any time. In this way we kept everyone aware of the implicit contract we had with Fagor about the process and could seek midcourse corrections regularly.

Second phase. In the second year, the team became active social researchers, administering questionnaires and conducting interviews and roundtables within the Fagor Group. González developed a pilot survey on some of the issues we had identified in the first year. After analyzing the results and puzzling about their meaning, the team decided to conduct an extensive set of interviews with Fagor members about the most troubling issues facing the cooperatives. The members of the PAR team collaborated in developing the interview protocols, were trained together, conducted the interviews, and debriefed each other collectively.

The interviews explicitly focused on the cooperative's problems, and we intentionally selected respondents from among those people most adversely affected by the problems. This approach grew out of an explicit commitment by the team to delve into the "night side" of the cooperatives. Such a commitment was an expression of the confidence Fagor members had in their ability to face the worst-case scenarios about themselves.

Quickly the team found itself awash in harsh and negative information. We document what we found in detail in our book. Many cooperative members used the interviews cathartically, painting a dismal picture of nearly everything.

As we examined the results, a number of things became apparent. Some of the criticism was certainly on the mark. There are defects in the Fagor system, and criticism of them is understandable. The intensity of the negative tone of the criticisms did not square well with the high degree of organizational discipline cooperative members exhibit. The specific tone of many of the responses led Fagor members to feel that catharsis had led to their taking exaggerated positions. Most important, the Fagor members of the PAR team had believed intuitively that Fagor's problems stemmed mainly from member apathy. The interview respondents were anything but apathetic. This caused an important reconsideration of their theory, thereby opening up the research process to other explanations.

In response to all of this, I suggested taking the conflictive issues identified and refined through the interviews into a different research context: roundtables (i.e., focus or theme groups) where cooperative members could discuss these issues in a more nuanced way while some members of the research team listened. The Fagor members of the team, through a process of reduction and synthesis, brought together the critical themes emerging from the interviews and converted them into a small, provocative set of subjects to be taken to roundtables of Fagor members, facilitated by a PAR team member.

The agenda for the roundtables was set by the Fagor members of the team, demonstrating their increasing control of the emergent focus of the research. The subjects selected were the "value-added" of being a member of the cooperatives; hierarchy and equality in the system; and the relation between participation and power in Fagor.

We held six roundtables, each with about eight people and lasting about 90 minutes. We taped the discussions, having assured participants that we would listen to the tapes and then erase them. We would use quotes but not attribute them to any individuals. For each session, two Fagor team members and I prepared a limited script of questions. One Fagor team member moderated the roundtable, the other kept track of the tape machine, and I took notes.

The sessions were lively in all cases. Almost immediately, the participants engaged one another directly and carried the discussion on. In contrast to the interviews, the roundtables provided much more detailed information about members' views. Many of the positions heard in the interviews were again articulated clearly, but, in the context of group discussion, they were answered by other members, modulated and elaborated, and ultimately clarified.

At this point, the context for the quotes I laid out in the beginning of this chapter should be clear. The PAR team was systematically pursuing divergent views of industrial democracy in Fagor and, accordingly, faced a puzzle. We encountered many intensely negative views. Yet the total membership, by any measure—absenteeism, voting, productivity, and so forth—was performing at a high standard. It was as if a perfectly healthy patient had come to the doctor, complaining that he was not feeling well although exhibiting no symptoms.

The roundtables provided an answer, because the roundtable technique is a closer approximation to the social reality of Fagor. Individual interviews provided uncontested and decontextualized opinions about matters having to do with cooperative relationships. The roundtables, themselves an egalitarian exercise in which everyone's opinion received roughly equal weight, revealed that the affirmative and negative views of the cooperatives were real but existed in a dynamic tension with each other. In response to nearly every affirmative statement made at the roundtables, someone raised a counter point. Most skeptical statements were also answered by affirmative visions. The roundtable leaders did not provoke this dynamic, and we did not expect this outcome. It had a dramatic impact on the PAR study.

The roundtables confirmed that apathy was not the problem in Fagor. Many members are strongly committed to the idea of industrial democracy, so much so that they are extremely critical when Fagor fails to live up to its announced standards. They also made clear that the affirmative and skeptical visions connect, in many (not all) cases, to specific, definable experiences the members have had. That is, the diversity of attitudes reflects the diversity of experiences members have in different roles in different parts of the system. Precisely because the cooperative structure compiles these different visions in general assemblies and other institutional contexts, the collective life of cooperation is necessarily filled with debate and divergence.

The roundtables also made clear that the most intense debates center around the most important basic commitments binding the Fagor members together: The value-added of being a member, surviving economic decline, and problems of equality are the touchstones of cooperation. They are the issues that generate the most energy, attention, and disagreement.

We learned through the roundtables that the members generally wanted to bring about positive change, that their critical spirit links to a desire for and proposals for action. This demonstration of the will to improve the system helps explain the ongoing success of the Fagor cooperatives as organizations.

The Results

From this point on, the PAR process moved in different directions. On the one hand, we reduced the PAR team to the smaller writing party that ultimately produced the book on the project. This process of converting the results into a book was trying for the Fagor members because of their lack of experience with this kind of writing. Nevertheless, the process produced a much more sustained analysis of the data and action implications than would have occurred otherwise.

Another thread involved a series of pilot PAR interventions to solve specific problems within member cooperatives. These were intended to convert PAR team members into leaders of subsequent study action teams as part of their personnel responsibilities. Selecting pilot interventions was a complex process. We selected some because a particular cooperative was in the midst of conflict in the relations between the leadership and the workforce. We selected others because a symbolically important "critical incident" had occurred there. Still others were selected because the problem in question was one shared by many co-operatives and a solution in one might help the others. Thus the selection criteria were a mix of ideological centrality and general organizational importance.

We viewed these pilot interventions as practice sessions, using members of the PAR team to create small study action teams within the cooperatives where the interventions took place. I served as a consultant for these interventions. The results were uneven, but the process enabled PAR team members to get a better sense of the process of managing study action projects themselves.

The PAR team utilized its new perspectives on Fagor to enter into discussions of the management of the corporate image and the then newly announced "total quality" program in Fagor. Using the results of the analysis, team members added new perspectives and raised questions about the way these programs were to be managed, attempting to make certain that the processes followed were consistent with the co-operatives' structures and goals.

The PAR process uncovered the need for the department of personnel to take a more proactive view of its role in the cooperatives. It emphasized the ever-present danger in any organization of rules and procedures taking precedence over sensitivity and good sense. It reiterated the problems involved in effectively informing members about complex organizational and financial matters so that they could effectively exercise their right to vote.

The most important overall analytical result of the project was the recognition of one persistent, negative dynamic in Fagor: the separation of democracy in governance from democracy in the work process. It became clear, as is widely recognized, that Fagor has achieved a remarkable level of democratization in the governance structure of its industrial enterprises. The system is elaborate, highly regarded, and functional. What is less clear is that many of the processes that occur in the workplaces are far less democratic. Hierarchical systems of supervision and management and impersonal personnel processes often make life on the shopfloor not very different from life on the shopfloor in any industrial firm.

This recognition is not entirely new to Fagor. But the PAR research project did more than identify this problem; it analyzed two key dimensions of it. First, individual members live the contradiction between democratic governance and life in the workplace as an existential contradiction. This fact surfaced in the skeptical statements found in the interviews and roundtables. Faced with the direct experience of democracy in governance and hierarchical control in the production process, members often feel oppressed by the "system" and yet know, on another level, that they *are* the system.

They attempt to resolve this contradiction in a variety of ways. Many attribute it to managerial duplicity or incompetence. Others say that the membership is not mature or educated enough to shoulder all of its complex responsibilities. Whatever the explanation, the contrast between democracy in governance and lack of democracy in the workplace is an intrinsic feature of life in Mondragón. To be committed to industrial democracy there is to struggle with these contradictions.

Fagor, however, does not pursue democracy in governance and in the workplace to the same degree. Our research made it clear that the Fagor system has developed a negative institutional dynamic needing correction. Problems emerging in the workplace, rather than being resolved where they emerge, are rapidly passed on to the social bodies and to the governance structure for solution. There is relatively little fundamental problem solving in the workplace itself.

This has a significant negative impact on Fagor, because the metabolism of any governance structure rests more on adherence to principles and rules than on resolution of individual problems. Thus the individual problems that originate in the production process are rarely resolved to the satisfaction of the parties involved, even if the governance structure is improved as a result. Once this dynamic is in place, it exacerbates the sense of contradiction between governance and work, between voting as an equal and being treated as a subordinate that fuels the skepticism the PAR team documented. Finding ways to get Fagor back to significant problem solving in the workplace became one of the key needs defined by the PAR study.

Reconceptualizing Fagor

The view of the Fagor system the team developed is quite unlike most of what had been written about Mondragón before. We stressed the notion that the Mondragón system is a process, a system undergoing continual development and change, not one founded by omniscient cultural heros. The team view emphasizes the ability of agreement about basic values such as democracy and due process to generate important tensions within the system.

We came to conceptualize Fagor as an arena of debate about the proper ways to embody industrial democracy rather than as a place where robot-like members enact a uniform ideological code. These debates, often high pitched and acrimonious, turn out to be possible because of an overall agreement that all members must follow the process rules of the system. Anything can be debated and changed, so long as no one violates the basic rules of one member/one vote, due process, and no strikes.

Fagor is, after all, built around a set of ethical commitments. While many members enter simply because the cooperatives offer good, stable employment, the institutional process involved in membership cause certain issues to come to the fore continually. Every year, the annual business plan must be voted on. Every year, the proposed distributions of profits and payments to capital accounts must be approved by the membership. Time and again, members must vote or otherwise express themselves as equal members in the cooperatives. Whether or not members take these responsibilities seriously, they form part of everyday life.

When the membership must decide difficult issues—such as the distribution of losses, changes in shifts that assign some members to unwanted time periods, investments in new infrastructure versus higher take-home pay—the process dramatizes the degree to which all share ownership in the system. Again and again, personal interests and the collective interest are contrasted, mediated, and debated.

As a result of these processes, Fagor is, in a sense, an environment of debate, not about the larger aims, but about how to accomplish them. Debates about the way to be most fair, most rational, most democratic occur continuously as a direct consequence of Fagor's being a democratic industrial cooperative.

Put another way, commitments to particular principles and process rules set the terms of the debates that will characterize the culture of any organization. If democracy and solidarity are key aims, then hierarchy and authoritarianism will be present as the "night side." Any incident, rule, or new process that appears to be tainted with hierarchy and authoritarianism will become the focus of a great deal of attention and energy.

When the PAR team initially was focusing its research, certain kinds of incidents immediately came up for discussion. The strike of 1974 represents the ever-present potential for a breakdown in solidarity. The poor handling of an original equipment manufacturer's demands for reorganizing a Fagor production line came up repeatedly as an example of authority out of control.

Thus a successful industrial democracy is not uniformly and peacefully committed to democratic ideals. It is occupied by the pursuit of democratic goals and the ongoing rooting out of practices and institutional features that inhibit this. This means that discussions with members and roundtables in which members exchange views are filled with expressions of dissatisfaction, with the measuring of the real against the ideal.

By the same token, the real for each member is somewhat different.

The specific experiences of life within each of the cooperatives, in direct production work, in supervision, in management, in personnel work are different. Members' daily experiences provide the material through which they measure the state of democracy in Fagor. When member reflections on these divergent experiences are brought into juxtaposition in the collective processes of cooperative decision making, in group meetings, or in research such as ours, a diversity of voices and views are heard. Each represents a different view of the world of Fagor, and most have some plausible connection with reality.

I want to stress that the lesson of Fagor is not that members respect all the diversity in the organization. Just as equality, in anything but its most mindless form, does not mean that everyone is equal, a respect for diversity does not involve respecting each and every way individuals differ. As I understand it, and as Fagor practices it, democracy is an attempt to both respect and benefit from significant and relevant differences between individuals.

What is significant and relevant is always a matter of debate, as the roundtables suggest. In Fagor, members feel it is important for every individual to have an equal right to participate and an equal vote, but not for every individual to have the same salary or the same job. Part of the reason for this is a commitment to the notion of human equality, and another part arises from the belief that different kinds of people have good ideas to contribute to the group. Openness in the process rather than radical equality is the aim.

This emphasis on respecting relevant diversity and capturing for the organization valuable differences among individuals does not produce an undisciplined anarchy in Fagor. It need not produce negative results in any organization. I think there are ethical reasons to use reflective practice in organizations as a means for seeking out diversity and trying to convince organizations that such diversity is a basic right of members and a potentially valuable resource for the organization. To our way of thinking, this diversity of views, disciplined by collective processes that work, constitutes organizational health. Creating a uniform organizational culture for Fagor would destroy it as a democracy and, in all probability, as a successful economic enterprise.

LINKS TO REFLECTIVE PRACTICE AND ANTHROPOLOGY

Many of the tensions we uncovered are an embodiment of "good dialectics" and "reflective practice," to use Donald Schön's and Chris Argyris's terminologies. The focus on organizational learning fits well with the PAR team's view that the essentials of the Fagor system lie in its ability to change responsively while not losing track of larger values. We also believe that the negative processes we identified correspond closely to the camouflaging and other mechanisms Argyris and Schön (1978) identify as inhibiting organizational learning. Here, however, I want to concentrate on the relevance of this case to Schön's ideas about reflective practice.

The term *reflective practice* invokes multiple meanings, according to one's point of reference. The dominant association is with Schön's highly regarded books (Schön, 1983, 1987). He has given reflective practice form and legitimacy, stimulating people in diverse fields to think along similar lines. The present volume exhibits this influence. But the term *reflective practice* also generates other, less precise associations.

Reflection, in our own culture, is supposed to be a good thing, so long as we do not reflect to the exclusion of action. *Practice* (as in "family practice" or a "legal practice") is a way of talking about disciplined action, based on a body of knowledge and learned through apprenticeship and experience, which we hope leads to excellence in action. It sounds like something that must be good, a process that happens inside the head of an individual, or between the heads and bodies of two individuals who find themselves in some kind of learning relationship. Who would advocate unreflective practice?

We assume that "time to reflect" is good time, peaceful time. Indeed, it is so peaceful that, for some social researchers and for a segment of the public, the linking of reflection and practice in a phrase appears to be an oxymoron. They believe that thinking is not a form of action, preferring to see many social problems as the result of too much reflection and not enough action. This notion of reflection both weakens it and sufficiently alienates it from practice that it is rendered meaningless.

One important association, however, seems not to spring to mind at all: the dynamic pluralism of reflective practices that make up any organization, any society. To my way of thinking, an important contribution that an anthropological approach to organizations and societies can make to the discourse on reflective practice is to stress the diversity of sense-making processes. These constantly occur in society; they are processes that interact with one another and yet cannot be reduced to one another.

A significant segment of contemporary anthropology views cultures as complex and dynamic fields of discourse and action, a perspective emphasizing a particular dimension of the concept of reflective practice. This chapter emphasizes this pluralism of reflective practices, seeing it as an extension of the concept of reflective practice itself. The focus on pluralism brings to the fore some of the social and political implications

of thinking about reflective practice in organizational context. Pluraliz-
ing the notion of reflective practice is politically important, as the Mondragón case example shows.

Of course, lack of sustained attention to the pluralism of cultural
processes within organizations is not unique to the literature on reflective practice. The burgeoning material on corporate and organizational
culture involves assessments of certain kinds of reflective processes in
organizations. It is fair to say that much of the popular literature on this
subject tends to portray "culture" within organizations as singular (see
Frost, Moore, Reis Louis, Lundberg, & Martin, 1985; Morgan, 1986). It
reduces culture to that which unites a group, gluing it together with
common presuppositions, values, and war stories. Failing organizations
are often viewed as ones in which a strong, unitary "culture" is lacking.

While this view captures one dimension of culture, such a formulation does a basic injustice to the richness of the concept of culture. I
cannot read this literature without feeling that management interest in
corporate culture links a desire for a quick fix to the U.S. competitiveness problem. There is a belief that organizational culture can and
should be managed from the top down and a hope that employees will
work harder for the same wages if they are "culturally" committed to
the goals (read "corporate culture") of the enterprise.

The political motives behind such a position are obvious. My worry,
and a key motive in writing this chapter, is that unless we tie the analysis of organizational culture to an explicit defense of the cultural pluralism in healthy organizations, the reflective practice approach can also
be appropriated as a managerial tool.

An essential point of this chapter is that the reflective process (like
a cultural system in general) is a multiple, diversifying, sense-making
process, even in close collaborations over long periods of time. Participants join in for differing reasons and leave with divergent lessons. Collaboration does not demand the development and enactment of a uniform cultural code, no matter how much certain schools of management
theory would like to have such a code to help control people. We must
conceptualize collective reflective practice in this way to avoid the ever-
present possibility that it will be "adopted" as a device for organizational manipulation rather than for organizational democratization.

What the study adds to Schön's perspective has to do with reflective
diversity in organizations. Our emphasis on the social and cultural heterogeneity in the Fagor system arose from a conviction that we cannot
understand systems unless we usefully capture the diversity within
them. We cannot make sense of the scope of a system, its potential for
improvement, its intrinsic limitations, or its likely changes without this.

The heterogeneity of the members and of their experiences within the system are part and parcel of the ongoing development of the Fagor structures. Nothing can erase the distinction between life experienced in the governance structures and in the workplace because it constitutes the institutional basis of the Fagor system. Fagor members cannot cease to compare their experiences in governance with their experiences at work because they are human beings for whom life is one multidimensional process.

Finally, their deepest commitments define which issues are most hotly debated. Participation is crucial; therefore there is never enough of it. Communication is the basis of responsible self-management; therefore communication must always be better. Industrial democracies must exist in the real world and thus compete by being economically efficient; but the social solidarity that forms the basis of democracy must not be compromised. Change is necessary for survival; but key institutional commitments to members must not be given up. Commitments to basic values dictate where attention will focus, what will be debated, and that these issues will be debated actively so long as Fagor is a vital organization. They also dictate what the "night side" of Fagor will look like. Authoritarianism, inefficiency, and insincerity have to be the daily worries of the members, given their commitment to the opposite values.

Thus a strong corporate culture does not mean enactment of a uniform ideological code or mandate, nor does it mean homogeneous reflective practices. Fagor's self-conscious commitment to organizational reflection as a way of life necessarily produces tension, debate, and change. These are signs of life, not of organizational failure. This kind of heterogeneity, reflection, and change is perhaps the defining feature of any thriving organizational culture.

Yet for all of this, Fagor is not an undisciplined organization. It has rigorous process rules and is orderly and predictable in its behavior. Fagor devises long-range strategic plans and has executed them well enough over the years to have survived the recession without laying off members and to have been consistently profitable over its history in highly competitive markets. This combination of organizational discipline and space for reflective diversity and fundamental debate shows that organizational success does not have to be bought at the price of destroying individualism.

THE POLITICS OF REFLECTIVE PRACTICE

Any linkage between reflection and action thus has a political dimension. What are the politics of reflective practice? The answer is not clear. If we place ourselves at a hypothetical distance from Schön's two books on reflective practice and try to visualize the model of organizations or societies that underlies them, we encounter the dominant paradigm as well as the main communication device: the teacher/apprentice relationship. Out of characterizations of these relationships is built the notion of reflective practice.

What, then, are organizations? Are they to be understood as the accumulation of such dyads? What is the character of collectivity? Since the books on reflective practice do not attempt to deal with this problem, I turned to Schön's collaboration with Chris Argyris (1978) on organizational learning about "theories-in-use," "espoused theories," and the distances separating them. This work, however, does not provide analysis of the diversity of espoused theories and theories-in-use or entertain the possibility that such diversity might be an intrinsic feature of all organizations.

Thus to extend and add political dimension to these very useful perspectives, we must address directly the issues of diversity and ideological hegemony in organizations. While I have not presented a theory about collective reflective practice in this chapter, I hope I have made the case for the need for such a theory.

CONCLUSIONS

The conclusions arising from this analysis are straightforward. Cultural systems are inherently diverse and diversifying. They respond to the ongoing sense-making activities of members of a society. They are a mix of shared and unique features, reflecting both the facts of social collectivity and the uniqueness of individuals and their experiences. While reflective practice is well defined and described as it applies to dyadic relations in a "reflective practicum," the cultural dynamics of the combined reflective practices that would arise in an organization dedicated to reflective practice need to be attended to explicitly. Without this, there is an ever-present danger that attempts will be made to deploy reflective practice in an authoritarian manner. At the very least, without attention to this, managers and consultants will probably fail to value the normal diversity of such processes in healthy organizations and end up treating organizational strengths as weaknesses.

ACKNOWLEDGMENT

My thanks to Donald Schön for very helpful criticisms of two drafts of this paper, to William Foote Whyte for both criticisms and corrections of the final draft, and to José Luis González for comments on the original outline.

REFERENCES

Argyris, C., & Schön, D. A. (1978). *Organizational learning: A theory of action perspective.* Reading, MA.: Addison-Wesley.

Caro Baroja, J. (1971). *Los vascos* (4th ed.). Madrid: Ediciones Istmo.

Frost, P., Moore, L., Reis Louis, M., Lundberg, C., & Martin, J. (Eds.). (1985). *Organizational culture.* Beverly Hills, CA: Sage.

Greenwood, D. J., & González Santos, J. L. (with Cantón Alonso, J., Galparsoro Markaide, I., Goiricelaya Arruza, A., Legarreta Nuin, I., & Salaberría Amesti, K.). (in press). *The corporate culture of Mondragón: Social and cultural dimensions of industrial democracy in the Fagor Cooperative Group.*

Morgan, G. (1986). *Images of organization.* Beverly Hills, CA: Sage.

Schön, D. A. (1983). *The reflective practitioner: How professionals think in action.* New York: Basic Books.

Schön, D. A. (1987). *Educating the reflective practitioner: Toward a new design for teaching and learning in the professions.* San Francisco: Jossey-Bass.

Whyte, W. F., & Whyte, K. K. (1988). *Making Mondragón: The growth and dynamics of the worker cooperative complex.* Ithaca, NY: ILR Press.

Whyte, W. F., Greenwood, D., & Lazes, P. (1989). Participatory action research: Through practice to science in social research. In W. F. Whyte (Ed.), *Action research for the 21st century: Participation, reflection and practice* [special issue]. *The American Behavioral Scientist, 32* (5), 513–552.

Part III

PSYCHOANALYTIC APPROACHES TO REFLECTION ON PRACTICE

5

Organizing Feelings Toward Authority: A Case Study of Reflection in Action

LARRY HIRSCHHORN

IN ASSESSING ONE'S HOPES for organizational life today, one might suppose that as people become more educated and companies become increasingly eager to compete in a global market, senior managers will increasingly value employee initiative. Organizational life will therefore become more democratic as people prove able and willing to accept more authority in their daily work lives.

But if we examine the psychology of authority, that is, people's feelings about leaders, their tolerance for risk, and their struggles with their own competitive feelings, we may find that such a hope is too one-dimensional. Instead, to assess the prospects for organizational democracy, we need a more complicated psychological understanding of work life, one that pays close attention to the psychodynamics of feelings as well as the exercise of apparently rational judgments and the pursuit of manifest interests.

This chapter, based on a "reflection in practice," suggests how a psychoanalytically informed consulting practice can illuminate the prospects and dilemmas of organizational democracy. It addresses the reader at three levels: first, describing a case of organizational consultation focused on the problem of authority; second, highlighting the choices that I, the consultant and author, made in taking up my consultant role; and third, examining the role that case narratives such as this chapter play in helping me reflect on my practice.

The chapter is divided into three sections. The first examines the dilemmas of authority by developing a "triangular" conception of

leader/follower relationships. The second presents a case of consultation. The third examines the case narrative as an example of one approach to reflecting on one's practice and learning from one's experience.

A TRIANGULAR CONCEPTION OF AUTHORITY

Consider the following common dilemma, which I have described
elsewhere (Hirschhorn, 1984): A plant manager introduces a system of
semi-autonomous teams so that workers have the opportunity to regu-
late themselves, but certain teams fail to manage their own internal processes. Consequently, latent team conflicts go unresolved, team productivity falls, and supervisors are forced to step in and take over. In such
a situation, team members would rather accept the authority of the
single supervisor than work to develop a more complicated group life
in which each of its members takes the authority for the successful functioning of the group.

Good and Bad Feelings

When confronting the dilemmas of self-management, team members realize that in order to gain the good feelings that come with a
successful group functioning, they must also face the bad feelings that
come with disciplining and evaluating one another. They want to trust
one another, but to function as a successful group they must also judge
one another. Instead of working to put these good and bad parts together within the microculture of a "good enough" work group, they
would rather abdicate—leaving the bad functions to the supervisor
while retaining the now watered-down and less task-focused "good"
interactions for themselves. (These basic concepts of splitting and ambivalence are drawn from Bion, 1959; Klein & Riviere, 1974.) They can
develop an informal group life that has considerable richness, but at the
cost of not fully experiencing and confronting one another as interdependent co-workers as well as shopfloor buddies. To survive, they have
to leave each other alone at some point. The group then becomes will-
fully dependent on its supervisor.

The Triangle

As this example suggests, people manage the problem of authority
and their feelings about authority in two interdependent ways. First,

unable to contain the good and bad together in one consistent set of relationships, they will often use the authority figure as a way of splitting up good and bad feelings. Thus in this example, the workers let the authority do the dirty work while preserving good feelings and good times for their teammates. Second, they manage their feelings about authority by constructing an imaginary emotional triangle that links *team members* to their feelings about *their supervisor* to feelings they have *about each other*. They distance themselves from authority—their own and others—in order to feel closer to their teammates. Their relationship to authority is *triadic* rather than *dyadic* in structure.

The Triangle and Ambivalence

I believe that this triadic structure is quite general, enabling people to manage their core ambivalences about authority in all settings. Authority evokes conflicting feelings in most adults. As competent adults, followers may resent a leader whose presumed competence and capabilities make them feel ashamed of their presumably more limited capabilities. Moreover, even when followers feel that particular leaders are authentically superior, they must take the risk of depending deeply on them when they have only a limited influence on them. Being a follower in the adult world means giving up control while acknowledging one's limits. Both of these feelings may prove difficult to sustain.

Yet on the other hand, people welcome the leader who frees them of the burdens of worry. Facing the core risks of the enterprise and containing the anxiety that these risks stimulate, the leader protects the followers and enables them to focus on their work. For example, I have found that very educated professionals in law firms and consulting companies are only too happy to let the firm's management committee worry about the strategic dilemmas so that they can get on with their work. They want the firm's leaders to take up the work of worry.

In effect, people both resent and feel grateful to leaders, and they will often manage this primary ambivalence toward authority by resorting to the triangular structure described above. For example, one person may manage contradictory feelings toward a leader by imagining that the leader is wonderful or terrific when compared to the hopelessness of her colleagues. She identifies with the leader's distinctiveness by psychologically devaluing co-workers and imagining that perhaps, unlike her colleagues, she has a very special relationship to the leader. This special relationship helps her tolerate her dependency more effectively.

Similarly, another person more stimulated by feelings of resentment than of gratitude may devalue the leader but then contain his anxiety by developing the psychological fantasy that he will galvanize his excellent co-workers to take over. He psychologically manages his feelings of being unprotected (after all, his leader is incompetent) by imagining that he can lead a revolution. In each case, these fantasies enable individuals to manage their feelings toward authority by invoking the core triangular structure linking these feelings with their feelings toward the work group.

A Culture of Feelings

I hypothesize that just as individuals develop particular solutions to the problems of managing their feelings toward authority, organizations develop cultures of feelings that reflect the reinforcing choices that individuals make. The group as a whole develops a consistent set of choices. These choices create a group process, group myths, and group behaviors that in turn help each individual resolve his or her feelings about authority. The following case study of a consultation to a not-for-profit agency shows how central agency staff developed a culture of feelings in which they idealized the leader, with each member valuing his or her special relationship to the leader while devaluing one another. (For a more elaborate discussion of a psychoanalytically oriented approach to consulting, see Hirschhorn, 1988.)

THE BELOVED LEADER

Family Services

Family Services, started by Peace Corps graduates in the mid-1970s and composed of about 40 central staff members and numerous field staff workers, established and managed family service clinics in poor communities in North America and parts of Mexico. Program staff at the central office established new clinics, introduced innovative service delivery techniques to fieldworkers, and worked to insure that viable clinics had sufficient year-to-year funding.

The agency was organized along both regional and functional lines, with some directors responsible for overseeing regions and others for managing services and programs (e.g., health education, family literacy, etc.). The work was rewarding but frequently difficult, since central staff, while feeling accountable for widely dispersed clinics and programs, often had little control over them.

The Leader's Centrality

I first entered the organization when George, a key program director in charge of health-education services, asked me to meet with Carol, the long-term executive director of the program. Carol, he felt, was overloaded and had become almost indispensable to the organization. Her staff highly valued her leadership and professional competence and came to her for advice on all matters of program development and clinic oversight. Carol, in turn, exercised complete control over the programs. She reviewed all grant proposals, edited all outgoing documents, and kept a close check on all developments in the field.

While the agency was ostensibly organized into regions and programs, Carol was in charge of all key program decisions. Directors functioned more as staff assistants to her. Thus, for example, when Carol met weekly with the staff responsible for a program or region, directors did little but assemble their own staffs, who in turn gave direct reports to Carol on the latest field developments.

Far from organizing the mass of details in the field and presenting key issues to Carol, the program directors simply functioned as administrators, bringing their own staffs to a meeting with Carol. They took on no executive authority themselves and felt no responsibility for developing a programmatic overview of their own area. Thus, while ostensibly in charge of their areas, they functioned as colleagues to their subordinates and as staff assistants to Carol. There was no functioning chain of command.

One manager expressed this feeling of lacking authority quite poignantly. At a group meeting of directors (eight in all), he noted that, when Carol was last absent on a trip, he felt stymied and did not know what to do in several program areas he was responsible for. This puzzled him, he said, "for I feel like a competent professional, like an adult." Why couldn't he act in Carol's absence? I suggested that perhaps he felt that Carol psychologically owned part of his job, that it was not entirely his. He smiled and nodded his head strongly.

The Presenting Issues

At the first meeting with Carol and George, Carol acknowledged the potential burden she faced as the organization, successful in raising funds and expanding its programs, simply became too large for her to manage. But while open to considering changes, she was skeptical that, after all these years, she and I along with her program staff could develop new ways of working. Nonetheless, she was willing to give it a try and agreed that I should begin by interviewing her staff.

My interviews with the program staff highlighted some of the structural issues that may have led Carol to manage the organization in such detail. Managing complex community service programs from afar in settings where local elites looked askance at services to the poor created substantial risks for Family Services. In parts of the South and Southwest, and in Mexico, such community clinics could and sometimes did become the basis for empowering poor people. Field staff committed to family functioning as well as social change thus had to navigate a midcourse between these two objectives. Moreover, since federal funding was scarce, Family Services had developed effective strategies for raising funds from regional elites who, while aware of the developmental impacts of such services, did not want them to become overpoliticized.

The program staff felt that Carol had the experience, capacity, and knowledge to take in an enormous amount of detail and felt safer in letting her make the critical and ongoing program decisions. She was simply too good. Nonetheless, all agreed that Carol was in danger of taking on too much work. A simple tabulation of the number of meetings she attended suggested that she spent close to 3 working months a year simply meeting with her staff, in addition to managing the organization's relationships with its funders and political supporters, writing proposals, and reviewing and editing everyone else's written work and correspondence before it went out.

The Emotional Triangle

Reviewing my interview data, I puzzled at the apparent anomaly of a not-for-profit organization, whose culture and history were rooted in the early spirit of the Peace Corps and the social values of the 1960s generation, tolerating such tight control by one person. I suspected that, in part, Carol's sheer competence, her commitment to her work, the political values that shaped that work, and the quiet and sustained quality of her concentration and attention enabled people to unequivocally submit to her judgment and authority. But I also believed that the relationships between her and her staff were partly shaped by the relationships among staff members themselves.

One vignette is striking here. When I first met Carol and George, the program director who first introduced me to the agency, they both emphasized the problem everyone was having with Bill, Carol's ostensible deputy. People felt that Bill, who had been brought in about half a year before to assist Carol, was trying to act too much like a deputy, trying to supervise the program areas by examining and correcting grants and reviewing field correspondence. As they spoke at length about the many problems he was causing, I imagined that Bill might have been obstructing Carol's increasing willingness to delegate some authority downward. Before meeting him, I half expected him to be a willful, strong-headed person intent on concentrating power in his role.

Nothing could have been further from the truth. He was a gentle and unassuming person, scholarly in demeanor, who felt pained and puzzled by people's suspicion of him and by the difficulty he faced in carving out a role. He thought he had been hired to relieve Carol of some of her work, as it had been explained to him by board members. He had no desire to be her deputy if she did not want one, he told me. Most of all, he wanted some role clarity and some real tasks, so that he could contribute to Family Services' mission while enjoying his work. I was convinced by his manner and moved by his genuine pain. So why had Carol and George created an image of Bill as the "bad guy"?

The relationship among the followers themselves seemed key here. I hypothesized that people tolerated, indeed welcomed, Carol's centrality because each director imagined or hoped that he or she had a special relationship to Carol. Realistically, since each person, regardless of formal title, had direct access to Carol and since she supervised them directly, each program staff in fact had the privilege of working directly with her. But I also suspected that many fantasized about having the most special relationship to her. Thus, for example (and this is poignant), George confidently told me that he would be the most appropriate deputy and successor to Carol if there were to be one. But when in the course of my interviews I asked some program managers about successors, no other program staff ever mentioned George as a potential leader. I suspected that he had distorted the reality of his situation in his mind, not because he was grandiose, but because his close working relationship with Carol stimulated his fantasy that he was in fact special.

Since all program staff members had special access to Carol and if we assume that each, like George, imagined that he or she was Carol's favorite, this would suggest that staff members had to jealously guard their link to Carol. Their co-workers were potentially their competitors. Bill's position, even if it only hinted at the emergence of a deputy role, threatened to undermine each person's special access to the leader. Moreover, people's heightened sensitivity, if not distorted view, regarding Bill's behavior probably reflected their awareness of Carol's overload.

The primary relationships at the agency, Carol's links to each of the staff members, were indeed fragile.

Competition: An Episode

This link between the competition among the staff for Carol's attention and the problems besetting the agency was enacted during the course of my consultation to the agency.

As a result of my interviews, I recommended, among other suggestions, that Carol institute a series of director meetings that she would run, Bill would staff, and only the eight directors would attend. Up to that point, all meetings had in fact been meetings of the entire staff, which all professionals, secretaries, and clerks attended. Carol never held a meeting that distinguished one level of the agency from another. I reasoned, and then told her, that by holding some strictly bilevel meetings, she would help the directors differentiate themselves from the rest of the staff. They would in turn begin to feel more accountable for the work of their own staffs, and they might be able to draw on each other rather than on her for advice. I acknowledged that the meetings could fail and suggested that she hold them over an experimental period of 3 months and then meet with me and her program managers to assess them.

Predictably, Carol and her directors had trouble holding such a meeting. As Carol noted, they met feeling as if there were "ghosts in the room," since the remaining (absent) staff seemed to "haunt them." They wondered if they could really hold any meeting of substance without including everybody.

The problems of holding such a meeting emerged at the end of my consultation, when I met with all the professional staff to assess the experiment. Marge, who officially reported to George, spoke up in anger. This whole process smacked of hierarchy, she noted; it went against the grain of the agency's egalitarian culture, and she had not been included in the decision to conduct this experiment. Moreover, she added, she never considered herself to be George's subordinate even if he formally appraised her performance once a year. She was his colleague. Marge's conception of the agency's culture, while simplified, was an egalitarian one; because Carol was so central and dominant, Marge would lose standing if Carol delegated authority.

Aware of Marge's anger prior to the meeting, for she had approached him to express her thoughts and feelings before the meeting, George replied in a tense voice that he had in fact been supervising Marge's work, though he acknowledged that he might have been lazy about this in the past because of Carol's close work with his staff. Carol replied a bit more testily, arguing that, however Marge felt, George was in fact her boss. I then noted that clearly all three of them had contributed to this dilemma and then suggested that, as one of the most long-standing trilevel relationships in the agency, it probably typified some of the central dilemmas in the agency as a whole. Marge concurred that it might, and then added that one reason she did not like these changes was that *she would find it very hard to give up her close relationship to Carol.*

In effect, George, as she had stated, was her colleague not her boss, but as she also acknowledged, he was her competitor, potentially blocking her relationship to Carol. This suggests that Marge and the other staff were willing to give up a lot of their own potential authority and forgo their own professional development—"become lazy" as George noted—if they could have a close and special relationship to Carol. Their willingness to forgo their own development, despite their competence and education, suggests that they not only idealized Carol but also identified with this idealization. They did not have to develop because in being close to Carol, they became her.

Feelings of Anger

Finally, I believe that the fantasy of anger played a critical role in shaping the group's feeling culture. As we saw, Marge was sensibly angry at the potential loss of her position, although she had worked to control it by speaking with George before the all-staff meeting. But I suggest that Carol and others had elaborated a fantasy in which angry and destructive feelings were always threatening to erupt throughout the agency.

As I noted, Carol felt that in holding the program managers' meeting she was confronting the ghosts of the absent staff members, as if by excluding them she had killed them, and they were returning like ghosts to wreak havoc on her.

Equally striking was my own experience of appearing like a bad and terrible person who would wreak havoc on staff members. After the program managers had conducted their experiment, I met with them to help them assess their experience. The discussion was a rich one in which the managers reviewed their own experiences of trying to take on more authority in their roles. Toward the end, I suggested that I come to the final all-staff meeting in which the full staff would assemble to assess the experiment. Carol hastily replied that such a meeting would not be possible, arguing that some of the people would not want me there. I had a quick flash of a scene, which I imagined was in Carol's

mind, of my presence stimulating an explosive encounter in which program staff would attack me. In Carol's fantasy, I thought, I was a potentially hated person. I remember, in fact, feeling angry and blurting out
to Carol, "Aren't these your meetings?"—to which she responded
somewhat huffily that indeed they were.

Catching myself, I then noted that I did not want to argue, but I
would like to think out loud with them. I said that to come to "take on
the staff, like a showdown at the O.K. Corral" would be foolish of me,
and grandiose to boot. But I then added, talking directly to Carol, that
through much of the consultation she had seemed to want to keep me
away from the staff, and that now I again felt she was extruding me
from a staff process as if I were dangerous or poisonous. She agreed
that she did seem to feel that way. I then said that perhaps the staff
needed to talk with me directly so that the difficulties I seemed to represent could be faced more directly. After all, I added, I was not so bad
in the flesh. A new program manager then chuckled, noting that she
too had heard all about this "strange person from the Wharton School,"
but now meeting me, I wasn't so bad. Carol then agreed to invite me to
the meeting and to talk ahead of time to staff members who might have
trouble with my presence. As it turned out, my presence at the all-staff
meeting stimulated serious and sometimes difficult talk, but certainly
no explosive attacks on me or anyone else. I suggest that Carol's fantasy
of the ghosts returning and her image of either my destructiveness or
vulnerability to attack highlighted an underlying tone and mood of the
agency. People walked carefully around each other, fearful that in stepping on one another's toes they might in fact stimulate the anxiety and
anger they all felt in competing for access to the prized leader. To erect
and support Carol as the sole authority, they had to distance themselves
from one another and in so doing had constructed a somewhat isolating
group life.

I witnessed a poignant consequence of this isolation when Bill, at
the last directors' meeting, sought feedback and discussion of his role.
He asked the group what his role in the program directors' meeting
might be in the future. If the meeting was to take on decision-making
responsibilities, would he have a say, or since he did not directly supervise professionals but was rather a direct assistant to Carol, would he
primarily support the meeting?

No one answered Bill, and he seemed alone and unsupported at
that moment. I felt that the group had not yet resolved its feelings about
Bill's positional proximity to the deputy role but did not want to say this
to him directly—perhaps imagining that if they said, "No, you don't
have the same power as we do," they would permanently damage him.

I then noted to the group that Bill's problem in obtaining clarification of his role was not unlike the problem the whole agency had in differentiating roles and drawing boundaries. Still, no one answered Bill. I turned to Bill and noted that his question reflected the continuing problem he faced in defining his ambiguous staff as opposed to line position and then, turning to the group as a whole, noted that it was very hard to say "no" aloud in this organization. One director then turned to Bill and said, "We will have to see how this meeting evolves. This is an evolutionary process." I then said that the group was avoiding the issue and that they had all learned to become good diplomats. Bill smiled and said, "Yes, we are all diplomats." The meeting ended shortly afterwards.

In short, Bill could not get an honest and direct discussion of his role. Fearful of drawing boundaries, establishing limits, saying "no" and therefore potentially stimulating explosive anger in others, group members could not treat one another seriously and honestly. They walked around each other. Consequently, group life had a somewhat ascetic quality. The feel of the group was serious, committed, and intellectual, but it lacked some of the nurturing qualities that help groups make it through difficult times.

In Sum

As I argued early in the chapter, people often face the problem of managing their ambivalent feelings toward authority, and they often do so by creating in their minds the fantasy of a triangular relationship that links them to their leaders through their co-workers.

My consultation at Family Services provides some insight into this process. Because they valued her competence and accomplishments, Carol's subordinates submitted to her completely and let her dominate their work. But to compensate for their resulting dependency, they developed a tense group life in which co-workers became competitors for the special relationships that each might have or hope to have with her. The resulting climate was one of isolation and suppressed anger in which competition among co-workers, though kept at bay, threatened to emerge through angry feelings. The resulting culture of feelings supported a system in which the leader was idealized, co-workers were regarded warily, and the tone was ascetic. Ironically, a beloved leader directing a program committed to empowering its clients was part of an authoritarian culture—one that repressed collegiality while stimulating the privately held fantasy that each subordinate was "special."

LEARNING FROM EXPERIENCE

Reflection in Action

Let us now examine the case as an example of reflecting in action. How do I, as a professional consultant, gain usable knowledge and insight through the process of consulting? I suggest that three moments of experience provide me with insight: "triggers," "patterns," and "affirmations." Let me briefly describe each one.

Triggers. By mobilizing and focusing my attention, triggers establish the relevant context for forming a hypothesis about the situation I face. The most common triggers are anomalies, contradictions, and metaphors. For example, the Family Services case as a whole has the character of an anomaly asking for explanation and understanding. How does a seemingly beloved leader like Carol shape a peculiarly authoritarian and ascetic climate, particularly when the agency has its roots in the "participative" climate of the 1960s? The anomaly triggers the consultant's attention. By creating a seeming disjunction between preconception and appearance ("Shouldn't 1960s people support participative organizations?"), it opens up a path for a deeper understanding of social reality that dissolves these disjunctions. Thus, as the case suggests, people can support a strong authority while emotionally identifying with a nonhierarchical culture by fantasizing that they have the most direct access to the authority figure.

Similarly, direct contradictions provide triggers for thought. When I expected Bill to be tough-minded and power-hungry and found him instead to be gentle and unassuming, I knew that the image of him, put into me by the other directors, served a psychosocial function that I needed to understand. People's inaccurate portrayal of Bill was integral to the agency's functioning precisely because it was so at odds with who Bill was. Like a beam of light, the contradiction illuminates an arena of feeling and thought that I believed would give me new insight.

Finally, metaphors provide access to the thoughts and feelings people have that are preconscious and that, therefore, they cannot and do not verbalize openly. The metaphor is the vehicle for a feeling, for the "color" of the situation that people experience but are frequently unaware of. When Carol said that there were "ghosts in the room" at the first only-directors meeting, she was invoking a feeling-tone as well as a thought.

This feeling-tone linked the meeting to the theme of creating ghosts, to the feeling of killing others, and to the anxiety of being haunted. Like a dream image, the condensations of meaning packed into a metaphor provide triggers for exploring the wider social field that produced the metaphor.

Patterns.   Patterns emerge when the consultant matches an event with his or her working theory of the situation. For example, when a program director complained that although he was a competent professional, he felt deskilled in Carol's absence, my prior theoretical understanding of the psychology of delegation led me to link his feelings to the ways in which Carol authorized him to do his work. By using the metaphor of "ownership," by suggesting that he did not fully own his job, I suggested to him that he could not feel competent if he were not fully authorized.

Similarly, I could examine the agency's culture of meetings through my theoretical understanding of delegation and organizational boundaries. While agency members could interpret their all-staff meetings as a sign of the agency's democratic nature, I interpreted it as a measure of people's unwillingness to delegate authority to one another. Because people could not trust one another, everyone had to be at the meeting. Boundaries, which divide work, rest on trust.

Affirmations.   Finally, I feel able to act, to take risks, when a hypothesis I have is confirmed. Three modes of confirmation are important. First, a hypothesis can be confirmed directly. For example, when Marge said she might lose her close relationship to Carol if she acknowledged George's role as her supervisor, she was directly confirming my hypothesis that the primary relationships shaping the agency were triangular in structure, that peers competed with one another for direct access to Carol.

Second, I can get confirmation from the feeling-tone of an encounter. When Bill asked for clarification of his role, the resulting painful silences, the feelings associated with avoidance and flight, confirmed that people could not comfortably be aggressive in public, could not directly draw boundaries. My other hypothesis was thus supported: Agency directors suppressed their aggressive feelings to avoid facing the competition that shaped their basic relationships. Aggression was "too hot to handle," because in mobilizing competitiveness, aggression might lead some people to realize that they were not Carol's most special person.

Third, affirmations can be provided by silence. When the program director, reflecting on his peculiar sense of inadequacy, silently smiled when I suggested he did not own his job, I felt that his silence was evidence of a satisfying closure to the conversation, the communication he had simulated. A silence can, of course, signify feelings of discomfort as well, but when the silence comfortably closes an encounter (and here the consultant must rely fundamentally on his or her felt connection to the conversation) rather than uncomfortably leaves it hanging, it is a sign that an interpretation has made sense and has helped clarify a piece of experience.

Reflecting on Action

The process of learning from one's experience does not, however, end with the action of consulting itself. Let us look at the case again. It is presented as a coherent piece of experience, as a puzzle solved, so that the different anomalies and contradictions described within it are finally brought into relationship with one another and with the basic theme of the case.

The reader might sensibly object to such a narrative. How can reality be so clean and coherent? Where are the messy edges? Are there not alternative explanations for what happened and what the author/consultant did? For example, when the other directors would not answer Bill as he sought to clarify his role, perhaps it was a sign that they really wanted to give him a chance to shape his role before prematurely defining it for him.

Such objections are sensible, but they miss the role that such case writing plays in the learning process. The case report is not an empirical finding or the definitive statement about "what really happened." Rather it is constructed as a model, an ideal-type picture of a particular kind of social system. Because it is coherent, because it tells a sensible story with a satisfying ending, it adds to the stock of models the consultant can use when confronting new situations and new social systems. Competence grows not when the consultant grasps more laws of behavior, but when he or she has access to a wider and increasingly diverse set of models or stories. Indeed, this distinction between laws and stories separates clinical from scientific practice. Scientists search for laws to reveal similarities that lie behind apparent differences. By contrast, case writers search for stories to reveal differences that lie behind apparent similarities.

The role that the case plays in learning from experience thus highlights the criteria we need to apply in assessing the case. If the case is to function as a model, it must satisfy four criteria. First, while based on a real situation, it must be abstracted from it. Unlike a verbatim report in which *all* events, thoughts, and feelings are simply linked by their appearance in time, in clinical narratives critical events, thoughts, and feelings are *thematically* linked, while other events are omitted.

Second, the case must be coherent. To function as a model or ideal type, its narrative must come to a close. As in a story or drama, the tensions and contradictions posed at the beginning must be resolved by the end of the case report. If they are not, the model will lack power and validity and the consultant will be reluctant to try it on in future encounters with a social system.

Third, the case must be plausible. Plausibility in turn rests on three criteria. First, while abstracted from details, it cannot appear evasive and vague. Second, if its coherence is not to appear false and "cooked," it must supply details that evoke the spontaneous and unplanned quality of social interaction. Third, while highlighting a unique situation, it must be attached to some commonly held beliefs about people and social processes, for example, people find competition difficult, or authority is a complex problem.

Fourth, to add to the stock of ideal types—to provide some genuine learning, rather than confirmation of past experience—the case, while plausible and coherent, must help the consultant link apparently contradictory phenomena together in new ways; it must pose and resolve some core paradoxes. Thus the case presented here plausibly clarifies how a "1960s" agency could support an authoritarian leader, how participative processes could mask a lack of trust, and how an idealized leader could stalemate the development of her subordinates.

In Sum

The case presented here can be used to examine the twin processes of reflecting in action and reflecting on action. The former is stimulated by triggers, patterns, and confirmations within the frame of action itself. The latter is stimulated by the properties of the case narrative. The case narrative potentiates later reflections in action by supplying a model that, while coherent, plausible, and abstracted, also resolves anomalies or paradoxes in new ways.

REFERENCES

Bion, W. (1959). *Experiences in groups*. New York: Basic Books.

Hirschhorn, L. (1984). *Beyond mechanization: Work and technology in a postindustrial age*. Cambridge, MA: MIT Press.

Hirschhorn, L. (1988). *The workplace within: Psychodynamics of organizational life*. Cambridge, MA: MIT Press.

Klein, M. & Riviere, J. (1974). *Love, hate, and reparation*. New York: Norton.

6

Trying to Grow at Work:
A Developmental Perspective
On Organizational Careers

HOWELL S. BAUM

OVER THE YEARS, I have been struck by the fact that many of us act differently inside organizations than outside. We do things we would never consider doing elsewhere, and we have trouble doing apparently simple things we say we want to do. In trying to understand why this happens, I have become interested in how people experience becoming members of organizations. What do people feel they are asked to do in order to become members, and what do they want in return for full participation? In what ways may people's actions in organizations express their satisfaction or disappointment with the outcome of tacit negotiations over membership conditions?

The organizational literature rarely addresses such questions. Most studies of organizational entry assume that individuals simply want to work loyally in the ways management wants, and socialization is seen as a more or less straightforward process of learning organizational norms. In this view, becoming a member involves little conflict or negotiation (see, e.g., Buchanan, 1974; Feldman, 1976; Porter, Lawler, & Hackman, 1975; Wanous, 1980; Wanous, Reichers, & Malik, 1984).

Some who write about organizational careers recognize that the course of a worker's relationship with an organization may reflect success in adjusting to a sequence of organizational expectations. For example, a new worker must apprentice before becoming a productive

This chapter is adapted from *Organizational Membership: Personal Development in the Workplace* (Baum, 1990).

contributor and contribute productively before mentoring others. Still, these writers, too, assume that workers' expectations largely respond to and are compatible with managerial requirements (see, e.g., Dalton, Thompson, & Price, 1977; Hall, 1976; Hall & Kram, 1981; Kram, 1985; Schein, 1978).

The literature on work motivation and job satisfaction recognizes that workers want more than simply being productive. For example, many look for interesting and challenging work and expect to be taken seriously. People are concerned about not only the content of work but also its social context. Though some writers acknowledge that these expectations may conflict with managerial interests, they say little about how initial satisfactions or frustrations of these expectations may affect organizational careers (see, e.g., Hage, 1980; Herzberg, Mausner, & Snyderman, 1959; U.S. Department of Health, Education and Welfare, 1973; Vroom, 1964; Yankelovich & Immerwahr, 1983).

What is missing is a view of a worker as a person whose work is part of a lifetime of interests and development. We need a theory of why workers come to have particular expectations of work organizations, why these expectations may change in specific ways, and why their satisfaction may have far-reaching consequences. Moreover, since people find themselves doing things at work that surprise them, we need a theory that considers workers' unconscious relations with organizations in addition to their conscious interests and calculations.

To explore these issues, I have talked with professionals and managers about their organizational careers—what they initially expected of their workplace, what they found, and how they reacted to their satisfaction or disappointment. Interviewing 50 people, I have looked for typical expectations as well as typical sequences of change in expectations. In interpreting people's accounts, I have relied on Erik Erikson's psychoanalytic model of development. Erikson describes a sequence of consciously and unconsciously shaped demands that people make on others in order to develop; among these expectations is competence at work. The model offers hypotheses about typical subtexts that may underlie a wide range of stories about organizational careers.

I will describe one organizational career here. It involves a puzzle: Why does someone who says he wants to be part of an organization to practice his profession nevertheless, for 6 years, hold himself apart from co-workers in an organization that offers precisely this possibility of affiliation? In order to answer this question, we need to attend to certain others. What does being a member of an organization mean to him? What personal goals or needs so strongly conflict with his stated interests in joining and advancing that he holds back from affiliating with the organization? And, above all, why do these conflicts arise for him when they do?

After presenting an account of his career, I will interpret it psychoanalytically in terms of unconscious developmental issues. Following that, I will reflect on my practice in conducting psychoanalytically informed research.

THE ORGANIZATIONAL CAREER OF CHARLES LATHAM

Formally, organizational membership is sealed with a paycheck. Socially, membership requires that a worker be included in others' activities. Psychologically, however, a worker does not feel like a member until he or she identifies with some part of the organization. The worker may collaborate with and feel close to co-workers and associate this relationship with the organization. In addition, he or she may identify with management actions or an organizational mission. In these cases, the worker thinks of co-workers', managers', or the organization's welfare as his or her own.

Psychological membership requires the wish and security to become intimately attached to an organization. It entails a willingness to compromise independence and accept collective norms. Some may find the rewards of affiliation, such as inclusion and warmth, sufficiently satisfying to warrant exchanging autonomy for membership. Others may hesitate about making such a deal, perhaps drifting from job to job, perhaps hovering on the periphery of an organization, or perhaps painstakingly negotiating entry into an organizational role. Charles Latham[1] offers an example of the third response.

Ten years ago he graduated from a professional program in city planning and took a job with a county planning department. He had interned there while in school and concluded it would be a good place to begin his career. He says he wanted to be a planner in order to promote urban development and help reduce poverty, and the job offered the chance "to deal with people directly." What he wanted from work was "more on the noble ideals side of the ledger than making money."

He liked his first supervisor, and yet, in describing his initial position, he emphasizes his separateness. He was hired to do social planning in a traditional physical planning agency, and his small section was located in a nearly inaccessible corner of the building. He felt others were "officious and aloof," that they considered themselves "a club you had to graduate into." He and other staff members spoke different professional languages and rarely consulted on substantive matters. He felt they regarded the social planning section as "a bastard child." They considered him "an outsider, a frill" and were "unaware of what we were doing." At the same time, he "felt deficient in physical planning areas" and "didn't know what a whole lot of maps were for."

Although he says he wanted to settle into the planning department, he spent more and more time with staff members of other, human service, agencies. While continuing to complain about exclusion from the organizational mainstream, he increasingly cherished his independence. He spoke of his identity as a social planner, in contrast with the physical planners of his department. He distinguished traditional planning's support for business interests from social planning's concern for minorities and the disadvantaged. He prized his outside contacts and valued their rewards more highly than departmental relations. Other agencies implemented some of his proposals, but that recognition did not improve his standing in his own department. As time went on, he lost interest in projects of the planning agency, and other staff members questioned his commitment to the organization. This situation continued for a half-dozen years.

Then a new position in community planning opened up, he applied for it, and he got it. The job required him to work with citizen groups, helping them prepare proposals to address problems they identified and getting their responses to development plans. He had to represent residents' positions to the department and present the agency's position to neighborhood groups. This role transformed his relations with the rest of the staff.

Immediately, he was central to the department. Not only was the community planner involved in physical planning, but he was the gatekeeper for other staff members when they contacted neighborhood businesses or citizen groups about plans. Others began to talk to him, both to inform him about their actions and to ask his opinions about community reactions. "All of a sudden," he says, "I was immediately connected to every section. I felt a little ridiculous, because here they were asking me all the questions, and I was new on the job." To his pleasant surprise, he found "there was no mystique" to the physical planning methods and maps he could not understand before, and he "learned all this quickly."

He sums up the crucial social and psychological meaning of this change: "It happened very dramatically and all at once. From the day I became a community planner, I was a member of the club—that simple." He became "an integral part of the department," "the eyes and ears of the department in the community." After 6 years of standoff, community planning provided an organizationally legitimate role in which he could function as both an outsider and an insider. He could throw himself into departmental work because it did not require surrendering his autonomy.

He continued in community planning for 3 years, until an episode in which his work with a community put him into conflict with the county council. Several council members pressured his director to replace him. The director kept him but moved him to another position. Although his next role was not as central to the department, and even though he left community planning under fire, his tenure there irreversibly led him and others to consider him a member. At last he identified with the organization. After all this, he says, "I feel very much part of the in-crowd. I feel my opinion is respected."

Although community planning is an evidently elegant solution to Latham's conflicts about affiliating, questions remain for later examination. Why did it take Latham 6 years to consider such a role? Moreover, after increasing his distance from the department in the earlier years, what led him to reverse directions and take this role central to the department? And what about this role so suddenly led him to identify with the overall organization? Answers to these questions depend on understanding the developmental meanings of work.

ERIKSON'S DEVELOPMENTAL FRAMEWORK

Psychoanalysis is the study of relations between unconscious thoughts and wishes and conscious intentions and actions. It explores the hypothesis that an explanation for many puzzling or seemingly contradictory actions is a conflict between conscious and unconscious aims, in which the latter may be more effective. Even when the two do not conflict, the strength and order of conscious actions may owe a great deal to unconscious origins.

Psychoanalyst Erik Erikson (1963, 1968) observes that human beings unconsciously and, increasingly, consciously follow a regular sequence of developmental stages. Maturing biological needs and potentials, shaped by cultural norms, create a series of challenges, each of which may be satisfied by a particular social relationship—with parents, peers, children, and others. Erikson argues that individuals manipulate the world to establish relations that will satisfy specific tests and make it possible to grow. Success at one stage permits advancement to the next, where mastery depends on continuing success at preceding tasks. The aim of development is to elaborate a personal identity—a sense of deepening continuity between who one has been and who one is and convergence between one's own and other's perceptions of oneself.[2]

Learning to work is a normal part of this growth. It requires an individual to have or develop *work ability* and to take or fashion a *work role or identity* acceptable to him- or herself and to co-workers. In addition, psychological membership in an organization calls for a worker to *affiliate with the organization*, feeling part of it and close to co-workers. These requirements correspond to the accomplishments of the fourth through sixth stages in Erikson's eight-stage model of development. The following discussion designates stages and work activities corresponding to them with parenthetical glosses showing their order in Erikson's model.

Developing *work ability* is normal for contemporary Western children between ages 6 and 11. They face the challenge of learning socially valued work skills, establishing what Erikson calls a *sense of industry* (stage 4) and avoiding a feeling of "inferiority."[3] Children find they can win recognition for channeling aggressive energy into work activities. Even after, they expect to exercise their competence at work, and adults express this wish in terms of "learning new skills," "using their abilities," and "solving problems."

A *work identity* is one aspect of a *sense of identity* (stage 5). Adolescence is the normal time for consolidating a personal identity and avoiding "identity confusion." Youths decide on the ideas and groups they want to identify with for the rest of their lives. Central to this commitment is establishing an identity as a "good worker" in a particular field. When adults speak of "putting themselves into their work" or "practicing their profession," they want to affirm who they are.

Organizational affiliation is one expression of *intimacy* (stage 6), a normal accomplishment of early adulthood, when people attempt to avoid "isolation." Individuals weigh the possibilities of closeness against the risks of exposure and loss. They try to act caringly in relations with others equal to them. The most important new intimacies are sexual, but friendships and organizational memberships also offer opportunities for attachment. Workers may express this interest in terms of "working closely with others" or "identifying with the organization."[4]

Erikson tells us to expect an individual's actions to be guided by conscious and unconscious intentions to progress in a regular order through this developmental agenda. Although some of these demands are especially appropriate to particular settings, such as family or school, every situation presents some opportunity to learn or maintain developmental accomplishments. The workplace, as an example, offers adults a location where they may practice various developmental tasks.

These observations on identity development suggest hypotheses for interpreting organizational careers. Events may be seen in terms of adults' efforts to consolidate and advance their developmental position within constraints set by co-workers and organizational policy. Insofar as workers succeed, their careers should reveal mastery of a series of developmental challenges. In particular, psychological affiliations or identification with a work organization should depend on a prior sense of identity as a worker and, before that, secure work ability, or sense of industry. These hypotheses suggest the outlines of subtexts in organizational careers.

REREADING LATHAM'S ORGANIZATIONAL CAREER

Latham wanted to become a planner but felt treated like "a bastard child" as a social planner in a physical planning agency. Veteran staff members presented themselves as "a club you had to graduate into." As years passed, club members did not legitimate the bastard child, but, equally, the child did not clearly try to graduate into the club. On the contrary, he spent more and more time with people in other agencies, doing work that was not only foreign, but also invisible, to the planners who could legitimate him. And yet this route outward eventually led him to the center of the organization. "Dramatically" and "immediately," he became "a member of the club."

One can see in the earlier account of Latham's career an ambivalence about becoming a member of a collectivity. He wanted to join the planning department but did not want to accept the organization's priorities or traditional professional norms and methods. He concentrated on deviant activities that, at best, could give him a peripheral role in the agency. Even when he moved to the center of the organization, he took a role that allowed him to retain divided loyalties. And yet he did become a social and psychological member of his department. His deviance was more than simply rebellion or withdrawal. Erikson's framework helps us understand why Latham found entering the organization so difficult and how this move outward may have involved a partly conscious, partly unconscious plan to become an organizational member after satisfying developmental prerequisites.

Latham had studied planning in graduate school. He had taken courses in planning methods and, as anyone taking a first job, was concerned about testing the usefulness of what he had learned. He wanted to know whether he could plan competently. In Erikson's terms, he wanted to build up a sense of industry in social planning and avoid feeling inferior to other practitioners (stage 4). Once he could consolidate his planning skills, he wanted, as he says, to establish a professional identity as a planner (stage 5). This would mean he could think confidently of himself as a planning practitioner, no longer a student, and others would consider him someone to be included in planning projects. Thus the planning department was an appropriate place to work on these related developmental tasks. As many others in the agency before him, he could learn work skills, articulate a work identity, and become socially and emotionally part of the organization. After all, as he realized from his internship, members of the department thought of themselves as a close and caring group, and they were open to new members.

Although Latham's ambivalence about joining the organization may have had several roots, some of his conflict may have arisen at this point. Developmentally, someone must have a secure work identity (stage 5) before feeling that closeness to co-workers and affiliation with an organization (stage 6) are possible. Otherwise, one simply feels overwhelmed, without a secure foundation for relations with others. Thus when Latham said he wanted to become a member of the planning agency and become a competent social planner, he was describing several accomplishments that had to follow a specific developmental sequence. In particular, he could not become a psychological member of the planning department if he was unsure of who he was professionally. Although in many cases a new professional may proceed through these three developmental stages relatively easily, Latham faced a realistic conflict in his department. He liked the emotional closeness of the staff enough to want to be part of it (stage 6), and yet this predominantly physical planning agency offered limited opportunities for establishing himself as a social planner (stage 5).

If he were ever to feel close to co-workers and identify with the organization, somehow he needed to establish a professional identity first. Turning outside makes sense in this context. Consciously, he described this move as necessary for becoming a social planner. Unconsciously, he seems to have recognized that he had to succeed as a professional on his own terms before he could join the department he wanted to belong to. Thus moving into a network of social agencies may be seen as part of an unconscious plan to develop in a normal sequence. His apparent ambivalence about membership in the planning department at least partly expressed this developmental need.

Once he had received the validation of other professionals and elected officials, he was able to join an organization, such as the planning department. The fact that he eventually became part of the agency through a community planner role reveals more of his developmental plan. This role makes sense as his compromise with the organization: He took a position as a mainstream physical planner in return for others' acceptance. Developmentally, once he had convinced himself that he had a professional identity (even if as a social planner elsewhere), he was psychologically free to take a range of planning positions. In addition, the community planner role makes sense as the department's compromise with Latham: In exchange for his moving into the professional mainstream, co-workers would let him have a role that allowed him time and loyalty outside the agency. It is as if unconsciously both he and they recognized that he had established a professional identity but had to practice at the next developmental task, collegiality and affiliation. Perhaps he and they felt he had special concerns about emotional attachment and autonomy. The role enabled him to deal with ambivalence about making a commitment to organizational peers.

This interpretation suggests that Latham's mixed reactions to organizational membership involved in part a conflict between more or less conscious wishes to become an active participant in a work organization and more or less unconscious needs to establish the developmental prerequisites first. One reason ambivalence about membership stands out in his story is that we generally consider joining an organization to be a simple matter. Any problems apparently involve willful resistance. Latham's career shows the psychological complexity of organizational entry. Although his hesitation might be interpreted as unconscious willfulness, his intentions were directed planfully *toward* growth rather than *against* membership per se.

Because of his developmental focus on professional identity when he entered the organization, affiliation would inevitably become an issue for him. Still, he was interested in becoming involved in the organization, and the staff "club" did encourage closeness among workers. Hence, once he satisfied the developmental requirements, psychological membership, although by no means certain, was likely. Significantly, even after he left community planning, neither he nor his colleagues doubted that he belonged.

CHALLENGES OF PSYCHOANALYTIC RESEARCH AND INTERPRETATION

Psychoanalytic Method and Evidence

This interpretation suggests that overtly contradictory actions may have an underlying consistency in terms of unconsciously guided plans.

How can we be confident of the validity—or completeness—of this interpretation? If there are other plausible interpretations, how can we choose one? What would constitute sufficient evidence to answer these questions? And what would be an appropriate methodology for collecting the evidence?

In writing of psychoanalytic evidence and interpretation, Donald Spence (1982) distinguishes historical truth and narrative truth. The former is what we conventionally mean when we refer to the "truth" of a story: It is a veridical account of past events. The latter is an account that makes sense of remembered events in contemporary terms. It is what we have in mind when we say a story is "good" but not necessarily fully "accurate"; the core of the story conveys an important truth.

Spence draws this distinction because many psychoanalysts, as well as historians, have confused the two truths, inferring the first from the second. But, he argues further, that historical truth is an inaccessible ideal. Many events of infancy occur before consciousness and language and cannot be recalled in later life. At best, observers of infants may draw adult inferences from what they see. Beyond this basic abyss between experience and description, Spence notes that each act a growing person performs to defend him- or herself from thinking of an unpleasant experience becomes a barrier to recalling events. One's account of one's life is a record shaped by self-deceptive distortions, which, if effective, prevent one from even recognizing that certain memories are only caringly constructed fabrications. As a result, those events that have created the most difficulties for contemporary life may be least accessible to investigation.

The structure and length of traditional psychoanalysis are designed to reach some truth under these conditions. In order to facilitate recollection of forgotten and repressed unconscious experiences, the analysand lies on a couch, facing away from the gaze of the analyst, and attempts to observe "the basic rule" of uttering every thought that comes to mind. The analyst speaks mainly on occasions where interpretations may shed light on the analysand's assumptions about the analyst, which, in turn, may be transferred from relations with parents or others earlier in life and, generally, where interpretations may help elucidate the past.

Analysis takes place 4 or 5 hours a week and may last for several years. The frequency is necessary to establish a close and eventually secure relationship in which the analysand may experience and grow to examine an intense relationship with the analyst. The duration is necessary because of all the unconscious obstacles people construct to avoid recalling painful memories. If enough time elapses, an analysand may become comfortable enough to recall, then relate, and then analyze important experiences. But, at least as important, years are necessary because many early recollections may be not simply incomplete, but completely distorted. The passage of time may enable analysand and analyst to discuss the various accounts and come to some shared conclusions about their accuracy.

Freud likened the progress of analysis to an archeological excavation: One digs through traces of the recent past eventually to reach their foundations in the distant past. And yet Spence's point is that, even with such a carefully designed analytic process, historical truth remains elusive. The best that analyst and analysand can expect is to construct a narrative truth that makes sense of troubling present and past experiences. This truth has no necessary historical veracity, but it may be pragmatically tested. If the analysand acts as if it is true and if, in so doing, acts more effectively than before, then it is a reasonable narrative truth.

Spence is correct in positing that the relationship between narrative truth and historical truth is probably unknowable. However, if the analyst or researcher sacrifices the rigor implied by the apparently scientific activity of mental archeology for the license implied by the artistic activity of constructing stories, it is easier to accept accounts that "sound right" despite weak empirical support. An analyst's authority by itself may persuade both analysand and analyst in cases where the evidence is fragmentary or contradictory. A researcher analyzing data in isolation is susceptible to similar self-deception. As a precaution, both psychoanalyst and researcher must be careful to distinguish preconceptions from evidence.

The psychoanalytic method provides checks against fantastic conclusions, but traditional psychoanalysis cannot be transferred intact into social research. Limitations of time, money, trust, and courage prevent that. Research into people's unconscious lives can be only psychoanalytically informed research. Interviews may be designed and conducted with the guidance of specific assumptions and hypotheses about human development and mental life. However, still much more than in the clinical setting, a researcher is unlikely to gain much from asking directly about early childhood experiences, unconscious reactions to other people, or such charged matters as the exercise of power and experience of intimacy. People will answer questions in ways that are comfortable and give the interviewer stories that the psychoanalytic framework may help interpret.

The Study of Organizational Careers

Understanding an organizational career, specifically, depends on knowledge of three things: an individual's overt actions; conscious and unconscious thoughts and intentions associated with these actions; and co-workers' actions, the network of social relations, and the organizational culture that constitute the individual's workplace environment. People talk most easily about what they have done, less so about how they thought and felt about events. They have more difficulty interpreting others' actions, especially their motivations. People give the least explicit information about the unconscious meanings of their own or others' actions.

In exploring these matters, I designed and conducted the 50 interviews whose underlying hypotheses were based on Erikson's framework. I looked for similarities between what people said they wanted from work organizations and what Erikson says people expect of others over their lifetime. In particular, I looked for correspondences between the course of organizational careers and the sequence of development Erikson observed. I asked questions to elicit unconscious issues as well as conscious thoughts or overt events.

I talked with people for 2 or 3 hours, occasionally longer. For most, this was as much time as they would spare for an interview. In response to my questions about the emotional meanings of work, some people did offer little more than the facts of a résumé or carefully circumscribed accounts of their past. A few told obviously one-sided accounts of grudges. But most, including Latham, seemed to talk openly, often enthusiastically, frequently with humor, sometimes with evident hurt. They talked not only of acceptance and triumph, but also of needs for friendship and romance, bouts of alcoholism, family mental illness, and depression about work. Several said the interview helped make sense of their careers. I think my tacit guarantee never to bother these people again encouraged them to trust me with some of the best stories they could tell.

As we talked, I listened for remarks suggesting that childhood events or unconscious aims may have influenced their actions as adult workers. For example, Latham several times characterized his agency as a "family," and I asked questions to explore how earlier family experiences may have influenced his expectations of the organization and his relations with others in it. I tried to test the emerging hypothesis that his apparent ambivalence about joining the agency reflected not simply a developmental plan but also conflicting feelings about authority and affiliation aroused in his family. He was the second child, the second son of nine children in a large extended family. I was curious, for example, whether his family position had led him not only to love, but also to resent, those who were around before he was, those who compete with him for attention, or those who bring others onto the scene.

I considered three contexts in analyzing an interview. The first is the interview as a whole: what the person said about him- or herself and apparent themes running through the comments. For instance, Latham's mixed wishes to join the organization and his disdain for other staff members suggested an ambivalence about belonging to something of which the agency was an example.

I examined such themes in a second context, psychoanalytic theory and case material, to see what general principles of conscious or unconscious thinking they might represent. Latham's ambivalence suggested the broader hypothesis that a conflict about intimacy could interfere with becoming a member of a work organization. Erikson, for example, speaks of organizational membership as one expression of intimacy and describes a developmental conflict between intimacy and isolation. Comfort with intimacy, he and others observe, depends on a lifetime of relatively unconflicted experiences with loved ones such as parents. This psychoanalytic literature, in turn, pointed to more specific questions to ask in analyzing the interview.

Sometimes I had answers for these questions, and often I did not. Still, I examined hypotheses further in a third context—all 50 interviews. For example, I looked for other interviews where someone seemed to have difficulty becoming a psychological member of an organization and where the person made mixed or negative comments about closeness with co-workers, family members, or other associates.

In Latham's case, I considered two tentative narrative truths. Before discussing them, I would just mention a third possibility, suggested by the mainstream organizational literature, that Latham's organizational career might be considered a conscious, deliberate, continuous, even if very slow, effort to learn what the organization expected and to adjust to it. This interpretation is incompatible with the evidence. It implies unconflicted, more or less steady progress toward organizational membership, and Latham's case involves not only considerable hesitation about becoming a member, but also unwillingness to take available opportunities to join.

One plausible narrative truth is the account of Latham's partly conscious, partly unconscious developmental agenda. The story is not complete; it would be helpful to know more about Latham. Nevertheless, the theme of a developmental agenda gives coherence to what he said. At the same time, his comments suggest a second narrative truth, portraying his ambivalence about joining the organization as an expression of lifelong conflicts about authority and belonging to groups. However, he did not say enough to construct a coherent story about this.

These two versions of Latham's career, both consistent with psychoanalytic theory, are compatible. They involve possible truths of different orders. The first concerns a sequence of tests one may pursue in order to grow. The second concerns conflicts about authority and intimacy that may affect the way one encounters such tests.

Even if Latham had said enough to construct both narrative truths, there are still other, compatible accounts of his career—some would emphasize conscious calculations; others, different unconscious aims and conflicts. In research, as in psychoanalysis, any interpretation is inevitably partial. I emphasize these two lines of explanations because, in complementary ways, they shed light on a conflict prominent not only in Latham's account of events but, as it became clear, in others' organizational careers as well.

The Future of Psychoanalytic Research on Organizations

All social research is exploratory in that findings are never certain. Moreover, psychoanalysis charts territory still less understood than the objects of other social investigations. Nevertheless, because it offers explanations where other frameworks do not, we should be willing to take risks, experimenting with imperfect but promising methods and speculating explicitly even where firm conclusions are unwarranted.

Research into unconscious organizational life will never have the length, intensity, or rigor of the traditional psychoanalytic method, even with its imperfections. But we can adapt this method to the constraints of social research. We should look for situations where we can talk at length with people who are willing and able to spend extended time with us. The specific approach depends on what we want to know, as well as the relationship available to us.

Comprehensiveness and systematic sampling are illusory. We should settle for samples of convenience, those who will talk with us. They will be biased in the direction of persons who are willing to speak relatively openly about relatively private matters, but the thoughts and wishes they share are certainly representative of others. In listening, we should be sensitive to both the differences among groups and the similarities among individuals. Over time, we can learn better whom to consider representative of whom else.

When we so briefly examine the manifestations of unconscious thinking in conscious life, we must be still more careful than other researchers to avoid projecting our own wishes and conflicts onto those with whom we talk. We will never conduct psychoanalysis with our research subjects, and we will end up with more questions than firm conclusions. But the virtue of psychoanalysis is that it offers robust hypotheses about the foundations and structure of organizational life. It holds that researchers must understand actions in the same ways the actors themselves do: both in terms of conscious contemporary intentions and in terms of unconscious, often seemingly ancient aims. These interpretations demand testing against alternatives in order to construct the most coherent, comprehensive, truthful accounts of organizational—and other—experience.

NOTES

1. "Charles Latham" is a pseudonym. Some identifying details in his career have been changed here.

2. Most of these are general psychoanalytic assumptions, and Erikson is not the only theorist to hold them. However, he stands out in his emphasis on the elaboration of personal identity as a motivation for development and his formulation of developmental stages in terms of social relationships.

3. Erikson formulates the developmental challenge of each stage in terms of a dilemma. Thus he labels the task of the fourth stage as choosing "industry versus inferiority."

4. To fill in Erikson's developmental framework, three prerequisites for a sense of industry are satisfying the dilemmas of basic trust versus mistrust, which occurs in early infancy (stage 1); autonomy versus shame and doubt, which occurs in later infancy (stage 2); and initiative versus guilt, which occurs in early childhood (stage 3). Two stages follow success at intimacy: generativity versus stagnation, which occurs in adulthood (stage 7); and integrity versus despair, which occurs in old age (stage 8).

REFERENCES

Baum, H. S. (1990). *Organizational membership: Personal development in the workplace*. Albany, NY: SUNY Press.

Buchanan, B., II. (1974). Building organizational commitment: The socialization of managers in work organization. *Administrative Science Quarterly, 19*, 533–546.

Dalton, G. W., Thompson, P. H., & Price, R. L. (1977). The four stages of professional careers—A new look at performance by professionals. *Organizational Dynamics, 6*(1), 19–42.

Erikson, E. H. (1963). *Childhood and society* (2nd ed.). New York: Norton.

Erikson, E. H. (1968). *Identity: Youth and crisis*. New York: Norton.

Feldman, D. C. (1976). A contingency theory of socialization. *Administrative Science Quarterly, 21*, 433–452.

Hage, J. (1980). *Theories of organizations*. New York: Wiley.

Hall, D. T. (1976). *Careers in organizations.* Glenview, IL: Scott, Foresman.

Hall, D. T., & Kram, K. E. (1981). Development in midcareer. In D. H. Montross & C. J. Shinkerman (Eds.), *Career development in the 80's.* Springfield, IL: Thomas.

Herzberg, F., Mausner, B., & Snyderman, B. (1959). *The motivation to work.* New York: Wiley.

Kram, K. E. (1985). *Mentoring at work: Developmental relationships in organizational life.* Glenview, IL: Scott, Foresman.

Porter, L. W., Lawler, E. E., III, & Hackman, J. R. (1975). *Behavior in organizations.* New York: McGraw-Hill.

Schein, E. H. (1978). *Career dynamics: Matching individual and organizational needs.* Reading, MA: Addison-Wesley.

Spence, D. (1982). *Narrative truth and historical truth: Meaning and interpretation in psychoanalysis.* New York: Norton.

U.S. Department of Health, Education and Welfare, Special Task Force. (1973). *Work in America.* Cambridge, MA: MIT Press.

Vroom, V. H. (1964). *Work and motivation.* New York: Wiley.

Wanous, J. P. (1980). *Organizational entry: Recruitment, selection and socialization of newcomers.* Reading, MA: Addison-Wesley.

Wanous, J. P., Reichers, A. E., & Malik, S. D. (1984). Organizational socialization and group development: Toward an integrative perspective. *Academy of Management Review, 9,* 670–683.

Yankelovich, D., & Immerwahr, J. (1983). *Putting the work ethic to work.* New York: Public Agenda Foundation.

Part IV

STUDIES OF PRACTITIONERS' LEARNING

7

Recipes and Reflective Learning: "What Would Prevent You From Saying It That Way?"

ROBERT W. PUTNAM

RECENTLY A COLLEAGUE wrote an article advocating an action research approach to stress in the workplace. He sent it to several practitioners he knew for their comments. One called to suggest revising the article to "instruct the reader how to do this exactly." While he did not say this to his caller, he wondered, "Is she looking for a recipe that people can use flawlessly? Can she be that naive?"

Many of us who seek to engage people in significant learning experiences disparage formulas, rules, or recipes for action as superficial. Practicing a skill requires judgment rooted in intuitive familiarity with the phenomena (Mayo, 1945; Roethlisberger, 1954). Conduct is guided by a system of values and standards; piecemeal changes in discrete techniques have limited impact (Lewin & Grabbe, 1948). Rules do not apply themselves; for every rule there must be additional rules on how to use the rule, and so on ad infinitum (Homans, 1950). For each of these reasons, novices are likely to misuse rules and recipes; they have not developed the know-how to use them correctly.

Yet well-intentioned learners do search for rules and recipes, especially early in a learning process. As one participant said after a workshop on promoting organizational learning, "If you could only give us a list of the eight things to say, that would be really helpful in getting started." This person was not naive; he understood that a handful of recipes was not a substitute for genuine mastery. The difficulty is that a new theory of practice cannot be acquired whole. Yet if it is acquired piecemeal, the pieces are likely to be used in ways that violate the whole.

Hence educators seeking to engage people in reflective learning are understandably ambivalent about teaching recipes. How much more ambivalent, then, might we be toward recipes designed to help bring about reflective learning? On the one hand, such recipes hold forth the promise of helping us with that difficult and uncertain task. On the other hand, they pose the specter of reducing the art of engaging people in reflective learning to technique.

This chapter considers the role of recipes in learning a theory of practice for engaging members of social systems in reflective learning. The new theory of practice is that described by Argyris and Schön (1974, 1978) as Model II. The chapter illustrates how recipes are used differently as a novice develops increasing mastery in using Model II. It also suggests how such shifts may be brought about. By reflecting on the use or misuse of recipes in particular situations, the learner develops understanding and skill in acting more consistently with the theory of practice from which the recipes were drawn.

THE LEARNING TASK: ACQUIRING MODEL II AS THEORY-IN-USE

Argyris and Schön (1974, 1978) propose that human beings hold theories of action that determine all deliberate behavior. These theories are of two kinds: espoused theories that individuals can state explicitly, and theories-in-use that must be inferred from actual behavior. While espoused theories vary widely, research suggests that virtually everyone acts consistently with the theory-in-use that Argyris and Schön call Model I (Argyris, 1982). Model I is a theory of unilateral control over others. Action is designed to maintain four underlying values: achieving purposes as defined by the actor, winning, suppressing negative feelings, and being rational. The primary strategies are those of unilateral advocacy, controlling inquiry, and protection of self and other. Consequences include defensive interpersonal and group relationships, limited learning, and decreased effectiveness.

Argyris and Schön have proposed an alternative theory-in-use, Model II, for creating learning systems. Model II is a theory of joint control and inquiry. Its underlying values are valid information, free and informed choice, and internal commitment. The primary strategies are to combine advocacy and inquiry, to make reasoning explicit and confrontable, and to encourage others to do the same. Consequences include an increasing capacity not only for learning to improve strategies for achieving existing goals (single-loop learning) but also for choosing among competing norms, goals, and values (double-loop learning).

Most people readily espouse Model II yet are unable to act consistently with it (Argyris, 1982). Learning to design Model II action, moreover, is not simply a matter of learning new techniques. It also requires changes in underlying values and assumptions that structure one's theory of practice. Hence there is a paradox in the notion that recipes, seemingly superficial techniques, could play an important role in learning a new theory of practice such as Model II.

RECIPES AND MODEL II

The concept of recipes can be understood in both a broad and a narrow sense. The broad sense includes a cluster of meanings embedded in ordinary language, with the core meaning perhaps that of a list of ingredients and steps for combining them, as in a cookbook. By extension, a recipe is a formula, or set of instructions, for designing action.

In this chapter, *recipe* is used in a narrow sense to refer to a sentence fragment with a characteristic wording that can be used to design interventions for some class of situations. The recipe that will be the focus of attention is "what prevents you from (. . .)?" This is a move for engaging people in reflecting on their reasoning. Other recipes in the Model II repertoire include "what have I said or done that leads you to believe (. . .)," and "what would lead you to (. . .)."

People who are learning Model II frequently use recipes in this narrow sense. They seem to notice phrases used by faculty and to adopt them. The purpose of this chapter is to describe how learners use such recipes as they gain mastery and to suggest how the shifts that occur may be brought about.

Educational practices for helping people learn Model II have not included explicit instruction in recipes (Argyris, 1982; Argyris, Putnam, & Smith, 1985; Schön, 1987). Indeed, learners are cautioned about using "gimmicks," or Model II strategies (such as the above recipes) in ways inconsistent with Model II values of valid information, free choice, and internal commitment. For example, if "what prevents you from (. . .)?" were used with the subtext, "come on, dummy, can't you see that you should (. . .)," it would be a form of covert advocacy designed to get the other to do what the speaker had decided should be done. The impact would more likely be defensiveness and polarization than mutual inquiry and reflective learning. This would be an instance of misusing a recipe, which is to say using it in ways inconsistent with the theory of practice from which the recipe was drawn.

To foreshadow the argument to be presented through the illustrations that follow: Novices use recipes such as "what prevents you from (. . .)" as one-liners. They lack skill for following through when the other responds unexpectedly. With increasing experience, the learner develops a repertoire of moves for using the recipe to implement a broader strategy, such as "help the client explore his reasoning." But this strategy may continue to be used within the system of values, assumptions, and frames characteristic of the learner's old theory of practice. Increasing mastery requires a second shift, as the learner becomes able to use the recipe and broader strategies consistently with the values and assumptions of the new theory of practice.

ILLUSTRATIONS: RECIPES IN ACTION

The data to be presented in this chapter are from my work with an organization development (OD) consultant whom I will call Paul. Paul and several of his colleagues participated in a series of workshops with Chris Argyris and me, seeking to learn Model II. After about a year and a half I arranged to work more intensively with Paul to study how he was using what he had learned and to help him continue learning.

First Episode: "I Think That's What I'm Supposed to Say"

This episode illustrates an early stage of Paul's learning to use the "what prevents you" recipe. It is from the first meeting that he tape-recorded for the intensive phase of our research.

Paul was meeting with a group of supervisors in the first of a series of meetings designed to help them learn leadership skills. One of the supervisors, Linda, said that she hoped to learn skills to help in situations such as a recent incident in which someone had been fired. After Paul asked what aspect of the situation she wanted to focus on, the dialogue continued:

PAUL: Is somebody going to use this as a learning incident?
LINDA: I'm not going to bring it up.
PAUL: What prevents you from using that as an incident?
LINDA: Nothing prevents me. I don't know, what do you want me to say?

PAUL: No, I'm trying to put together two things. I heard you say you want to learn how to deal with those situations. And then you said, right afterwards, you wouldn't bring it up.
LINDA: I don't think I want to talk about it now.

I have suggested that "what prevents you" is a characteristic wording, a verbal formula or recipe. To get some insight into what saying that sentence meant to Paul, let us shift from the action episode between Paul and Linda to the interview I had with Paul 2 days later in which I asked him to reflect on that episode.

We picked up the interview at the point where I was reading the data given above:

BOB: And then you said, "What prevents you from using it as an incident?"
PAUL: I thought that was a pretty good thing (*laughs*).
BOB: Say more about that.
PAUL: I was thinking to myself, "I think that's what I'm supposed to say. If Argyris was here, he'd say the same thing."

Consider what we discover from Paul's reflective talk. First, his "what prevents you" move was highly salient to him. He remarks on it; he evaluates it positively; and he laughs. Second, Paul says the move is "what I'm supposed to say" and that (or because?) Argyris "would say the same thing." It is almost as if it were Argyris talking, not Paul. This could be a cue to a particular kind of learning, or a particular stage of learning, that of identifying with a model. It is also possible that this aspect of "doing as Argyris would" was especially salient on this day, the first time Paul had taperecorded his work for the research.

Paul also felt some discomfort with imitating Argyris, as indicated by a comment he made later in our interview: "I said [to myself], I don't want to start sounding like a parrot or anything; I want to be able to know what I'm doing. It just sounded like, here I am using a new tool." The metaphor of a parrot suggests one who squawks verbal formulas without understanding their meaning. This lack of deeper understanding is the reason that recipes are so often misused.

Paul continued by describing his purposes in using the recipe:

It's a way to get Linda to look at what to me was an apparent contradiction. And it was a way for me to get real information that I didn't have. I didn't understand why Linda would not use that,

when she says she wants to learn how to deal with it. It still per-
plexes me.

This begins to identify the class of situations for which Paul sees
"what prevents you" as appropriate. In particular, he understands himself to be getting Linda to see a contradiction and to be gathering information.

Although Paul felt a sense of success when he used the "what prevents you" move, he did not see the episode as a success story. In fact,
when he first mentioned it as one we might discuss, he said, "I seemed
to get myself into trouble that I couldn't get myself out of." As he per-
severed in probing "what prevented" Linda from using the incident,
she became increasingly upset. Commenting in our interview on what
he was thinking during this part of the episode, Paul said:

> "I'm feeling stuck," is what I'm saying [to myself]. "I don't know
> how to get myself out of this one à la Argyris," I say to myself.
> "I'm not handling it right. Am I too concerned about what I'm
> doing? Am I getting stuck in the technique of what am I going to
> do about helping her learn? And that may be dysfunctional, so let
> me shelve it for a while."

Paul's reflections suggest just the difficulties we would expect in the
early stages of using a new technique. It feels unnatural to him; when
he gets into difficulty, he doubts his ability to follow through consistently with the new approach; and his self-consciousness makes it even
less likely he will be able to follow through competently.

I suggested in the introduction that if "what prevents you" were
used as a kind of covert advocacy, in this case as a way of getting Linda
to talk about the incident, then it would be inconsistent with the values
guiding Model II. Other data from our interview suggest that this was
what Paul was doing. What is interesting in the present context is that
Paul became aware of this while reflecting in our interview. The data
thus illustrate how reflecting on the use of recipes may contribute to
learning to use them more consistently with the practice from which
they are drawn. Consider the following two excerpts from the interview:

> I see now, if that's the way it went, maybe it wasn't inconsistent for
> her to say, "I want to learn from it, but I don't want to talk about it
> now." It [may have been] just a timing kind of thing. But I wasn't

hearing that. I was sort of forcing it into an inconsistency kind of thing.

I had already prejudged, "I'm sure she could have done something earlier to prevent the firing." That was my bias, okay?

Paul's retrospective critique of his action, I suggest, is important to his learning how to use the "what prevents you" move in the future in ways more consistent with Model II values. In the interview he described himself as prejudging the issue, forcing his interpretation, and missing relevant meanings. These errors can be understood as created by the frame within which he used the new technique. It would seem that his reflections should increase his ability to recognize such errors as they occur in the future and, therefore, to correct himself during an encounter.

Indeed, Paul was partially able to correct himself during this encounter by using another recipe, one he had developed more skill in using. As Linda became more upset at being asked what prevented her from using the firing incident for her learning, finally she said:

LINDA: It could have probably come up if you didn't mention it.
PAUL: I don't understand. Why—what is it in what I say or do that makes you say, "I don't want to talk about it"?

"What is it in what I say or do" is another recipe from the Model II repertoire. Unlike "what prevents you," which Paul was just beginning to use, this recipe was more integrated into Paul's practice. As he said in the interview:

There's another one of the [recipes]. That's okay, I felt comfortable with that one. I use that one a lot, now. It was more a part of me.

Paul's move seemed to help him and Linda recover from their growing impasse. Later in the meeting Linda volunteered to talk about the firing incident.

This episode has illustrated two features of how a novice uses recipes. First, attention focuses on the recipe itself, and there is little understanding of how it fits into a larger sequence. Thus the novice quickly gets stuck and, quite appropriately, lacks confidence in his or her ability to follow through. Second, the recipe is used within the context of existing skill, even when the larger practice from which the recipe is drawn is inconsistent with that skill. In this case, the existing skill is

Paul's ability to frame the situation as one in which Linda should talk about the firing incident, and his role is to get her to do so. Data from the interview show that Paul was able, on reflection, to become aware of this framing and to call it into question.

Second Episode: "I Was Really into the Meat of His Unawareness"

Eight weeks after the episode with Linda, Paul was using some Model II recipes in ways that showed both more flexibility and a deeper level of understanding. At the same time, he continued to be limited in his ability to build on the information he generated with his recipes.

Paul was talking with Mike, the operations manager at a manufacturing plant, about a problem with a subordinate. Stan had taken vacation days at a time that Mike had thought it crucial he be at work. Paul engaged Mike to role-play how he planned to talk to Stan. He learned that Mike had "strongly advised" Stan not to take vacation days but had "left it open" for Stan to evaluate the advice. When Stan chose to take his vacation, Mike felt he had "done me an injustice by not respecting my wishes."

In helping Mike reflect on how he planned to talk with Stan, Paul focused on what he believed was a mixed message: While nominally leaving it open for Stan to use his judgment, Mike then criticized Stan for not respecting his wishes. Hence Mike must have expected Stan to realize that it was not really an open question.

Over the next 20 minutes, Paul used recipes for inquiring into Mike's reasoning on at least five occasions. Here is the first:

> What would lead you to have every intention of having him here, and letting him know he had any leeway at all not to be here? What would lead you to do that?

"What would lead you" is a Model II recipe that can be reciprocal to "what prevents you." Thus, when Mike said "I couldn't have been any more direct unless I just said, 'Stan, you are not to take those two days off,'" Paul asked, "Why didn't you say that?" And when Mike later volunteered, "I guess I prevented myself from saying, 'Be here,'" Paul probed further: "And why is that? What is it that prevented you from doing that?"

Let us consider Paul's reflections in our interview on his "what would lead you" intervention:

> That's pretty good, I think. At the time, I know I was really into the meat of his unawareness. And I knew we were at the nub of something useful.

If we compare Paul's work with Mike to his work with Linda, we see both similarities and differences. In each case Paul identified an inconsistency and used "what prevents" or its reciprocal, "what leads you," to address it. In each case he spontaneously mentioned his sense of success at using a Model II recipe.

The two cases differ in what Paul understood himself to be doing by using the recipe. With Linda he was "getting her to look at an inconsistency" and gathering information. With Mike he was "getting into the meat of his unawareness." Paul was not only helping Mike to see an inconsistency, but also helping him to reflect on the reasoning that led him to create the inconsistency. Paul's work with Mike exemplified a major theme in Paul's learning at the time, that of "exploring the reasoning."

A second difference is what seems to be a lower degree of self-consciousness about "using a new tool" or "being a parrot." Data not included here show that Paul still had difficulty with getting himself stuck; but with Mike he found himself able to say that he was stuck and to find ways to resume the inquiry. These differences suggest that Paul felt more confidence in his ability to follow through after using a recipe.

A deeper parallel between Paul's work with Mike and his work with Linda has to do with his framing of the situation and his consequent inability to take advantage of meanings that would have enabled him to move on. Four of the five times that Paul probed Mike's reasoning for giving Stan leeway, Mike gave a version of the following reply: A manager in Stan's position should not have to be told such things; he should evaluate and decide himself. Each time Paul said, in effect, "But Mike, you weren't direct." Mike would then repeat that he was direct enough and that Stan should have understood. Hence the repetitive pattern emerged that gave Paul the opportunity to make the same intervention five times.

It is as if Paul framed the situation as one in which he had to get Mike to acknowledge that he had not been direct with Stan. Hence Paul understood Mike's reply that Stan should not have to be told as a defense against acknowledging his own indirection. In our interview I proposed another way that Paul might have understood and built on Mike's response:

BOB: My reaction is, Mike is articulating an important managerial dilemma. Which is, he's right. Managers at some level of authority ought to have space of free movement and should not be ordered what to do. So that's one thing I'd want to say to Mike: "I agree."

PAUL: And I do agree with that.

BOB: Okay. He's in a dilemma, because he believes he knows better than Stan what Stan should do. And yet he believes he cannot tell him, because then he will be undercutting the responsibility he believes Stan should have. That's a dilemma I'd like
to help Mike manage more effectively.

PAUL: So the strategy is to lift out the dilemma in Mike's situation.
And maybe the way to change his strategy would be, first, to
state his dilemma to Stan. That he does value allowing Stan
freedom. But that he's conflicted when Stan acts in a way that
he thinks is abusing his freedom. And to illustrate that.

Paul actively assimilated my coaching by inferring a maxim: "The
strategy is to lift out the dilemma in Mike's situation." Such maxims
might well help Paul transfer his learning to new situations. Indeed we
will see in the next episode that Paul was able to "lift out the dilemma
in the client's situation" on his own.

But "lifting out the dilemma" is more than a strategy. It requires
stepping out of the framing that led Paul to see Mike only as defensively
denying his own responsibility. In order to see Mike as caught in a dilemma, Paul would have to take the stance that Schön has described as
"giving him reason" (1983, p. 68). That is, he would have to appreciate
what is valid in Mike's reasoning, while not losing sight of its limits.
This is a sophisticated form of perspective-taking that is both difficult to
achieve in the rush of immediate experience and of great importance in
engaging people in reflective learning. Using Model II recipes appropriately requires developing the ability to take such a stance.

Paul offered an additional explanation for his not having been able
to lift out Mike's dilemma:

I was so caught up in the technique, and only looking at one thing
at a time here, that I didn't see the bigger picture of the notion of a
dilemma, which I am aware of and know about, theoretically. But
I'm caught up in the mechanics with Mike of looking at his reasoning and the hole in his thinking. In a very narrow way.

Paul's difficulty would seem to be characteristic of all forms of skill
learning. Competent performance requires following up any particular
move by noticing its impact, what Schön (1983) would call the "backtalk" of the situation, and shifting to any of several possible further
moves. Someone who is learning will tend to "fixate" on the move that
is at his or her learning edge. One way of understanding this tendency
is to realize that the move at the learning edge requires so much con-

scious attention, so much of the limited available cognitive capacity, that even well-learned moves may not be accessible. With further practice, a move that was once at the learning edge becomes more skillful, freeing up attention for noticing other aspects of the situation.

After our interview, Paul met again with Mike. Mike decided to talk with Stan about the dilemma he experienced. Mike later reported that the conversation had gone well and thanked Paul for his help.

This episode has illustrated a higher level of skill in using recipes as part of a broader strategy. Attention focuses less on the recipe itself and more on the strategy of inquiring into reasoning. While the ability to follow up the initial recipe and keep inquiry moving has increased, considerable attention must be devoted to the mechanics of implementing the strategy. Hence it is difficult to respond flexibly to the backtalk of the situation. The difficulty becomes acute when flexible response would require shifting from the familiar Model I stance of "getting him to see what I know he should see" to appreciating the possible validity of his perspective. At this stage of learning, while action has become more skillful, it remains consistent with the values and assumptions of the old theory of practice.

Third Episode: "Here's Where I Change"

Five weeks after the episode described above, Paul met with a plant manager, Greg, and his staff as they worked to downsize the organization. Greg's boss, acting on a financial model created by upper management, had told Greg that he had to reduce the size of his organization from 200 people to 150. Greg had told his staff to figure out how many people each could give up and still be able to do all the work the plant had committed to. The episode described here is from the meeting at which Greg and his staff were adding up the numbers.

Paul believed that this process for reducing the number of employees was a massive error, and one that had been made repeatedly by the organization. In Paul's view, the real problem was redundancies among the several plants in the division. Meeting the target, Paul believed, would require working across the division, instead of within each plant, and certainly not within each functional unit of a plant.

The plant staff spent the first 2 hours of their meeting going through each person's numbers. When they added them up, the total was 190, down a bit from the present 200 but well short of the target 150. Greg declared that this number was unacceptable.

Over the next 45 minutes, Paul made four attempts to advocate his view that the target could only be met by redesigning work across the organization. His hope, he told me in our interview, was to persuade Greg "to stand up in the division meeting" and advocate the need to work across the organization. Each time, Greg objected that redesigning work was not feasible. Three times the group then resumed arguing about the numbers, making little progress. Greg did allow that he would defend an argument for as many as 165 people, but others on the staff did not believe they could do the work with so few.

Paul felt increasingly frustrated as he looked for new ways to convince people of what he believed had to be done. As he made his argument for the fourth time, Paul was able to shift the discussion by using two moves from the Model II repertoire, including "what prevents you." What was especially significant in Paul's action was that he was able to follow up his use of the recipe by stepping out of his original frame and empathizing with Greg's dilemma. This led Paul to let go of his "convince them" strategy and instead to focus on helping Greg manage his dilemma.

The pivotal episode began when Carol, the finance manager, argued that it was impossible to meet Greg's target:

CAROL: (*Makes calculations.*) It is just not realistic to think we can do all we have to do with 165 people.

PAUL: An alternative is, yes we may be able to do it with those numbers. But, what it will take is going back and looking at how to reshape all of this work. And that's the kind of operation that I'm saying can't be done without a lot of hard work.

GREG: But I'm not disagreeing. I'm just trying to get you guys to realize the position that I'm in, while I agree with you, that's going to take convincing of others. Because I can't be the only one to do that. [Other plants] need to do that, too.

PAUL: Sure. What would prevent you from going into the division meeting and just saying it that way?

Let us turn to Paul's comments in our interview. As we reviewed the beginning of this episode, he said, "Here I go again, getting my advocacy in there." When we came to his "what prevents you" intervention, here is what Paul said:

Here's where I change. "Good intervention," I say to myself. I heard Greg saying something that he hasn't been saying so far. Now he's at least acknowledging that there are other parts of the system that are part of the problem. So maybe that's the timing of the intervention: [I see] some receptivity for this kind of [move].

As in previous weeks, Paul congratulated himself on his "what prevents you" move. His focus, however, was less on the wording than on making an intervention that changed his approach with Greg.

Let us dig further into how Paul saw the relevance of "what prevents you" in this situation. He suggested that the timing of the move was related to his perception that Greg was saying something that was new and that indicated receptivity. What was it that Greg now seemed more receptive to? The new meaning that Greg communicated was, in Paul's words, "other parts of the system are part of the problem." Recall that Paul's hope had been to get Greg to stand up in the division meeting and advocate that downsizing required redesigning work across the organization. It seems likely, therefore, that what Paul saw Greg as now more receptive to was the idea of his making this argument in the division meeting.

This interpretation suggests that "what prevents you" was used here in the service of Paul's original goal. It was, in other words, another way of convincing Greg to do what Paul believed he should do. Paul's initial follow-up supports this interpretation:

PAUL: What would prevent you from going into the division meeting and just saying it that way?
GREG: What [my boss] is going to do is bang the table, yell, and say, "Guys, you were told to get to a number. We've got to get to that number. I don't care whether we reshape work or not. That's a corporate number."
PAUL: And do you believe that [your boss's] reaction to you is a reasonable reaction?
GREG: It doesn't matter, at that point. See, the pressure of managing the numbers is being driven down by [high-level executives].

Paul explained in our interview that his strategy in asking "is it reasonable" was, "If Greg understands that what his boss is demanding of him is unreasonable, then he could more easily hold a position there." Thus, the question was designed to get Greg to see that his boss's reaction was unreasonable, thereby furthering Paul's objective of getting Greg to "stand up."

What occurred next, however, was something new. Paul was struck by Greg's reply, "It doesn't matter." Paul was receptive enough to this window into Greg's perspective that he allowed himself to be surprised and to shift out of his effort to convince. Paul's shift became evident as the conversation continued:

CAROL: The numbers coming down from corporate are not realistic. [Your boss] must be made to understand that he must make that argument at the corporate level.

PAUL: I just want to confirm Greg's position. If I put myself in his shoes, I'm going to go into the division meeting and from past experience I'm going to know I can't push forward a reasonable argument, because my boss will act unreasonably. And Greg's likely to lose his head. So, understanding that position, I will still say, somebody has to push these reasonable arguments forward. Or this nonsense, which happens at this level and the level above it, will keep happening.

GREG: The breakthrough in the division meeting will be if everybody comes in with the same kind of scenario, saying "we cannot do it."

Rather than join with Carol, Paul shifts to confirm the validity of Greg's dilemma. At the same time, he does not back off from his view of what would be best for the organization. This move is similar to that which he was unable to make with Mike. Recall that it was during our interview that I helped him see the possibility of building on Mike's reply to "what prevents you" (or "what would lead you") by identifying Mike's dilemma while also working on the limits within which Mike was dealing with the dilemma. Here Paul is able to do it during the meeting. How did this occur?

In our interview Paul suggested that the critical shift had occurred when he heard Greg say "it doesn't matter" if his boss's reaction is unreasonable: "I think this is where I began changing, and I eventually get to empathize with him."

Paul's comment is curious in that minutes before, commenting on his "what would prevent you" intervention, he had also said "here's where I change." It may be that both reflections are accurate, in the sense that Paul changed twice, in different ways. The first change, with "what prevents you," was one of strategy: Instead of advocating, Paul inquired into Greg's reasoning. The second change was deeper, as Paul began to empathize with Greg's position and therefore to question the strategy of "convince him." Paul continued:

As soon as Greg says, "Well, it doesn't matter," I begin to realize, "He's right. He's going to get his head squashed in anyway." So that's where I become much more sensitive to his position. This is why I don't pursue [my original strategy].

Paul could have dismissed Greg's answer as resistance. Instead he recognized what was valid and built on it. What seems to have happened is that Paul's Model II recipe, "what prevents you," even if originally used within his frame of "getting Greg to stand up," generated data and evoked a set of understandings that together catapulted Paul into another frame. From this alternative frame, Paul said, "I began to realize that I can't really convince people to do [what I thought best]. I mean, there is a real dilemma here. I'm caught in a system, Greg is caught in a system, where his head can roll."

Paul acted on his newfound empathy by confirming Greg's dilemma. This move appears to have been helpful in maintaining a learning relationship with Greg and in generating more productive dialogue in the meeting. Greg suggested a "breakthrough" scenario, and the group discussed how likely it was. Over the next several weeks, Paul helped Greg and others develop a plan for restructuring the organization that was accepted by the division.

This episode has illustrated how a learner may become able to do on his own what he earlier had seen only on reflection or with the help of a coach. The process is neither easy nor certain; in this case Paul pushed his point of view four times before he thought to use the "what prevents you" recipe to inquire into Greg's reasoning; and even then he was not immediately able to take a stance of "giving Greg reason." But this time, he was able to interrupt his perseverance and reframe the situation.

Generalizing from what happened in this episode, it may be that misusing recipes is a necessary part of the learning process. Recall that in this instance what helped Paul see the relevance of "what prevents you" was that it offered a way to achieve his original goal of "getting Greg to stand up." That is, from the frame he was embedded in, it seemed like it might work. What then happened was that the recipe generated surprising data that led Paul to reframe the situation. It may also be that the recipe served as a mnemonic, reminding Paul of the Model II stance of "giving reason," or perhaps reminding him of our earlier discussion about "lifting out the dilemma in Mike's situation."

Calling Recipes into Question

At this point in Paul's learning, he was beginning to question how he was using some of the Model II recipes. During our discussion of his work with Greg he asked, "Am I inviting enough inquiry in my own advocacy? I tried to, but I don't know whether it was just pro forma." Paul was referring to the way he had advocated his view that work had to be redesigned across the organization. He had prefaced his argument by saying, "Knock me down if I'm wrong"; and after explaining his view he said, "I don't know if that makes sense to you, or whether I'm fouling it up." He had not paused for reactions, however, but continued to explain his argument.

While the wording of these phrases is not standardized in the same way as "what prevents you," the phrases are recipe-like. They are intended to encourage others to confront or inquire into Paul's reasoning. But Paul wondered, "Maybe I'm using something, and not really allowing, not stating it in such a way that I'm inviting inquiry. Does that become one of the mechanisms that's not true, that might be a disguised way of not allowing inquiry? I'm not sure."

We see here that Paul was no longer feeling a sense of success simply because he had used a Model II recipe. He was aware of the possibility that he might misuse recipes by using them inconsistently with the values and purposes characteristic of Model II. He raised these concerns spontaneously in our interview, and we worked to design ways for him to create genuine opportunities for inquiry.

SUMMARY

This chapter has described three episodes from the work of a single practitioner to identify qualitative differences in how a novice uses recipes while developing increasing mastery. For convenience, let us refer to phases of learning corresponding to the three episodes.

In the first phase, novices use recipes as one-liners. Lacking expertise in the theory of practice from which the recipe was drawn, novices may get themselves in trouble they cannot get themselves out of. Nevertheless, they may feel a sense of success at having done what they are "supposed to do," what they believe an expert might have done. At the same time they may feel some discomfort or chagrin at imitating or "being a parrot."

The second phase is marked by a shift of attention to using the recipe to implement broader strategies from the new theory of practice. In this case, the new strategy was "exploring the reasoning": Paul used the "what would lead you" recipe to "get at the meat of Mike's unawareness." While the focus thus shifts to more general concepts and sequences of moves, learners may remain caught in a kind of tunnel vision, concentrating intently on the mechanics of implementing the new strategy. It is therefore difficult to respond flexibly to the backtalk of the situation. In particular, the data here show an inability to reframe the situation to "give reason" or empathize with the dilemmas of the other person.

In the third phase, learners become able, at least at times, to respond to surprising data by reframing the situation, stepping out of their original perspective to take account of another. Also in the third phase, learners may call into question their own use of recipes. Rather than feeling successful simply by using a recipe, they may consider whether that usage was pro forma or genuine.

The three phases thus show a progression from using recipes as one-liners, to using them as part of a new strategy but still within old frames, to using them more consistently with the new theory of practice.

How do such changes come about? The emphasis here has been on learning through reflecting on instances of using or misusing recipes. For example, while reflecting on his work with Linda, Paul described himself as having prejudged the issue, forced his interpretation, and missed relevant meanings. In other words, he became aware that the sequence of moves he organized around the "what prevents you" recipe was inconsistent with Model II values and purposes. A later echo of this kind of critique occurred in phase three, when Paul questioned whether his use of inquiry phrases was pro forma rather than genuine. Such reflections should increase learners' ability to recognize such errors as they occur and therefore to correct them on-line, as Paul seems to have done in his work with Greg.

Reflective learning can be promoted by the kind of coaching dialogue illustrated in the second episode. In that instance the researcher/educator recognized a point at which Paul was stuck. His learning edge seemed to be designing inquiry into Mike's reasoning, and he was unable to take advantage of meanings in Mike's responses. Moving further required reframing the situation to "give Mike reason." The coach modeled such an approach, and Paul actively assimilated the coaching by formulating a maxim: "The strategy is to lift out the dilemma in Mike's situation." Five weeks later Paul was able to implement such a move with Greg.

Using recipes would seem to be a form of imitation or mimicry. As Schön (1987) argues, imitation is not passive; rather it requires "selective construction" of what is essential in the performance to be imitated (p. 108). The phases of learning described here suggest a progression in what is taken to be essential. The novice takes the recipes themselves as essential and looks for opportunities to use them. Good results, however, often are not forthcoming. If the learner reflects on what is going wrong, another aspect of masterful performance may be taken as essential: the repertoire of moves for using the recipe as part of a broader strategy. And when results still leave something to be desired, further reflection may lead to focusing on the frame within which the recipe and strategy are used. Developing the ability to frame situations differently is closely related to shifting toward the values and assumptions of the new theory of practice.

What is it about recipes that makes them useful? First, even as a one-line intervention, a good recipe may elicit useful data. When Paul said "what prevents you" to Greg, he was told how Greg thought his boss would act. Paul was able to confirm for himself that Greg's concerns had validity. So the one-liner elicited data that triggered Paul's reframing of his work with Greg.

Second, recipes are memorable phrases. In moments of stress it may help to have recipes that come quickly to the tongue. Moreover, they may serve as mnemonics in the sense of cuing a set of understandings that help the learner remember what he or she is supposed to be doing. A one-liner may be more than a one-liner; it may be a retrieval cue for a set of concepts, models, and ways of acting.

The vividness of recipes may also aid in focusing reflection. Paul seemed to remember episodes in which he had used a new recipe and to propose that we discuss them in our interviews.

These considerations give a different perspective on the use or misuse of recipes as gimmicks. It is true that learners often use recipes within the context of their taken-for-granted framing of the situation. I have suggested that this is necessary, as the learner must see the relevance of the recipe from a perspective within the current frame. Seeing opportunities to use the recipe enables the learner to gain experience, thereby becoming more skillful. It also provides occasions for reflecting on how the recipe was used. With increasing skill, helped along by episodes of reflecting and by appropriate coaching, the learner may become able to jump from gimmick to genuine reframing, from superficial technique to action consistent with the deeper meaning of a practice.

REFERENCES

Argyris, C. (1982). *Reasoning, learning, and action.* San Francisco: Jossey-Bass.
Argyris, C., Putnam, R., & Smith, D. M. (1985). *Action science.* San Francisco: Jossey-Bass.
Argyris, C., & Schön, D. A. (1974). *Theory in practice.* San Francisco: Jossey-Bass.
Argyris, C., & Schön, D. A. (1978). *Organizational learning.* Reading, MA: Addison-Wesley.

Homans, G. (1950). *The human group.* New York: Harcourt, Brace & Co.

Lewin, K., & Grabbe, P. (1948). Conduct, knowledge, and the acceptance of new values. In K. Lewin (Ed.), *Resolving social conflicts.* New York: Harper & Row.

Mayo, E. (1945). *The social problems of an industrial civilization.* Boston: Division of Research, Harvard Business School.

Roethlisberger, F. J. (1954). *Training for human relations: An interim report.* Boston: Division of Research, Harvard Business School.

Schön, Donald A. (1983). *The reflective practitioner.* New York: Basic Books.

Schön, Donald A. (1987). *Educating the reflective practitioner.* San Francisco, CA: Jossey-Bass.

8

Reframing: The Role of Experience in Developing Teachers' Professional Knowledge

TOM RUSSELL and HUGH MUNBY

ASK ANY TEACHER or professor, "How did you learn to teach?" As likely as not, the response will be "by teaching" or "by experience," and little more will follow, as though the answer were obvious and unproblematic. While there is an implicit acknowledgment that actions and performances can be learned through or by experience, there is little understanding of how this comes about. Since 1981, our research has been directed at understanding how the interaction between a teacher and his or her experience gives rise to knowing how to teach. The studies we began in 1984 were based on the work of Schön (1983) because the epistemology of practice that he explicated offers a fresh level of discourse for understanding the place, rigor, and significance of knowing-in-action and reflection-in-action (Russell, Munby, Spafford, & Johnston, 1988). In this chapter, we focus on a pivotal part of Schön's theory: reframing.

Reflection-in-action is a process with nonlogical features, a process that is prompted by experience and over which we have limited control. Teachers at every level of education are familiar with the circumstance of being unable to get a point across to a whole class. Success may come suddenly and unexpectedly, through the teacher's somehow hearing what the students say in a quite different way. For us, the essence of reflection-in-action is this "hearing" differently or "seeing" differently, a process that Schön calls "reframing." Importantly, the form of reflection that involves reframing is very different from the more familiar form, which Schön terms "reflection-on-action" (Munby & Russell, 1989). This refers to the ordered, deliberate, and systematic application of logic to a problem in order to resolve it; the process is very much within our control. The sort of thinking characterized by reflection-on-action involves careful consideration of familiar data. In contrast, reflection-*in*-action presents the data quite differently, so that they appear in a novel frame. What control we can exercise comes through reflection *on* reflection-in-action, when we think systematically about the freshly framed data.

Reframing becomes less mysterious in the light of the writings of Toulmin and Hanson in the 1950s. Toulmin (1953) argues that science is a way of seeing, so learning science is not a matter of using old inferences to examine new data, but of learning to see data in new ways. The special nature of this form of "seeing differently" is the focus of Hanson's (1958) first chapter, "Observation." Readers will no doubt recall the intriguing puzzles presented in the reversible pictures (often found in psychology textbooks) that Hanson presents: the old woman and the young lady (p. 11), or the antelope and the bird (p. 13). Especially intriguing to us is the power of the processes that enable us to suddenly see data differently. For Gestalt psychologists, the processes are known as gestalt shifts; for Kuhn (1962), they represent paradigm shifts, in a much larger sense. For Schön, in the context of learning what is taught by experience, the process is reframing.

Data collection in our most recent study (1986–1988) involved interviewing each participating teacher immediately following a period of classroom observation; interviews were spaced at monthly intervals whenever possible. The 15 participants include teachers in a preservice teacher education program, teachers in their first and second years of teaching, and several teachers with a number of years of experience. In analyzing our data for evidence of reframing, we have been particularly attentive to the language teachers have used when talking about their work. Reframing involves "seeing" or "hearing" differently, so the process of perception is a unified process in which observation *is* interpretative, and this is reflected in language, in particular in changes in metaphors (Munby, 1986).

The two cases that follow focus on the puzzles of practice that confront two experienced teachers and give rise to reframing. Our goal is to open up the process of learning by and from experience, as well as to show the force of the construct of reframing in that process. The cases of Diane and Roger have been selected because they so richly illustrate the role of reframing in the development of professional knowledge, and two features are particularly important. Reframing of experience facilitates the use of pedagogical knowledge acquired in courses, work-shops, and conferences. Reframing also mediates between theory and practice, revealing new meanings in theory and new strategies for prac-tice.

DIANE

Diane is an elementary school teacher with 12 years of experience at various grade levels. She has enrolled in professional courses during most summers since beginning to teach. These first helped her to de-velop the technical skills of teaching; then, in a master of education program, she explored research and rationales for various teaching practices. The project's interviews with Diane began in her twelfth year of teaching, her second year at the Grade 1 level; she had taught kin-dergarten for the 2 years before moving to Grade 1.

Diane has a large class of 28 students, and it is obvious that she and her students have worked out the necessary classroom routines to ac-commodate everyone in an activity-centered program. There are many interest centers set up around the room, and the students move inde-pendently from one activity to the next with minimal direction from Diane. They have also established routines for group activities, for quiet reading time, and for entering and leaving the classroom. While the routines appear to function smoothly, the atmosphere is not rigid; the students are free to choose their activities, move about the room, and chatter if they are not disturbing the work of others. Diane respects the students and strives to allow them as much independence as possible. She gives them the feeling that while learning is pleasant, and even fun, they have a job to do and she is there to help them do it. "Calm, gentle, and caring" would describe Diane's interactions with students. She seems to be able to monitor all of them at their various activities while she focuses her attention on one individual.

Diane's puzzles about her practice focus on the students and on her role in finding what she calls their "learning paths," a phrase that re-flects her attention to individual development and styles of learning. These puzzles arise out of close attention to her students and her as-sessment of how her teaching methods are functioning to help the chil-dren learn. Diane's reframing of puzzles of practice adds to her knowl-edge about her teaching patterns, reshapes her beliefs about children's learning, and ultimately extends her repertoire of teaching methods. In the following sections, we examine three puzzles that are of particular interest to Diane.

The Puzzle of Finding a Suitable Balance of Activity

Diane's practice presents her with a persistent puzzle: What *balance of activity* are students most comfortable with? Her thinking about this puzzle appears in the following comments:

> That's what I find the hardest thing, is to get the balance of activity that they're comfortable with. They need their own free choice time. It gets to a point where you can't tell them to do something any more. The fourth time you say, "This is what you're doing now," they just can hardly sit.

> I think an interesting area of research at this level would be what kind of ebb and flow or what pacing do they need in a day. Because it would be different at different levels, ages. And that's really, I think, what I've been floundering around to find. Do they need quiet in the morning? Everybody knows they need quiet when they come in after the long recess at lunch. But should it be directed quiet where I'm telling them what to do, or should it be self-directed quiet like quiet reading where they have the choice? And if you can just find what suits the kids best, at what point in the day, boy, you've found out something that's really important.

Diane asks questions that are familiar to most teachers. At this stage in her professional development, the questions that dominate her thinking about her teaching show how she challenges herself to satisfy each individual as well as the entire group: "How do you accommodate everybody?" "How does one type of instruction not suit certain types of students?" "Why do I feel uncomfortable teaching kids this way?" "How do they think about science?" "I don't know if that was the best selection of words to get them talking." Diane believes she can help students by discovering their learning paths and making provision for their individual needs. She struggles to balance teacher-directed and student-directed activities, and the following examples of this puzzle illustrate how reframing contributes to a broader understanding of the "ebb and flow" that students require.

Managing independent reading. The first example concerns Diane's efforts to create a time and environment for independent reading. During one interview, she tells how she came to alter her strategy for building up 20 minutes of quiet reading time. During the previous year, Diane followed guidelines suggested by the reading consultant to establish the patterns for quiet reading time. The consultant prescribed a method whereby all students were punished for one child's inability to remain quietly reading. Here, then, the problem is framed as one of *class* management. Diane's dissatisfaction with this initial framing of the problem arose because she found that she was not comfortable with imposing arbitrary standards. She found that her students were unhappy with losing their reading time, and that the routines were not achieving their goal. As Diane reflects on her discomfort and the evidence from her classroom, the problem is reframed as one of *individual* management. Diane's solution is to quietly ask the offending individuals to give up their privileges of a personal space and return to their desks. This strategy is consistent with her beliefs in maintaining the dignity of each child and in providing an environment for students to accept responsibility for their own learning. Importantly, the solution emerges from Diane's "seeing" the problem differently. As the following shows, she is clearly satisfied with the new frame:

> In the afternoon we have "quiet book time," and they have to look at books all by themselves, no talking. They don't read, but they look at the books and I've read half a novel. I really like it. I think it's important to model. A lot of them at the beginning, they would look at the book, leaf through the pages, and throw it back in the library. And now they're sustaining; they're learning what to do with books. And even Michael, who is very active, he'll find a spot and he doesn't want anyone around him. They get behind the door or under a table. They can't even whisper. If they whisper or talk, I just go and put my hand on their shoulder and ask them to go to their desk. They take their books, but they've lost their personal space. Last year I did it differently. They sat in their seats. They had to have four books. I rang a bell, "Quiet." And if anybody talked—this is the way it was prescribed to us—if anyone talks, we then have to put our books away. The kids were so mad most of the time, and they weren't up to 20 minutes quiet time until Christmas. I think this is a more humane way of building up the time, and they're almost at 20 minutes now [beginning of October].

Establishing classroom routines. Diane's efforts to establish classroom routines provide our second example of her general puzzle of achieving a suitable "balance of activity." Part of Diane's problem seems to be the familiar conflict between respecting students' freedom to select their own learning activities and the importance of routines for classroom management and personal interaction. When Diane joined our study, her routines were observed to be effective, allowing her 28 students to move from activity to activity during the day with minimal disruptions to personal freedom. Diane talked about how her dissatisfaction with trying to set up routines the previous year had made her realize that she needed to change her strategy. Initially, she reported, she would introduce a routine; then she would observe that the students were not using it effectively; and she would abandon it and would try another routine. The cycle repeated, and she quickly became frustrated with her efforts:

> Last year I would get frustrated because the routines wouldn't work. And I'd have kids with their heads down on their desks. I'd say, "Put your heads down, I can't stand the noise." And I'd even put my head down too. . . . At the beginning of this year, I realized that I wasn't trying—if I had a new routine, I would start it and then say, "Oh, it's not working too well, I won't do it." I wasn't giving them long enough to learn it and to be consistent. Now I've learned to pick one, and stick with it, and insist. If I say, "Listen, please!" then we wait until everybody listens. And being willing to wait and having the patience—and, with Alex in there, you might have to wait 10 minutes.

Diane's resolution of the problem is described above in terms of learning. In the previous year, the problem seems to have been framed as a *management* problem, almost as if telling the students what to do is enough. This year, establishing routines is "seen" as a *learning* problem. Once in place, the new frame virtually solves the problem, because Diane can invoke what she knows about learning at this age: Practice, time, and patience are required. Importantly, this reframing appears to reinforce Diane's knowledge of her students' learning and her own teaching methods. She is reminded that students need time to learn new skills and that she needs patience to wait for signals that the new skills have been learned. This realization carries over into other areas of her classroom practice, and Diane becomes more conscious of providing students with a "second or even third shot" at learning something new.

While Diane has cast her puzzle in terms of finding a balance of activity suited to each child, it is also possible to see the puzzle in terms of finding a balance between theory and practice. Diane is attentive both to the theoretical consistency in her teaching and to the effects of her practices. These two examples can be interpreted as instances of practice initially guided by theory, which was later extended and elaborated by reframing that was driven by experiences. Many of Diane's professional courses have introduced her to theories that assume children can be more responsible for their own learning than "traditional" classrooms appear to assume. Diane has considered these theories carefully and finds them appropriate and worth pursuing, but she is also attentive to the "backtalk" from the children she teaches. Two additional puzzles of practice, concerned with when to intervene as teacher and how to involve parents, can also be interpreted in terms of reframing that brings theory and practice into balance with each other.

The Puzzle of Teacher Intervention

A second set of puzzles for Diane concerns a persistent dilemma arising in her practice: While she believes that her job is to instruct and to help each student develop properly, at the same time she believes that students should determine and direct their own learning. Not surprisingly, these potentially conflicting images of her role generate puzzles about the amount and type of intervention she should provide. She asks herself, "Do I alter instruction for him or do I just observe and record?" "Should I be pushing, intervening?" In the following interview segments, she voices the dilemma she feels between "letting the child choose" and "pushing the child to achieve."

> I don't know sometimes if we push them hard enough. You know as long as you're not asking them to do something that's too hard. Like spell all the words right. That's too hard. I told one boy that, "I want you to write like a Grade 1 student. I don't think you should have to write like you're in Grade 4." His brother's in Grade 4. You know when he writes, he gets negative feedback from his brother.

> Their writing journals are where they write about what they want. But you sort of have to *make* them write about what they want. I don't know what Dave [a colleague who specializes in the study of children's writing] would say about that, because I know that he would say that was intervention, that I was intervening. But you know, that's what we're here for. If you don't intervene in reading instruction either, they won't read until they are about in Grade 4.

The revisions she makes to journal writing exemplify how Diane works through the teacher intervention dilemma. Interestingly, her language changes over time as the problem is addressed and then resolved.

At the beginning of the year, Diane talks about encouraging students' personal writing in terms of "easing them into it."

> I'm trying to get them to write in their journals. We'll try to ease into it. "Is there a word around the room you can copy?" "It doesn't matter if it's messy." "Write it upside down." It's hard, this writing. They have to know so much. They have to know the letters; they have to know the sounds the letters might make. They have to know directions. And then they have to make the effort to write instead of draw. I think if you left them alone, I think most of them would draw for the whole year. I give them blank journals now and say, "Write or draw." And then in November, I'll say, "Try to write something in your journal." I won't use the word draw any more and they click into these little things. In December I might give them a journal that has lines at the bottom and that will tell them, "She's expecting writing on these lines."

In January, she tells how she has observed that students are reluctant to write in their journals under her "easy-going" approach. Many are still drawing rather than writing, and those who are writing are not able to sustain a topic. Essentially, students are not writing as much as she had hoped, and she changes her instructions in an attempt to encourage students to write more. She explains that she has abandoned her relaxed instructions and expectations and is now "pushing" each student to write.

> I'm changing my approach to journal writing too. I've said to them . . . Dave would say, "Let them write." Well, they don't write. They are just like adults; they are lazy. They like to draw. And sure, they get a chance to draw about things that are important to them and so on. But they need a little push to write. "You're going to write today! You're going to write and show me what you have written." I used to say, "Now maybe if you don't write anything today, that's okay." Not anymore. *Everybody* writes!

In Diane's language, we see reference to her more directive approach to journal writing: "I was being a little strict." "This is business." "Maybe I should be pushing a little more." "You sort of have to make them write about what they want." "I had them write a sentence about Adam." "That would be pushing writing." In her revised approach to journal writing, she is providing more detailed direction and offering students less free choice. She is imposing her expectations on students' writing, rather than having them write about what they want, when they want.

In part, this change in practice is prompted by her experience the previous year, when she kept students' journals to track their writing progress and discovered that they made little visible progress if left to their own choice of activity. Her "let them write about what they want, when they want" approach is consistent with her belief in children's abilities to guide their own learning, but it is ineffective with many students. Diane's language in the interview segments suggests that she has come to view the teaching of writing very differently. Initially, the focus reflects the idea that one learns to write just by having opportunities to write. Later language suggests the view that one can learn to write only by writing. Accordingly, there is a change in what it means to Diane to teach writing, and this reframing is evident in her revised approach to having students write. By revising her approach so that it provides more specific structure and less freedom of choice, Diane has begun to sort out her dilemma about teacher intervention. While she still believes that real writing is writing about what you want, when you want, her experiments with imposing her standards and expectations for journal writing indicate that most children seem to need that imposed structure.

The Puzzle of Parental Involvement

Diane's relationships with parents represent a third set of professional puzzles about practice. In her earlier years of teaching, Diane worked from a perspective that separated "school" learning and "home" learning. While she recognized the value of involving parents in their children's learning program, she made few provisions for contacting parents other than through formal reporting and interview sessions. Her professional attention was concentrated on setting up in-classroom activities. In the following statement, Diane discusses how she altered her patterns of interaction with parents.

I wonder if that's another really important thing I've done differently is to try to be on the right side of the parents. They come to pick up a kid in the middle of class and I just drop everything and say, "Hi, how are you? How is he today?" I always care about my kids, but before I would think, "I've got to get this lesson taught. I don't need any interruptions." But parents are crucial at this level, especially in the reading. They make the difference. It's like a partnership. That's a skill that's taken me a long time to learn. It's public relations.

Diane appears to have switched from seeing parents as people to whom she is accountable, to seeing them as potential partners in her professional work. This change occurred over time, and was initially prompted by noting the progress that a few "special-needs" students had made with the help of a home support program. She realized from this experience that all students could benefit from parental assistance in their learning and decided to focus her energies on establishing more active parental involvement. Possibly, her increasing confidence as a Grade 1 teacher contributed to the change. She is now willing to risk opening her practice to parental examination, and she now takes more time to talk to parents informally when they come to the classroom to pick up their children, even if the conversation interrupts her planned lesson. Her reading program is designed so that students take home books to share with an adult nightly, and she supports this program with frequent letters to parents offering suggestions for reading activities. She carefully structures formal parent interviews so that she is interviewing the parent about the child's learning habits at home. This restructuring was influenced in part by an interview with her son's teacher. As a parent, she appreciated the teacher's interest in her child and saw the value of parental cooperation and support.

The new perspective on the role of parents in the enterprise of schooling appears to have opened up possibilities that seemed unavailable to her beforehand. Nevertheless, new problems also emerge in the new frame:

> What I think I should do now is to contact the parents of these kids who are taking the books home every night and bringing them back unread. . . . What made me think I should be looking into this a little bit is that one girl said, "Oh I like taking them home. I don't get a chance to read them, but I like taking them home."

Thus a new frame does not mean an end to puzzles and problems; the scrutiny of one's own practice continues, but it moves to more elaborated views of practice. Theory has played a crucial role in Diane's professional development at every stage, and yet she is just as clear about how she has found that theory must be worked out in practice. Diane has moved recently to the role of principal, and we can anticipate that her attention to experience and to consistency not only within theory but also between theory and practice will continue to be a dominant feature of her professional activities. When we sent her a draft of her case report for comment, she wrote the following reply, indicative of the value she places on gaining greater understanding of her own reframing of experience:

> Thank you for sending the copy of the case study; you know how I enjoyed talking with you about teaching Grade One. I enjoyed reading the case study just as much. Reflecting on the development of my teaching skills will be helpful for me now as I support teachers who must continually be learning how to teach. Already I have drawn on my experience with you to help me be more understanding and tolerant of a teacher who is still in the "What do I do on Monday?" stage.
>
> The day your material arrived I had been dealing with one problem after another until I was feeling rather discouraged. Some feedback about myself at this particular time gave me a real boost and will help me further define myself as a teacher. Thank you for involving me . . .

At this point we conclude our discussion of reframing and the development of professional knowledge in the case of Diane and turn to the case of Roger. Again, we find that reframing is driven by efforts to work theories of learning into practice while also attending to the actual effects of practice on students.

ROGER

Now in his sixth year of teaching, Roger teaches science to Grades 7 and 8 in a special program for gifted students. All the children in these two grades at the school have been identified as "gifted"; the most immediate impact of this is that Roger works with class sizes of 16 and is the science teacher for these students over a 2-year period. Roger could be said to have been preparing himself for a teaching career since the age of 12, when he first realized that he had an ability to relate well to children in his capacity as a volunteer leader with community groups. He continued to pursue his interest in teaching and learning throughout his high school and university years by reading about and experimenting with various learning approaches. By the time he entered his preservice education year, he felt very comfortable in a teaching situation and found that his experiences with children helped him make sense of the education courses.

Roger credits his first 2 years of classroom teaching as being valuable for helping him to better understand the learning process. Because he taught only half-days in a high school setting in his first year, Roger had time to think about his practice, time that is not available to most beginning teachers simply because they are so busy. The experience at the secondary level also gave him insights into the restrictions that covering a common curriculum can impose on teachers. In his present position, Roger experiences few such restrictions. The administration and staff provide collegial support for teachers who want to develop programs tailored to students' interests. Roger appreciates the freedom and flexibility available to him.

Roger spent his second year teaching Grade 6 core subjects in the school where he now teaches. From the Grade 6 work, he learned more about how students think about their school experiences. Aware that he did not know all he would like to about children at the Grade 6 level, he asked them to tell him how they best liked to learn. Roger was able to design a program in which students were free to explore areas that interested them. He acted as a resource person, offering guidelines and suggesting approaches for solving problems. This experience reinforced Roger's understanding of the importance of working cooperatively with students.

In Roger's discussions of his professional growth, we see him reframing various puzzles of practice. These puzzles arise from his interest in the teaching/learning process and have to do with both students' learning and his own learning. The ways in which Roger addresses and works through these puzzles tells us much about the development of his professional knowledge. His specific instances of reframing of teaching practices occur within the broader context in which he listens to his students, watches them interact with materials, and attempts to resolve gaps and inconsistencies he perceives in his rationale for his practices.

Three puzzles are ongoing in Roger's teaching experiences; these concern the nature of "inquiry-based learning," the contrast between "inquiry" and "traditional" learning, and the nature of students' understanding. We see Roger pose a question about his practice and attempt to answer it by experimenting, just as his students are asked to experiment with interesting and puzzling phenomena. The experimentation may result in answers but more often triggers further questions, which in turn initiate another cycle of inquiry. Roger describes in interviews how listening to the backtalk from events in his classroom alters his view of learning and consequently his approach to teaching.

The Puzzle of Inquiry-Based Learning

Roger entered teaching with a firm belief in an inquiry-based approach to learning. His experience with an inquiry-based research course in university and several years of experience as a Scout leader provided him with "a large knowledge base of how kids learn" prior to his preservice teacher education. His preservice courses helped to confirm for him the value of experiential learning. However, attention to backtalk from the events of his classroom showed him that "learning by doing" was less effective than he had believed. He discovered that inquiry-based learning needed to be associated with content if students are to learn the concepts of science. At the same time that his experiences were generating puzzles about the question of students' learning, Roger was exploring similar questions in the work of both Driver (1983) and Barnes (1976). The parallels between his reading and his experimentation with practices generated a new frame for his understanding of practice. In the following comments, Roger describes the chain of events that led him to question what appeared to be a firm personal belief in the value of inquiry-based learning.

> When I came here [to the Faculty of Education] I was very much experiential, very discovery-, inquiry-, process-oriented. And that was great because that was very much the kind of approach and philosophies that were being used here, particularly in science. And when I went to try it, it worked very well. The kids love it, they really enjoy it, but what I noticed was that they were having a lot of fun and they loved science but they weren't learning anything! And so I began to develop strategies that would deal with that as a side issue. "Yes, we'll have some fun, but now we've had some fun, we sort of have to learn some things!" I thought, "This is really stupid. You can't have two parallel approaches to teaching." Anyway, the more I started to read about teaching, and think about it, I really began to look at trying to sort out that dilemma of how is it that people learn so much by *doing* things and yet, when you give kids things to do in science, they don't really learn anything about science other than "science is fun," and "science is enjoyable," and that kind of thing, which is very worthwhile, too.
>
> And I guess the thing that really struck me was I read Ros Driver's book, *The Pupil as Scientist?* At first, I was really annoyed with the book because basically what it says is that inquiry is screwed up, [that] kids can't do anything if they don't know anything, and they can't discover anything or plan their own experi-

ments or whatever if they have no background. It was so obvious that it annoyed me: Basically, she's saying that inquiry doesn't work. *But I didn't want to know it.* It was almost as if I believed in it so strongly that there must be a way to make it work. Anyway, the outcome of that book, really, was to lead into the whole, I guess, "cognitive science" approach to teaching, and looking at how people learn. And I basically got involved in that sort of thing. . . . And that has led to all kinds of reading on top of that. And discovering, actually, [that] there are a lot of people who feel that way. Not that the sort of philosophy or the spirit of inquiry is wrong, but just that there has to be some associated content to go with it, and that this can happen in specific ways so that people have some things, some tools to work with when they go to do this experiential kind of thing. So that's what I played with last year, with my kids, and it was dynamite.

When we asked for an example to illustrate what he meant, Roger selected a topic that he particularly enjoys because it is intriguing to children but not familiar to most of them. They have some relevant background knowledge, but the phenomena are open to multiple interpretations. Corrugated plastic tubing used with pumps is readily and inexpensively available in hardware stores. When a section about 3-feet long is swung by one end, the tube "sings," and the pitch one hears can be varied by swinging faster and slower. Roger describes his strategy in the following excerpt from an interview:

I managed to get hold of some corrugated plastic hose which when you whirl it around has the property of giving off a sound, or "singing," and it struck me that this would be a very interesting way to begin to explore the whole idea of scientific inquiry with Grade 8 students. I gathered together about 10 tubes and demonstrated the fact that they "sang" and left them with the challenge of developing an explanation for why the tubes sang. What they were able to do, very quickly, was to make small discoveries of what affected the tube; for example, the idea that if you cover up one end of the tube that it won't sing any more, and that led them to the idea that the air has to—obviously there's air involved in this—that air has to go through the tube, and typically that's ended up with a very lively discussion of which way the air goes through the tube, and often the class will separate into two "camps"—those who believe it goes from the hand out and those who believe it goes from the swinging end in. When we got together to discuss that, it was quite apparent that there were various ways of proving that, as far as they were concerned. They were sent off to find more conclusive evidence and to begin to pull together their explanations and also encouraged to use other examples of things they were familiar with. . . . The kids were very much encouraged to experiment on their own and to try things based on reading that they had done, things that they would look up, because there are very few places you can go that have an explanation for how this tube works, but there are places you can go that talk about sound and soundwaves. We did some work with tuning forks, and the kids played with those and tried to look up how that was similar and out of that built up some very interesting explanations of how this tube worked, several of which happened to be very close to the accepted explanation.

Roger displays a clear understanding of how his perspectives on teaching have developed. His firm belief in an inquiry method made him reluctant to alter his belief in its value, but, by being open to the events of his classroom and the views of others, he has a new, broader frame for this teaching strategy. Puzzles about the practical limitations of experiential learning led Roger to a new perspective on science teaching, which is now cast to include critical concepts necessary for student understanding. Both puzzling experiences and relevant arguments about the rationale of inquiry methods were crucial in the reframing process. He offers the following account of the teaching actions that emerge with the new frame.

I spent a lot more time myself trying to identify the really critical concepts or ideas that I was trying to get across. And I found that it was a lot more difficult than I initially thought, even with a background in science, to distill things down and say, "What is *really* important about this area that the kids need to know in order to make any sense out of it?" So that's basically how I started and then decided to present all that, up front, to the kids, right at the beginning of any work.

The Puzzle of Inquiry versus Traditional Teaching

Another puzzle that Roger sees recurring in his practice involves his gradual shift through each school year to what he terms "more traditional lecture-style teaching." While he strongly believes in "messing about" inquiry and an activity-based approach to learning science and includes these in his lessons, he finds that as the year progresses he uses more lectures and question-and-answer lessons and provides fewer opportunities for students to mess about. As Roger works through the puzzle of why he drifts toward more traditional teaching strategies, we see him come to a deeper awareness of his personal teaching patterns. The discussion of this puzzle is initiated in an interview at the end of his fourth year of teaching when the research team asks him to discuss areas of his practice that are particularly puzzling.

> One of the puzzles that I have is more about me than my teaching. I find that gradually through the year, I drift more toward a traditional method of teaching. I don't know whether there's some influence on me that suggests, "You're not covering enough or you're not doing enough." It's certainly not an external influence. Nobody comes into my classroom and says, "These kids are not learning." It just happens and I don't know why. When I sit back and look at it, I say, "Why are you doing this? Because it's not really what you believe in."
>
> That one [the puzzle of why he drifts to traditional teaching] still baffles me, but I think part of it comes from confidence in seeing the thing work, because I'll have units that will just go exceptionally well, and I'll have others that really kind of flounder around a little bit, maybe because I didn't think them through very well or because the kids weren't ready for the way I was doing it. So then I'll start to doubt whether what I'm doing makes sense.

Roger is encouraged to rethink his activity-based approach by the knowledge that other teachers are also experimenting and discovering many of the same sorts of dilemmas that he faces. His participation in a master of education program is particularly influential in restoring his confidence in his experimental approach to teaching science.

> The nice thing about doing the master's program is that you begin to be exposed to other people who are thinking in similar ways and they're finding that, "Yes, some of this works and some of it doesn't." That I find gives me more confidence. I can say, "Oh, somebody else is trying it, and they believe in it too, so maybe I *am* on some kind of intelligent approach here."

Late in his fifth year of teaching, we again ask Roger to discuss the puzzle of his shift to traditional methods during the school year. While he acknowledges that the puzzle persists, he seems to have found a better way to view the underlying issues.

> I'm beginning to resolve it. That seems to have most to do with the degree of planning that I've put into the thing. So what I'm getting to sense more and more is that, when I'm working on a unit maybe that hasn't been particularly well developed in my head or on paper, that I tend to fall back to traditional teaching. So I'm more conscious now of saying [to myself], "No, you can't do that." I really have to think these things through before I try to use them. But I've also found that before I can really develop a unit, and before I can put it together in the way that I want to, I virtually have to run it just sort of off the top of my head to start and see how it goes and see what kind of directions develop naturally. And so the next class, the following year, ends up with something developed out of that as to what caught people's interest and what sorts of conceptions did the kids have that were worth pursuing.

Here Roger's reframing of his own practices enables him to extend his professional understanding of the relationship between planning and lesson delivery. By working through the puzzle of why he drifts to traditional teaching, his practice leads to new theory. He originally framed the puzzle in terms of doubts about the value of activity-based learning. As he explores those doubts in his science classes and in his M.Ed. program, he reframes the puzzle in terms of planning, preparation, and awareness of students' conceptions. The new frame for the drift to traditional teaching makes him more attentive to the role of lesson preparation and more aware of the importance of understanding students' conceptions of topics so that he can plan for future activity-based lessons.

The Puzzle of Students' Understanding

A need to understand students' conceptions of science is at the core of a third puzzle in Roger's practice. His perspective that learning is making sense of one's world leads him to question how to present curriculum units in ways that allow students to make their own sense of science concepts. Two themes recur in the analysis of his reframing of students' understanding of science: Roger steps back from his practice and listens to backtalk from the students, and he reinterprets his strategies for planning units and lessons.

> It's so much easier now to step back and look at what's happening as opposed to [wondering] "Where do we go next?" I'm also able to predict fairly well the kinds of things that will come up and get a sense of the kinds of things that the kids will or won't understand. . . . Because things are fairly well laid out now and I can stand back from things a bit, I concentrate on the kids who aren't getting into it as much and look at some aspects of why they don't. And how you can move them from this very structured position to one where they're quite willing to suspend things. One girl when she started out in Grade 7 was lost without any kind of a structure. Now she really enjoys being confused! And it provides a challenge for her. But it took a fair bit of work to get her to that stage, and a lot of that comes in the feedback that I give in the reports. Once the kids are allowed to *believe* that they have some ability to solve these kinds of problems, then everything opens up.

One clue to Roger's attention to backtalk from his students appears when we isolate phrases in which he talks about what his students do: "kids were incredibly responsive," "kids were telling me about how they liked to learn," "talked to them and found out what they were used to, and how *they* saw it, because I already knew how I saw it," "make much more effort to get to know the kids," "with concept mapping, it's very easy to spot that kind of misinterpretation," "easy to identify kids who are linear thinkers."

By stepping back to observe students' reactions, Roger establishes written and oral dialogue with individual students in which he clarifies his own understanding of their views of science and also challenges them to rethink those views. The technique of concept-mapping (Novak & Gowin, 1984), which he initially used in his own planning, evolves into a strategy that helps students learn as it helps him recognize which students are experiencing difficulties with the concept.

> This concept-mapping idea takes loose ideas—and it doesn't have to be a highly fluent sort of thing, even kids who are not very fluent writers and who couldn't write a page on how a cell reproduces or whatever can take the major ideas and at least show you how they tie them together in their mind. And it's fascinating because I use them in assignments. And at a glance, I can see where the misunderstandings are and it's great. . . . What you get out of concept-mapping—it becomes very easy to identify the kids who are very linear thinkers, who have real trouble tying these ideas together. I end up learning so much, working this way, about how

the *kids* learn and it helps me enormously. I end up going back and changing all my things immediately and saying, "Well, I'll have to change that around!" because something that I thought was fairly obvious clearly wasn't. . . . I identify the sort of key areas, the things like energy, and force, and friction and try to present some sort of integrated representation. I've been using concept-mapping to represent how I see the overall picture of how these things are related. Now the other thing that I've spent quite a bit of time doing is trying to identify how kids see those ideas. I present what *I'm* thinking of, get them to present what *they're* thinking of, and then we have a place to start negotiating.

Roger's reframing of student understanding reminds us that our own formal learning experiences tend not to create an understanding of the learning process that can assist us as teachers. Roger's belief that he wanted students to make their own sense of science concepts was initially constrained by the ever-present images of students' "taking in" what teachers talked about. Assisted by the technique of concept-mapping, Roger watched what his students did and listened to them, trying to establish connections between his beliefs and the events of his classroom. By trusting that students could make progress on their own, and by adjusting the levels of structure and control in his teaching, Roger came to understand what his personal belief meant at the level of classroom actions as a teacher. The payoff to Roger of a broader perspective on how students understand science is apparent in the following account of how he has come to see his planning and presentation in interaction with each other.

What happens tomorrow depends mostly on what happens today, and so that's how I plan. What I end up doing now is I look ahead and say, "Here's a general thread, a general direction of where I'd like to be. Not exactly step-by-step how I'm going to get there, but I want to work with singing tubes and at some point I want the kids to have some work with tuning forks because I think that introduces sound, and then eventually I'd like the kids to make a presentation on why the thing works." And that's about the extent of the structure because what happens in between depends on what the kids do. . . . I think planning can consume you to the point that you don't see what's really happening. So I'd rather put more of my energy into thinking up ways in which I can reinforce this process and providing materials that will allow that to happen.

Roger's language illustrates his reframed view of presenting curriculum units. Phrases such as "work together," "designed the program around how they liked to learn, how they didn't like to learn," "have them use what *they* know to make sense of things," "worked really hard at trying to identify kids' interests" suggest that Roger's attention is focused more on how students view and understand science and less on his own views of curriculum topics.

The three aspects of teaching that Roger has reframed over several years of science teaching appear to have run independently, but with obvious overlaps. The puzzle of inquiry-based learning was probably inevitable for Roger, given his background upon entry to a preservice teacher education program. That puzzle had to be worked out on its own, but it also interacted with his efforts to understand those times when strategies that he terms "traditional" appeared naturally in his work. Finally, the strong concern for inquiry by students led him from his own learning experiences as student and teacher to the process by which his students come to understand concepts in science.

REFLECTION AND PROFESSIONAL KNOWLEDGE

Our accounts of reframing by Diane and Roger in response to puzzles arising within their teaching actions and in the relationship between beliefs and actions illustrate how we have attempted to understand the process of reframing as it applies to teaching and the development of teachers' professional knowledge. The 15 case studies in our 1986–1988 study provide valuable insights into the development of professional knowledge by teachers. Each case is consistent with the familiar view that teachers learn to teach by teaching. More importantly, each suggests the significance of reframing puzzling experiences, particularly those that involve consistency between theory and practice.

Kennedy's (1987) definitions of "professional expertise" as discrete technical skills, application of theory or general principles, critical analysis, and deliberate action (drawing on Dewey and Schön) suggest one framework for describing our findings. Our 15 cases show some predictable (Fuller, 1969) developments in teachers' attention to the class, to individual students' differences and needs, and then to teaching for these. Understandably, the beginning teachers in our study have limited knowledge of formal learning and instructional theories and limited ability to display corresponding knowing-in-action in their teaching. Some of our participants provide evidence that their teaching is guided by other considerations, such as the prescribed curriculum. In two cases, there is clear tension between expressed ideals about teaching (the focus on individual needs, teaching children to learn for themselves, etc.) and their interview language, which contains metaphors associated with covering the curriculum. Here the metaphors seem "stale"; the teachers seem unable to break from them and thereby productively reframe the problems and inconsistencies of their practice. Thus critical analysis and deliberate action do not ensue, and ideals are not translated into teaching. Alternatively, Diane and Roger, two of our more experienced participants, illustrate considerable professional growth; interview data show important characteristics. First, the metaphors in the language used are fresh ("generative," in Schön's terms): Roger uses metaphors that are consistent with the idea of inquiry, coming from the physical sciences; Diane uses metaphors that describe how she thinks she has learned. Second, both teachers have pursued further academic study with the express intent of trying to understand classroom phenomena better.

These cases and others have advanced our understanding in two ways. First, we have come to see Schön's reframing as an integral part of a cycle in the development of teachers' professional knowledge: When an initial theory-in-action encounters puzzles or surprises, backtalk stimulates reframing, suggesting new actions that imply a revised theory-in-action. Second, we have come to see that reframing and the appearance of a revised theory-in-action are accompanied by changes in teachers' descriptive language. We do not yet understand what experiences prompt these changes, nor do we understand fully what capabilities are needed for teachers to be able to reframe. Seeking consistency between theory and practice and better theories to guide practice appears to be an important element in productive reframing.

REFRAMING A RESEARCH AGENDA

Our work with the reflection-in-action perspective in the context of teacher education now spans a period of 5 years. We have been increasingly aware of and interested in the evolution of our understanding of that perspective as a frame for research, as we have engaged in several studies of teachers' professional development. Russell initially developed an agenda of questions related to the education of beginning teachers. Later this was merged with Munby's interest in metaphor to generate a study of both beginning and experienced teachers. It is stressed in Schön's perspective that new meanings and insights arise as one pursues the avenues of inquiry that are suggested in a particular professional domain. We now understand this point at the level of action. When we began, our understanding of Schön's distinction between reflection-in-action and reflection-on-action was incomplete. The contrast is plausible as Schön (1983, pp. 61–62) presents it, but exploring the meaning of those terms in the context of individual teachers' development is quite another matter. We continue to discuss the distinction as we organize the data presented in this chapter. We have come to understand that the central feature of this concept is "in-action," not the familiar sense of "reflection" that most of us take the word to mean. As we now understand Schön's argument, reflection-in-action emerges within a teacher's activities of teaching: Actions and the responses to them are closely intertwined with a reframing of the teaching situation. For Diane and Roger, reflection on this process involves resolution of puzzles about how theory can be played out in practice, as actions generate new meanings for theory. *New actions and new frames for practice go hand in hand.* Some actions survive and others do not, as their consequences become more clearly understood, both in practice and in theory. From the researcher's perspective, reflection-in-action is difficult to detect and challenging to document. While we find observation of teaching essential to the process of interviewing teachers about their professional activities and their professional knowledge, we would not expect to observe directly the "event" of reflection-in-action. Our most recent strategy involves a combination of teachers' own reports of changes in their teaching approaches and views of the classroom context with analysis of teachers' interviews over time in search of shifts in the imagery they use to describe their work.

Our conceptualization of the nature and development of professional knowledge in terms of reflection-in-action and metaphor is immediately applicable to the study of how teachers learn to teach. Teacher education seems to rely on the premise that propositional knowledge from lectures and books can be translated directly into practice. This premise fails because it cannot explain how the act of teaching is used by the beginning teacher to acquire practical knowledge. In our recent studies, we have seen novice teachers, as they begin to teach, explicitly reject what they have been told in the Faculty of Education; yet their teaching does develop and improve.

While we recognize that Schön's (1983, 1987) formulation of professional knowledge is complex, controversial, and incomplete, we are convinced that it offers an important guide to further understanding of professional learning. The relationship between teaching and research continues to elude teacher educators, and there are many attempts to explain why. Billups and Rauth (1987) tackle the matter directly in a discussion of "professionalism in teaching":

> Even as relevant information about effective ways of teaching emerges from research, methods of disseminating and applying the concepts at the classroom level remain antiquated. Teacher disinterest in research is in vogue, reflected in the reaction, "What do researchers know about what goes on in classrooms?". . . . Many supervisors and administrators are comfortable repeating the same ineffectual process imposed on them in the past, which did very little to improve their teaching or supervisory skills. (pp. 636–637)

While we accept this analysis, we notice how easy it is to speak of "dissemination" and "application" and to overlook the matter of *teachers' professional knowledge,* and how such knowledge is acquired, held, and developed.

ACKNOWLEDGMENTS

This chapter draws on the work of a 2-year research project, "Metaphor, Reflection, and Teachers' Professional Knowledge," directed by the authors and funded by the Social Sciences and Humanities Research Council of Canada. Phyllis Johnston prepared initial drafts of the two cases described here.

REFERENCES

Barnes, D. (1976). *From communication to curriculum.* Harmondsworth, England: Penguin.

Billups, L. H., & Rauth, M. (1987). Teachers and research. In V. Richardson-Koehler (Ed.), *Educators' handbook: A research perspective* (pp. 624–639). New York: Longman.

Driver, R. (1983). *The pupil as scientist?* Milton Keynes, England: Open University Press.

Fuller, F. (1969). Concerns of teachers: A developmental conceptualization. *American Educational Research Journal, 6,* 207–226.

Hanson, N. R. (1958). *Patterns of discovery: An inquiry into the conceptual foundations of science.* Cambridge, England: Cambridge University Press.

Kennedy, M. (1987). Inexact sciences: Professional education and the development of expertise. In E. Z. Rothkopf (Ed.), *Review of research in education, 14* (pp. 133–167). Washington, DC: American Educational Research Association.

Kuhn, T. (1962). *The structure of scientific revolutions*. Chicago: University of Chicago Press.

Munby, H. (1986). Metaphor in the thinking of teachers: An exploratory study. *Journal of Curriculum Studies, 18*, 197–209.

Munby, H., & Russell, T. (1989). Educating the reflective teacher: An essay review of two books by Donald Schön. *Journal of Curriculum Studies, 21*, 71–80.

Novak, J., & Gowin, D. (1984). *Learning how to learn*. Cambridge, England: Cambridge University Press.

Russell, T., Munby, H., Spafford, C., & Johnston, P. (1988). Learning the professional knowledge of teaching: Metaphors, puzzles, and the theory-practice relationship. In P. Grimmett & G. Erickson (Eds.), *Reflection in teacher education* (pp. 67–90). Vancouver: Pacific Educational Press & New York: Teachers College Press.

Schön, D. A. (1983). *The reflective practitioner: How professionals think in action*. New York: Basic Books.

Schön, D. A. (1987). *Educating the reflective practitioner: Toward a new design for teaching and learning in the professions*. San Francisco: Jossey-Bass.

Toulmin, S. (1953). *The philosophy of science: An introduction*. London: Hutchinson.

Part V

CRITICAL ANALYSIS OF PRACTITIONERS' UNDERSTANDINGS

9

Anticipating Implementation: Reflective and Normative Practices in Policy Analysis and Planning

JOHN FORESTER

ON A SABBATIC LEAVE several years ago, I had the opportunity to do extensive fieldwork in local city planning departments. I interviewed suburban and urban planners, and I watched in their conference rooms as they negotiated for design and project changes with real estate developers. I sat in, periodically, on raucus zoning board hearings. Mostly, I watched for the ways the planners handled local land-use conflict.

Local planners had a delicate balance to strike, for they were caught in-between developers who wanted to build, neighbors who were wary of disruptive new projects, and other agency staff who were protective of their turf. I wondered how the planners managed. When, too, I wondered, did they have influence? And because the image of technical problem solving seemed to fit their work so poorly, I wondered how better to describe what the planners really were doing as they worked.

At one memorable meeting, I watched from the corner as a planner met with two developers who wished to build 70–100 units of low- to moderate-income housing in a certain part of their city. The meeting took about 2 hours. The developers and planners talked about potential building sites as they looked over a couple of maps in front of them. After the initial introductions, the meeting became quite boring, actually. After all, there was no project yet for anyone to be particularly upset about. But I knew that my boredom itself meant that I was a captive of my conventional understanding of planners' practice. Here was that practice in front of me, and I seemed to see little of interest. I was missing most of what was significant in front of my own eyes.

About half-way through the meeting, then, I became perplexed: Just

what is really going on here? Where is the action? Where is the professional practice?

I thought I would try something. What I saw and heard in front of
me was just talk. I realized, of course, that many people's minds boggle
at the thought that professional action is intricately wrapped up in
speech, that it is complex talk through and through. So I wondered
what would happen if I simply stopped listening—midway in this meeting—so I could observe just the raw behavior, and thus potentially the
real practice, that would be left. If I just *kept watching, but stopped listening*, it seemed that I would then be observing the real practice in front
of me, without the superficialities of its talk.

I tried it. What was left was a bit of lip motion, some shifting of
bodies, and mainly index fingers pointing to various spots on the map
on the table. The index fingers pointed here, paused (accompanied by
lip and body motion), then went there (same accompaniments). The
most striking thing I saw when I stopped listening, then, was the professional work of index-finger pointing. Now surely, I thought, this is
not "the action" in this meeting.

Or was it? I began to listen again and think about just what the
developers and the planner were doing with those index fingers. They
were pointing, to be sure, but their work together seemed far richer
than that. They seemed to be anticipating complex worlds of future actions and interactions: "What if we go *there?*," the developer would ask.
"Or you might go *here*," the planner would say. And so on.

All of a sudden this boring meeting was transformed before my
eyes. Now I saw that with each motion of a finger pointing to a different
spot of the map, the planner and developers were imagining future
worlds (that did not yet exist, obviously) complete with possible project
designs, possible interventions (we would have to talk to this guy across
the street or meet him in court!), and so forth.

I left the meeting transformed. Always interested in the ways that
professionals theorized in practice, now I had a better idea about how
they did it. Anticipating future worlds, they had to theorize to imagine
those worlds plausibly, present them plausibly to anyone else, and
gauge their actions and strategies with respect to those future worlds.

I explained my hunch about "anticipation" to Lloyd Rodwin of
MIT's planning faculty. What is the difference, he wanted to know, between that work of anticipating and the work of expecting and predicting that we have always thought professionals did, the work our positive predictive theories were designed to inform? My intuition told me
that the grammar of "anticipate," "expect," and "predict" did overlap,
but that there was more to the story. When we anticipate events we

seem peculiarly engaged with those events; when we predict or expect events, we are more detached, more like spectators, less responsibly involved. Checking the dictionary, the thesaurus, and books on usage suggested that my hunch was right—but how could I go about developing it?

I had a deadline approaching for an essay I was to write about the normative work done by planning practitioners. I thought I could take my hunch about professionals' anticipatory work and test it in this essay. Would the idea help me understand planners' work in a powerful way? Did the anticipatory work I thought I had seen have an important normative part to it? (Wouldn't it have to have a normative part if it was interested activity, judgmental activity, evaluative activity?)

I had recently observed another meeting in another planning department. A planning director had met with a developer and the developer's engineer who proposed to build a new office complex on an old warehouse site. If my hunch made sense, I could analyze that meeting in "anticipatory" terms and perhaps come up with some surprising results. If my hunch was off-base, I would come up empty-handed when I looked closely at this meeting.

This chapter presents the results of what I found (although other results are also reported in *Planning in the Face of Power* (Forester, 1989; cf. Alterman & MacRae, 1983). The first section presents the data: a partial transcript of the planning meeting and an early slice of the process of project review. Listening to the developer's proposal to put two office buildings on a large land parcel near a major arterial street, the planner does much more than "review" the developer's intentions or the project's specifications. The second section sets out the "working hunch": Facing a complex environment and an uncertain future, must the analyst practically *anticipate* possible outcomes of the construction and thus respond accordingly—taking steps early on not only to foresee and evaluate potential consequences, but to shape them as well? If this work is inescapably normative, just how is it to be done?

The third section, then, explores the structure of anticipatory analysis and its requirements. My foray into the dictionary, thesaurus, and usage books told me that in ordinary language *to anticipate* and *to expect* do share meanings but that they diverge significantly as well. Fowler (1965) captures the distinctiveness of *anticipation* by telling us that "to anticipate a crisis" (or a project, a policy) is not simply to foresee or expect it, but to take steps beforehand to meet it. But we must ask how this is possible in analysts' practice. Before steps can be taken to deal with potential outcomes, strategies must be prepared. And surely before strategies of action and analysis can be organized, possible implemented futures must first be imagined. What are the practical requirements involved in this work?

The third section answers these questions in two ways. First, it shows what types of working theories analysts must have if they are to envision: (1) policy or project consequences, (2) the normative and political world in which implementation is to occur, and (3) the interorganizational world of actors who must be involved for project review, analysis, and implementation to proceed. Second, this section explores how analysts can strategically manage arguments in the decision-making process. Let us begin with the transcript from the meeting.

THE TRANSCRIPT: INITIAL PROPOSAL AND PLANNING ANALYSIS

Planning director Tom Johnson, in his early 30s, moved to the planning department after spending 10 years in the city's community development office. Gerald Sullivan, a ruddy-faced real estate developer in his mid-50s, proposes to tear down an existing warehouse in the city and erect two office towers in its place. The existing parking lot would remain, drainage would be maintained, and new landscaping would be provided. Developer Sullivan and his engineer, Bert James, have come to Johnson's office to ask for advice before applying for a building permit. Next, they will go to the city's planning board for a decision about any special conditions that may need to be attached to the permit.

On paper, the process is straightforward. Johnson will write up an analysis of the project. He will submit it to the planning board, who will decide about the conditions to attach to Sullivan's permit. But the planning board may or may not read Johnson's analysis, and may or may not care much if they do, Johnson's recent experience suggests. *Powerful* is not an adjective Johnson would use to describe his distinctly advisory role in the decision-making process. Decisions are made by the planning board. But some boards take staff advice seriously and some do not. Here, Johnson knows, the board has strong "pro-growth" sentiments. As a result, they may attach few if any impact-mitigating conditions to the requested building permit.

The meeting takes place at a small conference table in a corner of the planning department's offices. It is mid-morning. The developer and planner are friendly, cooperative, and attentive to one another. They are also wary of each other, though, keenly aware of the potentially adversarial relationship between them.

After initial greetings and a reference to an earlier telephone conversation, Sullivan says to Johnson, "We wanted to review the city's criteria with you, to look at the process, to get your advice about whether we're going in the right direction or not."

As this meeting progresses, we will see that planning analysis is not simply the frozen content of a static document (Johnson's recommendations to the planning board). We will see, too, how much the planner does before ever presenting "an analysis" to the relevant decision makers. The meeting continues:

JOHNSON: What's your timetable?

SULLIVAN: We'd like to break ground next fall with the first phase. All together there'll be half a million square feet of office space.

JOHNSON: Okay, how about showing us what you've got?

SULLIVAN: Let me introduce Bert James, our engineer. He'll show you what we have.

JAMES: Yes, these plans are very incomplete, but they'll let us get started. They're at 40 scale; do you need 20?

JOHNSON: The planning board can waive that; it looks like it'll all fit at 40.

JAMES: *(Pausing over the site plan)* Do we need a separate application for the parking lot?

JOHNSON: No, since the new ordinance was passed, the forms haven't been done yet.

SULLIVAN: The new review process supersedes the old parking application, but not the traffic review, right?

JOHNSON: Right. *(Looking at the plans)* The only thing missing is the indication of the existing buildings nearby . . .

SULLIVAN: Let's write that down *(as much to himself as to Bert)*.

JOHNSON: The way most people do that is by taking the assessor's plans . . .

SULLIVAN: As far as this is concerned, should this include existing or proposed buildings as well?

JOHNSON: Proposed as well . . .

JAMES: *(Motioning over the site plan)* So this is the site. This shows the amount of paving, and the coverage by the buildings. We'll be reducing the present footprint. We'll have data on this with the new stats about footprint area, amount of landscaping . . .

JOHNSON: *(nodding at each point)*

JAMES: . . . and the plans for the drainage—we propose maintaining the existing outlets. . . . So let's go on to the parking. This pavement would be maintained; the existing access would remain; we show two loading docks here—the zoning bylaws say that's required, . . . 12 × 25, right?

JOHNSON: Right. (*Moving from the question of access to the broader transportation issues*) Do you know about what the state is doing with the Route 3 improvements nearby?

SULLIVAN: What are they doing? Can you brief us?

Here the planning analyst describes the three phases of the road improvement project that the state has initiated near the developer's site. Phase one is 100% designed and due to begin construction in the coming year. Phase two is 75% designed, but phase three is hardly on the drawing boards. Even with these improvements, though, the large intersection close to the site will still rate an "F" (over capacity at peak periods) on the state's rating system—it will have improved from 160% (over-) capacity to "only" 110% (over-) capacity after the phase one improvements are made. Getting this intersection below 100% capacity would require a major commitment of funding that no jurisdiction is presently willing to consider.

SULLIVAN: I've never heard of an "F." What about phase three's schedule?

JOHNSON: Depends on phase two. By the way, do you know about [the regional shopping center's] plans?

SULLIVAN: No. (*Wondering again what information the planner might have*)

JOHNSON: They'll impact the transportation situation in a couple of ways, but if you stick to your timetable you'll be in the ground long before they make their changes; they have lots of environmental problems.

JAMES: (*Joking*) We don't have any runoff problems, it's all paved! (*They all laugh.*) So let's get back to the plans here . . .

They go on to review the parking layouts, required dimensions, and the way the plans should look to be reviewed by the planning board.

JOHNSON: (*Pointing to the edge of the site*) Is this going to be the principal access?

SULLIVAN: Yes. [He explains that the other entrance would be used less; it lies at a steeper grade, but will be altered, too. The engineer continues to present plans for drainage and landscaping.]

JAMES: (*Probing*) We haven't seen any problem with drainage in that area, right?

JOHNSON: Not in that area, no.

After this initial review of the site, the conversation turns to the review process itself. The developer and engineer go item by item through the steps listed as recommended or required in the city's documents describing the project review process.

JAMES: On this "development impact statement"—we're ready to go to the state for a new driveway . . .

JOHNSON: A "curb cut permit," yes.

SULLIVAN: The impact statement seems to cover air, water, traffic on the site. How deep do we really have to go into all this?

JOHNSON: Let's take it one by one. On traffic it should be a full-blown analysis. This is like what you'd do under NEPA.

SULLIVAN: Oh, don't give me those monograms—or whatever they are! *(He then laughs at what he's said.)*

JOHNSON: For environmental impact assessments, what we've accepted before is a short narrative, or even an outline—unless you think there's a real problem. For example, because of that intersection, you'll probably need an air quality study for the state; so when you file it with them, just give it to us too. *(Moving through the other items to be considered in the application process.)* Talk to Joe Hart, the director of public works, and make sure that he understands what you're going to do with the sewers and all . . . *(Continuing with more general advice:)* Talk to anyone who has jurisdiction beforehand—public works is just one who will be reviewing this. *(Turning to the question of fiscal impacts noted in the city's documents.)* A statement of fiscal impacts is recommended, not required . . . there are standard methods for calculating them; I can give you an example if you want.

JAMES: I'd appreciate that. *(Taking prodigious notes all the while)*

JOHNSON: *(After discussing other possible impacts)* Do you know about the [regional planning association's] growth impact study?

SULLIVAN: No. Are they part of the state?

JOHNSON: No, they're an organization of several of the municipalities here, without formal authority, but you might review their study . . .

SULLIVAN: How do we get it?

JOHNSON: Talk to Jeanne Wall on their staff.

JAMES: Who else gets all these plans for review? *(The planner lists several other city departments.)* Would it behoove us to meet with all of these departments?

JOHNSON: Yes, especially with the city hall departments.

SULLIVAN: After we've filed the plans?

JOHNSON: Better before, so you can incorporate their comments
     into your plans; we can set up a meeting and do it all together.

SULLIVAN: Is that a new process here?

JOHNSON: No, it depends on the size of the project and the site; we
     like to encourage it . . .

SULLIVAN: Well, that would really help—it could save several
     weeks. That's super; if we had to go to each one of them alone
     [it could get all tangled up]. So we go through you to do this?

JOHNSON: Yes, we'll try to set it up; we'll need a couple weeks
     probably.

SULLIVAN: (*Surprising the planner*) Well, we'd like to submit the
     plans next week . . . then let's meet with all the departments.

JOHNSON: Okay, sure, but the planning board won't want to sched-
     ule a hearing on this without hearing from the other depart-
     ments . . .

JAMES: (*Drawing the obvious implication*) So it'd be good to meet all
     together earlier.

JOHNSON: Yes.

This meeting continued to cover other questions of project consequences, relevant officials for the developer's team to contact, and requirements imposed by the city upon new developments of substantial
scale. At the end of this project review session, it was clear neither when
the developer would formally file his plans, nor how those plans might
yet change, nor just what analysis and recommendation(s) the planning
analyst would forward to the formal decision makers, the planning
board.

If Sullivan really intended to file his current plans for the project
"next week," had this whole meeting been pointless, an empty ritual?
Hardly, for 3 months later the plans had still not been filed. "Why?" I
asked Sullivan. "Well," he said, "the city changed the law on us. We're
taking the new site plan review process into account now; in another
month or so, we'll file." In fact, though, the "new" site plan review
procedure had been adopted by the city council 5 months earlier, but
Sullivan apparently—and significantly—had only realized this in the
course of meeting with planning director Johnson. Even so, that review
procedure could be satisfied in a wide variety of ways, as Johnson knew
only too well, and regretted. It seemed to Johnson that Sullivan would
try to push ahead quickly, but to Johnson's surprise once more, Sullivan
did not.

This suggests that not only are project consequences uncertain, but that elements of the review, decision-making, and implementation processes can be uncertain, too. Analysis calls for attention both to "the project" and to the practicalities of "the process." Considering the work reflected in this transcript, just what has the planning analyst actually been doing in this case?

ANALYSIS: DOES THE ANTICIPATORY HUNCH HELP US?

Notice first what the planning analyst is quite obviously not doing in this case. He is not "solving a technical problem" as an engineer or a statistician. He does not gather data with a formula or a set of equations ready at hand with which to generate an "answer" or a "solution." Indeed, before the planner can think about solving anything, he needs first to find out, or better, to formulate, just what the problems here might be.

Notice second that the planner is not simply trying to *predict* project consequences. Beyond attempting to forecast project impacts, the planning analyst actually calls the developer's attention to other actors' plans—to those of the state and of a nearby shopping center that may affect the current proposal. Here the analyst is indeed looking ahead to possible outcomes, but for the purpose of changing—potentially improving—the developer's proposal in light of shifting environmental and economic conditions.

What the planner is doing in this case, then, is neither solving a technical problem nor simply predicting and evaluating the consequences of a proposal. Instead, it appears, the planner is working to *anticipate and respond* to future implementation possibilities—in which versions of the presently proposed project would actually be on the ground, implemented, inhabited, socially and functionally interdependent with the surrounding land, community, and organized public and private bodies. To *anticipate and respond* to development possibilities, the planning analyst appears to think politically as well as technically, to probe political questions as well as functional ones, to attempt to learn not only about consequences but about what is consequential, to learn not only about impacts but also about a wide range of political and community concerns.

But what does such practical anticipation involve? Consider carefully what the planning analyst actually does in this case.

The planner does not equate "the problem" he faces with the project or the site alone. He works to find out what the developer is proposing and also to construct a sense of the overall project context. So he asks questions about the current proposal. But he also suggests that the developer find out about the state's plans to improve local traffic conditions and about another developer's plans to enlarge a nearby shopping center—an expansion that could well affect the present project. The planner here tries to envision the developer's site as proposed, but in conjunction with the developing physical and socioeconomic context encompassing it.

The planner places the proposal in "institutional space" as well as in geographic space. So he tells the developer about the growth impact study of the regional planning body, about the jurisdiction of other city agencies, and finally about the standard procedures of the planning board, who "won't want to schedule a meeting without hearing from the other departments." Surveying the institutional world that the project proponent must yet navigate, the planner can suggest, for example, what the planning board might waive—and what they might not waive.

Placing the project in institutional space, the planning analyst anticipates the official concerns that other agencies and public bodies are likely to have with traffic, air quality, water quality, and adjoining properties, and he acts beforehand to try to persuade the developer to address those concerns. So he recommends a "full-blown analysis" of traffic impacts, a study on air quality (that the state, he predicts, will likely require anyway), the inclusion of existing buildings near the site when the plans are forwarded to the planning board, and so forth. Similarly, the planner anticipates the mandates and official interests of other city departments, and he acts to respond to those; so he encourages the developer, for example, to meet with the relevant city departments before filing plans, so that the plans to go before the decision-making bodies can incorporate the comments of the department's staff reviewers.

Besides placing the proposal in its functional and institutional contexts, the planner also addresses questions of the relevant actors to be consulted or taken into account. Notice that "talk to Joe Hart . . . and make sure he understands what you're going to do" is politically and practically a very different piece of advice from "satisfy the standards of the department of public works." In a similar way, without naming names or specifying a formal rule, the planner anticipates the planning board's reticence to act on a project without having letters of review from certain city departments. Here the planning analyst provides the developer with a practical analysis not of institutional rules or procedures but of the operative political culture animating the relevant institutions that will determine the proposal's future. The planner provides information not only about formal rules but about the informal ways that such rules may be applied or interpreted or waived by significant actors in the project review process: decision makers or "influentials."

At a basic level, then, the planning analyst here listens to the developer and his engineer and tentatively seeks to answer three questions: What are the important facts about what is being proposed? What mandates, procedures, rules, and official requirements are relevant? And who are the actors that need to be involved; which particular social relationships count here? Because these three questions raise quite different concerns, we will consider at greater length below how planning and policy analysts might pursue these issues in practice as they anticipate possible project or policy implementation.

Notice, now, that the planner in this case acts more like a practical participant, anticipating future implementation and seeking to shape it, than like a disengaged observer or spectator looking ahead to problematic consequences, violated standards, or disgruntled actors. The planner wants to make a difference, not just to make an analytical argument (as essential as that is). What does he do?

The planner's contribution in this case centers on several functions:

1. Providing counsel about the navigation of the application process ("the planning board can waive" the scale requirement)
2. Helping the developer prepare (and perhaps improve) the project proposal by suggesting tools to use ("most people do that by using the assessor's plans")
3. Sharing his knowledge of contextual changes with the developer to allow or even encourage the developer to fit the proposed project more appropriately (if perhaps opportunistically as well) into its actual physical, functional, and social context (thus the planner describes the state's road improvement plans and the plan of the nearby shopping center)
4. Directing the developer's attention to real problems, to the critical issues (not drainage but traffic, air quality, perhaps fiscal impacts as well)
5. Referring the developer to other agencies and actors whose "comments" about the proposal may be important (to the developer or to the planner and Planning Board)
6. Managing the review process; he details and interprets requirements, suggests particular staff to contact, proposes a follow-up meeting with the other departments, and generally organizes the tasks to be performed before the proposal is to be decided upon (in this case, first by the planning board)

What ties these six activities together? Throughout, the planner seeks not so much to make an argument about the proposal as to manage the process of argumentation concerning it. The planner is concerned both with getting the developer's proposal "in shape" and up-to-date and with attending to the arguments ("comments," "concerns," "feedback") of other agencies, actors, and departments whose word(s) will make a difference. Indeed, at the early stages of project review, the analyst is more attentive to managing the process of argumentation than to formulating his own argument (the so-called "analysis," "report," or "recommendations"). Seeking to manage these arguments is no act of altruism, for only by doing so can the planner in turn get sufficient information for his own "analysis" to be sent to the planning board and ultimately, perhaps, to other decision makers as well, for example, the zoning board of appeals.

Thus the work of "analysis" involves far more than performing calculations and writing "the analysis"; it requires not only making reasonable judgments about likely futures but also attending to and indeed shaping a range of other actors' arguments and "inputs" to the process. In the meeting that the transcript reflects, notice that the analyst's attention was focused first on the proposal, the site, and its environment, then on a range of other actors whose "comments" might be relevant, and only then on the actual moment of decision before the planning board.

THE STRUCTURE OF ANTICIPATORY ANALYSIS

The planning analyst, then, is involved in at least three phases of anticipatory analysis. First, the analyst must envision possible futures of the (implemented) project in its physical, institutional, and cultural context. Second, the analyst must prepare and manage arguments both supporting the proposal (the analyst thus seems to assist the developer) and seeking to modify the proposal (the analyst thus sets the stage for the comments of the public works director and others). Third, the analyst must seek to effectively present (and perhaps negotiate with) his or her own formal analysis of a final proposal and alternatives to it. Within the limited space of the present chapter, we consider only the first two, usually most neglected, phases of analytical practice (cf. Forester, 1989).

If analysis involves these three components (envisioning, managing, presenting), notice that neither of the image of "technical problem solving" nor that of "prediction and evaluation" adequately captures what analysts actually do. The work of planning and policy analysis can no longer be narrowly equated with the calculation and presentation of results. Instead, this empirical, "micropolitical" look at an analyst's practice suggests a different understanding of what planning analysis, and by extension policy analysis, really involves.

Planning and policy analysis can be understood not solely as the work of calculation but also as the practical anticipation of potential project (or policy) implementation. Analysts must thus in part formulate the very problems that they may act to meet; prepare, solicit, and manage the arguments evaluating those problems; and then present synthetic arguments (an "analysis") proposing one or more courses of action. Before an analysis is presented, it must be prepared, its complex and potentially conflicting components managed; but before its component arguments can be prepared and managed, the scope of the project (natural, social, political-economic) must be first envisioned. How is this "envisioning" possible? Consider each requirement in turn.

Envisioning Possible Implementation:
Implications for Problem Formulation

This analysis extends and refines the familiar argument that in planning and policy analysis "problems" must be formulated before they are "solved" (Seeley, 1963). Engaged with a prospective project, the analyst must not only present the facts of what may happen, not only interpret and explain what is likely, but also try to respond practically to anticipated problems and so seek directly to influence, to alter, to shape now what will happen later.

Thus, paradoxically, an influential planning or policy report might anticipate a transportation problem and prevent the problem from ever occurring. Notice that this can make success quite difficult to show: How does one measure something that never happened? Showing what a project or policy does (housing units or inoculations or jobs provided or regulated) can be difficult enough; showing a (nonexistent?) problem that has been averted is far more difficult. The planning analyst needs to be as interested in what should not be as in what should be, in what will never exist as in what does or will exist. For the analyst, the anticipated world, including potential problems to be prevented, is every bit as real as the existing, observable world—even though, if the analyst succeeds, this potentially problematic world might never exist! No wonder these professions have been difficult to define: They are as much about preventing worlds as they are about creating them—but what has been prevented does not exist, cannot be observed, is difficult to measure, and is perhaps still more difficult to appreciate!

The planning or policy analyst's work, nevertheless, may affect proposals by refining them before decisions are taken, influencing the decisions about them, or affecting the conditions ("mitigation measures," "contingent contracts," and so forth) that may attach to implementation. The analyst must respond to the problems he or she can envision were the project at hand to be implemented. This work of anticipating problems—envisioning hypothetical futures and responding by fashioning desirable ones—is interventionist through and through.

Such analysis is far from conventionally technical or rule-bound; it appears instead to involve an intimate mixture of descriptive and normative elements. Yes, problem formulation was always understood to be a value-laden, selectively descriptive activity, but now we are in a position to understand that problem formulation is not just arbitrarily, but rather systematically, normative. Analysts' anticipation of implementation and response requires that a definite series of normative choices be made. In addition, as we shall see, the work of planning and policy analysis is inescapably (and influentially) theoretical—for without a range of substantive theories, the analyst could never (1) envision future implementation situations and their consequences, (2) prepare and manage the arguments exploring implementation alternatives, or (3) present either a cogent analysis of several alternatives or a recommendation specifying "what ought to be done."

Consider now, briefly, the theoretical competence that the planning analyst in our case must have in order to envision and shape the future as he listens to the developer and engineer present their plans (Bolan, 1980). He works from experience, to be sure, but from the experience of what? How does he learn from that experience and draw implications prospectively about this particular project? Facing a new and arguably unique situation, the analyst must use the rough theories he has. Three types of theories come into play: behavioral or functional, normative, and moral-cultural. Consider each in turn.

Behavioral theorizing. Imagining the site in question, the analyst sees that drainage has been adequate, that the amount of paving on the site will not expand, and that the building footprint will shrink. Without further changes, he infers, the existing drainage system should work and present no new problems. The road system in the surrounding area is already overstressed. The projection of 500,000 square feet of office space translates silently into numbers of likely employees and then numbers of trips-to-work generated daily. The planning analyst easily predicts aggravated traffic congestion, and so he moves directly to call for a "full-blown" traffic impact study.

To envision such functional problems at the site, then, the analyst relies in this meeting on relatively simple physical and behavioral theories: A change in paving will change drainage requirements; an increase in office space will generate jobs that will in turn generate traffic in the immediate vicinity (whether the increase in jobs is "net" to the region or not). Further studies can explore and begin to specify these problems, and then suggest solutions or mitigation measures; but first the planner needs basic behavioral theories—if only "rules of thumb"—to begin to envision and imagine the "problems" that will need further attention.

Normative theorizing. Yet the analyst's basic behavioral theories only help when they are joined with the normative political theories that he brings to bear on the case. In this meeting he interprets and formulates a whole series of requirements, obligations, and needs that he asks the developer to respect: The planning board may waive a procedural requirement, but they may not consider it proper to review the full proposal before considering the evaluations of other city departments; the applicant should "talk to anyone who has jurisdiction beforehand"; the developer is encouraged to review the study of the regional planning association; he is assured that the air quality study done for the state will be good enough for the city—and so forth. Here the planning analyst uses elements of practical normative theory: He recognizes discretion, not just the "letter" of the regulations; he points to the normative, not just functional, interdependence of the planning board and the city departments, and he thus invokes the legitimacy of the departments' reviews; furthermore, he invokes the legitimate authority of "anyone who has jurisdiction" and encourages the developer to seek them out early, or risk surprise—the normative arguments we call "opposition"—and subsequent delays; he appeals to the legitimacy of the regional planning association's concerns, without making an argument to take those concerns seriously.

The analyst's normative political theorizing here is also conspicuous for what it lacks: He makes no mention of a broader public, or of active citizens' groups concerned with regional growth, or of the strongly progrowth attitudes of the planning board itself. Given those latter attitudes, the analyst's silence on this point reflects part of a deliberate political strategy to push the project toward as much analysis of potential impacts as possible in the hope that other actors' arguments for mitigation measures might then arise—for lacking that, the planning board might just pass the project along with its blessing, leaving future city residents to pay for its neglect. The analyst's silence about the decision-makers' real attitudes, then, reflects a normative political theory and a series of calculated judgments about (1) the limited power and lack of legitimacy of certain official bodies and (2) the proper ethical and professional role of a planning analyst (Tong, 1987).

The point here is neither that the analyst is right to make these judgments in this case nor that his performance here is exemplary. Rather, the point is that such normative judgments, and more fundamental normative political theories, are necessary to planning and policy analysis practice at the level of detail, not simply at the level of broad generalities and homilies pledging allegiance or resistance to democratic capitalist regimes.

The still stronger point to be made is this: In the existing literature discussing planning and policy analysis, little seems to be known about the day-to-day work of analysts, and still less seems to be known about (1) the variety of normative judgments they must perpetually make, (2) the normative political theories of all sorts they employ to make and defend such judgments, (3) the ways that such judgments might be rationally criticized and refined, and (4) the ways that such normative theories might also be criticized and improved (Bernstein, 1983; Fischer, 1985; Johnson & Blair, 1985). Can practitioners, researchers, teachers, and students afford to continue to ignore these questions, pay them lip-service as barely discussable "value-judgments," and suppose that in the thoroughly evaluative professions of planning and policy analysis the work of valuation must then be either strictly utilitarian or irrational?

The simple case discussed here suffices to show both (1) that analysts need normative theories to make the judgments necessary to do their work, and (2) that those judgments are poorly rendered as utilitarian ones. The planning analyst in our example makes arguments and gives reasons; only in a trivial sense is he calculating benefits and costs and reporting the results.

Cultural theorizing.   In addition, the analyst in our case brings to bear practical cultural theories that he has tacitly developed in the course of building and maintaining working relationships with many others over the years. He knows that Joe Hart at the public works department is someone who will want to be consulted early on. He knows that Jeanne Wall of the regional planning body hopes to be helpful in such cases. He knows that different participants in the planning process have different values and concerns: The developer may be interested in trading design improvements for assurances of speedy review; the majority of the planning board may only be interested in "growth," and so forth.

The analyst's cultural theories that come into play here focus attention upon the webs of local political culture and morality in which the planner operates; these are working theories of political culture and morality writ small, not large. The analyst's practical theorizing here concerns particular people's personal identity and reputations, their concerns, interests, sensitivities, quirks, biases—any special characteristics of people (for example, having fought past turf battles) with whom the developer and analyst alike might work. Will last year's planning board scandal lead anyone to be more conscientious this year? Will Peabody push for more information when Tuttle wants simply to approve the works—or will Peabody just shrug and defer again? Practical cultural and moral theories allow analysts not just to fantasize but to imagine ahead of time what it might be like to work with particular people in a wide range of possible situations.

In every meeting that a planning or policy analyst has with others, such practical theories of identity, of culture and morality, come into play as the analyst makes judgments about the likely candor, duplicity, support, reliability, cooperation, opposition, interests, or commitments of other participants in the planning or policy-making process. Is it even possible to work with others and not have such questions arise? Planning analysts, then, need to gauge not only (1) behavioral consequences of possible courses of action and (2) the normative mandates and procedures shaping possible alternatives, but also (3) the realistic character and identity of other participants in the planning and policy process.

Consider, then, the lessons to be derived about "problem-formulation" from this case. What do analysts initially require to do their work before writing their reports—to anticipate and respond to the range of practical futures that can be envisioned? First, to envision consequences, analysts need behavioral theories. Second, to envision mandates, procedures, obligations, and their own legitimate roles, analysts need normative political theories. And third, to envision the character of those they must listen to, watch out for, and build durable working relationships with, analysts need cultural and moral theories of their institutional worlds.

Let us turn now to the second requirement of anticipatory analysis. After envisioning potential futures, analysts must prepare and manage arguments strategically.

Managing Argument Strategically

Notice that as the analyst brings these three types of working theories into play, the analysis is just beginning. How are these practical theories to be built upon? How may analysts work to prepare the initially embryonic analysis, to explore the substantive grounds for the arguments to be made, and to manage the process of analysis and review?

These questions about the preparatory or management aspects of analysis have unfortunately been widely neglected. Two common academic views of analysis distract attention from what analysts actually do. Analysis has been considered either as a purely cognitive, problem-solving activity, or as one of structured social interaction (Lindblom & Cohen, 1979). The problem-solving view of analysis essentially reduces the practice of analysts to mental processes such as calculation (and guesswork); the interactionist view focuses upon processes such as voting or market exchange, thus ironically finessing the question of an individual analyst's practice altogether (cf. Wildavsky, 1979).

Yet insightful alternatives stand out. Peter Szanton's *Not Well Advised* (1981), for example, neglects political and normative questions that haunt policy analysis, but it shows the essential significance of the analyst's relationships to others with whom he or she must work. Analyses must not only be thought, they must be argued. Then, as practical arguments, they must be managed in the form of strategies as well.

Notice how much the transcript shows us about what the planning analyst does. He asks, suggests, explains, checks, agrees, refers, warns, and promises. His words matter. Failing to respond, or responding inconsistently or too brusquely, he might be held responsible later—say, if the developer adds one such complaint to others in front of the planning board or the city council. So the analyst chooses his words carefully. He seeks to be clear, responsive, but also at other times not altogether clear—for very specific reasons, as we shall see. He does not want to be held to predictions (for example, about timing) whose validity he cannot assure; he wants to promise cooperation, but also to be professionally critical without being (overly) threatening. Thus, in speaking, the analyst is acting. His actions are "speech acts," actions that are not only purposive, but more practically communicative, conveying meaning and shaping expectations as well (Forester, 1982, 1985).

The analyst manages practical arguments in several ways. He directs attention to issues ("Is this the principal access?" "Show the existing and proposed buildings"). He also manages the developer's perception of the review process: He makes an argument providing potential roles for representatives of the state, other planning bodies, local agencies and departments, and neighboring developers. The analyst manages arguments not only about participation but also about the timing and sequence of the process. He recommends early reviews by other city departments, and he backs up that recommendation with the conjecture that the planning board will not move ahead until such reviews are completed. He suggests a process for the review, for the development of the project itself ("so you can incorporate comments"), and for the analysis that will follow. He suggests not only the joint review, but a series of consultations—with Joe Hart, with Jeanne Wall, perhaps with a representative of the neighboring shopping center, too. The analyst offers to provide an example of a fiscal impact analysis; he suggests, in effect, that the developer do the analysis (even if it is "recommended," not "required") rather than risk delay later should someone become concerned about the possible fiscal consequences of the project for the city. Here the analyst faces and even creates uncertainty: Is the risk of delay sufficient to induce the developer to submit an analysis for public scrutiny? The analyst manages arguments that direct attention to issues, shape participation and involvement by affected parties, gauge the timing of the process, and fit this project into the larger context of local and regional development.

Actions fit together into arguments. Arguments fit together—are managed—into larger pieces we can call "strategies." In this case the analyst's strategy in part is to involve other established bodies and focus their analytical attention upon this proposal before the planning board ever sees it. That strategy consists of a set of related arguments: Check with the regional planners because they might help you do the impact analysis; check with Joe Hart because he is central to the process; traffic's a real problem here, so do a full-blown impact study of it; and so forth. Perhaps, this analyst hopes, if other established city departments raise concerns about potential project impacts, the planning board might (have to) listen—something their pro-growth sentiments would likely prevent were just the lone analyst to raise exactly the same concerns. Managing argument strategically here, then, the analyst seeks to enhance his own limited influence—and resist the planning board's pro-growth ideology as well.

Recall now the developer's move that surprised the planner: "Well, we'd like to submit the plans next week." The planner's strategy in the meeting had been designed, of course, precisely to forestall such a quick submission that might push the project through. Three months later, it turned out, the developer had not yet submitted the plans; he was preparing the documents required by the public review process. "In another month or so," he then told the author, "we'll file."

To assess and study analysts' strategies of working on project or policy proposals, then, we must study the arguments they fashion in practice. This means, of course, studying not simply the content of their arguments, what they claim, but the pragmatic force of their arguing, how they make persuasive arguments in real time. Studying arguments practically, in turn, will mean studying actions, the communicative actions of analysts in practice (Forester, 1989). Understanding that actions may add up to arguments and that arguments can be managed as strategies should make vitally clear that "the social construction of policy and planning problems" is not simply a matter of academic sociological interest. This social or communicative construction of problems is deeply political, for it is necessarily selective, allocating attention and concern to some issues but not others, shaping the agendas of consideration (and participation) for a range of actors and decision makers alike.

So analysts must both argue and manage. Without an argument to consider, we have process without content. Without a strategically managed process, the most lucid and insightful analysis may be altogether ignored, produced too late to be useful, or manipulated for extraneous ends. Planning and policy analysts thus must learn not only to explore substantive issues but also to strategically and ethically manage the process of analysis and public scrutiny.

CONCLUSION

This analysis began as an attempt to explore a hunch about the anticipatory character of planning analysis. That exploration led both to a set of findings that can be summarized here—and to a surprise: the realization that so much of what planners do involves preventing worlds from coming into being, work whose success will not be visible, work whose appreciation may suffer as a result. I have continued to explore this hunch in related essays and in a collaborative book with Norman Krumholz (Krumholz & Forester, 1990). Let us review, then, the results about planning practice that we have put forward for further study.

First, the work of the analyst is not simply to solve "the problem" at hand but also to formulate initially just what "the problem" (traffic? scale?) might be.

Second, the analyst wishes not just to formulate the problem but also to intervene to meet it ahead of time: to anticipate implementation and so respond to the particular opportunities and problems presented—by involving other city departments, for example.

Third, this work of anticipation has a logical structure. If analysts are to anticipate implemented projects or policy outcomes and seek to shape them, they must do several things. They must envision the functional, normative, and cultural worlds in which proposed projects or policies will have meaning. They must then prepare and manage the arguments, and the process of argumentation, available to consider potential outcomes. In this process, analysts must then devise arguments as technicians just as they simultaneously manage those arguments strategically as political organizers. Analysts may then present their analyses to decision makers.

Fourth, to anticipate project alternatives, analysts must make a wide variety of normative judgments—ranging from their interpretations of mandates, rules, regulations, and procedures to their strategic choices about information or arguments to offer or to withhold.

Fifth, and finally, to understand planning and policy analysis as deeply anticipatory encourages further research clarifying how skilled practitioners' actions can fit together into arguments, and how those arguments can in turn fit together into normative strategies of effective planning and policy analysis.

ACKNOWLEDGMENTS

I would like to thank Simon Neustein, Frank Fischer, Rick Taintor, Larry Susskind, Aaron Fleischer, Alan Mandell, and Davydd Greenwood for their comments. This essay is adapted from an earlier work (Forester, 1987). Note that because all the participants in the meeting considered were men, the masculine pronoun is used frequently throughout this chapter.

REFERENCES

Alterman, R., & MacRae, D., Jr. (1983). Planning and policy analysis. *Journal of the American Planning Association, 49,* 200–215.

Bernstein, R. J. (1983). *Beyond objectivism and relativism.* Philadelphia: University of Pennsylvania Press.

Bolan, R. (1980). The practitioner as theorist: The phenomonology of the professional episode. *Journal of the American Planning Association, 46,* 261–274.

Fischer, F. (1985). Critical evaluation of public policy: A methodological case study. In J. Forester (Ed.), *Critical theory and public life* (pp. 231–257). Cambridge, MA: MIT Press.

Forester, J. (1982, summer). Toward a critical empirical framework for the analysis of public policy. *New Political Science,* pp. 33–61.

Forester, J. (1985). The policy analysis-critical theory affair: Wildavsky and Habermas as bedfellows? In J. Forester (Ed.), *Critical theory and public life* (pp. 258–280). Cambridge, MA: MIT Press.

Forester, J. (1987). Anticipating implementation: Normative practices in planning and policy analysis. In F. Fischer & J. Forester (Eds.), *Confronting values in policy analysis: The politics of criteria* (pp. 153–173). Beverly Hills: Sage.

Forester, J. (1989). *Planning in the face of power.* Berkeley: University of California Press.

Fowler, H. W. (1965). *A dictionary of modern English usage* (2nd ed.). New York: Oxford University Press.

Johnson, R. H., & Blair, J. A. (1985). Informal logic: The past five years, 1978–1983. *American Philosophical Quarterly, 22*(3), 181–196.

Krumholz, N., & Forester, J. (1990). *Making equity planning work: Leadership in the public sector.* Philadelphia: Temple University Press.

Lindblom, C., & Cohen, D. (1979). *Usable knowledge,* New Haven, CT: Yale University Press.

Seeley, J. (1963). Social science: Some probative problems. In M. Stein & A. Vidich (Eds.), *Sociology on trial* (pp. 53–65). Englewood Cliffs, NJ: Prentice-Hall.

Szanton, P. (1981). *Not well advised.* New York: Russel Sage.

Tong, R. (1987). Ethics and the policy analyst: The problem of responsibility. In F. Fischer & J. Forester (Eds.), *Confronting values in policy analysis: The politics of criteria* (pp. 192–211). Beverly Hills: Sage.

Wildavsky, A. (1979). *Speaking truth to power.* Boston: Little, Brown.

10

The Assessment of Hearing-Impaired Children

MALCOLM PARLETT

"I CAN'T GIVE you a list—you look at a child and see his needs," reports a head teacher impatiently, having been quizzed for some minutes about how precisely he goes about identifying the special educational needs of the children for whom he is responsible. Another teacher backs him up: "Based on 25 years of teaching experience, I know what these kids are like." In these and other encounters, my colleague Keith Pocklington and I have come up against a significant phenomenon: Not only are professional practitioners often inarticulate about their practice, but they also display some reluctance even to make the attempt to say what it is they do and how they do it.

Those who examine how skilled practitioners work are well aware of the difficulty people have in making their "tacit knowledge," as Polanyi (1967) calls it, manifest. Everyday professional practice includes much that has been overlearned, skills and perceptual judgments that have become habitual, and procedures that have been totally integrated into people's "automatic" repertoires. Asking somebody to pay attention to these, by now, commonplace phenomena can easily appear intrusive: The inquiry may be seen as unnecessary or uninteresting. If, instead, one were to ask somebody to discuss, say, a newly introduced procedure, or a new item of equipment delivered, such an inquiry would be understood and the practitioner would probably welcome the invitation to talk.

Keith Pocklington and I were conducting the interviews mentioned above at a point several years into a research program in Britain. Hitherto we had been mainly gathering reactions toward certain new developments in the education and management of children with sensory impairments: We had, in other words, been dealing with "news." We

213

had been consistently pleased with the articulate, thoughtful, and lively interviews we had held; often it was very difficult to terminate discussions, so keen were teachers and others to voice their opinions. Now we were intentionally moving into an area of investigation that was less a matter of opinion and more a matter of what people actually did; we were looking at some of the very ordinary and very unnewsworthy aspects of daily professional practice. This was when we noted a shift—not with everybody, but certainly with some—toward a more resistant stance. And yet, as will become clear in the following account, there was a strong case for examining the details of practice, for opening up to closer inspection certain features of the everyday world of practice. In this we were attempting to render the taken-for-granted once again newsworthy, to raise critical consciousness with a view toward practical improvements.

The focus of my account is on professional practice related to the education of children with impaired hearing. The professional groups in question include teachers with specialist skills in teaching this category of pupils, medical and audiological staff, psychologists, speech therapists, social workers, and officials in the local education authorities. This is not an exhaustive list.

Even more significantly, I shall be examining two tasks, or functions, performed by this group. They are closely linked. The primary activity is in Britain called "assessment" (in the United States it might be called "evaluation"), wherein professionals examine a child and come to certain conclusions about him or her. The second, adjunct activity occurs when the professionals engage in "educational placement"—deciding what kind of educational setting is most suitable for the child who has been assessed (for instance, in an ordinary school with an itinerant support teacher or in a special unit, or perhaps in a school for the deaf or partially hearing).

What I shall be discussing, therefore, is a common variety of multidimensional and multiprofessional review process. Although this chapter concentrates on children with special needs, similar reviews of children are common throughout education and indeed throughout the helping professions for both children and adults. The account may be considered as an exercise in reflecting on practice with a view toward heightening the professional awareness of educational, medical, and other relevant personnel.

Although we originally began our investigation from a research stance broadly aiming for impartial description, rather than taking an explicitly political, normative, or overtly critical stance, there was a discernible shift in our outlook as the work progressed. The ideal of an entirely neutral observer is obviously false. At the same time, there is an honorable tradition in most spheres of organized knowledge that encourages objectivity, straightforward description, and the "bracketing off" (to use a term from phenomenology) of the preconceptions and assumptions of the writer/investigator. Such was the starting-off point for the work contained in the case study that follows. The change referred to was that in the course of the study we became somewhat more "normative" and critical, concerned with the lack of attention given to procedures that had major implications for the future lives of an underprivileged group, and at times angered by the seeming lack of concern for critical self-examination of the kind we came to realize was necessary if practices were to be improved.

THE ASSESSMENTS

The following assessment (spoken not written in this instance) is an example of how a dense summary of impressions is put together to depict an individual child, whom we shall call Jane. Jane, who was 7 years old, was described by a senior teacher of the deaf in the following way:

> A canny little child, a pleasant bairn, far too reserved, inwardly enjoying things, a complete introvert with adults but less with other children. . . . She tends to play, read, on her own, she works hard. . . . In one-to-one situations, I feel she is working to potential, but we cannot whip up any drive.

Some assessments are extremely brief, yet—like the one above—they appear to "sum up" the boy or girl being assessed. Thus a specialist teacher of the deaf depicted one child in a few words: "a bright girl who happens to be deaf." Another teacher encapsulated a boy in this way:

> He's got concentration, willingness, application, but on the other hand, he has a very limited background, a lack of experience of anything wider. . . . You cannot talk to him about anything outside his normal experience.

Some of these summary descriptions refer to the present, attempting to report the state of play at the time they are formulated; such as this statement by a teacher of the deaf:

His language is normal, he's a bit slow, he's got quite a bit of hearing, he makes the odd mistake, his social development is normal.

Others refer to why past decisions were taken, such as this comment by a teacher in charge of a partially hearing unit:

Academically speaking, he could have been transferred to an ordinary school but this would mean that he would not get home support as there is a marital breakup. In order that he not be deprived of the constant daily attention of a stable person, he was retained in the unit.

Such summary pictures of children—occurring frequently throughout the educational world—are built from components that, in these cases, range from medical information and audiometric data of a "scientific" and supposedly incontrovertible kind, all the way through to descriptive and personal remarks at the least technical and more ambiguous end of the continuum. These are typical assessments, even if more vividly expressed than some. Brief statements are woven together to build an overall impression. The assessor is selecting certain items and excluding others. How is the choice of "elements" in the assessment made? What is going on in the practitioner's mind when choosing what to report? These are starting points for the inquiry here.

CONSTRUCTING THE ASSESSMENT

Professionals, in formulating an assessment of a child, appear to make two types of choices. First, elements are selected to make the child differentiable. Second, the wording of constituent statements is affected by the context of the assessment; for example, for whom it is intended, for what purpose, with what set of implied understandings between the parties involved. These two processes, *differentiation* and *sensitivity to context*, are closely related but will be examined separately.

A child is observed performing a task or test; case records, reports, and selections of classwork are scanned; parents, teachers, or others are questioned. The assessor is confronted with a mass of potentially relevant information and some ordering is called for: He or she cannot report every single detail, even in a lengthy case report.

Selections are based on what stands out about the child being assessed. Some items are judged "newsworthy," others not. The professional searches for order among the myriad details of the child's case by noting the newsworthy. The process is akin to everyday thinking, although here it is more formalized.

To take a trivial example, the table at which I am writing is circular, made of wood, and has a central pedestal. The top has a diameter of 3.5 feet. The characteristics commented on help differentiate this table from others. I have not remarked upon its surface being flat and smooth or its being at the ordinary height of a writing table; in this crude depiction of the table, these do not serve to differentiate this table from others— they apply to too many. Similarly, the elements in an assessment are chosen to render the child distinctive.

Of course, in order to select the appropriate elements, the assessor draws upon a lot of background knowledge (of the experiential, tacit kind). In choosing "table elements" for my description, I draw upon my knowledge of tables in general and what confusions might arise if certain items are left out.

There exist for children with hearing defects numerous categorizations, some within official terminology (for example, "middle-ear deafness") and some much more unofficial (for example, "partial deafness"). Some are shared nationally or internationally among the relevant specialists, others have local meaning only. The process of differentiation involves detailing not only how the child is different from but also how he or she is similar to others within a general category.

I am drawing attention to how differentiation occurs, realizing that a case can be made that it is an unorganized procedure. Attempts have been made to promote systematic checklist procedures, so that capricious or overspecific assessment elements can be avoided. With standardized, comprehensive checklists, the categories of comment are supplied and, in theory, full coverage is approached. Yet we found, when checklists were introduced, that busy specialists tended to rush through the "inapplicable" characteristics, giving the barest response possible, slowing down only to add comments under the category they felt was important in the particular instance. So there was not a lot of difference in the final result. Report forms try to order professional behavior and are frequently resented. If noting what is special is intrinsic to the assessment process, standardization of the procedure may not be an improvement.

Differentiation is to be expected, given that assessments contribute to decision making. "Is the child suitable for school X?" requires weighing up this child's suitability against some kind of implicit norm. Indeed, on becoming aware that there may be embedded comparisons, one soon realizes that assessments are riddled with them. In both medical and educational spheres, the implied standard is normal development. Medical reports, in particular, concentrate on discrepancies or departures from this standard. Take, for example, an ear, nose, and throat surgeon's assessment of Peter, age 3:

> Slow talking, parents complained of deafness. Supernumerary thumb removed from right hand. Right pinna is smaller than left. Query child post-mature one month. Query low-tone deafness of congenital origin or due to catarrhal condition, etc.

Clearly, what are commented upon are departures from "normality," along with speculations as to causes: Normal features are not thought necessary to note.

Comparisons are not always made with an external referent (for example, the "healthy child") in mind: The child may be compared at one point with how he or she was at another time or with other children in the same setting, or the child will be depicted in terms of how he or she responds to one classroom setting compared to another.

Comparisons are also often related to stage of development. Indeed, being "ahead" or "behind" of an hypothetical standard is a common differentiator. We encountered many assessments of this kind: "Slower than children of 9 and a half"; "Very immature . . . tends to need a tremendous amount of attention . . . needs prodding"; "Although his progress is behind the other children, it is parallel."

The "ideal child" is a particularly potent standard against which to compare children—ideal, of course, as seen by the person making the assessment. Understandably, children regarded as "high achievers," "confident," or "cheerful" are often spoken of warmly: They correspond to many teachers' notions of the ideal child. Other children are compared to them, often unfavorably, and—again—usually by implication only. A teacher of the deaf, for example, described a 7-year-old girl attending a unit for the partially hearing as follows:

> Not making good use of her residual hearing. . . . Does tend to give up early . . . doesn't like it when she's wrong . . . needs a lot of encouragement . . . you have to be very careful how you correct her . . . lacks confidence. . . . She's not willing to try new things.

Although the elements here are presented as merely features observed and noted, there are implied comparisons throughout. Take the statement: "tend(s) to give up early"—early compared to whom? Or "needs a lot of encouragement"—what kind of child does not need encouragement? Or "you have to be very careful how you correct her"—how much more careful does one have to be than with other children, and, specifically, which other children, anyway? The answers are not clear. One senses the presence of a contrasting case in the teacher's imagination: a child who does not give up easily, does not need encouragement, and with whom the teacher can be relaxed at times when she needs to correct the child. In other words, the confident, cheerful, high-achiever types mentioned above are present as some kind of model or point of reference, but without acknowledgment, or perhaps even awareness, that this is being done.

To keep the above remarks in perspective, let us remember that most practitioners are skillful: Inevitably and properly, they draw upon extensive experience to make the distinctions and shadings of meaning that add the subtlety and precision, as well as the vividness, to their appraisals of children. Also, to introduce lengthy histories that assemble information and comments on symptoms, behavior, circumstances, history, and prognoses in a less selective fashion, while perhaps desirable in principle, are not welcome in practice: Most receiving assessments want to grasp quickly the essential nature of the child under consideration and—in order to come to decisions—prefer that professionals report in summary form. There is usually insufficient time to reflect upon each case in great detail.

In addition, professionals are usually confronted with complex, ambiguous, or incomplete data. Inevitably, a sense of uncertainty is engendered. Both for the professional's peace of mind, and to meet the demand for a clear summary, there is an attempt to reduce ambiguity. An obvious way to do this is to place the child in a context of meaning, to make the case coherent. To do so, professional workers draw upon their acquaintance with other children to provide a basis for comparison. There are implicit references to other children, and there are less obvious contrasts, as shown above, when the child is compared to certain shadowy background images.

THE DANGERS IN DIFFERENTIATING

So far I have concentrated on aspects of assessment that are routine and basically benign. However, there are obvious dangers of these components of practice becoming distorted or exaggerated in ways that make a mockery of the whole procedure.

First, differentiation. Producing an assessment is clearly not a mere technical recording of a child's characteristics. As noted above, features of the child are singled out, given weight, judged to be suitable for inclusion. Active involvement of the assessor is inevitable, and one can see how the process may go too far, with too great an interpretive influence and too little documenting of actual observations.

Projection

The personal quality of what we notice is, of course, powerfully demonstrated in various projective tests devised by psychologists—for example, when we are invited to report what we "see" in the Rorschach inkblot. The rationale of these tests is that people reveal their preoccupations in how they react to supposedly neutral inputs. Projection is not, however, merely a psychological condition with morbid overtones; it is, in a more general sense, a process in which we all engage most of the time. Since we all have different tacit knowledge, different formative experiences, and different outlooks and values, it is hardly surprising that we interpret what we see (or hear) in ways that are different, sometimes strikingly so, from how others do.

We can say that it is not only beauty that lies in the eyes of the beholder, but also conscientiousness, laziness, liveliness, deprivation, naughtiness, passivity, and so forth (all of which are featured in the kinds of assessment looked at here). These amount to being personal constructions (Kelly, 1955) used to organized selectively the perceptions of information taken in.

Projection of this kind is thus normal, indeed, inevitable. Where the process can get out of hand is when these constructs act as filters, so that certain definitions and attributions are introduced that are almost solely a product of the assessor's personal way of looking at the world. Thus a very orderly individual who tends to feel uneasy in the presence of disorder is more likely to notice—and perhaps to feel strongly about—individuals who appear to him or her to be untidy or disorderly. Other professionals, lacking this particular preoccupation, might not comment at all on the child's disorderly habits; they simply would not judge them to be sufficiently noteworthy—they might not even "notice" them.

Examining what people said in their assessments suggests, in a number of instances, that professional workers sometimes actively disliked or disapproved of some of the children they were assessing, just as they seemed heartily to approve of others. There is no evidence to suggest that they were consciously or deliberately trying to introduce positive or negative bias; they were simply reflecting what they discerned or had concluded about a child.

Here is an extract from the report of a peripatetic teacher (a teacher who regularly visits different local schools) on a 6-year-old girl, Laura:

> An extremely pleasant child who readily cooperates. . . . Eagerly watches for speech and any new skills which she quickly grasps. She makes a good attempt to copy sounds of speech. . . . Mixes freely with the other children, talking with them and integrating well. . . . Keenly interested in the spoken word . . . continually asking questions and showing a lively interest in everything around her. . . . Can concentrate for quite long periods.

Whatever characteristics Laura has, one inevitably is drawn to the conclusion that the teacher's own personal feelings toward Laura are very positive. Equally, the opposite seems to be the case in a teacher's report on an 11-year-old boy:

> David is not a likable boy. He is obviously very intelligent and with his nature it can make him very sly. He is often disruptive in class and a nuisance. He is really his own worst enemy. . . . [He] can be very cruel.

I do not wish to say that all strong reactions to children are products of assessors' irrational personal reactions. But assessments do seem to differ in how much they are value-laden and vividly impressionistic, as opposed to being articulated in a more moderated style, factual and, supposedly, value-free. An example of a more neutral-sounding kind of assessment is the following report from a psychologist:

> Danny is a child whose level of ability is probably within the dull/normal range. . . . [He] seems intellectually to be functioning like that of a child of 6–7 years. [Danny was in fact almost 9.] He clearly has a very limited input and output of language because of hearing loss. Danny seems to have some difficulties with visual memory (only functions at 5-year level), and it may be that this contributes to some of his educational difficulties. . . . All this adds up to a child with substantial learning difficulties which may be very difficult to meet adequately.

The dividing line between "healthy" and "unhealthy" degrees of interpretation is impossible to define exactly. Readers will draw their own interpretation of how value-free the remarks about Danny are—and whether true neutrality is indeed possible.

Stereotyping

A variant of projection is stereotyping. This occurs when an assessor projects onto the child a number of features or qualities that he or she associates with a type—the type or grouping under which the child is subsumed. Stereotyping, of course, is the foundation of prejudice and stigmatization.

Racism, sexism, and prejudices about age and social class are well known, both for their prevalence and effects. Not surprisingly, they sometimes appear in assessments as well as in informal discussions among professionals. In our study we noted references, for instance, to a child having "mixed parentage" or coming from "a poor home" when such information seemed very tangential indeed to the discussion in hand.

However, more prevalent is a more subtle form of stereotyping. Making a child differentiable—in the sense earlier discussed—can easily turn into mere tagging, typing, or labeling of the child, with evidence contrary to the chosen type being underplayed or overlooked. Every time a child is categorized (for example, as "difficult to reach") there is a natural tendency thereafter for the label to dictate what is perceived and reported. The categories themselves become fixed ways of conceptualizing that are applied unthinkingly.

Donald Schön (1963) has described the ways in which categories are used to examine "things" but are not themselves examined as ways of thinking—they have become fixed and stay fixed:

> In the ordinary process of applying concepts to things no new concepts emerge. When we identify something as an instance of the concept . . . we simply order experienced things in terms of it. . . . A girl says to a boy, "I know your type," and she has him typed. Her perception of him has changed but not her category. In the ordinary application of concepts to things the concepts leave the process as they come in. (p. 28)

By a similar process, the conceptual range of a group of professionals can progressively rigidify. Types get set, and experimental generalizations in local circulation are reiterated to the point where they are no longer examined afresh. "Typical" deaf children come to be thought of as having standard reactions. "All hearing-impaired children," stated one teacher of the deaf, "can switch off, more so than a normal child." A head of service remarked of one boy: "He is very deaf-oriented . . . deadpan, dead-passive." A head teacher commented on another child:

"He has a surprising command of written idiomatic language considering he's so deaf." Notions of what it means to be deaf, to "have a deaf
attitude," to have a "deaf voice" to be one of the "normal deaf," even
among the most knowledgeable specialists, seem to become almost
fixed categories or divisions. Any child who comes, then, to be labeled
a "typical deaf child" by one professional is likely to be a recipient of a
number of other attributions through simple association.

SENSITIVITY TO CONTEXT

Assessments are produced within an organizational framework.
They contribute to decision making; or they are written for a file that
will be read by other professionals who have (or will have) responsibility
for the child's education or medical/audiological care; or they form the
basis for reports to go to a review committee, to parents, or to other
local education authorities if the child's family is moving. In short, there
is a purpose for assessments and also an audience addressed, think-
ingly or not.

Assessors act under constraints related to expectations embedded
in their job definition. For instance, they are not generally expected to
comment on the child in areas beyond their expertise (and if they do,
they are sometimes resented for doing so). Moreover, the language they
use—how much they resort to jargon or to a layperson's translation—
is chosen with the audience in mind.

Here is part of a report on a 4-year-old child written by an audiologist in a hospital and sent to the divisional medical officer, with copies
to the child's family doctor and to the head of service in the local education authority:

> The audiogram . . . shows thresholds in the region 65 db across
> the speech frequencies. The difference between the two ears today
> is not of any significance, and bone conduction thresholds follow
> air conduction quite closely. It is very pleasing to see a young fel-
> low with this loss using so much speech and language, and he ap-
> pears to be making very good progress especially when I under-
> stand from his mother that some 2 or 3 years ago he was not
> saying a word.

Although there is more formal language here than in other assessments quoted, there are many elements chosen on grounds previously
discussed (for example, what is special about this boy?). Yet the point

here is that the audiologist's choice of elements is also heavily influenced by the terms of his commission: No terms are introduced that would be "beyond" the other professionals he is writing for.

In speaking to parents, the language of assessment is usually quite different. For instance, here is how one school medical officer explained to a parent that her daughter had more than a hearing loss: "There is a central factor involved here. . . . The sound is coming in but the brain can't make use of it."

To make sense or meaning of such assessments, one needs to know who has made them, for whom they are intended, and what expectations people have about what is an "appropriate" report from this individual. The specialist is influenced by a series of conventions about form, length, language, and focus, all of which may be taken for granted.

There is another component to being sensitive to the context. The assessment evokes certain associations in those hearing or reading the report. Just as creating an assessment draws upon the tacit knowledge of the assessor, so understanding it draws heavily upon similar knowledge on the part of the receiver. Especially when summary assessments are brief, as they often are, much is left to the reader or listener to complete—to fill in the details.

The notion of "filling in" is taken from the work of the sociologist Aaron Cicourel (1976). He has argued that in reports made by professionals (he examined the area of juvenile delinquency) a lot is left out, with reliance being placed on the report's readers to be able to supply interpretations that the report writer has in mind but does not spell out explicitly.

Again, this is an everyday aspect of discourse: There is no way a flow of communication can occur without much being taken for granted by both parties. If speakers had to spell out all the implications embedded in their speech, conventional communication would grind to a halt. What is of interest here is to realize how elements of a summary assessment convey, and are often meant to convey, additional meanings— more than those stated explicitly in the actual chosen words. This comment by a medical officer is but one of numerous possible examples:

> He's missed a lot of schooling. And there are problems at home.
> Mother is very ambivalent. He could not take any more rejection.
> His father has already rejected him.

This is a sketch of the child's overall position. There is very little in the account that is concrete or factual—yet it has a poignancy and persuasiveness that is hard either to question or to refute.

The assessor, sensitive to the context in which the report is produced and read, does not need to spell out every implication, elaborate on each nuance, and draw the conclusions for the reader/listener: That would often be superfluous and could be regarded as insulting—as if the professional were talking down to his or her colleagues. A shared professional culture and background knowledge presumes certain understandings; effort is saved and decisions are reached more rapidly using an effective shorthand.

THE DANGERS OF SENSITIVITY TO CONTEXT

Just as there are possible dangers in differentiating, to which I have alluded above, so there are possible dangers to sensitivity to context and evoking associations.

We have noticed how the assessor judges what is relevant and appropriate to include, as well as what linguistic form to use. The possibility exists that the assessor can become oversensitive to the context in which the assessment will be viewed or heard; it may become an attempt not to depict accurately but rather to bring influence to bear. Over time, assessors realize that certain information, if included, is likely to result in one decision, while other details may spur action in another direction.

Assessment in many areas of professional practice, including the area studied here, is closely allied with decision making. In this case, many of the decisions relate to what school a child should go to. Inevitably, this close association makes "adjustments" in the reporting more likely. There are many separate ways of arranging test data, observations, and conclusions in a report; and those presenting reports cannot fail to realize after years of experience what the implications are likely to be when couching the report in one form rather than another.

Here is a short extract from a medical officer's report on a 12-year-old boy at a committee meeting where placements were being decided:

[The mother] now feels very positively about residential school because she's finding it increasingly difficult to cope with him. He's already been in some trouble with the police. The marriage is still very bad. Grandmother has now gone to an old people's home, and this has helped a bit. The older brother is not attending school, and there is tension between the brothers. Mother finds it a strain. *Could we get him into a residential school as maladjusted?* [Emphasis added.]

The sting is in the last sentence. Is there a way, the medical officer is asking, that a "case can be made" for a particular course of action? He has, in fact, largely made that case by including in his remarks information that supports placement in a school for the maladjusted.

In similar fashion, a psychologist present wonders whether a different school (for the same boy) might not be preferable:

> Could he go to an ESN school because his achievement is so low, having missed so many years of schooling at junior level?

Again, the small slice of information introduced here provides the rationale, or legitimation, for an action proposed. (In the end, the case was referred elsewhere, on the grounds that "hearing [was] not the major factor" for this boy.)

Related, but distinguishable, are the problems for assessment when the process of evoking associations becomes magnified. The assessment does not merely evoke certain kinds of association in passing but is deliberately and specifically structured to conjure up associations in the minds of those receiving the assessment; it has become an attempt to persuade.

I noted earlier that when people hear or read a summary assessment, their own tacit knowledge and background thinking is stimulated: They fill in details not included in the report itself. If a great deal is left to the imagination of the reader or listener and innuendo and implication are manifestly built in, the likelihood is that persuasion is the goal. In the fuller statements made, on which I have concentrated so far, we came upon no instances of outright attempts to persuade. But there is a fine line, and some of the examples already quoted may be thought to fall near to persuasion.

With shorter comments, particularly those advanced in informal meetings between practitioners, the dangers are greater. In discussions between professionals, abbreviated, potent images abound. Examples of some of those heard in this study were as follows:

> "A walking hurricane"
> "A featherbedded child"
> "A bit clingy"
> "She soaked up language . . . ate it up"
> "This child is literally going to waste"
> "Effervescent"

Although such phrases were usually embedded in slightly more extended comments, these were the information-carrying words. Here one sees both the filling in and the evoking of associations carried to an extreme degree. There is almost complete reliance on the receiver's contributing the meaning. That so much is communicated (apparently) in these evocative one-liners is a measure of how "re-constructive" our thinking and perceiving can be.

ASSESSMENT AND DECISION MAKING IN A PROFESSIONAL GROUP

I have concentrated so far on the individual professional. In reality, at least in the field studied, assessments are rarely carried out in isolation. Instead, there is a collaborative review process in which opinions are exchanged, reports combined, and a composite picture painted. A likely potent influence on decisions is the power of group consensus and the suppression of individual differences. In general, professionals seemed unwilling to challenge what a colleague said. This may have been because professionals concentrated on particular features of a case (as befitted their specialties) and did not feel entitled to question the judgment of a different specialist. However, there also seemed to be no tradition of challenging assessments advanced; nor was there any requirement to present evidence to back up statements made. Even contradictory data, when included, seldom appeared to be recognized as such.

What was common, in fact, was a tendency for general images of children to become shared among a group of collaborating practitioners. In many cases, as described earlier, a child becomes either favorably or unfavorably regarded. "Halo effects" are further sustained when different professionals hear one another's opinions.

Sometimes, when there is a strong positive halo, contradictory or "negative" information may be alluded to but also discounted. Thus, with one boy, Robert, there were strongly positive feelings toward him on the part of his teachers, despite his severe difficulties. When Robert was almost 11, his specialist teacher noted that

> [his] speech is still very poor, but he's outgoing and will persist until he's understood. He has an insatiable curiosity. [Later the report goes on] Robert does not find numbers easy but works hard and consistently . . . his eagerness to learn is a great pleasure.

In Robert's case the general expectation is couched in optimistic terms. Contrast this with how another boy, Ian, is talked about by a teacher of the deaf:

We don't feel there is anything to build on or that there ever will
be. . . . If parents are not interested and involved in their child, we
don't expect very much.

Against such a background expectation about Ian, indicators contrary
to the unhopeful picture would, one suspects, have to be very pro-
nounced indeed to be "credited" to the child, so emphatic is the negative image.

During one clinic session observed, the cases of three individual
children, all from the same school for the deaf, were gone into in depth.
The head teacher was present, as were the school medicine officer and
the school nurse; individual teachers and parents were brought in for
parts of the discussions. Here are some of the statements made that (in
the observers' views) seemed most significant in defining an overall
view or image of each child.

First Child

> "She behaves like an ordinary hearing child—says 'what' and lis-
>   tens." (medical officer)
> "Emotionally she is not the right sort of child for a residential school
>   . . . not fair to her." (head teacher of special school)
> "I think she would rise to the challenge [of a special unit in an or-
>   dinary school]." (area school psychologist)
> "Pleasant, forthcoming, and she would fit in." (teacher)
> "I think she would need a fair whack of peripatetic help." (head
>   teacher)
> "She is mixing with normal children, she's got friends outside
>   school." (medical officer)

Second Child

> "We can contain him until summer." (head teacher)
> "We took him virtually off the scrap heap . . . an absolute cabbage
>   . . . we have more or less socialized the child." (head teacher)
> "The parents have no illusions." (head teacher)
> "Mother is very sensible about the handicap." (medical officer)
> "At his level . . . it's not important to have a teacher of the deaf."
>   (head teacher commenting on the fact that the child is severely
>   subnormal in addition to being deaf)

Third Child

> "He is kept as a baby." (head teacher)
> "He seems to be a very spoilt child." (teacher)

"Speech is not too bad [emphasis on *too*]. He responds well to sound. He's very deaf." (teacher)

"He can't concentrate . . . very poor academic progress . . . he's very poor all around . . . he sticks out in the class as a baby . . . he is never allowed to do anything on his own." (head teacher and teacher)

"I wouldn't say he's got a particular friend." (teacher)

What appeared to happen in the meeting, evident in the comments presented, was that those taking part thought aloud and, by stages, came up with a shared view of the case. Thus the first child is regarded favorably and is a candidate for integration; the second is viewed as severely handicapped, and there is a suggestion that he is being written off as a "hopeless case"; the third is regarded unfavorably, as immature and isolated.

The emergence of a single image or definition reduces complexity. There is a natural inclination on the part of decision makers to achieve clarity and closure. Given large caseloads, often complex and uncertain data, time pressures, and a wish not to vacillate, it is inevitable that professionals wish to eliminate confusing side issues and to highlight principal points. They naturally prefer, in their decision-making capacity, to work with edited accounts rather than uncondensed, richly textured descriptions. In one review meeting those involved were asked to present a "brief but comprehensive thumbnail sketch" in order to facilitate a more rapid discussion.

The inevitable reduction of complexity has led Cicourel (1976) to draw a connection between what happens in discussions of cases and what happens in the transmission of rumors. There is "leveling," with the material becoming "more concise and more easily grasped"; there is "sharpening," meaning that perceptions and reports are increasingly selective; and there is "assimilation," with reports becoming "more coherent" and "consistent with presuppositions." In these ways, Cicourel claims, a complex picture is whittled down to a simpler one, the out-of-character statements are reduced, and the general stereotyped image of a child is built up and then becomes *the* definition. In freezing the image, observational data—already multiply transformed—are set down and become part of the child's history and record. These in turn can become the currency of interchange between professionals, particularly over time and with changes of personnel. As a picture is built up, it gathers a momentum of accumulated opinion that becomes difficult to countermand, especially where there is little tradition of professionals' challenging one another's judgments.

PROFESSIONAL SELF-STUDY

In the present account I have examined what is included in an assessment; how reports are communicated to different audiences; what interpretations are made by those who receive them. I have also looked at how fixed images arise and how judgments or interpretations can govern ways in which a child is subsequently perceived.

In this section I consider briefly how practitioners might begin to study such phenomena for themselves.

Videorecording in particular provides a powerful medium for exploration. Suppose that it were possible to video a particular child in, say, a classroom setting or—if the whole process was not too threatening or difficult technically—to video a meeting between the child's parents and, say, the specialists involved in the case.

If videotapes of a particular child were viewed by a group of professional workers, it would be interesting (and revealing) for them to note:

1. Their professional views of the child and his or her condition, development, and potential
2. Their private and personal reactions to the child and family
3. Their perception of the child's educational needs
4. What kind of educational setting they would consider appropriate
5. What advice they would give the parents
6. How they would word a "thumbnail sketch" of the child
7. What they would be likely to include and leave out if the child came up for discussion at a case conference—based on their past experience of such meetings

It would be important that these perceptions and responses be recorded privately by each observer. Having done so, the next stage would be to compare notes.

Practitioners would rapidly have to come to terms with how many different points of view they represented as a group; how their personal reactions were often not shared by others; that discrepant data were often side-stepped or omitted; that professional attitudes differed markedly about what should be done in particular cases; and what advice should be given to parents.

Whether or not specific experiments or demonstrations are conducted along these lines, videorecordings of areas of practice can provide a focus for detailed, and probably lively, discussions. They permit observation of private events in a more public forum, and they are vivid and appealing. At the end of a discussion period in which respective outlooks on an observed case have been aired, the tape could be viewed again. Successive viewings of the same videotape could reveal more and more detail that had formerly been overlooked. Nothing would bring home more vividly how much assessment is based on creative projections and filling in, and how few actual data are required for the practitioner to assume he or she "knows" what a child is like.

A second domain of possible exploration relates to examination of case records. For instance, the accumulated case records of particular children (preferably unknown to those examining them) might be carefully scrutinized. Again, each researcher could record his or her overall impressions of the child or go through an extensive checklist of questions to be answered on the basis of the records. The likelihood is that practitioners:

1. Will end up with varying kinds of reactions to the child
2. Will be sensitized to the extent to which concrete evidence is available and drawn on for conclusions presented in the case report
3. Will be able to identify the predilections, points of view, and biases of the writers
4. Will be better able to assess the potential usefulness of different kinds of information.

More elaborate experiments are obviously possible. It would be particularly interesting, for instance, for a group of teachers and specialists to review a child's records before viewing a tape of the child either undergoing assessment or playing with other children. The twist could be that half of the group would read a case record written in a "negative" tone; the other half, a record that was full of "positive" remarks. What would be the differences between the viewings of the two groups? Almost inevitably, taking part in such a simulation would heighten each professional's own awareness of how he or she constructs records and is affected by reading accounts in advance of working with a child.

Activities such as those suggested here, following on from or in conjunction with reading the earlier study, are likely to provide a means for cross-communication between different specialists, officials, and teachers who normally never discuss with each other precisely how they work, interpret reports, or assess children who have special needs.

ACKNOWLEDGMENTS

I would like to express my appreciation and thanks to Keith Pocklington, who was my collaborator in the research study from which this article grew. He was also co-author of unpublished material that I have drawn on extensively here. He bears no responsibility for any inadequacies in the present manuscript. I should also like to thank the National Foundation of Educational Research in England and Wales for their support of the research and permission to publish this article.

REFERENCES

Cicourel, A. V. (1976). *Social organization and juvenile justice*. London: Heinemann.

Kelly, G. A. (1955). *The psychology of personal constructs*. New York: Newton.

Polanyi, M. (1967). *The tacit dimension*. London: Routledge & Kegan Paul.

Schön, D. A. (1963). *Displacement of concepts*. London: Tavistock.

Part VI

STORIES TOLD AND LIVED

11

Narrative Reflections on Practical Actions: Two Learning Experiments in Reflective Storytelling

CHERYL MATTINGLY

"We had the experience but missed the meaning."
T. S. Eliot

WE TELL STORIES for many reasons: to entertain, to gossip, as evidence for our arguments, to reveal who we are. Sometimes we tell stories, especially about experiences that are puzzling, powerful, or upsetting, in order to render those experiences more sensible. Telling stories offers one way to make sense of what has happened. We may even catch a level of meaning that we only partially grasped while living through something.

For 5 years, from 1983 to 1988, I helped conduct two action research studies in which professionals were asked to tell stories about their work and then to analyze those stories in order to investigate underlying values and assumptions—the implicit problem settings guiding what they saw and how they acted. In these studies I combined an ethnographic investigation of storytelling as it occurred naturally in the practice with an intervention that used storytelling as a learning tool. The first of these studies was done with project development officers at an international aid agency, the World Bank. The second was a study of occupational therapists working in an acute care hospital.

In this chapter I consider the everyday sense-making role storytelling played in both these practices. I also examine what happened when this ordinary mode of talk was used as an action research tool to help professionals reflect on their practice. The impact of these experiments in which professionals were asked to tell stories and analyze them in a highly self-conscious way turned out to depend largely on the role already played by their ordinary storytelling in their work environment.

WHY STORIES AS A BASIS FOR REFLECTION?

Storytelling and story analysis can facilitate a kind of reflecting that is often difficult to do, a consideration of those ordinarily tacit constructs that guide practice. Stories point toward deep beliefs and assumptions that people often cannot tell in propositional or denotative form, the "practical theories" and deeply held images that guide their actions. Michael Polanyi (1966), Donald Schön (1983, 1987), and many others have argued that much practical knowledge is tacit. Actors may not be able to present their practical theories or guiding images propositionally, or may offer explanatory theories that do not seem to reflect the assumptions actually influencing their actions. But they can always tell stories about what they have done and what has happened to them, and others, as a result.

If actors are more aware of the beliefs and assumptions underlying their actions, they are more likely to recognize when their beliefs are unfounded or when their theories lead to consequences they did not want or could not explicitly espouse. Such reflection can have moral consequences. Both the project officers and the occupational therapists tended to intervene with clients less powerful than they. There is a constant danger that the professional's hoped-for story will be imposed on the client without the professional's recognition or acknowledgment of the imposition. Under such labels as being pragmatic, facing the facts, or doing what is technically required, professionals can imagine future scenarios that embed a host of implicit beliefs and attitudes that would look questionable were these made explicit. Since stories reveal the way ideas look in action, showing what experiences emerge when certain ideas are followed (Burrell & Hauerwas, 1977; Murdoch, 1956), analyzing stories can allow a moral investigation of the practical consequences of beliefs and theories that are otherwise decontextualized abstractions.

In these two action research studies, one rationale behind using a narrative approach to reflect on practice was that telling stories in a forum, where the group of occupational therapists or project officers was reflecting on their practice experiences, might provoke a powerful consideration of the ordinarily tacit body of constructs (beliefs, metaphors, images, strategies, values, and the like) that inform practice. The deeper rationale was rooted in the fact that everyone tells stories. While narrative (or story, and I use these terms here interchangeably) is only one mode of representing action, it is a very basic one (Bruner, 1986; Carr, 1986; MacIntyre, 1981; Ricoeur, 1980, 1984).

Within Western cultures at least, the language competence that allows us to recognize and produce narratives appears in children at about the age of 3 (Brooks, 1984). We seem to need narrative to make sense of situations, moving back to beginnings to discover where we are and where we might go. Narrative provides an explanation that "seeks its authority in a return to origins and the tracing of a coherent story forward from origin to present" (Brooks, 1984, p. 4). Narratives also help tell us *who* we are. They are perhaps our most fundamental form for communicating the sense of a life and thus a sense of the person who lived that life (Arendt, 1958). Stories not only give meaningful form to experiences we have already lived through. They also provide us a forward glance, helping us anticipate meaningful shapes for situations even before we enter them, allowing us to envision endings from the very beginning.

If storytelling is a natural way we represent experiences to ourselves, might it not provide a quite natural basis for learning from experience? Experience is obviously an inconstant teacher; it is perfectly possible to live through something and not learn much as a result. One motive for telling stories is to wrest meaning from experiences, especially powerful or disturbing ones. Even everyday experiences are continually imbued with meaning, rendered more coherent, more vivid, even more real, through storytelling. "When we return home and 'tell our day'," the philosopher and novelist Iris Murdoch said in an interview:

> we are artfully shaping material into story form. So in a way as word-users we all exist in a literary atmosphere, we live and breathe literature, we are all literary artists, we are constantly employing language to make interesting forms out of experience which perhaps originally seemed dull or incoherent (Magee, 1978, p. 266).

Since storytelling is an everyday way to make sense of or add sense to things that happen to us, it can presumably be employed more self-consciously as a learning tool.

EVERYDAY STORYTELLING: THE SHAPING POWER OF STORIES IN PROFESSIONAL PRACTICE

Reflecting on and communicating about actions formed a large part of the work of both these professional groups, and telling stories was one way to do this. Storytelling was common among both the project officers and the occupational therapists. But telling stories was not the only way they communicated what was going on in a development project or a clinical case. It was just one form of talk among others, and an "unofficial" mode at that. Both groups of professionals had multiple modes of discourse to choose from to describe the same patient or development project, and the kind of discourse they chose determined which features of their practical experience they attended to in their practical experience.

One important question in understanding the role of storytelling in a practice is what function it serves. When and why are the professionals telling stories? I do not answer this question in this chapter, or at least not directly. Here I consider a second important line of questioning, one addressed less often. What is the nature of the practical problem when it is framed in a story? How does this differ from the way that problem is understood when it is communicated in non-narrative form? How does story, as a form of discourse, shape the content of what it narrates? I examine these questions about the role story plays in shaping practical problems by looking at cases where project officers or occupational therapists shifted between narrative and non-narrative discourse in addressing the "same" problem.

Storytelling among the Project Officers

Once I asked a project officer I was interviewing to tell me how he had come to understand a particular urban project when he initially joined it, one in a city with a long history of World Bank interventions. He replied, "Definitely not by reading aide memoires or briefs—the message is there but it is implicit." He told me that teaching new team members what the project was about was one of the responsibilities of the project leader. "How does he do that?" I asked. "Does he sit you down and outline the main objectives?" "No, not that," he said. "He tells you a story. We talk a story together."

The work of "talking a story" happened extensively in the field when the project team gathered together in the evening and worked out a series of decisions about what to recommend, negotiate, and demand of their counterparts in the field about how a project should be designed. Project officers associated telling stories with their work in the field and with the informal talk among team members in which they tried to devise a "collective story" that gave coherence and consistency to each of their individual actions.

Urban projects became significantly different entities when represented through stories rather than the formal written documents re-

quired by the World Bank. Bank documents followed a required structure that was almost invariable from city to city or project to project.
Rural projects in East Africa had a way of sounding rather like urban
projects in Latin America or power projects in South Asia. One striking
difference between informal storytelling and official Bank representations of projects was the very different way a complex project was given
a sense of coherence when rendered through a formal Bank document
(say, the project appraisal report) and when depicted in a story.

In a project report, various project components (a sewer line, a new
fleet of buses, an upgraded housing project) were discussed and justified in comparative isolation, with little or no reference to the behind-
the-scenes events that strongly influenced how they were actually designed in the field. However, project team members often relied on oral
storytelling to understand what the vision behind the project actually
was and how a project had come to take the shape it had. Each urban
project could be considered to have a certain story logic shared by team
members but not necessarily by their managers.

The following example illustrates the difference between a project
component depicted through a story and that same component depicted in project documents. The example concerns a plan to create incentives for joint government and business development ventures in
sections of a South Asian city where a new subway was being put in.
The project appraisal report described this component of the project as
follows:

> Selective intervention by [the metropolitan planning authority] (or
> agencies on its behalf) will be made at strategic areas, already subject
> to speculative pressures, for example, adjacent to the Metropolitan
> Transport Project (underground rapid transit) stations to facilitate the
> further development of these areas by the private sector.

This brief description is rather like the conclusion of the story with no
description of the events that led up to it. For the seasoned reader of
Bank documents, the rationale for "selective interventions"—by which
the report means "real estate ventures"—is indicated. This "selective
intervention" will stimulate the private sector, which will in turn generate money for the public sector. As described above, this component
primarily responded to the need to bring more money into the public
coffers by having the private sector get more involved in urban development. But when the project team told stories about the purpose of
this intervention, the problems this component addressed shifted and
broadened significantly.

In their storytelling about the design of this project component, the direct economic rationale for its inclusion in the overall loan proposal was clearly important not as an end in itself but rather as a catalyst for even more important goals. As narrated, this project component represented a successful conclusion, an "ending" to an interesting process of negotiation with local city planners. As recounted in their stories, this component was not so much a means for generating more revenue for the city as a means for training local city planners and managers. The underlying problem they identified in their stories was that the local city officials needed to reframe the way they tackled their urban problems. From the perspective of their stories, this real estate venture represented a successful move in using project design to "train" local government agencies about urban development. It was more a training venture than a real estate venture. In this case the "trainer" role involved showing a Marxist government how to act like a capitalist entrepreneur, taking advantage of an investment opportunity that could be advantageously exploited to serve socialist objectives. The significance of this training aspect was shown by the joking of the team leader when describing the real success of this land development component: "Selling capitalism to the Marxists—that I see as my biggest success."

The "story logic" underlying the technical description in the project report began to be revealed in a session with members of the research team and members of the mission team. Team members described this same plan to create real estate ventures around the subway. In the excerpt below, transcribed from an audiotape of the session, the team leader gave a graphic and funny description of the urban problem the project team confronted with this subway construction:

> TEAM LEADER: Now you get a situation where, for whatever reasons, somebody else is funneling a subway right through the center of town. Because it's not a state government agency, it's a gift from the center of [the country], these guys are taking a center and blocking all the already limited space. Now, no amount of World Bank intervention or God or anybody else is going to change what this does to the transportation, the performance of the public buses and trams. And certainly it will come on paper with numbers well below what we should have got. Or a sewer caves in because traffic has been rerouted to get away from the subway, and as a result of that they kick out three other streets to deal with an emergency of infrastructure, the repair [of] which is already a hundred years old and hasn't had any maintenance for most of those hundred years. So one's dealing with problems that books don't write about.

RESEARCHER: That big tunnel—that was from the central government?
TEAM LEADER: Yeah, that was a gift originally from the Russians.
  They got the plan underway and then realized what they'd
  gotten themselves into and I think abandoned that. But then
  there was enough commitment to carry on. And then that's
  made more complex by the [country's] ideology generally,
  [which] is to go for low technology, so where everywhere else
  they bring in excavators and dig the hole in a fraction of the
  time, you've got thousands of guys there with teaspoons
  scratching the dirt 50 feet deep on the roadside.

The rationale behind the proposed real estate venture was not that it
would solve the problems created by the subway but that it would turn
an inconvenience into an opportunity. These project team members particularly prided themselves on being able to seize opportunities—and
more important, to recognize opportunities—even in what at first
glance looked like complete disaster. The vivid description of the chaotic
introduction of a subway that only exacerbates downtown congestion
paints a picture of an increasingly disordered urban scene. Against this
dark comic backdrop of general confusion, the real estate venture can
be seen as an imaginative insight into how all this increased chaos can
be turned to some advantage. Third World cities are notorious for their
overwhelming problems and small resources. What the team members
most wanted to teach their Third World counterparts with this project
component was to see their cities with just this opportunistic eye.

The team leader went on to describe the reasoning of the project
team:

This metro, for whatever trouble it caused, was still happening
and somebody else was paying for it in cash terms. We said,
"Don't let's sit around and wait for it to finish. There are lots of
opportunities to be made, lots of money to be made out of having
the first bite of the cherry in terms of overbuilding on stops—if
you look at the Toronto experience or Boston or other[s]." So
through this we got them [local planning authorities] involved
much more in our broader program, in helping the planning of the
city. We got them to include a program for urban renewal in a
number of critical sites where they're going to capitalize on the investment of the metro. And we're talking to a Marxist government.
(Laughs) All this is nonsense compared to selling capitalism to
Marxists. That I see as my biggest success. Now what we did is we

persuaded them [that] in fact this was one way to get the private sector to develop along these sites. So again they weren't using government money. Somebody else was paying for the metro but by auctioning the development rights they could make sufficient subsidies to move across to their social program, which fit much more with their ideologies . . . so they began to see that it did make sense.

There are two striking differences between the narrative and non-narrative accounts given in this example. The first is that the narrative account focused on people. The second is that in the narrative, people did things and as a result things changed. Narrative descriptions highlighted the role that particular actors played in shaping the project component. In the non-narrative account no actors were identified. The project component was announced as though it emerged from nowhere. In the team leader's story there were two groups of actors, two collective characters, a project team and local city officials. These two groups clearly had differences in perspective; theirs was an uneasy alliance. The story itself centered on building this alliance between two unnatural partners, the capitalistically minded project team and local officials of a Marxist government. The success of this alliance, as portrayed in the story, came about because the project team persuaded their Marxist counterparts that a capitalistic eye for economic opportunities could serve socialist ends (which the project team also approved)—social programs for the poor.

This example reveals a fundamental feature of narrative accounts. Narratives, first of all, concern action. In stories people do things and as a result situations change, or things happen to people and as a result the people change. Speaking of the "eventness" around which narratives are organized, Genette describes narrative as a kind of monstrously elaborated verb (1980, p. 30). To say that stories concern action is not only to say that they are dynamic accounts where people do things but that the motives and intentions of particular actors are a focal point of concern.

Storytellers need not provide complex psychological accounts of their characters' intentions, but stories do foreground intending, purposive agents in presenting how things have come about. Stories are investigations of events as actions; they are, to use Burke's (1945) vocabulary, "dramatistic" investigations. Following Burke, drama stands for the paradigm of action in its full sense as connected to intentional agents.

Stories recount actions through a strategy that Aristotle, in the *Po-*

etics, described as imitative. Stories recount actions by imitating them; they tell how (and why) something happened by *showing how.* Stories present actions through a diachronic rendering that, in the process of unfolding, reveals contexts and lives. They create a "chronological illusion" (Barthes, 1975). Even in the simplest story, this chronological structure is likely to be complex, for stories chain events together in a sequence that is not reducible to sheer linear sequence, to the next-nextness of a series of discrete actions. The temporal movement of a story is much more complicated, connecting particular events chronologically, thematically, and teleologically. Stories unwind along a temporal axis and yet display a wholeness in which each particular episode takes its meaning as part of the larger whole. We intuitively recognize that a story ought to hang together as a whole when we ask what the point of the story was.

In the team leader's story a temporal structure suggests the more complex dramatic and thematic structure. The temporal structure is quite simple. As the project leader tells the story, the team first confronts an overcrowded Third World city where a new urban disaster is in the making, the misguided gift of a new subway. In describing the difficulties this "big tunnel" creates, the narrator also manages to describe an inept, if well-intentioned, local planning mentality wherein highly labor-intensive efforts are preferred. Therefore, rather than use excavators, there are "thousands of guys there with teaspoons scratching the dirt." But in this story the team also sees that this subway has its possibilities, specifically "overbuilding" on prospective metro stops. "Metro overbuilding" is described as both a good idea in itself and a way to entice the local planning authorities into taking a different approach to city planning, one more congruent with the planning approach of the project team. The quickly narrated sequence of events—seeing a problem, seeing a potential opportunity created by the problem, convincing the necessary authorities to agree to act on this opportunity—reinforces the morals of the story. One moral is that the real benefit of this project component was its potential effect in energizing a local planning authority to take a more aggressively opportunistic stance toward city planning. This moral is foreshadowed in the first event described, the comic portrayal of the subway building, which is an indirect and witty commentary on the planning mentality of city officials. The ironic buildup helps create a more dramatic effect when, in the final event, the project team has somehow persuaded these planning authorities to adopt a more Western attitude—to think more like the planners of Toronto or Boston.

The project officers themselves were of two minds about their own storytelling. On the one hand, they relied on it to make sense of what they were doing within their project teams. They often complained about having to describe project designs through the "product"-oriented project report, because it was much more difficult to justify their rationale for any design decision if they could not relate the story that led up to it. But on the other hand, they also worried about telling stories, because these revealed the complex politics involved in designing projects. Storytelling was a less controlled discourse; and because it focused on the motives and intentions of the actual people involved in the design process, it was also a more dangerous form of talk. (This feature of storytelling became even more evident in the stories project officers told in one-on-one interviews, when the vague "theys" were named as the particular directors of particular local planning authorities.) The morals of project officers' stories had an uncomfortable tendency to conflict with the espoused stance of the World Bank, which was that projects were created on the basis of rational planning, not such personal intricate maneuvering.

Storytelling among the Occupational Therapists

Discussing clinical cases with colleagues played a substantial role in the occupational therapists' work day. They had two dominant ways of describing a clinical case. One was a biomedical discourse, a language I came to call "chart talk" because it conformed to discourse in the medical charts. The other was a narrative discourse, a language of personal experience. These two modes of description played a powerful role in giving therapists two languages for making sense of patients, two ways of envisioning clinical work. The same patient could be described through both forms of talk. "Chart talk" was the kind of discourse one learned through being taught how to record a clinical case properly in the medical charts and present a case properly in a formal staff meeting, particularly one where a physician presided.

The most obvious feature of "chart talk" was that it made the diagnosis, rather than the individual patient, the center of description. When a patient case was presented in this way, therapists typically outlined a list of general problems clustered around a particular patient. The tendency toward an atomistic portrayal of clinical problems also characterized the way they described the treatment process. Treatment was depicted as a serial collection of therapeutic interventions, a linear sequence of events. General functional problems relevant to occupational therapy (say, lack of trunk stability, visual and motor impairments on the left side, inability to dress independently, and the like) were connected, one by one, to treatment interventions, with intervention outcomes matched against the initially identified problem categories. When a history was given, either of onset of disability or of treatment process, that history was of the pathology and its course through treatment, not of the person who possessed it. The particular experience of the patient was downplayed or left out altogether.

Alternately, when therapists told stories about their work with patients, clinical problems and treatment activities were presented as part of an unfolding drama. A cast of characters emerged. Motives were inferred or examined. Feelings often dominated the drama, with the storyteller interspersing descriptions of what happened with interpretations of how the patient felt or of his or her own emotions when certain events transpired. Both the patient's illness experiences and therapist's experience of treating the patient took center stage.

The case example below illustrates this difference in the two forms of discourse. This example is taken from field notes of a weekly departmental staff meeting at which a student intern gave a formal case presentation as part of her internship requirements. Her presentation ranged from a description in which Parkinson's disease was the main character to one that introduced a patient, his wife, and the therapist (or a more vague therapist team, a "we").

The presentation divided dramatically. In the first half, the student therapist discussed the general medical characteristics of Parkinson's, with emphasis on those aspects of the disease relevant to occupational therapy. Her disease-centered discussion was organized as follows:

1. She began by describing general functional problems characteristic of Parkinson's disease, for example, "Major dysfunctions which come with the disease are personal changes, depression, drowsiness."

2. She then discussed management of the disease. She told the group, "The disease is lifelong since there is no cure. The person becomes increasingly inactive, so keeping active as possible as long as possible to keep up general health is essential. Maintenance is really important."

3. She described various ways to assess and rate a patient's extent of impairment. She reviewed a scale developed by a physician for delineating rate of severity along ten impairment dimensions.

4. Finally, she returned to her earlier management and treatment theme as she discussed the role of drugs and rehabilitation in treating the disease. She emphasized certain rehabilitation tasks that were the

special domain of occupational therapy: "Things to be done with patients are moving arms in big circles so that a person can write bigger.
This helps in writing. Also [do] passive range [of motion] for rigidity."

The presentation then shifted markedly as the student began telling
the group a story of her work with a particular Parkinson's patient. She
introduced her narrative by saying, "It is hard to see a patient dependent at one time and independent at another. This is one of the most
difficult aspects of this disease for everyone, the patient, the family."
Here is the story she told:

> When he [the patient] was on drugs he could do all the ADL [ac-
> tivities of daily living]. When he was off, he couldn't do anything.
> He had a mask-like facial expression. His changing ability to func-
> tion was frustrating for him and for his wife. The only adaptive
> equipment I gave him was a shoe-horn, because it was difficult for
> him to reach down to put on his shoes. I suggested . . . [unclear]
> but he didn't want that. He said that something would have to be
> changed because his bedroom was downstairs in the basement.
> His wife wanted to keep him downstairs but finally agreed that he
> could have a bedroom in the livingroom. He progressed rapidly
> and after a week and a half he was smiling, becoming more social.
> His wife told me, "He does nothing at home." I don't know if she
> could hear what we were telling her. We said, "He is not just sit-
> ting around. Many times he simply can't do anything because of
> the disease." When the wife heard that he would be on medication
> and that this would improve his functioning she said to him,
> "Good. There's a lot of chores around the house you can do." I
> don't know how much she heard of what we were telling her.

What was most notable was the response of the audience to this
cueing that talk was entering another domain. The affect of the group
changed dramatically. Several leaned forward and focused more directly
on the speaker's face. The structure of conversation shifted. During the
first half of her talk the audience was quiet, respectful. Everyone assumed some appearance of listening, if distant listening. The speaker
was not interrupted. During the second half, the audience paid increasingly close attention to the speaker, mirroring her facial expressions on
their own faces in sympathetic accompaniment to the unfolding story.
Talk changed from a strict monologue to an increasingly flowing, overlapping dialogue, with nearly all audience members participating in the

end. The audience became a chorus, first in largely nonverbal expressions that marked their strongly felt participation in the story, quickly followed by storytelling of their own at the conclusion of the speaker's story.

This talking flowed into a storytelling exchange in which others around the table offered their own experiences with Parkinson's patients, emphasizing the "feltness" of the disease for patient, family, or themselves rather than its objective medical features. Nearly all speakers narrated small stories that picked up and elaborated some themes raised by the initial story given above. Initial narratives followed the themes in the first story somewhat closely, while later storytelling tended to follow previous stories thematically in a contiguous fashion but did not necessarily remain faithful to key themes raised in the first story. Here are some excerpts from the dialogue that followed the presenter's story:

> "I remember there was this patient, when she was on she could talk about how crabby everyone thinks she is. Then she would go off."
>
> "I had this man. He's alert but he has no way of communicating. No method of communicating at all. *(Sounds of horror by listeners)* He's allergic to every medication used. He's the worst case of Parkinson's I've ever seen."
>
> "I think it affects the emotions of patients a lot."
>
> "This is awful to say but, this man was completely intelligent but his hygiene, he couldn't control himself. It was hard. It must be hard on a family member. *(Turning to student presenter)* Your example is extreme, but often the family doesn't understand."
>
> "My friend had a grandparent. This guy would take showers at 3 in the morning, wake everyone up. His wife would yell at him. It was terrible. Finally they found a nursing home for him, level one, where next to it there was a self-care home. His [the friend's] grandmother moved into that one next door. It took them 3 years before they could come to terms with it and finally put him away. The guilt."

This collective storytelling continued until the staff meeting finally broke up. One of the key differences between the narrative and non-narrative parts of the presentation was that when discourse moved into the narrative mode, the atmosphere became much more highly charged and impassioned. While narratives center on actions, they often tell more than what someone does. They nearly always recount not only doings but also experiences, what happens to the actors, that is, how events act on the actors and what meaning this carries for them.

To say that stories are about experience is to say that they deal with events from a particular perspective; they tell us about "life divined from the inside," in Bettelheim's wonderful phrase (1977, p. 23). Events in a story are construed as a passage, a movement from some initial situation through various twists and turns to some final situation. Stories are about experience as a movement through time. Walter Benjamin (1968) has said that stories are the ways we tell about how life goes forward. While narratives may not explore this inner world with any great depth, they nearly always contain an evocative element that draws listeners into an empathic identification with the protagonist that allows them to experience something of what being in this sort of situation would feel like if they were actually there.

Another characteristic of the narrative discourse in the example above is how strongly moralizing it is. There is little or no effort to exhibit a value-neutral stance toward the events depicted. Even in these extremely brief stories, certain moral themes are built; often themes begun by one speaker's story are elaborated or reinforced by another speaker's story. Sometimes the moral is made explicit, but more often it is simply given in the very way that the events are described and sequentially ordered, a feature also well illustrated in the storytelling of the project officers. Aristotle, in the *Poetics*, saw the organizing of story events by plot as a structuring that turns a mere sequence of events into a unified whole governed by a moral. For Aristotle, the plot is a type of moral argument. Hayden White (1980) follows Aristotle in his discussion of historical narratives by describing a story's plot as the structuring device that provides the meaning of particular events through the part they play in a larger, integrated whole. White sees this ordering as not merely formal but moral, in fact, as formal in service of the moral. And in our ordinary descriptions of stories we have preserved this Aristotelian notion, as when we speak of the "moral" of the story.

REFLECTIVE STORYTELLING AS ACTION RESEARCH

Aristotle saw narrative as a natural framework for representing the world of action. The simplest version of this view is that narrative mirrors the world of action. It just tells what happened. In modern and postmodern times the notion that stories mirror the world of action (the mimetic view) has fallen into disfavor because it has become apparent (and has taken on epistemological weight) that any representation of action is also an interpretation, one story among others that can be told.

Both these action research studies relied on the pluralism inherent in storytelling, the fact that different actors will tell different stories about the "same" situation. Professionals met as groups to tell stories about their practice and to reflect on the multiplicity of versions they generated about the same patient or development project. The occupational therapists rarely treated patients as teams, so these multiple versions were based on group sessions at which therapists told stories about what they saw occurring in videotapes of patient treatment. The fact that project officers worked in teams allowed collective storytelling about projects they were working on together.

The results of these studies could hardly have been more different. The storytelling experiments generated reflection and intellectual excitement among the occupational therapists but not the project officers. In the following sections I examine these differences and consider how the role that storytelling ordinarily played in the practice influenced the success or failure of an action research intervention based on taking a more reflective stance toward one's practice stories.

Reflective Storytelling in the World Bank

The World Bank–funded study was designed as an innovative participatory form of process evaluation in which the World Bank project team members would collaborate with outside researchers in an investigation and assessment of the project development and lending process while they were still in the midst of carrying out their work on the project. The research team consisted of members of MIT's School of Architecture and Planning.

Two project teams volunteered (somewhat warily) to take part in the research. One team handled urban projects in a large Asian city. The second team was at the early stages of designing an urban project for several middle-sized cities in the Middle Eastern country. The four primary vehicles for this in-the-midst scrutiny of the project process were:

1. Debriefing sessions, which occurred before and after the team left to make a site visit of the project
2. Individual semistructured interviews with each team member in order to capture their perceptions of the project process
3. Observation of project-related meetings in Washington and at the field site in the developing country
4. Review of project-related Bank documents

Group debriefing sessions were organized as structured reflections on brief discussion papers that the research team produced. These discussion papers were based on individual interviews and field notes. In interviews team members were asked to tell stories about their experiences working on the project, and the papers were thematic analyses of these stories. The papers themselves were used to trigger a revisiting of the stories individuals had told and to generate alternative stories as team members reacted to our way of analyzing their stories and categorizing them by theme. Often debriefing sessions involved a collective retelling of the same stories that individuals had told us in interview.

The World Bank exercises were not successful experiments. The project officers never became partners in the research. They never felt they had enough to gain, and the risks were very high. For them, reflecting on practice was exceedingly dangerous, essentially prohibited within the organizational culture. I sometimes felt I was the only learner, and one thing I learned was how effective storytelling could be for avoiding reflection on experience.

I began to confront the tremendous power of stories to obscure the meaning of experience, in fact to disguise the experience altogether, not only for the audience but for the storytellers themselves. I also confronted the power of the institutional context to determine the kind of stories that could be safely told. In the context of the World Bank, tellable tales were versions of heroic romance where Bank project teams were the missionaries of economic enlightenment and rational planning. Darker, ironic tales that conveyed the immense difficulties, misunderstandings, and dissimulations that plagued international development projects—the "culture of dishonesty," as one Asian official put it to me—were much more taboo. Even when such stories were told in private interview sessions, they were denied or downplayed at any group meetings. Consequently there was little chance for the project officers to reflect seriously on their work—including its difficulties—as they actually experienced it.

In the World Bank the work of the project officers was monitored by numerous layers of higher-level bureaucrats within the system. These project officers belonged to a small contingent of World Bank professionals who actually spent a significant part of their work time (one-third to one-half) in the developing countries. They then reported their findings and decisions to higher-level management who rarely left Washington. Project officers described themselves as caught between the demands and concerns of counterparts in these developing countries and the institutional interests and perspective of the upper-level Washington management who controlled their salaries and career advancement. They said they "worked in a fish bowl," where every action they took was subject to potential reprimand by their superiors.

Consequently they worried about their storytelling, particularly about any written transcripts of audiotaped interviews. While it is often surprising and disturbing to see one's oral expression transfigured by writing, where it seems to take on a different meaning, there was more to it than this. Written discourse in the Bank was not the place for experimental accounts or for just saying what one thought. It was a highly controlled discourse.

The project officers were unnerved by "fixing" their talk into a form that could then be examined in a more public way. Both these action research studies depended on researchers' capturing ephemeral moments of ongoing practical actions and oral expression in ways that allowed them to be examined. These studies were not only ethnographic in the sense that an ethnographer (myself) was on the scene taking notes. They were also ethnographically based action research in the sense that they relied on the ethnographer's tool of "fixing" actions that would otherwise disappear, of recording practices for perusal (Geertz, 1973; Marcus & Fischer, 1986). In this case, we were asking those we were studying to reflect with us on these captured moments of practice.

This was an invitation the project officers felt they had to refuse. In so doing, they rejected their own stories as objects worth serious consideration. This refusal may have indicated a concern not to take their practical experiences too seriously, at least not in public. But it also reflected a concern to protect the stories they were willing to tell from too close an inspection. Often the stories they told us were not, as it turned out, stories of their experiences in the field at all but narrative versions of the project reports. Sometimes they told stories about things the project had accomplished, in narrative past tense, and we discovered later that these were illusory stories, stories of what the project was designed to accomplish but never had, narrative reflections of a paper reality that bore little resemblance to the on-the-ground facts in the field. They told us about low-income housing projects that had been built, cattle that had been moved from the center city to the periphery, new industries begun to increase the urban tax base. And when I visited the city where all this was supposed to have taken place, I found that the housing settlements were not there, that the cattle were still clogging traffic in the central city, and that there were no new industries. But they existed on paper, in the project appraisal report.

Project officers also sometimes forgot what they had experienced. When asked to tell stories about the process by which key components of the project had been designed, often they simply could not remember. It is as though there were a cultural restriction on remembrance. Remembering could endanger; one might remember experiences that did not conform to Bank policies and Bank procedures. The capacity of project officers to function as "urban cowboys," as they sometimes called themselves, depended on their being able to protect the Third World frontiers from too much prying by higher-level Bank managers.

Reflective Storytelling among the Occupational Therapists

The action research project with the occupational therapists was conducted from 1986 to 1988. Like the World Bank study, it was funded from the inside, this time by two national organizations, the American Occupational Therapy Association and the American Occupational Therapy Foundation. From the beginning, several of the most experienced therapists in the setting saw this exercise in reflective storytelling as a place to do some much-needed reflection on their practice, a luxury their daily work schedule did not permit. While they often expressed worry about being criticized by the research team or their peers, they were actually anxious to describe their practice experiences and the problems they faced and were much less invested than the World Bank practitioners in using their stories to hide what they did and how they felt about it.

This greater success most likely reflects differences in power positions of the two professional groups. The occupational therapists were not under organizational scrutiny in the hospital context and appeared to feel little risk of exposure at the institutional level. They were not considered a threat to operations of the clinic. Occupational therapists often complained that no other health professionals knew anything about what they did. Their anonymity and relative lack of power gave them a certain freedom.

A primary way practice was "fixed" in this study was through videotaping clinical sessions. Videotapes became the main vehicle around which reflective storytelling occurred. During group sessions, therapists were asked to "tell the story" they saw in a videotaped session of a therapist treating a client. Invariably the therapist told a different story. I often asked therapists to watch a videotape of a clinical session as though it were an unfolding story they were reading, or perhaps even a whole novel. I then asked them to give a title to the novel and name the chapters. This interpretive strategy highlighted the differences in the overall meaning each participant assigned to what was going on as well as the differences in how the videotaped session could be divided into parts that contributed to the general themes they had identified in their story titles.

Looking at their practice as a series of unfolding stories provided an unusual vantage point for reflection for these therapists. While they frequently told stories about their clinical work in a casual, lunch-talk kind of way, they had never tried to look carefully at their own work using a narrative mode of analysis. Stories were something one told informally at the end of a staff meeting, or to communicate a bit of patient information to a fellow staff member, not an analytical mode. By stopping to examine their own way of seeing practice when they told stories, occupational therapists were reflecting on their narrative reflections. This shifted them away from thinking of their practice as the employment of technical skills (ranging arms, assessing trunk stability, and the like) and placed their technical skills and problem solving within a context of a historically unfolding interaction between themselves and their clients and an evolving sense of the story they were living out in their work with a patient.

Probably the most useful role reflective storytelling played was in helping the therapists "denaturalize" their way of seeing their own practice. The liability of storytelling is that so many versions are possible. This worked to advantage in heightening therapists' recognition of the interpretive nature of their work. They became much more conscious of the immense assumptions they were making (had to make, in fact) about the lives of their patients, about what mattered to them and what they ought to care about. Because occupational therapists help handicapped clients improve their self-care and their ability to live as independently as possible, the assumptions they make about what constitutes independence and what competences their clients ought to have are critical to their effectiveness.

The videotapes that were viewed were always of an occupational therapist who was a member of the group. This meant group members were offering multiple interpretations of a session that one of them had conducted. Often the therapist whose tape was being viewed commented later that others saw aspects of what was going on that he or she had never noticed. Overall, the multiplicity of interpretations allowed therapists to view their own interpretations of their clinical sessions as just that—interpretations, rather than clear mirrors of how things just are.

This narrative reflection also encouraged them to see practice as unfolding and necessarily responsive to unexpected contingencies—a process not altogether preordained in the initial treatment plan and only very partially shaped by their original assessment and planning. Many were initially uncomfortable about thinking of themselves as clinicians who continually, in small and large ways, ran into trouble with clients, so the "getting stuck" analyses were often highly charged. A year later, when they reported on how this research had influenced them, nearly everyone mentioned their relief at being able to speak of their practice as a place where things often did not run smoothly and where they and their patients often did not seem to agree about what should happen in therapy. Many appreciated the recognition that part of their clinical skill involved the capacity to continually improvise in order to best respond to what was happening in the immediate setting, and they all grew intrigued with how this capacity to improvise could be better taught to new therapists.

By the second year of the project, occupational therapists other than those participating in the study heard about what we were doing and asked various members of the research team to give presentations and workshops across the country. Although the research project has formally ended, interest among occupational therapists is still growing. Other hospitals have asked for similar studies, and academic programs have asked for courses based on the research team's descriptions of findings.

I was completely surprised by this national response. I was hoping not to replicate the difficulties of the earlier World Bank study, but I certainly had not anticipated this general level of interest. Why has this happened? I think the answer lies in the meaning everyday storytelling has in the practice of occupational therapists. It has something to do with the kind of thinking therapists already do when they tell stories.

Therapists are telling something important about their work in their stories, and this is what our study unearthed and helped articulate. The therapists who participated in the research and those who have come to workshops say that our work is "empowering." The sense of power comes, I believe, because their ordinary storytelling had already captured a level of complexity in the clinical problems they were treating that was ignored in the usual biomedically oriented accounts of clinical work. In their stories, therapists reveal the depth of the problems their patients face and, in so doing, the depth of their own interventions.

In the medical culture, occupational therapists are often seen as technicians, or even "play ladies," who occupy patients' hospital time with checker games and craft groups. From a biomedical perspective, chronic illness and disability are physiological problems. But from an occupational therapy perspective, disability is not only an injury to the body, it is an injury to a patient's life. Occupational therapists have the task of helping the handicapped become more "functionally independent." This can be treated as a technical task, one of helping clients improve their motor skills and learn to use special adaptive equipment. Or it can be treated as addressing the profound difficulty of how disabled persons are going to be able to continue to live meaningful lives burdened with bodies that no longer allow them to carry out those occupations that gave their lives meaning and purpose, which in turn gave them a sense of self.

When occupational therapists describe their work in the language of "chart talk," they are able to convey their reasoning as it relates to the physical body, but they can say little about how they are intervening to help the patient with a disabled life. Telling stories gives them a way to examine the disability as an "illness experience," to borrow a phrase from the medical anthropologists (Good & Good, 1980, 1985; Kleinman, 1988). They can examine how they treat disability phenomenologically, as a meaningful experience that reverberates throughout the life of the handicapped person. Occupational therapists have told us they see this research and the notions of clinical reasoning that have emerged from it as giving them a new language, a medium for talking about what they do in ways that the traditional, medically derived form of talk does not.

I would say that the language is not new at all. What we have done is merely take seriously a form of construing clinical problems that was part of their practice all along.

CONCLUSION

In action research the "subjects" are no longer subjects but rather find a way to become researchers of their own practice. More than many research traditions, action research represents a kind of ideal practice. Those studied must come to see something at stake in examining their own practice, they must be willing to risk a certain exposure to themselves and to colleagues, they must even be willing to chance the possibility of changing and taking new actions. If the research subjects remain just subjects, then there is no action research.

As storytellers, practitioners are already incipient researchers into their own practice. Ultimately, the potential power of using storytelling as the basis for action research is that storytelling is something practitioners already do. An action research design that makes practitioners self-conscious about their storytelling reframes this undervalued mode of oral discourse as a form of reflection on practice. Simply asking practitioners to reflect on the stories they already tell can provide a natural bridge to a serious inquiry about the very deepest layers of value and belief that undergird the decisions they make.

But there is nothing inevitable about the shift from storytelling as lunchtime entertainment or behind-the-scenes politics to storytelling as a self-conscious mode of practical reflection. There are many dangers inherent in taking stories seriously. Stories tend to focus on the roles particular actors played in bringing about some conclusion. People are held responsible. One could say that in stories the storyteller is always implicitly answering the question "Who is to blame here?" Stories are often emotional, even impassioned. They convey what individuals feel as well as what they do. Having strong feelings can look unprofessional. It might appear that decisions are being made from personal experience or intuition rather than from level-headed technique and theory-driven expertise.

Although the project officers relied on stories in shaping their decision making every bit as much as the occupational therapists did, their stories were not something they wanted to reflect on. The kinds of issues that are the stuff of stories—actions, accidents, alliances, and enemies—were particularly dangerous material in an institutional climate governed by a high level of delicate international politics. A reflection on practice from a narrative vantage point can be infinitely more worrisome than a reflection that presumes that practice is merely a matter of making the correct technical decisions.

REFERENCES

Arendt, H. (1958). *The human condition.* Chicago: University of Chicago Press.

Aristotle (1967). *Poetics* (G. Else, Trans.). Ann Arbor: University of Michigan Press.

Barthes, R. (1975). An introduction to the structural analysis of narrative. *New Literary History, 6,* 237–272.

Benjamin, W. (1968). *Illuminations.* New York: Schocken.

Bettelheim, B. (1977). *The uses of enchantment: The meaning and importance of fairy tales.* New York: Vintage.

Brooks, P. (1984). *Reading for the plot: Design and intention in narrative.* New York: Knopf.

Bruner, J. (1986). *Actual minds, possible worlds.* Cambridge, MA: Harvard University Press.

Burke, K. (1945). *A grammar of motives.* Berkeley: University of California Press.

Burrell, D., & Hauerwas, S. (1977). From system to story: An alternative pattern for rationality in ethics. In T. Engelhardt & D. Callahan (Eds.), *Knowledge, value and belief.* Hastings-on-Hudson, NY: The Hastings Center.

Carr, D. (1986). *Time, narrative, and history.* Bloomington: Indiana University Press.

Geertz, C. (1973). *The interpretation of cultures.* New York: Basic Books.

Genette, G. (1980). *Narrative discourse: An essay in method.* Ithaca, NY: Cornell University Press.

Good, B., & Good, M.-J. DelVecchio. (1980). The meaning of symptoms: A cultural hermeneutic model for clinical practice. In I. Eisenberg & A. Kleinman (Eds.), *The relevance of social science for medicine* (pp. 165–196). Norwell, MA: Reidel.

Good, B., & Good, M.-J. DelVecchio. (1985). *The cultural context of diagnosis and therapy.* Unpublished manuscript.

Kleinman, A. (1988). *The illness narratives: Suffering, healing, and the human condition.* New York: Basic Books.

MacIntyre, A. (1981). *After virtue: A study in moral theory.* Notre Dame, IN: University of Notre Dame Press.

Magee, B. (1978). Philosophy and literature: Dialogue with Iris Murdoch. In *Men of Ideas* (pp. 262–284). New York: Viking.

Marcus, G., & Fischer, M. (1986). *Anthropology as cultural critique: An experimental moment in the human sciences.* Chicago: University of Chicago Press.

Murdoch, I. (1956). Symposium: Vision and choice in morality. *Aristotelian Society, 30* (Suppl.), 32–58. London: Harrison & Sons.

Polanyi, M. (1966). *The tacit dimension.* New York: Doubleday.

Propp, V. (1986). *Morphology of the folktale.* Austin: University of Texas Press.

Ricoeur, P. (1980). Narrative time. In *On Narrative* (W. J. T. Mitchell, Ed.). Chicago: University of Chicago Press.

Ricoeur, P. (1984). *Time and narrative* (Vol. 1). Chicago: University of Chicago Press.

Schön, D. (1983). *The reflective practitioner: How professionals think in action.* New York: Basic Books.

Schön, D. (1987). *Educating the reflective practitioner.* San Francisco: Jossey-Bass.

White, H. (1980). The value of narrativity in the representation of reality. In *On Narrative* (W. J. T. Mitchell, Ed.). Chicago: University of Chicago Press.

White, H. (1987). *The content of the form: Narrative discourse and historical representation.* Baltimore, MD: Johns Hopkins University Press.

12

Narrative and Story
in Practice and Research

D. JEAN CLANDININ and F. MICHAEL CONNELLY

Story . . . is an ancient and altogether human method. The human being alone among the creatures on the earth is a storytelling animal: sees the present rising out of a past, heading into a future; perceives reality in narrative form.

(Novak, 1975, p. 175)

PHIL BINGHAM,[1] an experienced inner-city school principal, was transferred to a troubled K–8 school as part of a board of education inner-city school renewal program. He became principal at the school, Bay Street, in 1980, the year prior to our arrival as participant-observer researchers. At the time of the appointment, Bay Street had a culturally and linguistically mixed student body and had the board's maximum socioeconomically based inner-city rating for purposes of special funding. The school had a reputation that the board, teachers, and others wanted to change.

Many of Phil's administrative actions were directed toward "establishing a community feeling among the faculty and then moving out into establishing a positive school community relationship" (notes to file, May 15, 1981). He worked to establish a "warm, friendly, pleasant, and secure" environment that would promote "mutual trust" (notes to file, October 27, 1981). We saw him change the school's physical environment by displaying more student work as well as having halls and rooms painted and new lighting installed. He organized grade and division meetings to encourage teachers to work collaboratively, and he invited parents to participate in school events and in daily school life.

Teachers were also encouraged to participate in community events. We came to see these practices as an expression, in part, of an image of community that was rooted in his past experiences as the son of Irish immigrants to Toronto and in his personal way of life as a resident in a small, relatively isolated community of homes on Toronto Island.

One of the lessons to be learned from the work with Phil is the sense in which school life is a form of living. In school, as in life generally, one's personal history, the traditions of which one has been a part, and the social and community relations in which one engages form the plot outlines of day-to-day life. This is a powerful notion for anyone setting out to understand schooling or to bring about school change. But it is not a new idea. At the beginning of this century, Dewey wrote that education is a form of social life. Narrative inquiry is one way of translating this Dewian conception into practical methods of educational research and reform.

In the following pages, we advance some preliminary ideas on narrative inquiry in educational studies and educational reform. Our work with Phil will appear and reappear as these ideas are developed.

INTRODUCTION

Narrative, or *story* if one wishes to be modest and unpretentious (Carr, 1986), names a primary phenomenon in education and a basic phenomenon of life.[2] Whatever may be said about narrative as "method" follows from its character as phenomenon. If we accept that one of the basic human forms of experience of the world is as story (a point requiring more discussion than part of the argument of a single chapter) and if, further, we take the view that the storied quality of experience is both unconsciously restoried in life and consciously restoried, retold, and relived through processes of reflection, then the rudiments of method are born in the phenomenon of narrative.

Deliberately storying and restorying one's life (or, as we shall see, a group or cultural story) is, therefore, a fundamental method of personal (and social) growth: It is a fundamental quality of education. So-called narrative research builds on this process of growth. Narrative method is the description and restorying of the narrative structure of educational experience. A researcher's narrative account of an educational event may constitute a restorying of that event, and to that extent it is on a continuum with the processes of reflective restorying that go on in each of our educational lives.

Some of this is seen in Phil's narrative. While we cannot see here that Phil's primary experience was a storied one, his own later telling of his life in terms of community is evident, as is the added retelling that developed and grew out of our work with him in Bay Street School. There is an important degree of symmetry between the language he uses to tell his story and the language used in the research narrative. Both have a nonabstract quality; a quality that Crites (1975) says makes it possible to "render the concrete particularities of experience" (p. 26). Narrative as research method is, therefore, less a matter of the application of a scholarly technique to understanding phenomena than it is a matter of "entering into" the phenomena and partaking of them. Narrative is part of the phenomena of educational experience.

ELEMENTS IN AN IDEA OF NARRATIVE METHOD

We have not comprehensively thought through the meaning and significance of narrative and narrative method in education, nor have we anything by way of a technology to propose. Rather, as we worked with teachers in schools and graduate courses, and with prospective teachers in classes and practicum settings, we became aware of some matters that alternatively, like the figures in figure-ground exercises, struck us either as prosaic and unworthy of attention or as significant and fundamental to the understanding of curriculum. We saw ourselves turning these matters into subjects of inquiry in ways that allowed us to keep the magic in the foreground and the prosaic in the background. Our list of such matters follows.

Experience

Our imagination has been captured by the possibility of studying experience rather than using experience as a contextual given for educational discourse. We have been impressed with how universal the word *experience* is in education. But, to use Adler and Van Doren's (1972) distinction, it tends to function as a word, not a term. It is mostly used with no special meaning and functions as the ultimate explanatory context: "Why do teachers, students, and others do what they do? Because of their experience."

The problem of studying experience is, for us, a problem of laying claim to the integrity of experience itself and of fending off either its formalistic denial through abstraction and the hegemonies of social organization and structure or its reduction into skills, techniques, and tactics. To do so is partly a matter of participating in the "politics of method" (Eisner, 1988; Pinar, 1988).

For us, keeping experience in the foreground comes about by periodic returns to the works of Dewey. For Dewey, education, experience, and life are inextricably intertwined. In its most general sense, when one asks what it means to study education, the answer is to study experience. Following Dewey, the study of experience is the study of life. One learns about education from thinking about life, and one learns about life from thinking about education. Keeping this sense of the experiential whole is part of the study of narrative.

Time

Time, like experience for the most part, remains invisible to an inquiring mind. There are works on time in sociology (e.g., Young, 1988; Young & Schuller, 1988; Zerubavel, 1979, 1981, 1985) and in the philosophy of phenomenology (e.g., Ricoeur, 1984), but for the most part they have not found their way into educational inquiry.

What might it mean to give time the magic of playing a role, being a "figure," in inquiry? One approach is a phenomenological one in which the idea of time is built up from the experience of it. According to Carr (1986), if we focus on our moment-by-moment experience, we discover a "prethematic" awareness of history. Quite apart from its intellectual and cultural content, we sense the passing of time, an experience that Crites (1975) claims has the simultaneous qualities of memory (of the past) and anticipation (of the future). This phenomenological approach to time, though limited (Carr, 1986), links the notions of time and experience. Experience, in this view, has the quality of an event or action. It is something that, at all times, has a past-future structure.

The relationship of past and future may be more or less passive or active (Dewey, 1916), a distinction that creates the potential for reflection and deliberate restorying. The central significance for the study of narrative is that the study of experience as figure is simultaneously the study of time as figure. Dewey's (1938) idea about time was expressed in his notion of "continuity," that is, the succession of situations within which experience occurs. Without continuity, there is no such thing as experience. Every experience is what it is in part because of what is brought to it, via prior experience, and in part because of its influence on the future, which is brought about by the alterations that occur in what Dewey calls the internal and environmental conditions of an experience.

Time, for Dewey, is more than an endless sequence of experiences.

Dewey (1934) developed the "tick-tock" metaphor of the clock to show how time, while having the quality of continuity, is experienced cyclically and rhythmically. Cyclic repetition is one of the bases for rhythm, and it is in rhythm that "there is that sudden magic that gives us a sense of an inner revelation brought to us about something we have supposed to be known through and through" (Dewey, 1934, pp. 170–171). Keeping the continuous, cyclic, and rhythmic sense of time is a second task associated with the study of narrative.

Personal Knowledge

One of the most persistent educational polemics is that of the sanctity of the individual child. However, with some noteworthy exceptions catalogued in works such as Eisner (1988), Pinar (1988), and Elbaz (1988), the study of what an education is or means for individuals is mostly absent in scholarly discourse.

One of our questions in narrative inquiry is how to make the study of a person's education theoretically interesting. First, the individual to be educated already has an educational history. Even at its simplest level, the learning of a new technique consists, as Oakeshott (1962) says, "in reforming knowledge which is already there" (p. 12). Second, an adequately conceived biography is as much a representation of a culture as it is a revelation of a unique individual. Culture is in the foreground along with the individual. The social, as Johnson (1987) shows, is embodied in the individual, though not only, nor even mostly, in simple social reproduction terms. The relationship is a dynamic one in which the social is reconstructed for a personal life story and in which the larger social structures themselves are influenced by personal action. A third matter is seen in revisitations with Dewey. For Dewey, experience is always social, such that a person is never an individual only. Nor is a person merely social. Rather, a person is a dialectic blend of the individual and the social, a notion akin to Polanyi's (1958) concept of the personal. Dewey characterizes an education, both teaching and learning, in both social and individual terms. There is agency in this view of education, since the wellsprings of the process are ultimately individual, not social.

Thus, when the individual is treated as figure, the personal emerges, which is both individual and social. The primary language of the personal needs to be simultaneously individual, social, cultural, and personally historical, as in biography. Keeping these marks of the personal before us is a third task associated with the study of narrative.

Reflection and Deliberation

Reflection and deliberation, methods of practical inquiry, are springboards for thinking of narrative and story as method. The two terms tend to point in different temporal directions, with *reflection* commonly implying a preparation for the future and *deliberation* implying past considerations. Since narrative requires a treatment of past, present, and future, we consider both terms.

Both terms refer to practical reasoning and yield uncertain results. Inquiry has always placed a high value on security and certainty in inquiry. These values, as Dewey, Schwab (1970, 1971, 1973, 1983) in his arguments for deliberative method, and Schön (1983, 1987) in his arguments for reflective practice show, are part of a long tradition of socially embodied theory/practice divisions.

Dewey's aim is to bring about a "destruction of the barriers which have divided theory and practice" (Dewey, 1929, p. 24). He conceives of a dialectic wholeness of theory and practice. For him, social movements, such as education, constitute the whole in which "conflicts and controversies" (Dewey, 1938, p. 4) define the practical and theoretical starting points of inquiry. In addition, within any inquiry the theoretical and practical dimensions are in interaction. Furthermore, every such inquiry has contexts of tradition and social direction and interacts with the surrounding social setting. Thus every social movement is a dynamic mix of theory/practice elements, and every inquiry within it has theory/practice set within the larger movement. Following Schutz and Luckmann (1973), we could say that every inquiry within a social movement has a horizon beyond which matters are taken for granted and considered certain but which, at any moment, may be doubted and opened for inquiry. Shifting the horizon shifts the course and outcomes of inquiry.

In Dewey's dialectic, doubt and uncertainty are the hallmarks of any meaningful social inquiry. Meaning and certainty tend to be inversely related in social inquiry so conceived. Deliberation and reflection are methods for charting a meaningful though uncertain course in social affairs.

For purposes of narrative, these considerations remind us that reflection and deliberation are methods that move back and forth in time, carrying with them uncertainty. A narrative is always tentative to a degree. It "produces likehood" (Polkinghorne, 1988, p. 175), not certainty. Furthermore, a narrative is both inescapably practical and theoretical. Practitioners and researchers commit themselves to reflection and deliberation in the construction of stories and narratives. A narrative construction is practical because it is concerned with a person's experience in time, and it is uncertain because the stories that are told and retold could be otherwise, as indeed can the narrative threads and the intentional futures to which they attach. The uncertainty is principally dependent on two things: (1) the specific practitioner and/or researcher interest in constructing the narrative and (2) their horizons, which wall off both the continuous temporal domains of personal biography and social tradition and the social domains of community and culture. Finally, reflection and deliberation are the methods by which one's life, and the stories of it, are restoried for purposes of reliving. It is the way to chart a course amidst biographic, cultural, and traditional bonds. Reflection and deliberation treat these matters, both for a person and for a researcher's account of a person, as theoretical elements in the telling of a story and as practical elements in the living of a story.

The elements of experience, time, personal knowledge, reflection, and deliberation, which we want to keep as figure in inquiry, are played out in the narrative work with Phil. This work revealed some of the important ways in which his education, experience, and life were intertwined. His life as community-oriented principal was inextricably intertwined with his adult way of life as a resident in the Toronto Island community and with his childhood and school experiences. We saw his administrative practices as the way these past experiences were "recollected" and "reconstructed" (notions we attribute, respectively, to Crites and Dewey) for the purpose of shifting Bay Street School's direction to a more desirable future. In terms of narrative these administrative actions are both flickerings of the past and rudimentary scenarios of the future. Both the past and a possible future are visible in the actions of the present. We see the personal knowledge of the individual as figure at the same time as we see the professional and social culture in which Phil, the person, has come to know his practices as school principal. And in the narrative inquiry process with Phil, we came to understand reflection and deliberation as the way in which he stories and restories his life for purposes of acting.

We now turn our attention to a more detailed working out of some methodological aspects of the process of narrative inquiry. We treat matters of data collection, interpretation, analysis, reflection and restorying, and audience, and we use our work with Phil at Bay Street School as illustrative of aspects of the inquiry process.

THE PROCESS OF NARRATIVE INQUIRY

The preceding sections provide some sense of the complexity of the phenomena of narrative and of ways of thinking about narrative as educational research method. Given the nature of narrative, one of the primary tasks for anyone undertaking a narrative study is to design a strategy for continually assessing the multiple levels (temporally continuous and socially interactive) at which the inquiry proceeds. The central task is evident when it is grasped that individuals both live their stories in an ongoing experiential text and tell their stories in words as they reflect upon life and explain themselves to others. More dramatically for the researcher, this is the smallest portion of the complexity, since a life is also a matter of growth toward an imagined future and, therefore, involves restorying and attempts at reliving. A person is, at once, then, engaged in living, telling, retelling, and reliving stories.

Seeing and describing story in the everyday actions of teachers, students, administrators, and others requires a subtle twist of mind on behalf of the inquirer. It is in the tellings and retellings that entanglements become acute, for it is here that temporal and social/cultural horizons are set and reset. How far of a probe into the participants' past and future is far enough? Which community spheres should be probed, and to what social depth should the inquiry proceed? When one engages in narrative inquiry, the process becomes even more complex for, as researchers, we become part of the process. Our narratives are lived, told, and retold in the research process. Thus the two narratives of participant and researcher become, in part, a shared narrative construction and reconstruction through the inquiry.

Narrative method involves participant-observation, shared work in a practical setting. The process is a joint living out of two person's narratives, those of researcher and practitioner, so that both participants are continuing to tell their own stories but the stories are now being lived out in a collaborative setting. The data for this collaboratively lived narrative involve field notes of the shared experience, journal records made by one or both of the participants, interview transcripts of discussions between the two participants, researcher and practitioner, and the stories shared.

In our work with Phil, we have the ongoing data of the joint living and telling of the shared story, which is an account of the narrative experience. As researchers we had shared in Phil's storying and restorying of his past experiences as we shared in the work of his present practices at Bay Street School. He used stories to explain present actions to staff, parents, and others, including ourselves. But as the following field notes from a Bay Street School staff meeting indicates, we also shared in the stories he was creating as we lived out our lives as participant-observers in the ongoing work of the school. We made the following record of an exchange at a staff meeting where the ideas of a community Spring Festival and a Friends of Bay Street Ball were first presented.

Dorothy then said that she wanted to say something about Bay Street's first annual Friendship Ball. Phil, I think, had introduced her by saying Dorothy wanted to take a couple of minutes to say something about this. Dorothy responded by saying, "Why am I always timed?" She said that they needed dollars for computers. She said something about a ball. There was lots of joking and going on about it being a dance. She said they planned to hold it in Silver Springs Court, the nearby community center, and that they would get interested people together and plan it. She said they planned to have it at the end of May, or close to June, and they would sell tickets. She said the people who had agreed to help organize it were Charles, Susan, and herself. She said that's all we have and she wondered if anyone else was interested. (notes to file, February 22, 1983)

Our expectation as researchers was that Phil would like this. He was always anxious to earn money for the school, to encourage the staff to work together, and, most important, to improve the community. But instead of enthusiastic support, he raised questions.

He asked how much money they were hoping to raise, and Dorothy replied, "oodles." Phil asked, "How much is an 'oodle'?" (notes to file, February 22, 1983)

Susan tried again to initiate some enthusiasm for the idea.

Susan said that she thought they would be having the friends of Bay Street School and that's what they would call their ball. She said that they wanted to have a profit margin and they hadn't worked it out yet but they would be charging $15.00 per head, with food. (notes to file, February 22, 1983)

Phil continued to raise doubts and then unexpectedly mentioned a festival.

Phil said he thought it was feasible and he wanted to talk to them about May and June. He said it was not about the dollars but the ways of doing it. He said he liked the "friendship" idea but he was concerned about the festival. He suggested that maybe they tie the ball to Sesqui (a city celebration) and that he would like to talk to them about it. (notes to file, February 22, 1983)

Phil went on to talk about a possible Spring Festival in which he wanted the school to be involved. He made reference to his participation in a local community advisory committee for Pincher Creek Park, a high-rise housing development close to the school. The community advisory committee had planned to hold a Spring Festival. Phil talked about this Festival as a response to the staff proposal to sponsor a Friends of Bay Street Ball.

> Phil said they [the advisory committee] have been very concerned about the "bad" press they [the housing development] have had and wondered why they can't see the good side. Phil said that on "your behalf, meaning on behalf of the school," he sits on the Pincher Creek Park Advisory committee. He said the people there wanted to know how they could change their image. They said something about the police only coming in on a crisis. They have decided they wanted to have a festival in the spring that would have both the police and the press involved and they would have a street dance here. The band would be the "Copper Tones," the police band. (notes to file, February 22, 1983)

Later at the same staff meeting, our field notes indicated the following.

> He said that Bay Street School is part of this community too. He then said it would be good to have a multicultural festival in the school yard and have Portuguese dancers, and it would be a fund raising event as well. He said something about the multicultural restaurant, and they would have ideas too. He then said, "I did this once before at Okotoks School and we made $1900." He said Dorothy had been involved in that and it had been amazing and it had been a multicultural festival and for that they didn't have a street dance. (notes to file, February 22, 1983)

These notes are excerpted from the record of the ongoing narrative, the telling in practice, in which we participated with Phil and other Bay Street School staff. After the staff meeting we, with other Bay Street staff, told ourselves stories in which we expressed surprise that Phil had not supported the first idea brought up by a group of staff members for a Friends of Bay Street Ball. He had, instead, talked about his interest in, and support for, the Spring Festival. We tried, with members of the school staff, to make sense of Phil's support for the community's Spring Festival rather than the staff-initiated proposal for a dance. Eventually, on Saturday, June 4, 1983, the festival Phil referred to in the staff meeting took place. It was a day-long event on the school grounds and involved the police, press, community groups, community agencies, school staff, and people from all parts of the community.

It was a very different activity from the one proposed by the staff as a Friends of Bay Street Ball. It took place in a different location (the school grounds rather than Silver Springs Court); the cast of involved characters were community members, including the school staff, rather than school staff only; and the roles each group played and the purposes served were different. We noticed that the primary role of the school staff shifted from contributing to the school to contributing to the community, even though, of course, they still obtained funds for school use. But the essential purpose of the activity was given meaning and contextualized within problems identified by the Pincher Creek Park Advisory Committee, that is, "bad press" was avoided, while the "good things happening" and the "image" they wished to create of their community were conveyed.

As researchers, we were participating in the ongoing daily work of Bay Street School and collaboratively trying to make sense of ongoing practices with Phil and other staff members. We were part of the unfolding story Phil was creating. We were also making sense with Phil in our conversations of the ways in which his present practices were a restorying of past experiences.

In narrative work on personal practical knowledge, data can originate in researcher observation, participant-observation of practice, and observations by other participants. Data may also be generated by the participants through personal reflective methods such as journal keeping, storytelling, letter writing, and autobiographical work such as that involved in the writing of personal annals and chronicles. In the research process, the researcher adds his or her own reflective voice. For example, the researcher voice in working with participants may respond to a teacher's stories with questions about why the story was told in the way it was. By answering the researcher's question, the participants may penetrate more deeply to other experiences to trace the emotionality attached to his or her particular way of storying events; this, from the point of view of research, also constitutes data.

In narrative inquiry data also include a whole array of nonstoried material, such as classroom plans and class newsletters. Teachers also write in nonstoried ways about rules, principles, pictures, metaphors, and personal philosophies. Beyond that, narrative researchers are concerned with the moral, emotional, and aesthetic qualities of all of these forms of data.

The process of narrative inquiry is characterized by movement first from experience to researcher and practitioner field notes, transcripts, documents, and descriptive storying of the experienced narrative and then to a mutual reconstruction of a narrative account. As participants, both researcher and practitioner, engage in the collaborative process of narrative inquiry, they work through a mutual reconstruction of the telling of the story in practice that has been captured in field notes, transcripts, and documents. This process is illustrated in our work with Phil. We began with the descriptive storying captured in our field notes, interview transcripts, and other data and then moved to a mutually constructed narrative that offered a way of giving an account of our work together. We began to reconstruct Phil's narrative around an image of community that found expression in his practices. We saw, for example, the narrative reconstruction of the staff meeting practices as part of an image of community. The experiential threads of the narrative were found in Phil's stories about his childhood and school experiences in inner-city Toronto; in his stories about his experiences on Toronto Island as a child and as an adult; in his and others' stories about his first teaching experience in the Island school and his later experiences at Okotoks and Lundbreck Schools. Phil's personal narrative was embedded within the cultural and historical narratives of his immigration to Toronto as the son of Irish parents, the Toronto School Board, inner-city Toronto schools, and, more generally, Ontario education.

When we began to offer Phil a narrative interpretation of his practices at February 22 staff meeting as an expression of an image of community, he began to story his early school experiences of home, family, school, and work. He told us stories about his family's summer and weekend excursions to Toronto Island, a small, vibrant community, and about their later move to the Island. The following is a brief narrative account of Phil constructed from his stories.

As a small child, Phil immigrated to Toronto with his parents from Ireland. Some 50 years ago the family rented accommodations in a part of Toronto that would hardly be recognizable to the inner-city youngsters who now live in the area, not far from Bay Street School. Phil's own experience could have included the high school to which students living in the Bay Street area would now go.

This dwelling, however, was not the first home his parents purchased. Their first home was on Toronto Island in a small community of homes that still exists today, a short ferry ride away from downtown Toronto. Even before Phil and his family had a home on the Island, they spent their summers and weekends as day visitors there. Phil's parents had been drawn to the Island from their first arrival in Toronto because, for them, it was a reminder of Ireland.

Phil went to school on the mainland, not on the Island. He shared stories with us and others such as the following one about his own school experience in a school with a large Jewish population.

> He had been sent to school in short pants. He and another boy in short pants were caught by older students who put them in a blanket. Phil had escaped, while the other boy was trapped. He went home saying he was never going to go back to that school again. He said he understood about being a member of a minority group, but he said he didn't look like a minority. He said you understood if you've had the experience. (notes to file, April 15, 1981, and November 23, 1983)

In Phil's stories, his most constant community was not the community in the area of Toronto where he and his parents lived and in which he went to school during the week. It was the Toronto Island community. It is this community that we came to see as significant in his narrative and that is central to the image of community at work in Bay Street School and its February 22 staff meeting. What are the characteristics of this community that make it so important to the unity of his life and that form the central core of his image of community?

We cannot know the Island that Phil knew as a child. Still, many of its features remain. It is geographically small and separated from mainland, downtown Toronto. Residents still commute by a ferry boat. There are no cars, so there is a common meeting ground as residents walk to and from the ferry dock to catch the early morning and late afternoon ferry. The community has always been small. In Phil's youth, the community faced problems faced by all rural communities, problems such as fire and police protection. Security was then, and remains still, a community responsibility. In Phil's youth the residents were a mixed group. They could have been, as Phil's parents were, new immigrants to Canada buying their first home, or they could have been people who already had a home in Toronto and for whom this was a summer home. The Island had a small elementary school administered by the Toronto Board of Education. Residents tended to come from different ethnic backgrounds and, in the early days, were from a broad economic cross-section.

Readers familiar with small, semiclosed communities will sense the difference between such a community and those where the boundaries are unclear, where neighbors may not know each other, and where there is reasonably clear stratification along economic and cultural lines. Such readers will sense the influence such a community has over one's outlooks on such matters as "community spirit," the role of social activities in the community, and the place of the school in the community.

Dewey conceived of the community as an organic entity with characteristics of its own. These characteristics are no mere sum of its parts. Just as the heart serves the circulatory functions of an organism, so, too, the school serves the educational functions of a community. This is how a community is perceived in Phil's stories of the Island community: an organic entity; an organism to which its residents, and their institutions of school, fire control, and self-policing, contribute.

Phil's first teaching job was in that Island school. He both lived in the community and taught in its school. We first learned this in a June 1981 lunch discussion, but at the time we paid little attention except to note it of general interest. The lack of attention we paid to it at the time can be seen in our field notes of that date:

> Somewhere in the discussion, I think it was in connection with the fact that Phil had taught at the Island school for a couple of years, we talked about where he lived. Phil has a place on the Island that he keeps open year-round. He lives most of the year, however, in Agincourt and really only moves out to the Island in the summer. We again talked about mutual acquaintances. (notes to file, June 16, 1981)

We began to appreciate the significance of the remark sometime later when the three of us were speaking to a group of administrators on July 14, 1983. Phil commented that the Island school was his first teaching assignment. In response to our remarks that he was a community-oriented principal, he said, "It all goes back to my family and to my early life on the Island" (notes to file, July 14, 1983). He went on to say that "the Island school was a real community school."

In these observations Phil, unprompted, is pointing to significant events that he believes contribute to the way he thinks about schooling in the way he stories his own life. For him, as it is in our interpretation, what he is and does at Bay Street School is part of a narrative with origins in the Island. He is, then, in his practices at Bay Street School, engaged in living, telling, retelling, and reliving his stories.

Phil left the Island school and moved to the mainland schools of Toronto for the next 25 years or so of his teaching career. He became an assistant principal and principal. As his career progressed, he moved from school to school. Of particular significance were his experiences at two inner-city schools and an alternative high school, Hill Street. All three schools were noted as community-oriented schools.

Thus, when we first came to know Phil, his reputation was twofold: a community principal and an exemplary inner-city principal. These can be seen as the two main themes in his narratives. But they are both given meaning in ways we could not have begun to understand when we first heard about them. Their meaning emerged from understanding the narrative unity of Phil's life and, in particular, the way in which it has crystallized into an image of community.

What should be clear from this temporally muddled set of data collection events is that the narrative inquiry process is not a linear one. There is data collection, mutual narrative interpretation by practitioners and researchers, more data collection, and further narrative reconstruction. The narrative inquiry process itself is a narrative one of storying, restorying, and restorying again.

In our work with Phil, we understood the image of community with new meaning when interpreted in light of his narrative. We are led to another restorying when we view Phil's image of community as one in which the school serves and performs functions for the community.

Phil believes the school itself should be conceived as a community. The following is typical of the way Phil talks about the school:

> Phil talked for a few moments about the importance of establishing a community feeling among the faculty and then moving out into establishing a positive school community relationship. (notes to file, May 15, 1981)

He worked hard to establish a congenial environment within the school and a sense of community in the staff. He supported a staff bus trip to Florida during the holidays, cozy potluck lunches, food served at evening staff meetings, support for a school radio station, establishment of a communications committee within the school, exchange visits by students and staff across the K–8 levels within the school, and school tours for all staff.

For Phil, however, focusing on the school alone separates it from the community and is therefore something he works against. He works toward a sense of community in the school and uses every opportunity to encourage it, as, for example, in his support for the year-end school-community picnics sponsored by the school and to which staff, students, and parents are invited. But Phil creates opportunities when he can, as he did with the Spring Festival, to more fully express the image by making the larger community central and the school in service of it.

So far our account of Phil's image of community has considered personal and administrative threads in Phil's narrative. We have focused on his home on the Island and on his administrative role in community-school activities. We now shift our focus more directly to educational matters, in particular to what the image of community means for the education of a child at Bay Street School.

Readers will recall that Phil attended school not on the Island but in inner-city Toronto. The story quoted above is only one of the stories that Phil tells that illustrate his feeling of being different from his school peers. He experienced the school as an outsider, but from the security of his "personal community," a community established for Phil by his parents, who knew "who they were and how they fit into the community" (notes to file, November 23, 1983).

We use the term *personal community* in the sense developed by Henry (1963). According to Henry, a person is born into a personal community, "a group of intimates to which he is linked for life by tradition" (p. 147). This personal community may be more or less stable in one's life. Phil senses the importance of personal community for the children of the transient families who surround Bay Street. The idea that children should have a sense of personal community is clearly expressed in an address to Bay Street School parents. His way of talking about what we call a learning community is one that fosters a personal community for the children. Learning communities are above all personal communities, a place where the bonds of intimacy are strong. The gist of his address to the Bay Street parents was as follows:

> The school environment should be warm, friendly, pleasant, and secure. He said that the environment should be this way for the children, for you, and for the teachers. He said that the environment should promote mutual trust; must make users feel welcome and feel that they belong; that every student should participate in creating and maintaining that environment and that there should be many places to display accomplishments of every child. Every child should have recognition. He made reference to the fact that they could see that tonight in the hallways. He said that every student is a part of the school environment. (notes to file, October 27, 1981)

The emphasis on a warm and supportive environment colors virtually all of his statements and actions on the students' curriculum. Even though Bay Street is a language project school, highly visible to the board of education and to the press because of its location and because of its special project status, Phil does not define the purposes of the school merely in terms of content learning.

When we think of Phil and his early school years, we see that his own experience of schooling is not the one he thinks children should have. His notion of what a child's education ought to be is, rather, tied to his life, both personal and professional, on the Island. In an important sense these two events, the child who enjoyed his childhood freedom in the Island community while attending an inner-city school and the Island resident principaling an inner-city school, are storied and restoried in Phil's life.

Part of the narrative reconstruction of Phil's image of community is understanding its expression in the ways in which school and community are connected. When we returned to the notes of the February 22 staff meeting, we sensed more deeply the importance for Phil of Bay Street School's becoming a part of the community during the conceiving, planning, and execution of the Spring Festival. We sensed the importance he attached to the view that the festival not be the school's festival, but the community's.

From the above, it should be clear that we did not set out to understand Phil in terms of the concept of narrative unity, or even in terms of an image of community. Instead we observed particular practices and were surprised by ones that we saw as inconsistent. In trying to make sense of his practices, we sensed a tension that alerted us to the possibility of there being something important in the ways that Phil's practices were expressions of his personal practical knowledge. It was in working from our sense of tension or incongruity in his practices through the personal knowledge account that we began to develop a construct to account for the underlying unity in his action.

Narrative inquirers tend not to begin with a prespecified problem and set of hypotheses. Instead they are inclined to begin with an interest in a particular phenomenon that could be understood narratively—such as teachers' personally held instructional knowledge in the work of Elbaz (1981, 1983), translation in the work of Enns-Connolly (in press), second language learning in Conle's (1989) work, or collaboration and practice in our own work (Clandinin, 1986; Clandinin & Connelly, 1988)—and then to try to make sense of the practice from the perspective of the participants, researcher, and practitioner.

INTERPRETATION IN NARRATIVE INQUIRY

In narrative inquiry, we hold that human experience has a storied quality. One of the consequences of this view is that the descriptions that each of us gives of our experiences as children, teachers, researchers, and members of school and community groups are descriptions of these narrative phenomena. These descriptions are a way of telling a story of our experience. Initially a narrative researcher is concerned with description, that is, a recording of events in field notes, a recording of participants' talk in interviews, and a recording of their stories. But even in these descriptive records, there is an interpretive quality, for when we tell stories of ourselves to others, as in Phil's story of his experience as a minority student in school, we are engaged in offering an interpretation of the stories we are living. And when we, as researchers, record field notes of participant-observation, there is an interpretative quality that enters into the notes we keep.

In narrative inquiry, the research act of coming to a participant's storied account is also an interpretive one based on field observations, participant-observation work, interviews, and participants' stories. As researchers participating in the narrative inquiry process, we tell our own interpretive stories of our experiences. The construction of a narrative account arising from the database also has an interpretive quality. We offer other ways of telling the story that offer constructs such as narrative unities, images, rhythms, and so forth as ways of giving an adequate, telling account.

In narrative accounts, ways of telling an individual's story as embedded within particular cultures and histories are offered. Accounts of how the individual is shaped by the larger professional knowledge context, as well as the ways in which the professional knowledge context has been reshaped in the unique situation in which the individual lives and works, are constructed. In narrative inquiry, the individual is shaped by the situation and shapes the situation in the living out of the story and in the storying of the experience.

These interpretations are offered because one of the main functions of research from a narrativist point of view is to foster reflection and restorying on the part of participants. The first, and central, contribution lies in the interactive relations between practitioner and researcher that lead to a mutual, collaborative telling and retelling of the participants', both practitioner's and researcher's, stories. This leads to a consideration of the way in which participation in a narrative inquiry opens participants to understanding change in their practices (Clandinin, 1989; Connelly & Clandinin, 1988).

We have written about change in practice that occurs within the collaborative relationships of narrative inquiry as a process of "giving back a story" (Connelly & Clandinin, 1985). In our inquiry relationship with Phil, we gave back a story in which we saw his practices as an expression of an image of community. We can, however, tell another story of two missed opportunities in our collaborative relationship with Phil. We missed an opportunity to give back a story of administrative hegemony, one in which Phil imposed his image of community on the staff as part of his practice in organizing the Spring Festival rather than the staff-initiated Friends of Bay Street Ball. In this telling of the story, we see his rejection of the staff's proposal as undermining the community in the school in order to enhance the school's participation in the larger community. Giving back this story to Phil would, we suggest, have led to another restorying and reliving of his practices.

We see a second missed opportunity as we retell the story of the inquiry process. We see in Phil's practice a possible story in which he continues to relive an image of community without retelling it in ways that take account of the changed and more complex social contexts of both Bay Street School and its community. If we had given back these two stories, Phil may have restoried his practices differently, a way of enabling still more change in the inquiry process.

Practitioner/participant and researcher/participant have different goals in narrative inquiry. Those goals are meaningful only within a large social narrative shared by both. The practitioner continues to work, and so the restorying is expressed in reshaped relations with children, school, community, and so forth. We see this in Phil's story when he begins to restory himself more explicitly as telling a story of community-school relations, as he did in the joint presentation to the administrators. The researcher also has this goal of restorying his or her narrative in his or her practices. A second goal for the researcher involves the more formal aspects of the story: a story that the researcher has confidence may be read with meaning by others. This question of audience is what primarily separates the interests of researcher and practitioner in narrative inquiry. The practitioner, in the end, is storying his or her experience and so must live out the experience. The researcher, while also restorying his or her own experience, wants others, an audience of other practitioners and researchers, to read narratively the one narrative presented in the research account. A third researcher goal is to develop theoretical constructs, such as that of "narrative unity" developed in our work with Phil, that offer a language for thinking and talking about experience, practice, and teacher knowledge.

NARRATIVE AUDIENCE

Researchers write narratives for a larger audience than their participants. Issues around the ways in which researchers should write accounts of narrative inquiry and the ways in which such accounts should be read are thus raised. Something of the spirit of action of the participants, practitioner and researcher, needs to find a place in the research story. Issues of representation and audience are central concerns.

One purpose of narrative research is to have other readers raise questions about their practices, their ways of knowing. Narrative inquiries are shared in ways that help readers question their own stories, raise their own questions about practices, and see in the narrative accounts stories of their own stories. The intent is to foster reflection, storying, and restorying for readers. Rose (1983) remarks that "the work as a whole will suggest new truths especially the extent to which all living is a creative act of greater or less authenticity, hindered or helped by the fictions to which we submit ourselves" (p. 17).

To be a reader of a narrative is to be drawn into a story, to find a place or way of seeing through participating in the story. Crites (1975) reminds us that the completeness of a story consists

> in the immediacy with which narrative is able to render the concrete particularities of experience. Its characteristic language is not conceptual but consists typically in the sort of verbal imagery we employ in referring to things as they appear to our senses or figure in our practical activities. Still more important the narrative form aesthetically reproduces the temporal tensions of experience, a moving present tensed between and every moment embracing a memory of what has gone before and an activity projected, underway. (p. 26)

In this Crites gives a sense of what narrative researchers try to capture in their narrative writing. They attempt to have the reader understand enough of the participants' experiences so that the reader can share something of what the experience might have been for the participants. In order to do this, a reader must make a genuine effort to share in the experience of the participants. It is something akin to what Elbow (1973) calls the "believing game," "an act of self-insertion" (p. 149). At its best it is a dialogue that allows a reader to share some qualities of the participants' experience. Narrative researchers need to consider the ways in which readers are drawn into the narrative and to see the potential for possible alternative stories. There are several. One is where the piece is read within the same researcher/participant purposes, as, for example, a reader who understands Phil's work with various community ethnic groups from a reading of Phil's narrative. Another reading would be for a different purpose, such as, for example, to see Phil's narrative as a way of illustrating administrative hegemony. This reading would highlight a dilemma for other administrators who may share Phil's communitarian goals. It was important to Phil that the festival be the community's festival. We see how he asserts a kind of administrative hegemony as he imposes his own plan in order to enhance the school's involvement in the larger community. Reading the narrative for this latter purpose allows us to see issues of leadership and administration with new insights.

What narrative authors can do is make very clear their own narrative purpose and, therefore, set what they deem to be the appropriate context for storying the data. However, as researchers and practitioners know, we must be sensitive to the legitimate alternative stories that might be told, given the data as presented and the purpose of the research.

The text, however, may be used for multiple purposes and for purposes unimagined by the original authors. As Novak (1975) reminds us:

> A story, once told, no longer belongs solely to the storyteller. It has existence independently of his will, intentions, or analysis. It is an object accessible to others. Others may see in it what the storyteller does not. Story is not narcissism or subjectivity, but its opposite: the making of an independent object. (p. 199)

And so it is in writing, and reading, narrative research accounts. Ultimately every narrativist researcher will suffer both blessing ("She saw more in what I wrote than I ever imagined") and blight ("She saw my participants as no more than blind reproducers of social inequity"). Narrativist researchers set out their narrative purposes and an appropriate context and counsel readers to play the believing game to ascertain the truth of the story. Readers assuming this way of participating in the narrative experience of another need to be prepared to see the possible meanings there are in the story and, through this process, see other possibilities for telling their own stories.

NOTES

1. The illustrations from Bay Street School are drawn from a 9-year research project on professionals' personal practical knowledge and narrative. To ensure privacy "Phil" and "Bay Street" are pseudonyms.

2. There are important distinctions that might be made between the terms *narrative* and *story*. In social science research the two terms are often collapsed with no great loss of precision. Polkinghorne (1988), for example, reviews possible uses of both terms and ends up treating them as equivalent, a position close to that adopted by Carr. We have an in-between usage. When referring to

participant situations—for example, classroom field records or interview data— we tend to use *story* to refer to particular situations and *narrative* to refer to longer-term life events. Thus we would tend to say that "Phil told us a story about a child in our meeting this morning," but that "The meaning of this morning's story in Phil's narrative of community relations is. . . ." Everyday speech patterns modify this loose distinction, and we would more often say "Deliberately storying and restorying one's life" rather than "Deliberately narrating and renarrating one's life." We would, however, follow Carr and Polkinghorne here and treat the two expressions as equivalent. When we refer to research, research method, and researchers we use the term *narrative* exclusively. For example, we could say "Narrative researchers, as Mishler (1986) shows, are engaged in the collection of stories when conducting interviews." Our ideas on narrative method are elaborated in Connelly & Clandinin (in press).

REFERENCES

Adler, M. J., & Van Doren, C. (1972). *How to read a book*. New York: Simon & Schuster.

Carr, D. (1986). *Time, narrative, and history*. Bloomington: Indiana University Press.

Clandinin, D. J. (1986). *Classroom practices: Teacher images in action*. London: Falmer.

Clandinin, D. J. (1989). Developing rhythm in teaching: The narrative study of a beginning teacher's personal practical knowledge of classrooms. *Curriculum Inquiry, 19*(2), 121–141.

Clandinin, D. J., & Connelly, F. M. (1988). Studying teachers' knowledge of classrooms: Collaborative research, ethics, and the negotiation of narrative. *The Journal of Educational Thought, 22*(2A), 269–282.

Conle, C. (1989). *Stories toward an interpretive thesis*. Toronto: Ontario Institute for Studies in Education.

Connelly, F. M., & Clandinin, D. J. (1985). Personal practical knowledge and the modes of knowing: Relevance for teaching and learning. In E. Eisner (Ed.), *Learning and teaching the ways of knowing* (Eighty-fourth Yearbook of the National Society for the Study of Education, part 2; pp. 174–178). Chicago: University of Chicago Press.

Connelly, F. M., & Clandinin, D. J. (1988). *Teachers as curriculum planners: Narratives of experience*. New York: Teachers College Press.

Connelly, F. M., & Clandinin, D. J. (in press). Stories of experience and narrative inquiry. *Educational Researcher*.

Crites, S. (1975). Angels we have heard. In J. B. Wiggins (Ed.), *Religion as story* (pp. 23–63). Lanham, MD: University Press of America.

Dewey, J. (1916). *Democracy and education*. New York: Macmillan.

Dewey, J. (1929). *The quest for certainty: A study of the relation of knowledge and action*. New York: Paragon.

Dewey, J. (1934). *Art as experience.* New York: Capricorn.

Dewey, J. (1938). *Experience & education. The Kappa Delta Pi lecture series.* New York: Collier.

Eisner, E. W. (1988, June/July). The primacy of experience and the politics of method. *Educational Researcher,* pp. 15–20.

Elbaz, F. (1981). The teacher's "practical knowledge": Report of a case study. *Curriculum Inquiry, 11*(1), 43–71.

Elbaz, F. (1983). *Teacher thinking: A study of practical knowledge.* London: Croom Helm.

Elbaz, F. (1988, September). *Knowledge and discourse: The evolution of research on teacher thinking.* Paper presented at the conference of the International Study Association on Teacher Thinking, Nottingham, England.

Elbow, P. (1973). *Writing without teachers.* London: Oxford University Press.

Enns-Connolly, Esther (in press). Translation and the translator: A narrative study of personal practical knowledge in the construction of meaning. *Curriculum Inquiry.*

Henry, J. (1963). *Culture against man.* New York: Random House.

Johnson, M. (1987). *The body in the mind: The bodily basis of meaning, imagination, and reason.* Chicago: University of Chicago Press.

Mishler, E. G. (1986). *Research interviewing: Context and narrative.* Cambridge, MA: Harvard University Press.

Novak, M. (1975). "Story" and experience. In J. B. Wiggins (Ed.), *Religion as story* (pp. 175–200). Lanham, MD: University Press of America.

Oakeshott, M. (1962). *Rationalism in politics.* London and New York: Methuen.

Pinar, W. F. (1988). Preface. In W. F. Pinar (Ed.), *Contemporary curriculum discourses* (pp. v–vii). Scottsdale, AR: Gorsuch Scarisbrick.

Pinar, W. F., Reynolds, W., & Hwu, W.-S. (in press). *Understanding curriculum: A comprehensive introduction to the study of curriculum.* Scottsdale, AR: Gorsuch Scarisbrick.

Polanyi, M. (1958). *Personal knowledge.* Chicago: University of Chicago Press.

Polkinghorne, D. E. (1988). *Narrative knowing and the human sciences.* Albany, NY: SUNY Press.

Ricoeur, P. (1984). *Time and narrative* (Volume 1). Chicago: University of Chicago Press.

Rose, P. (1983). *Parallel lives.* New York: Vintage.

Schön, D. (1983). *The reflective practitioner: How professionals think in action.* New York: Basic Books.

Schön, D. (1987). *Educating the reflective practitioner.* San Francisco: Jossey-Bass.

Schutz, A., & Luckmann, T. (1973). *The structures of the life-world.* Evanston, IL: Northwestern University Press.

Schwab, J. J. (1970). *The practical: A language for curriculum.* Washington, DC: National Education Association.

Schwab, J. J. (1971). The practical: Arts of eclectic. *School Review, 79,* 493–542.

Schwab, J. J. (1973). The practical: Translation into curriculum. *School Review, 81,* 501–522.

Schwab, J. J. (1983). The practical 4: Something for curriculum professors to do. *Curriculum Inquiry, 13*(3), 239–265.

Young, M. (1988). *The metronomic society: Natural rhythms and human timetables.* Cambridge, MA: Harvard University Press.

Young, M., & Schuller, T. (Eds.). (1988). *The rhythms of society.* London: Routledge.

Zerubavel, E. (1979). *Patterns of time in hospital life: A sociological perspective.* Chicago: University of Chicago Press.

Zerubavel, E. (1981). *Hidden rhythms: Schedules and calendars in social life.* Chicago: University of Chicago Press.

Zerubavel, E. (1985). *The seven day circle.* New York: Free Press.

Part VII

THE RESEARCHER'S EVOLVING STANCE TOWARD THE RESEARCH SITUATION

13

Shifting Stories:
Learning from a Reflective
Experiment in a Design Process

GIOVAN FRANCESCO LANZARA

INTRODUCTION: PURPOSE AND CONTEXT

THIS CHAPTER REPORTS on an intervention and an experiment within a design process. It focuses on the design and the adoption of a computer music system at a major educational and research institution, which will be referred to as "the Institute." The opportunity for this study was provided by a large-scale, multimillion dollar project that the Institute has undertaken to develop new computational facilities and educational software for undergraduate education. Within the context of a broad evaluative study of the impact of individual projects on teaching and learning in a number of departments, I participated in the computer music project as a team member, playing the role of the observer/evaluator. For over a year and a half I worked closely with the project leader, Jeanne, and the software developer, Armando, helping them with observation, description, and assessment of project activities, recording and analyzing their interactions with other faculty members, and keeping track of the process of design and adoption within the Music Section of the Institute. I have tried to interpret the process through the experiences and the stories told by the participants. Particularly, I have tried to explore and account for the multiple and shifting understandings of events generated by the different actors at different points in time as they were engaged in designing.

The project's main goal was the development of Music LOGO, a computer system and language designed to help students explore musical structures and extend their musical understanding.[1] The developers' role was to create a system that would enhance the teaching of music courses (theory, perception, appreciation, performance, history) at all levels. My role was to help the project members carry out evaluative and self-evaluative functions that they might find difficult or even impossible to fulfill *while* they were engaged in action. We came to call this special kind of inquiry, jointly conducted by the observer and the designers, a *self-study*. A self-study is an on-line inquiry and intervention into a situation of practice (for instance, a project) in which an observer/agent facilitates his or her partners' reflection on their own practices and experiences. But a self-study may also be regarded as a technique to develop knowledge about design processes by allowing people to recognize features that would not be easily discoverable otherwise. Its units of analysis and time boundaries are variable: They can range from a "snapshot" episode drawn from a broader process or practice to more extended longitudinal records that trace the entire "history" of a project.

However, how the observer was supposed to operate was by no means clear at the outset. My role and activities had to be discovered and, in a way, designed *in itinere*. Also, they kept shifting as the project progressed. At the start the self-study work required mainly documenting the software development proper from the beginning through field testing. But when the Music Faculty decided to introduce Music LOGO into the official curriculum, the scope of the design and of the entire self-study had to be broadened, and their focus shifted partially from software development to curricular reform and institutional adoption of the new system. In the interaction between the project developers and the Music Faculty, further and broader educational, cognitive, and institutional issues were raised. Thus what was originally thought of as a pilot project turned to be a major effort at computer-based educational innovation.

As it progressed, the self-study disclosed new purposes, gained more complex meanings, and yielded different understandings of the subject matter. Throughout the inquiry, theories and assumptions were formulated, discussed, and tested about what music is as a performing art, a domain of cognition, and a field of education. What it is important to teach and learn in music, how the computer can help students extend their musical understanding and acquire musical skills, and how the new educational software should be integrated into the music curriculum were some of the issues debated. Furthermore, this activity provided an opportunity to explore the complex and multiple threads binding the intentions and strategies behind the development of educational software, the subtle implications for music education and practice, the students' experiences with the system, and the patterns of adoption of the new system at both the individual and institutional levels. At the same time, an awareness developed of how pre-existing imageries and cognitive frameworks, habitual patterns of behavior, and established institutional settings for teaching and learning may influence and become embedded in new computer-based thinking and practical routines. Finally, even the observer's mode of inquiry became subject to inquiry and evaluation. Both my underlying assumptions and my earlier understandings had to be scrutinized, leading to a revised picture of the entire process in which I was engaged. In this respect the computer music project itself became a sort of ongoing practical experiment in self-evaluation, a laboratory for self-questioning and learning about issues of design, educational innovation, personal and institutional change, and methods of conducting an on-line, close-up inquiry into those matters.

Perhaps one of the most interesting and unexpected outcomes of the self-study was my discovery of my own changing role, activities, and understandings in the course of the process. To my surprise, I discovered that as I was helping my partners reflect on their own practice, I was also reflecting on my own. The reflective nature of our social interaction—one person's questions and observations stimulating another person's questions and observations—led me to do with my own research work what I was doing with that of my partners, that is, to conduct a self-study of my own modes of inquiry and shifting understandings. This discovery was by no means a painless or easy task. First, for quite a few months I resisted changing my previous interpretations of the process, even though, in light of new events and of the Music Faculty's feedback, they no longer seemed adequate. Changing them involved abandoning a number of ingrained assumptions that I had unreflectively brought to the inquiry and the situation. Then, when I was finally ready to make myself "vulnerable," I did not know how to deal with the uncertainty generated by such change, especially with its ambiguous consequences for the real purpose and relevance of my inquiry.

While some aspects of the process described are particular to the Institute and to the Music Faculty, many of the issues raised are common ones that must be taken into account when any educational (or other) technology is introduced into an institutional setting. I believe that they lend themselves to insights of a general kind. Thus my purpose in doing this work was at least twofold. First, I wanted to learn about what happens when a new technology is adopted within a complex institutional setting—how individual agents and the institution as a whole learn about the technology and its educational implications.

Second, I wanted to develop a prototype of an inquiry into a process of design and innovation that could be a guide to further studies of the same kind in other organizational and institutional settings.

DESIGNING THE EXPERIMENT

How, then, was I supposed to proceed? How could an experiment be designed that would enable both the observer and the project members to develop relevant knowledge about the design process and to reflect on their own theories, strategies, and experiences while they were actually engaged in action?

The First-Order Inquiry

By first-order inquiry, I mean an investigation into the perceived facts of a design process or organizational setting. Of course, such facts may come in different forms; for example, they can be, as they mostly were in our case, the actors' descriptions and interpretations of events, processes, and behaviors. A first-order inquiry aims at providing an overall description or explanation of the course and direction taken by a process. In a second-order inquiry, by contrast, attention is focused not on the actual or perceived sequence of events themselves, with the intent of extracting a "true" or plausible story from the data, but on the varying criteria, categories, and procedures used by observers and actors in approaching and comprehending their materials. It deals, in short, with interpretations of interpretations. Historiography, for example, is typically based on second-order inquiries. Van Maanen (1979) illustrates a similar distinction in ethnographic research.

The methods of the orthodox approaches to social research lend themselves well neither to the kind of reflective inquiry I wanted to do nor to the on-line observation and analysis of process phenomena. To the extent that process is studied, it is done through quantitative measure of predetermined categories that purport to define what is "real" about the social world. According to this view, the analyst must remain aloof from the social phenomena themselves in order to measure and categorize them objectively and tell "the true story." Though some research frameworks point to the importance of behavioral and process variables in social phenomena, as Boland (1979a) rightly points out, research that actually studies the process itself, not just the outcomes, is almost nonexistent. Where such research does exist, it only looks at the process in retrospect, after it has occurred.[2]

My inquiry, on the contrary, involved *living with the process* for a while, somehow letting myself *be seized* by it. The whole point was to observe events and situations as they evolved through time in order to explore the kind of knowledge that could be drawn from them. This was not an easy task. Because situations shifted all the time and nothing seemed to be "fixable," I kept pursuing the actors' changing perspectives and descriptions. Indeed, the process was to be recorded *as seen* through the eyes of the actors themselves as they engaged in social interaction; and the conditions for this kind of inquiry were to be realized on-line, while the process of experimenting itself unfolded. Thus an interaction had to be designed that would make relevant data accessible to observation and analysis. In inquiries of such a kind, the accessibility and quality of the data are *not* independent from the kind and quality of the social interaction that is established between the observer and the observed.

Throughout the self-study, according to intentional design, I actively intervened in the ongoing design process by continually, insistently, sometimes obsessively asking questions on issues of design, music, and education, gently forcing the project developers and the faculty involved in curricular reform to make their views and choices explicit and to become accountable to one another and to themselves. This perpetual questioning and self-questioning activity, carried out throughout the entire study, turned out to play an important role in the design process itself, as the participants acknowledged later on. The first-order inquiry developed through a number of various activities:[3]

1. I had extensive conversations with the participants about their design assumptions and strategies, problems encountered, options for solution, things that did not seem to work and were discarded or put aside, things that were recognized as important but were forgotten in the process.

2. Project developers and members of the Music Faculty engaged in joint evaluations, trying to assess the meaning of events or choices that were perceived as relevant to the development of the project specifically and to music education generally.

3. The participants were asked to account for their own and the others' evaluations of the system and its educational implications or expected impacts. When possible, I elicited and analyzed cross-evaluations among the different actors, trying to highlight, compare, and discuss divergent views. We tried to use the differences and the affinities that emerged as a source of insight both into the subject matter and into one another;

4. Along the same lines, I conducted on-the-spot experiments in self-observation and self-evaluation, which I called "self-experiments," in order to help the actors see more clearly and explicitly into specific design problems or into their own and others' pictures of shared objects, events, and situations.

At the outset of the self-study I only had a vague idea of how to design these self-experiments, but during the course of the project I realized that I was using some specific events or interactions as occasions for designing small, on-line, practical experiments to help people throw light on particular issues or problems they confronted, evaluate what was being done, and explicitly say what they thought about it. In all these self-experiments I would record the backtalk given by the participants involved. We all realized at one point that our experiments on educational, cognitive, and institutional issues were turning into an opportunity for learning about a process of learning. Indeed, we were doing an experiment on an experiment, submitting events and situations to a particular kind of reflective and reconstructive treatment.

Backtalk and the Second-Order Inquiry

As a preliminary outcome of my first round of observations and self-study activities, I wrote a report telling a story of facts as I perceived them, using people's experiences and evaluations as data sources. By writing this story I wanted to establish a perspective on the data, give a description of the design process, make an argument, and develop a conceptual structure for organizing and interpreting my findings. But at the same time I wanted to draw a picture of events and actors, as I first saw them, that could be "inspected" and tested by the people who were involved in the process and portrayed in the picture itself. So I submitted the report to the participants—project developers and Music Faculty—in order to get their *backtalk*.

The "story of facts" is not a simple narrative. Rather, it resembles what Clifford Geertz (1973, 1983) has called a "thick description," in which descriptions of events and situations are given through the words, the constructs, and the formulas that the actors use to define and tell what they do and what occurs to them. The observer "inscribes" in the story a multiplicity of complex conceptual structures, trying to elicit layers of meaning and to extract what is being "said" and meant in an event. By so doing, the observer transforms transitional events or actions, which exist only as instant occurrences, into narratives that exist in their "inscriptions" and can be inspected and revisited. Thus momentary, spot-like events and actions reveal to observation their complex specificity, their dense structure.

In this spirit, I used my report as a testing device, a tool for making a large-scale self-experiment, this time extended to the entire design process. My purpose was to test how people would respond to my story and to the pictures I had made of them, what they would have to say about the events reported, and ultimately whether their perspectives and evaluations would converge with the ones reported in the story. Letting the actors read the story and talk back to the observer was a strategic move that, almost unexpectedly, gave a methodological turn to my inquiry. The backtalk was both extensive and penetrating, providing new contextual data that otherwise would not have been readily accessible and leading to a more complex picture of the educational and institutional implications of the computer music project. Note that the new data were generated in an interaction between the observer and the actors and might, in part, have been generated *because of* the interaction. Further inquiry became possible because people were given a chance to read the story, see themselves portrayed in it, and respond to the observer.

Particularly, the backtalk and the extensive discussions that followed allowed the actors, including the observer, to go back to past events and see them in a different light, thus generating different interpretations; and some of the interpretations did not converge with what I had described in the report. What made the new materials interesting was not so much that different actors held multiple and conflicting perspectives on the same event at a specific point in time (*quot homines, tot sententiae*—"as many opinions as there are men"—is what social research usually tries to account for), but that the same actor would shift his or her perceptions and cognitions of the same event as time elapsed, producing different descriptions of it at different points in time. Observing the backtalk led me to redefine contexts and events and to revise my own perspective. As the actors talked back and told different stories about past events, my job became one of accounting for both the shifting stories and my own evolving understanding of the process, accounts that I then discussed and tested with the actors themselves. As a result of this second round of observations, a new story was generated, which I labeled "a story of shifting stories and shifting minds." My inquiry thus turned into a sort of historiography.

In this second-order perspective I had to play two different games at the same time, alternately switching from the role of a project staff member, that is, an *agent of the process*, to the role of a *reflector on the process*. Being an insider and an outsider at the same time was by no means an easy task. One game involved looking at events and situations with the mind of the project developers, that is, as they experienced them; but the other game involved looking at the same events and situations with my own mind, putting them at a distance and in a varied context. One game required penetrating deeply into the minds of the people and into the culture of the Institute as a whole, looking at events *through* their minds and culture, while the other game required studying precisely *that* mind and *that* culture, taking the role of an ethnographer visiting an alien culture and interpreting people's multiple and shifting interpretations (Geertz, 1973, 1983). Depending on the perspective from which they were viewed, facts, actions, and situations fit into different contexts and acquired a different meaning and relevance. Also, their meaning and relevance—and even their perception as identifiable unities bounded in space and time—shifted, depending on how much time had elapsed between their occurrence and their retrospective assessment; their place and boundaries shifted in people's memory.

In the following sections I shall try to better illustrate my argument by showing how the backtalk helped both the actors and the observer reshape their perceptions of major events in the design process. The focus will be on what I perceived to be a key event in the overall process of the system's design and adoption, namely, a "demonstration" of Music LOGO that the project developers gave to some members of the Music Faculty. Depending on the specific interpretation of this demonstration, the understanding of the whole process changed. I shall report and discuss the multiple and shifting stories that people told about the event at each subsequent round of testing in the self-study, and I shall try to account for the actors' and my own evolving understandings of the phenomena observed. The stories now become the materials of our inquiry, and the remainder of the chapter will show how they were generated, compared, and tested throughout our self-experimental activity.

INTERPRETING AN EVENT: SHIFTING STORIES

The Event: The System's "Demo"

Shortly before the Music Faculty's formal decision to adopt Music LOGO as a teaching tool, a number of Faculty members got together and sat around a table to take a closer look at the system. "What does the thing do?" they wanted to know, "What is it for?" For about 2 hours Jeanne showed the group how the system could be used, focusing on some of her students' work, and then engaged them in actually working on a couple of her composition-like projects. Some of the participants tried musical experiments with the system and got quite involved in making tunes; some started to debate the educational vices and virtues of "the thing"; others simply sat and watched in silence.

After the demo, the project developers and I sat down to thoroughly analyze and assess this 2-hour meeting. We tried to define what the discussion was about, how people responded to the system, and what different points of view and evaluations they held. In the subsequent stages of the process, the demo became a continuing source of reflections and afterthoughts for the developers, the Music Faculty, and myself. At different stages of the self-study, a number of distinct descriptions were generated about this simple, apparently harmless event. Below I discuss the three descriptions that seem to me to be the most significant. The first description, which arose in my first round of observations, is named the "controversy" story. The second, which originated from the participants' backtalk to my first story, is referred to as the "learning experience" story. The third, which resulted from a further round of backtalk, is labeled the "cooptation" story. Each new description was generated a few months after the previous one, and with each new description a different view of the whole design process emerged. Let me now tell these stories and show how they shifted into one another.

The Making of a Story: The Demo as a Controversy

As I was sitting in the demo meeting and watching what was going on, I perceived the discussion to be a controversy about Music LOGO, and I pictured it as such in my first story (in the report). In going over the protocol immediately after the demo, it seemed to me that a confrontation had taken place and that a substantive argument had developed, especially between Jeanne and Bruno, a music historian. As I initially perceived it, the demo was a situation in which the participants were asked to evaluate the system and make a yes-or-no decision about its adoption in the Music Section's introductory course for beginners. This perspective rather smoothly led me to center in on and highlight those instances in the protocol where a disagreement, or a rift in positions, or an explicit statement for or against the system could be easily detected. Consider, for instance, the following piece of dialogue, where the debate reached its climax and the issues at stake were more directly addressed:

BRUNO: Jeanne, this is where [Music LOGO] eludes me a bit, because now I see, it's at this level that I don't see the utility, because I see it as a game that turns music into numbers instead of really getting people going on music.

JEANNE: Well, I see it as a way of describing structural relations at a higher level.

BRUNO: Quite higher. It's just another system.

JEANNE: No, I don't mean higher in that sense, I mean structurally more aggregated, so that instead of writing 123 234 345 you could say: "I want a sequence made up of this motive, and I want to . . ." You are describing the structural relationships.

BRUNO: I guess what I'm asking is: What are they getting their hands on? Are they learning something about music from this, from using it, I mean? I would argue probably they aren't!

JEANNE: It depends on what you mean by making music: If you mean making music in a way it's usually used, as "let's play sonatas, let's make some music in that sense," or if you mean "making a thing, making an object, making something that has some coherence," or at least exploring what that means.

In this lively verbal skirmish, and throughout the whole discussion, Bruno and Jeanne explicitly brought to the surface a set of sharp dichotomies:

"Turning music into numbers" versus "going with music"
"Describing structural relationships" versus "listening and singing"
"Playing sonatas" versus "making something that has some coherence"
Procedural description versus feelingful perception
"Working with materials" versus immersion and exposure.

Bruno and Jeanne seemed to disagree on the meaning of "making music" and on the kind of teaching that better helps students gain access to relevant musical experience. They brought to the demo different assumptions about music, education, students' skills, and teachers' roles. Bruno saw the system as being an analytic and manipulative game, turning music into programming and keeping students away from "real" musical matters, while Jeanne, on the contrary, stressed the idea that it might help them discover and develop their own intuitive rules for making music. For Bruno, Music LOGO was basically a "listening device," a surrogate teacher, or, at most, a sort of smart taperecorder. For Jeanne, instead, it was a playground for conducting experiments with musical structures and for exploring the meaning of musical coherence. In his teaching, Bruno valued style, repertoire, cultural and historical context; he tried to fit Music LOGO into his own musical world and way of teaching by ascertaining how he could use it in designing student projects that would reflect and integrate his habitual ways of thinking and practicing. The main argument running across the demo—the one raised by Bruno and the one most visible to me—seemed to be about education: How good is the system for music education? How beneficial would it be for the students?

The rift between Jeanne's and Bruno's positions became even clearer to me when I separately asked them to cross-evaluate each another's teaching methods and ways of thinking. This is how Jeanne saw Bruno's way:

> He wants students to get excited, to love music; he wants to inspire them, to create a cultural and emotional sensibility, to create a desire. It's a sort of immersion into music. He says: "surround yourself with that and something will happen."

And, in turn, this is Bruno's view of Jeanne's way:

> Jeanne wants them to go into philosophical questions, into cognitive questions. I mean, it's a different order of experience . . . not what the students are expected to do in the introductory course, that is, basically, listening.

Commentary: Mapping the events. Using these and other pieces of "evidence," I proceeded to chart the demo as a controversy. Then I looked for any other pieces of evidence that I could interpret in the "controversy" perspective. As I saw it, Jeanne came to the demo as the "proponent": She wanted to show her colleagues that Music LOGO is a valuable teaching tool, and, obviously, she had the burden of the proof. So I portrayed Jeanne as the project champion. She had an interest at stake. A number of things depended on her "victory" in the debate: mobilization of additional resources for her project; installation and operation of the Computer Music Lab; curriculum reform; good relationships with Music Faculty; acceptance, visibility, and adoption of Music LOGO, and so forth. Having identified a proponent, it was natural for me to look for the opponent, and the obvious role of opponent in a formal debate is to question the proponent's claims. In the demo this role was by all evidence taken by Bruno, since it was he who raised several objections to Music LOGO and to the validity of Jeanne's claims.

Throughout the whole discussion, and later on in the subsequent stage of curriculum development, Bruno made a series of points that consistently challenged the system. His questions touched upon the educational value and use of the system, the "weird" numerical notation adopted, multiple solutions, the significance of student exercises and protocols, the sort of exercises that should be designed for the course, the kind of musical training the students should get, the role of "listening" and other performing activities. What Bruno was questioning was the appropriateness of Jeanne's project to the introductory music course. He voiced his doubts about a specific use of the system and tried to suggest other kinds of applications. By doing so, he revealed a different way of thinking about music and education.

I interpreted Bruno's argument as a way of "resisting," or even "rejecting," the system, using it to support and validate my controversy frame. In a way, I noticed those things in the protocol that matched the assumptions I had inadvertently brought to the demo. These, quite naturally, became "evidence" for me. Later on, as the discussion expanded in the subsequent process of developing the teaching materials for the Computer Music Lab, I still kept using the polarized arguments and dichotomies (and sometimes exaggerated them) to make sense of what looked to me like an ambiguous and at times erratic design process. In retrospect, I might say that my first "chunking" of the flow of events and the work that I did with it were attempts to construct a story that would make sense, that would have a coherence in its own terms. "Polarization" was a useful organizing device. And indeed the data seemed to fit the controversy story nicely, to the point where I was able to project onto the story an "aura of obviousness." The story represented what I held, at that stage, to be a plausible and coherent picture of what had happened in the demo. That became *the* reality for me. All the rest fell in between. But when, later on, I presented this picture of the demo to the participants for testing, a somewhat different story emerged from their comments and evaluations. The once "obvious" controversy story did not hold up anymore, at least not in the form I had initially framed it.

The First Backtalk: The Demo as a Learning Experience

In the backtalk, both Jeanne and the Music Faculty members provided additional cues that helped me see the event in a new light. Further complexities and dimensions surfaced, elements that had gone unnoticed or been underplayed in the first round of observation and analysis. For example, it was really amazing to hear Jeanne say, after reading the story: "I have been looking for what is *not* there!" Most of the participants seemed to agree that there were important features missing in my first-round description. Gradually I came to realize that the controversy was neither the only nor the dominant aspect of the demo. Indeed, after going through my description, most of the Music Faculty members said, quite simply, that the demo was most of all a learning experience, least of all a confrontation.

To be sure, the backtalk and the second round of observations became occasions for new discoveries about the different attitudes of the Music Faculty, the role of the composers in the discussion, the influence of academic ranking, the function and meaning of the demo within the entire design process, the place of Music LOGO with respect to the curriculum and the Music Section, and, finally, my own way of understanding what had happened. For example, Simon, a composer, said that in the first story the discussion had been narrowed down to an argument between Jeanne and Bruno, while, on the contrary, it had been more general and articulate:

> From reading this, one doesn't get the impression that there was a bunch of other people sitting there. . . . It is not clear why you selected Bruno as the main character.

He pointed out that, although there was indeed a substantive argument going on, the demo had the character of a collective inquiry, with people forming opinions there rather than bringing preconceived notions with them. A similar point was made by Paula, a junior faculty member, who resented my portrayal of junior faculty as resisting Music LOGO. On the contrary, she claimed:

> We came to the demo to learn and search out, to discover possibilities, because most of us had not been previously exposed to the system and had a question about it.

"Most of us were silent," she explained, "because we were 'taking in.'" Rather than falling into two opposing camps, she added, the general feelings, though unexpressed in words, were in the middle, a blend of curiosity and cautiousness. For most of the people, the underlying question was: What is this thing about? "The purpose of the demo," Bruno pointed out, "was to get us thinking: Some of us were thinking out loud and some were not."

The backtalk gradually revealed that the previous story did not reflect the different ideas and attitudes of the Music Faculty generally, not even those of the individual members who attended the meeting. It was not apparent from my previous version that people exhibited different ways of approaching Music LOGO, depending on their various cognitive imageries, professional backgrounds and histories, academic roles and ranks in the Music Section. I had particularly failed to grasp the open and exploratory attitude of junior faculty and to appreciate the distinctive role played by the composers. Several distinct issues were being articulated in the discussion: I had chosen to highlight the educational issues raised primarily by Bruno, perhaps because he was the most talkative, but I had underplayed the more technical, musical ones that were implicitly raised or elliptically hinted at by the composers in their hands-on trials with the computer-based compositional projects. On the contrary, I had arbitrarily attributed Bruno's educational ideas and arguments to the other participants, casting him as the champion and the voice of the entire Music Faculty. If I wanted to give a more accurate account of the complexities of what had happened in the demo, most people suggested, I had to chunk it in a different way, breaking down the different responses of the participants.

First commentary: Discovering new features. These comments made me go back to the protocol and rework on it. I began looking for what I had "left out," for things in the protocol that I had not "seen" earlier. I tried out new ways of highlighting and grouping the phenomena observed in the demo, looking for places where an attitude of discovery or an activity of joint learning could be detected. As a result of this second-round, reflective work, the same piece of dialogue would now be connected to different fragments of dialogue and would convey new meanings. What I had taken as a "given" in telling the previous story now came to the foreground as a subject for inquiry. Some new features, such as the more technical musical issues and the composers' response, became visible; some, like Bruno's and Jeanne's argument, received a different treatment; others, like the supposed decision-making function of the meeting, were eliminated. I started paying attention to different things than in my previous description, and I used the materials in a different way, striving for a new kind of coherence. In the process, I made what I perceived to be important discoveries.

First, in encountering "the new thing," the participants responded in a variety of ways. There were different kinds and modes of learning taking place. While some sat silently on the backstage, others got more involved, albeit in different ways. The teachers who were composers and music theorists did not talk much; instead they immediately engaged the materials as musicians. They started making tunes right away, using what they had done to go very smoothly into inherently musical issues, without explicitly questioning whether the tool was in principle good or bad for music education. They tended to pay attention to the more musical, domain-related aspects of the compositional exercises designed by Jeanne, raising issues of periodicity, symmetry, kinds of groupings, musical coherence, accentuation, metric problems, and so forth. Their main problem seemed to lie in discovering what they could do with such a system as practitioners. They would tacitly ask: What can we do with this tool in music? How can we make music with it? To the contrary, other teachers, such as Bruno, who placed more value on a historico-cultural orientation and teaching method, tended to argue about matters of principle and to raise questions of a different kind, revealing a different way of thinking about music. So, while Bruno resisted entering the compositional experiments and even experienced them as a sort of manipulation, the composers went very smoothly into Music LOGO, immediately relating it to their domain of practical knowledge. One might say that while Jeanne and the composers were talking about *music*, in some ways using the system as an additional medium and in other ways ignoring it, Jeanne and Bruno were arguing about the system itself. To borrow Seymour Papert's expression, for the composers the system soon became a thing to think and act with (Papert, 1980), while for the music historians it was a thing to talk and think about. One might also say that Music LOGO did not threaten or sensibly affect the composers' basic ways of doing things in music, their compositional routines; it seemed to "fit" reasonably well into their habitual world of practice. For Bruno and the other historians, however, it interfered with objects and activities that their discipline holds dear: established rules and codes, terminology, language and symbols, style and repertoire. When Music LOGO intruded into their familiar world of music, they got displaced from the images, entities, objects, routines, and relationships that constitute the cognitive and institutional setting—the preexisting "formative context"—in which they usually practice and teach music (Ciborra & Lanzara, 1987; Unger, 1987).

Furthermore, through the backtalk I came to realize that the attitudes of the Music Faculty with respect to Music LOGO differed notably depending on their academic roles and ranks; thus I could not put them all in a group, as I had in the previous story. In the past, most of the senior faculty had shown themselves to be strongly prejudiced, or at best skeptical toward, such experiments, sticking to their beliefs that the Music Section is *not* the place for technology within the Institute and that music and music education are *not* the places for introducing computers. They actually regard the Music Section and themselves as the

Camelot of the Humanities, surrounded by hordes of technologists. But junior faculty "did not share that history," as Paula remarked, and were not in principle opposed to innovation. On the contrary, they showed a mix of curiosity and cautiousness, of interest and perplexity. The question for them seemed to be whether Music LOGO would present an opportunity for or a threat to their professional growth and career advancement. Their cautiousness in the demo and in the subsequent stages of the design process seemed to stem from their legitimate suspicion that they could not really be sure whether the work they put into learning the system and into educational innovation would be institutionally appreciated and academically rewarded in the Music Section specifically and in the Institute at large. To be blunt, the willingness of faculty on the tenure track to learn and be involved with the system depended on whether that involvement would "count" in their academic careers, and the interest and positive response of lecturers not on the tenure track depended on whether their work with Music LOGO and educational innovation would positively affect their uncertain future in the Institute. However, given the Institute's pervasive value system, which puts a premium on leading-edge scientific research rather than on education or research in education, that does not seem to be the case; hence their ambivalent feelings and lukewarm interest. The subsequent events in the process more clearly showed how people's responses are extremely sensitive to this mix of subtle cognitive and institutional factors, continuously shifting over time as these factors themselves shift.

Second commentary: Sources of the "controversy" story. By the same token, the participant's backtalk led me to ask what had originated my controversy story. Why did I have *that* specific way of looking at the demo? What criteria did I use for selecting events, drawing boundaries, articulating observable phases, and identifying main characters and leading themes? Revisiting the demo, I gradually began to see what I had been doing with my materials. I came to see that in my earlier account, I had placed the event in a sort of narrow and misplaced context. Broader contextual data, inaccessible at that time, were missing from my picture. So I tacitly filled in the gaps with assumptions that would hold my story together. I assumed, for instance, that through the demo Music LOGO was entering the Music Section and being tested by the Music Faculty; thus it could only be accepted or rejected. I took as "givens" of the situation that the participants were a decision-making group; that, in general, the Music Faculty were skeptical about, if not openly opposed to Music LOGO; that they needed an evaluation of the system from the teaching staff; that the demo was a regular debate with proponents and opponents; and that the outcome of such debate was to be a yes-or-no decision. By bringing and unreflectively enacting this frame of mind in the situation, I gained access to the event and selected what I held to be relevant data.

Yet as I see it now, there was another major influence on my first description of the demo. My view of it as a controversy was supported and partly shaped by what Jeanne had to say, before the demo, about her attitudes and feelings toward the Music Faculty. In describing the historical antecedents of Music LOGO and of her relationship to the Music Faculty, she gave me a "me-and-them" story: Despite many efforts in the recent past to win the Music Faculty's attention and interest, they had remained indifferent to her work and suspicious of such experiments; while Music LOGO was widely known and used in the outside world, it was stuck in a sort of private garden within the Institute and hardly known in the Music Section. This story fitted perfectly into my frame, and I quickly picked it up. From this I inferred that the demo was occurring at a crucial point in the history of Music LOGO and its designer, and I interpreted Jeanne's sometimes defensive and contentious behavior in the discussion as reflecting, in part, her negative views of the Music Faculty and the whole situation, rather than a response to the participants' actual behaviors in the meeting. In this sense, the demo was an event in which other events and other stories from the past—a history—were deeply embedded.

Thus what constituted "evidence" for me and, most importantly, the various efforts by which I tried to carve a coherent story out of the protocol, were influenced both by my own mistaken or untested presuppositions and by the actors' observable behaviors before and during the demo, which in turn depended on *their* presuppositions and interpretations of the situation. It is difficult to say to what extent my interpretation of the demo was shaped by the participants' interpretations of the same event and by their descriptions of their own roles and behaviors in it. At this point, my only access to the event was through the actors' perspectives and behaviors. But, again, I was able to discover the extent and the character of the actors' influence on my selection of relevant materials only through the backtalk, not *while* I was actually selecting them.

Taking these antecedents as "givens," it was natural for me to frame the demo as a controversial debate; it was easy to identify a rift in the participants' positions. That seemed to me the most "straightforward" way of interpreting the data. This specific mode of description was built into the way I tacitly chunked the protocol and selected the relevant data. Among the many events that were happening and the many

themes that were being touched upon, I selected the confrontation between Jeanne and Bruno as the leading theme of the meeting, using it
as the ordering device of my story and argument and the major key for
interpreting the facts.

Third commentary: Reinterpreting "the facts" of the demo.   Through
the backtalk, however, a new and richer map was generated: People
came to the demo in order to learn about the system, discover possibilities, and be informed, not to make a yes-or-no decision. Now the story
becomes one of discovery and learning about unknown matters. The
controversy was still there, as the data seem to confirm, but now it became "included" in the learning story—a feature to be dealt with within
a broader set of features. It certainly seemed less "obvious" than before,
taking on a different function in the new context. One might then rein-
terpret the controversy as a way for the actors to make their respective
assumptions and stances clear as they struggled to develop a joint
agreement on how Music LOGO should be used. In this perspective, the
polarized argument—as in the "hot" dialogue between Bruno and
Jeanne—works as a natural vehicle for learning and designing in pursuit of a common target. Elements that were used in the controversy
story to identify a rift between a proponent and an opponent in a win/
lose game were now interpreted as argumentative devices that the actors spontaneously used to give one another access to their respective
views and ideas. For example, Bruno and Jeanne in their verbal transactions might simply be "explaining" to one another what they hold
dear and relevant in music education. Bruno, in his later reinterpreta-
tion, pictured himself as "challenging and experimenting," trying to
find out what the system was good for from an educational point of
view, whether it matched his educational ideas and desiderata, and so
forth. Jeanne, responding to the challenge, provided examples of how
the system could be used for or adapted to the specific educational requirements that Bruno posed. In the process, some of the participants
moved from an initial rift to a creative shift in their position. Challenges
and arguments, then, were to be taken not as a rejection of the system—
an *a priori* denial of its utility—but as a way of getting a sense of it, of
exploring its possibilities. It was a way, as Bruno put it, "of construc-
tively probing the system."

   In responding to my controversy story, people tried to account for
their own behavior in the demo in terms that sometimes differed remarkably from my picture of it. Bruno, for example, as he looked back
at the demo as described in my report, provided a more articulate view
about why in the meeting he seemed to be making an argument against

Music LOGO. He said he was trying to force the issue, to make the discussion focus on education. Being concerned mainly about the students, he did not want to go into technicalities; he wanted to probe the system, to try to understand what it could do for students in the introductory course. Thus, in his later account, he pictured himself as not really "resisting" but rather "challenging" the system in order to discover and test its educational potential.

Fourth commentary: Redefining the context.   Later on in the study, as new events took place, my view of the place and function of the demo within the design process changed. I came to see that in the first story I had treated the demo as a self-contained episode in space and time. I had kept it disconnected from other related events, failing to see its function in the broader context of the Music Section and of the overall process of educational adoption of Music LOGO. Most people agreed that I had been correct to emphasize the demo as an important event, but the drama and impact I had assigned it seemed to be askew. Simon said that the impact of Music LOGO was not on the Music Section as a whole but on the teaching of a specific course. "The demo," he remarked, "was an important event because it was a *seed*, a beginning that made other things possible." At the demo, the Music Faculty only *began* to discover Music LOGO. Along the same lines, he went on to evaluate my whole picture. Bruno set a new meaning and context for the event:

> You put too much emphasis on the demo, you give the demo more meaning than it had for us. . . . Maybe that is important for the purposes of your analysis . . . but we forgot about the demo, now we are looking forward to the introductory course. . . . The demo was for us only the beginning of an ongoing process of adjustment, reflection, and remodeling of the course.

At this point, the participants were looking back at the past from the perspective of what they were doing *now*, reflecting a climate of growing curiosity and involvement bred by the approaching deadline for beginning to prepare the teaching materials for the Computer Music Lab curriculum. To the participants' eyes, and consequently to the observer's, the demo had acquired different qualities and meanings because it had become an event placed in a temporal chain of events punctuated in a different way. The demo was now perceived as having changed the institutional setting of the project in such a way as to create a new set of institutional possibilities, a new interpersonal atmosphere, and a new world of action and inquiry for the people involved. It opened up a new

space in which the developers and the teaching staff could work together. The importance of the demo was that, as Jeanne said, "it pushed
over the edge, into another world." Perhaps precisely because of that it
tended to be "forgotten."

The Second Backtalk: The Demo as Cooptation

Several months later the "learning" story was submitted to the project developers for a second round of backtalk and testing. In reviewing
the story, meanings shifted again and a new story emerged. In the
meantime, new events had occurred: The Computer Music Lab had
been installed, the teaching materials prepared, and Music LOGO used
for the first time in the introductory course. But apparently the promises and possibilities that the demo had opened up had not yet been
fulfilled. In the first semester, some 150 students were using the lab.
Faculty, in an effort at evaluation, were paying attention to students'
log-in and log-out times, and some even asked students to write comments on their experience in the lab. However, following an initial stage
of engagement, the teachers had not pursued their adoption of the system to the point where they could autonomously teach with it, and, for
one reason or another, they had gradually dropped it. For various reasons they found it difficult to relate the lab to their teaching, and they
had not been pushing the students hard enough to use it. As a consequence, in the following semester the course curriculum had not been
substantially changed, the teachers continued to adhere to their old
ways and practices, very few students were using the lab and experimenting with the system, and the whole project, in the words of its
developer, was "falling off." So far the project seemed neither to have
produced much educational impact nor to have built up much institutional knowledge about the system. The attempt at integrating Music
LOGO and the Computer Music Lab into the introductory course had
substantially failed, or at least it was perceived so at that time.

In this changed context, when the project leader went through the
second story and started making comments about it, she said that the
demo had had no factual consequences, either educational nor institutional, and that it was indeed a plain case of *cooptation*. Here I report
this new story, as I heard it from Jeanne. The demo was a "formal gesture" to the junior faculty on the part of the chairman of the Music
Curriculum Committee in order to make the introduction of Music LOGO
more acceptable to the faculty and, in particular, to staff who taught the
introductory course. The meeting had rather the character of a social
rite of integration within the Music Section. The real reason for having

the demo had to be understood within the context of departmental politics; the demo had had a social and political function, and the discussion turned out to be a "pantomime," a ritual, with no real substance to
it. The argument that was developed was a fake one, and the controversy was insubstantial, merely reflecting underlying stances and positions within the Music Section that were "political" in essence. The real
issues at stake were smooth acceptance and legitimation of Music LOGO.
By making his argument, for instance, Bruno was simply resisting this
cooptation. Indeed, the whole process of designing the lab teaching materials subsequent to the demo was one of political transactions and
trade-offs. There had been no real experimentation by teachers, nor had
there been a "creative shift" in their positions: They were just "coping"
with the situation. The only shift that had occurred was political, the
consequence of a trade-off. Indeed, the demo had been neither a learning nor a "seminal" event, as it was interpreted in the second story. It
had not had any significant or lasting impact on the attitudes of the
participants. In Jeanne's words: "Nothing really happened in the demo
and after! People have not learned anything!"

Commentary: Testing the validity of the story. Jeanne's new story
put me back to work. What were the reasons for this further interpretation of the demo? If the demo was a pantomime with a fake argument,
what would be the meaning, then, of what was being said in it? Within
the "cooptation" story, what would be the significance of Jeanne's and
Bruno's argument and of the composers' activity? While the learning-
experience story did not wipe out the controversy, but rather included
it by assigning the argument a new function and meaning within a varied context, the cooptation story contained features that did not cumu-
late well with the two previous stories. On the contrary, it tended to
deprive the demo of some of its most significant features as recorded in
the protocol. The value of the demo as a learning experience for the
participants and as a substantive controversy on musical and educational matters tended to be denied or downplayed. If one took this perspective seriously, the entire history of the design and adoption of Music LOGO—developing the lab materials, integrating them into the music
curriculum, setting up the lab, testing with the students—would be re-
written as one of political conflicts, transactions, and manipulations.

Sticking with the original data, there was no evidence in the whole
protocol that the demo was merely a political event, the discussion
pointless, and the argument fake. There was no way to assert that
people were not really meaning what they were saying, nor that they
were meaning more than what they actually said, although these are

both entirely possible in principle. There was no way to support or validate the cooptation story using the data of the demo protocol. On the
contrary, this data indicated forcefully that people were taking their discussion very seriously. An interpretation of the demo as a cooptation
would not account for the rich and articulate behavior displayed by the
participants in the demo. One might say, in the first instance, that the
argument was substantive and meaningful in terms of its literal content
and, in the second instance, that it *also* reflected stances and positions
that were "political." In other words, according to this view, the argument between Jeanne and Bruno could also *stand for* an underlying political contention that could not be explicitly spelled out because the
context, the occasion, and the state of interpersonal relations among the
Music Faculty did not allow it. But there was no way to test the validity
of this view by starting from the demo protocol. This interpretation
could not be drawn directly from the data provided by the discussion;
it derived from the new situation that later emerged. This new way of
looking back at the demo seemed to reflect not the actual data of the
demo protocol but rather the growing sense of disenchantment with the
slowing-down of the project. In other words, the cooptation story
seemed to be a response to a new situation that originated in later
events and experiences. Thus, in her new interpretation, Jeanne used
the project's present situation and outcomes to review the meaning of
the demo. But in doing so she tended to wipe out many of the features
that made the demo an interesting and important opportunity, in its
own right, for learning about issues of computers, music, and education
and for the development and educational adoption of Music LOGO—
irrespective of its political valences and independent of its apparently
weak impacts on people's modes of thinking and on the follow-up of
the project.

ACCOUNTING FOR THE SHIFT

Emerging Questions: Toward a Second-Order Inquiry

When the participants were asked to "talk back" to me, they tended
to develop stories that were reflective responses to the backtalk experiment. These stories sometimes differed remarkably from my account of
past events. Also, although these stories tended to be internally coherent and *unique* in their own terms, they were often inconsistent with
one another. Each story reconstructed the demo in different ways,
bringing new meanings to the event and revealing shifting criteria for

description at work. Not only would different participants give the same event multiple interpretations at a specific point in time, but also the same individual would construe different stories about the same event at different points in time. Consequently my perception of some key events, such as the demo, changed. The shift of the stories affected my understanding of the entire design process, forcing me to go back and reconsider my manner of making descriptions and conducting inquiries.

On the one hand, the new stories provided further contextual data that were relevant to a deeper understanding of the setting and background of the project, leading to a more articulate picture of its institutional context and educational significance; on the other hand, they evoked several unexpected questions and puzzles that, when taken seriously, opened up an inquiry of a different order. Why would people tell me all these different and shifting stories? What makes them change their perception of the same event at different points in time? Why do they chunk the flow of events in different ways when they go back to reconsider the past? How can I account for the shift? And to what extent is my own understanding affected by all this?

Sources of the Stories

The stories seemed to stem from the complex interaction of three distinct sources: previous stories, later events, and backtalk. Let me now try to describe this phenomenology.

The stories as transient constructs. The actors gave different meanings to the demo by making coherent universes within which the demo gained meaning—universes that could include the demo in different ways.[4] In each new story, the demo acquired a varied "position"—a specific valence—within the broader context of the design process. The uses people made of the demo as a significant event shifted with the evolving situation; and as the uses shifted, so did the modes of description. In shifting from one story to the next, new features, relations, and behaviors were "liberated" and rearranged in different ways, while previous ones may have been kept or wiped out. Each story thus became a sort of "reference entity" for the actors—"an embodied and enacted description of what the participants know so far" (Bamberger & Schön, 1983, p. 70)—that helped them establish some transient order, construct some transient meaning, and undertake some exploratory action in a shifting, ambiguous situation. When the situation changes, the descriptions have to be revised if they are to make sense in the new situation.

The shifting stories are transient constructs, intermediary arrangements that, in their various transformations, help the actors and the observer make sense of a complex situation; they are continuously rearranged, or discarded, or put aside, as situations evolve into new emerging states. Once constructed, a story becomes a point of reference, a "hook" to fix what the actors and the observer know so far about the evolving situations that they have to face and account for.[5]

When the actors were asked to talk back about the episodes they had lived through, they kept shifting their boundaries to account for later, incoming events. Depending on the situation at hand and on the current context, they recontextualized and reconstructed the demo in different ways, modulating or accentuating peculiar aspects of it. Thus the event itself was *extended* into an ever-evolving sequence of descriptions. For example, when the first backtalk took place, a few months after the actual occurrence of the demo, new events had occurred, the situation of action had changed, and perceptions and perspectives had shifted. Thus when the "learning experience" story was generated, some of the faculty who had attended the demo were engaged in developing new teaching materials for the Computer Music Lab. They were busily experimenting with different kinds of solutions to the problem of integrating Music LOGO into the introductory course and its established activities. They seemed to be in an experimental and learning mood, and the deadline for completing the teaching materials was close. Consequently, they needed to build a coherent picture of what had happened and what they knew so far. The demo was an event that had to make sense *in the present context*. It was used and reshaped to fit present interests and perspectives. It had to be connected and grouped with other events and situations that had occurred so far. The demo was now "a piece of material" distant in time and, in order to gain a new meaning, needed to be situated in a temporal and logical chain of events. For example, it was now seen as the beginning—"the seed"— of the development of the Computer Music Lab and of "many other events." The actors reinterpreted and justified their earlier behaviors through the present situation. The demo was reinterpreted and given meaning in the light of the present situation, and the latter, in turn, was "explained" by reference to the demo. By grouping it with what came next, the actors constructed a chain of events—a plot—that made sense and had a coherence *now*. This plot, which could have been temporary and makeshift or stable and resilient, was a cross-temporal structure, connecting many events, whose main function was to confer coherence, meaning, orientation, sense of place and direction, motivation for undertaking action, and even identity.

Producing the shift. In our self-study, this process of revision and reconstruction was facilitated by the backtalk. The new stories about the demo were generated by allowing the participants to look back at the stream of past events in which they had been involved and to see themselves *while* they were engaged in action, as they were depicted by the observer. This move gave them an opportunity to test their own perceptions and interpretations against mine, to see the ways they saw and behaved at different stages of the process, to recall things they had forgotten, to appreciate the differences between the situation *then* and the situation *now*, and, finally, to construct new stories of "what really happened." The move opened up a space for discussion and reflection, creating a mirror, or rather a video, in which the actors could see themselves portrayed or, to stay with the metaphor, "featured." So the stories were generated by commenting and reflecting on previous stories, producing extensions, revisions, evaluations, variations, recontextualizations, and so forth. In this process, one may really build on previous stories and data by adding further dimensions to an event, as in the learning story, or else one may refer to data that were not in the original protocol but stem mainly from later occurrences, as in the cooptation story.

The shifting stories are also, in part, a consequence of the backtalk, in the sense that they were literally "produced" *through* the reflective activity, although it is certainly difficult to say to what extent. But one thing can be stated with certainty: Had my report not been handed back to the actors and had the actors not been given the possibility of shooting back to me, no story other than the "controversy" would have become visible and made available for public inspection and inquiry. For example, the learning-experience story was composed from additional data generated within the conversational, interactive research framework of the self-study. These data would most probably have been lost otherwise; they would have not fallen into my visual field. Thus the backtalk created the conditions for the shift in the previous story to take place, and that shift, in turn, was the source for liberating/annihilating features, thus leading to a new story. In this sense, I might well say that, through the backtalk, I have "produced the effect I wished to observe" (Schön, 1983).

Nature and Consequences of the Reflective Move

The backtalk was the methodological kernel of the self-study. Although its research implications were still unclear at the beginning (and some are still unclear now), it turned out to be a strategic move. I could have clung to the first story as the true and definite picture of reality, an accurate account of what happened in the demo. Or else, as is common in most social and action research, I could have used the backtalk only as feedback, that is, a correcting device or control mechanism to get to a more rigorous picture of the situation. In such cases, the discrepancies between earlier and later data are indeed considered, but only as corrective inputs to more refined, "first-order" descriptions; they are made to converge to an end-of-the-line description that presumably represents "the true reality." In this perspective, each subsequent description would be a closer approximation to the true story. In our self-study, additional data were certainly used to produce better stories, but I also made a different, more "radical" use of the backtalk. I used it as a reflective mechanism to inquire into the categories and procedures by which the stories were generated. In other words, the discrepancies between the new data and the previous stories were treated as springboards to jump to a "second-order" inquiry into how stories are made and into why and how they shift in time. In this perspective, the research focus is not simply upon the fixing of a plausible story out of some first-order data, but rather upon the process of making and changing stories in time. To do this, I had to treat the stories as "data" for a second-order inquiry. And this, in turn, involved being able to disconnect from and gain access to the different assumptions underlying the generation of different stories.

By such a move, a complex conversational structure was enacted, with several distinct conversations simultaneously taking place at different levels. To begin with, there was a conversation between myself and the actors (project developers, faculty members); another conversation was going on between the actors and their materials (Music LOGO, the project, music, education, curricula, and so forth) and a third one, between myself and my materials (my own representations of the design process). But at the same time, the reflective move also engendered "second-order" conversations between the actors' and the observer's stories, and between the actors' current and their own earlier stories.[6] This complex conversational structure incorporates an important time dimension that must be discussed in more detail.

The move opened up the past (and the present) to discourse as a common domain of reference for the agents of the process. As they intentionally gained access to prior events in the same process, they were also able to converse with themselves. Looking back at past events and reflecting upon them had the effect of making the process "double back on itself," thereby enabling it to live off itself (Olafson, 1979). By that move, an abstract self-referential time dimension was embedded in our small experimental world and in the research method, and a sort of "historicity" was grafted onto the design process. The move enabled the participants to make use of their ability to refer to events in their own pasts (Olafson, 1979). Revisiting prior events was for the actors a way of keeping and renewing the memory of what often gets lost in a design process, that is, the process itself as well as many of its previous "branchings" that do not converge or fit with the final outcomes. Thus an intelligibility, or different kinds of intelligibility "across time," could be imputed to the process by eventually unifying individual time frameworks. The influence of previous events, choices, actions, and descriptions on the present situation, and even on the present ways of perceiving the situation, could be appreciated. "I see now how I could have done it differently" said the project developer referring to the demo. The "doubling back" of the process on itself was not produced by duplicating it, by making replicas, but by remaking and rewriting previous stories. Events were interpreted and reinterpreted *through time*, not only *in time*. By bringing selectivity, and adding or subtracting depth, time itself became both a sort of "material" by which shifting stories were constructed and an inner component of the research method.

Looking backward at the process pulls events out of the world of action, where they have been "lived," and inscribes them into the world of memory and discourse, where they can be remembered and told. But the time structure of the description never matches the time structure of the event as it occurred in the domain of action. Events and actions are punctuated in different ways, they are given a different tempo, depending on whether one is *going forward with them* as the process unfolds or is *looking back at them* from a temporal distance. To an actor involved in a situation of action, his situation is a self-contained microworld, bounded in space and time, where he temporarily lives. He tends to (and has to!) appreciate it from within, and he will punctuate the flow of experiences according to his changing goals and perspectives. His focus of attention is pointed to the future, and his job is to act in order to make something happen *next* out of *that* situation. That is whence he gets purpose and meaning for his actions. On the contrary, when he looks at the same situation in retrospect, he comes to see it as a spot in a set or sequence of many other happenings. Now he is looking from a present that is the future state of those previous actions and events, and he will tend to treat them as causes or conditions for what he has got in the present (Schutz, 1973). He will try to cut out of the past an ordered sequence or plot that should be coherent and make sense *now.* Accounting for those events and actions in terms of their *function* in a plot is now what helps him make meaning and shape coherence in retrospect.

Thus "what happened," as it is experienced by an actor, never coincides with a specific description nor with the totality or the sequence of descriptions, even if the one who makes the description has been a witness and an actor in that happening, as it is well known to contemporary historiographers. When the elements and the features that were acted upon within a situation of action are transposed to a domain of description, they are subject to a different kind of treatment and become different things. Now the making of the description becomes the locus of action. This was clearly perceived and stated by Jeanne:

> By putting the demo in a different space, a space of discourse, it becomes something that is talked about, it becomes the focus of attention, not something whose reality exists only in the temporally and spatially bounded domain of action, something which is locally acted upon and lived through for a while, and then—puff!—disappears.

An event is identified by means of (and evolves through) time and space, but whether the multiple and shifting descriptions will ultimately converge to a shared, "objective" story—a story that is reported as the true one—is a matter of fiction and choice, not a matter of fact and truth. That amounts to saying that the truth of an event can never be accessed through a sort of composition or combination of the innumerable stories that can be told about it. The truth of an event is itself a makeshift artifact that must be jointly constructed and tested in practice and has only a practical, local validity.

Evolving Understandings of the Design Process

As the reader might have realized already, the backtalk also had important consequences for my understanding of the design process. It helped me reflect upon my own criteria for interpretation and revise my conceptual structure. As the actors, responding to the controversy story, added new data and basic features that did not fit with my previous account, I gained insight into my own ways of looking at things. If, when asked about things past, the actors respond with descriptions that, although internally coherent in their own terms, pay attention to different features, what does this tell me about my own way of making a description? What does this tell me about what I take to be significant or even observable in a phenomenon?

These emerging questions made me look back for the criteria I had quite spontaneously (unreflectively) used in chunking the protocol of the demo and in interpreting the overall flow of events and actions in

the design process. That involved making myself vulnerable to the possibility of restructuring the assumptions tacitly embedded in my earlier
description. As a consequence, both the mode and the object of my
inquiry shifted, eventually raising questions that went far beyond the
immediate, first-order objective of capturing the "real" facts and the
presumably "objective" sense of them. From trying to fix the events
given a certain way of chunking a flow of data, my inquiry shifted to
assessing the multiple and shifting ways of chunking and interpreting
the events at different points in time throughout the process. While in
the first round of observations and analysis I was using the observed
data to make a story, now the different stories generated in the process
became second-order data for inquiry. The various ways of organizing
reality and making sense of it *in time* themselves became new materials
for inquiry, not stable maps in terms of which I tried to fix the facts *"wie
es eigentlich gewesen,"* to recall Leopold von Ranke's expression. The inquiry into "facts" shifted to an inquiry into multiple, time-dependent,
evolving descriptions. Both the knowledge embedded in my previous
description of the demo—that which I was taking for granted and in
terms of which I was "seeing" the demo—and the limitations of such
knowledge became visible and a matter of discussion with my partners;
they could be tested against other modes of description. As a result, it
was possible to gain insight into how the complex, evolving social artifact that we usually call "reality" is constructed and transformed
through an endless process of discovery, production, and reflection.

In the process that I have studied, making, testing, and revising
descriptions were crucial activities toward building a shared sense of
reality among the participants in the project. At one stage such activities
could not be kept separated from the actual process of designing the
system and the new educational environment associated with it. The
design of the system itself evolved through making, evaluating, and
remaking descriptions. To be sure, generating stories that are meaningful and powerful, as well as usable in practice, is an important aspect of
the design activity; it is a way of acting with the materials of design.
There are stories that are better than others, in the sense that they help
us understand and act more effectively in a situation of action. For instance, the learning-experience story that came out of the backtalk is
definitely a richer artifact than the controversy story: it incorporates features that were cut out of the previous story, conveys more complex
meanings, refers to a broader context, and points to potential actions
and choices that were not visible before. Briefly, the story conveys a kind
of intelligibility of the design situation that broadens the range of possible actions for the designers.[7]

Interestingly enough, I came to see that the very same process of accruing/wiping out features characterized different kinds of "design" activities: the construction of the system's evolving configurations, the various interpretations of the demo, the generation of multiple and shifting stories, and even my own inquiry into such matters. In each case we were dealing with "ways of making artifacts," albeit different kinds of artifacts (Goodman, 1978). In other words, I performed as an observer the same kind of reflective activity that the designers did in their design work. My purpose at one point became to help them do with their materials the same thing that I was trying to do with them. In helping the actors perform a self-reflective activity, at the same time I reflected upon my own research method, categories, and materials. It is important here to remark that the help was mutual; in other words, I could do my job *because* they did theirs and because of the special kind of access they allowed to me. As the actors could see themselves reflected in my description, so I could see myself reflected in their comments to my description, or, to be more precise, in the discrepancies between their comments and my description.

To put it another way, the self-experiment was *built into* the design process; for the agents in the process, the design activity developed, in different degrees, by means of a reflective, self-evaluative work. Thus the history of the project also merged with the history of the self-study. The design process itself was structured as a self-study, consisting of a number of self-experiments conducted at different levels, both in local situations bounded in space and time *and* on the whole process. It is interesting to notice that the direction and the outcomes of the process were in part dependent on the self-study work, even though it is difficult to assess to what extent that was true. This is why incorporating an explicit reflective function into the design process and the research method should indeed be regarded as a reality-building strategy, not as a superfluous ornament of a narcissistic watcher or designer.

SOME CONCLUDING REMARKS

Coming close to the end of my inquiry, I shall try now to draw some conclusions from the kind of work I have done. As I reflect upon it, going back in rapid flashbacks to events, episodes, and situations that punctuated the design process, I am struck by the multiple aspects and the shifting character of my work. What I perceived to be the object of my inquiry changed over time as the self-study progressed. As new events and problems challenged the project developers and the Music

Faculty involved, my focus of attention shifted and my research questions had to be reformulated. Although I was expected to keep track of a linear sequence of events, I often proceeded in cycles—through evolving questions. I often found myself rehearsing questions that had been asked already at previous stages of inquiry or in different contexts. But the answers given to those questions were never the same. In keeping track of the process, I was often frustrated by not being able to cope with the sudden and unexpected shifts of events and situations, and I sometimes felt inadequate at connecting and at making sense of the unfolding complexities, intricacies, and multiple dimensions of the process. It was difficult, for instance, to map out the changing points of views and the shifting interpretations of the people involved in the development and adoption of Music LOGO. I felt as if I had been unwillingly dragged into a game where the rules, the "things" and the "ground" of the game itself were changing all the time, *while we were actually playing*, as in *Alice in Wonderland*'s Queen's croquet-ground.[8]

For instance, one of the basic problems that I faced was fixing the object of the self-study and drawing its boundaries. At the beginning of the experiment, my intended job was to analyze and document the computer music project, that is, the Music LOGO software development proper. But when Music LOGO was unexpectedly adopted by the Music Section to be used in the introductory course, broader educational, interpersonal, and institutional complexities came into the picture, and very much into the project's scope and activities. Consequently the scope of the self-study changed, too.

Turning the demo into a subject for a reflective experiment was crucial to that change in scope. In a way, the shifting descriptions of the demo reflected the actors' and my own evolving understandings of the design process and our repeated attempts at fixing its shifting boundaries. As I initially perceived it, the demo marked, so to speak, the crossing of a boundary between the project's "inside" activities and the "outside" institutional setting: With the demo, Music LOGO started its "long journey" into the Institute. But later I began to see the demo and the subsequent curriculum development as essential components of the design process. As designing activity extended into educational and institutional matters, I began questioning where its real boundaries were. Together with the developers, I kept redefining the scope and the contours of the self-study as we went along.

By the same token, the scope and meaning of the project were reassessed. For the project developer, as she often pointed out, the real outcome of the project became the integration of Music LOGO into an educational and institutional context, not so much the software technology and facilities per se. The project was placed within the broader context of curriculum reform, professional music practice, academic roles and ranks, institutional dynamics and constraints. New insights and options for action were discovered. For example, the continuing interaction with the Music Faculty led the project developer to readdress some of the uses and applications of Music LOGO and to see the Computer Music Lab not as a fancy, specialized computer environment, but rather as a general facility for generating music education, open to a variety of uses and novel possibilities. Both Music LOGO and the Computer Music Lab underwent a process of reinvention—a process of creative adoption wherein some of the originally planned applications were dismissed, while new functions, uses, and meanings came into being (Rice & Rogers, 1980).

As I perceive it now, at the completion of my work, the self-study was an occasion to extract a considerable amount of knowledge about the multiple and subtle threads binding design intentions and choices, educational options, and patterns of adoption within a given institutional setting. This knowledge is often difficult to access, because it is not embedded in the outcomes of the design process and tends to be obliterated by the outcomes. Rather, it is "anchored" to the shifting stories that people tell at different stages of the process—stories that people tend to forget as they proceed in designing.

Here a very important function of the observer becomes clear. He becomes a sort of storyteller: By reporting these stories, he keeps the memory of the process, a memory that is often fragmented in many different, sometimes incompatible, ever-evolving stories. His task is to put these fragments together to compose a picture—a story of shifting stories—that no single actor probably shares. The observer records features of the design process that would have been left buried or forgotten under the surface of pressing events and actions or under the urge to search for solutions. Yet these features, though pushed to the background of action and awareness, can never be completely wiped out: In some special sense they stay with us in a sedimented, objectified form that tends to hide its origin, and they have a subtle influence on our ways of thinking and acting. They become embedded in what we choose to forget and take for granted in our designs.

ACKNOWLEDGMENTS

Many thanks are due to the project developers for having helped me design the research conditions that made this type of inquiry possible and to the members of the Music Faculty for having been very collaborative. In a way, they are indeed "technically" responsible for what I wrote, although not morally. Also, I wish to thank Donald Schön, with whom I have had long and helpful discussions on the methods, the problems, and the findings in my work.

NOTES

1. The project did not start from scratch, but had some important antecedents. On the one hand, it originated in Jeanne's previous research into the cognitive aspects of music perception and understanding, as well as in her strong interest in education and learning as a field of research in its own right; on the other hand, based on the results of these studies, and unsatisfied with traditional teaching styles, Jeanne has undertaken the development of a computer music system. The system exploits the high-level capabilities of the LOGO language (Papert, 1980), allowing for a powerful procedural description of musical structures and facilitating composition-like student projects. Music LOGO employs a notational system that allows students to represent and manipulate elements and relations in ways that standard music notation makes difficult or impossible. Sequences of pitch and duration can be constructed, named, combined, and transformed, helping students with little or no previous musical training move quickly to engage in composition-like activities.

2. The question of how to gain access to and develop relevant knowledge about social processes has always been a matter of debate in social research. A number of approaches and methods have made different claims. Certainly such knowledge is very much dependent on the method of inquiry, that is, on the specific modes of observation and analysis that the observer chooses to adopt. Cross-sectional approaches, which are very much in vogue, focus on what might be called "static photographs" of a social phenomenon; they tend to develop knowledge relating to these still pictures, not to the evolution of the phenomenon *in time*. Nevertheless, the findings that result from such a research strategy are often generalized across time in an arbitrary manner. Such cross-sectional analyses, however, make it difficult or impossible to grasp the "motion picture" of a phenomenon and to develop process-related knowledge. Yet the process may reveal features that are embedded neither in its outcomes nor in the still pictures, and these features may be extremely relevant to the understanding of the phenomenon. But how can one gain access to phenomena that are highly volatile, intrinsically unstable, or even ephemeral—phenomena that have often been "obliterated" by the time the process has reached its final state? This question becomes crucial in the analysis of complex design processes, where analysts and designers need a kind of knowledge that is quickly and effectively usable in the process in which they are engaged. In this chapter I try to give an example of how one could go about addressing this question. For

more research work from the same perspective in the field of systems development, see Boland (1979a,b), Salaway (1985), and Lanzara and Mathiassen (1985).

3. The fieldwork consisted of on-site observations for several hours weekly, close monitoring of the software development activities, review of documentary materials, and extensive taperecorded interviews with the project developers, with some faculty members variously involved with curriculum design, and with several students who used the system in their classes. Also, a 2-hour demonstration of Music LOGO given by Jeanne to some members of the Music Faculty was recorded and thoroughly analyzed, together with a few other backtalk sessions and a 1-week workshop, attended by the designers, the Music Faculty, and myself, on Music LOGO and its educational applications.

4. Some of the terms used here are borrowed from Bamberger & Schön (1983). All the discussion of stories as transient constructs draws heavily on their work.

5. Winnicott (1953), in his study of children's play behavior, first introduced the notion of "transitional object" that I am here transposing and adapting to a different context.

6. The notion of conversation is used here in a broad metaphorical sense. See, for this, Schön (1983) and Bamberger and Schön (1983). I should say that I see it as a way of acting rather than a way of speaking. This whole self-study proceeded by means of conversations and explored the meaning of conversation.

7. The question of the validity of the stories, of whether a story can be tested rigorously against observable data and can be said to be "better" or "more valid" than another, bothered me a great deal during my research work. I was particularly puzzled by a statement made by a project developer about the shifting stories: "Yes, the stories are different . . . yet they are all true!" If all views are valid, then questions of validity disappear and we are inevitably led to take a relativistic position. But if we admit that some stories might be more coherent or complete, or more powerful, effective, and more usable in practice, then there must be a way to compare and test them. I claim that, in fact, we do compare, test, and evaluate stories all the time in the practical and argumentative routines of our real-life situations. Furthermore, the stories that are generated also depend on the kind and depth of testing done during the backtalk. This, in turn, raises questions about the criteria for testing: When is a test of previous stories fully adequate or complete? If seen in a temporal perspective, I would argue: probably never. Because tests are themselves events in time, on which multiple stories can be told, their validity is perceived differently across time and can be—in fact, is—continuously questioned and requestioned across time. In this context, I wish to remark that questions raised by Putnam and Schön about my present account—during workshop discussions they suggested that I should not accept at face value my subjects' later revisions of their stories—are precisely a test of the adequacy of my testing criteria, and if this test on the one hand helps me see *now* what I could have done better *then*, on the other hand, by creating with its very occurrence a possibility of its own disconfirmation, it is,

in my view, *also* a powerful instance of the argument that the pursuit of validity is necessarily time-related and time-bound (which does not imply relativism). This line of reasoning leads me to see testing as a generative and projective activity, as a way of generating further, eventually richer stories (I should say: a way of making history) rather than checking and stabilizing some "valid," conclusive interpretation of the past. Obviously, the issue of validity is here raised only at the local, practical level, not in the sense of establishing a universal scientific truth.

8. See Lewis Carroll's (1865/1982) *Alice's Adventures in Wonderland.* The strange croquet game imagined by Carroll may be taken as a metaphor for the problems and puzzles that social research is bound to face in the study of ambiguous, shifting real-life situations, where the subject matter is hard to harness to the rules of method. Such situations may lead the observer to try to either control or reflect on the rules of the method and on his own role as an observer, in short, to acknowledge the fact that he, as well as the objects of his inquiry, stands on a moving platform.

REFERENCES

Bamberger, J., & Schön, D. A. (1983, March). Learning as reflective conversation with materials. *Art Education*, pp. 68–73.

Boland, R. (1979a). The process and product of system design. *Management Science, 24* (9), 887–898.

Boland, R. (1979b). The process and product of system design: A phenomenological approach. In *Proceedings of the Third International Conference on Information Systems,* Ann Arbor, MI, December 1982 (pp. 31–45).

Carroll, L. (1982). *Alice's adventures in wonderland.* Oxford, England: Oxford University Press. (Original work published 1865)

Ciborra, C., & Lanzara, G. F. (1987). Change and formative contexts in information systems development. In *Proceedings of the IFIP Conference on Information Systems Development for Human Progress in Organizations,* Atlanta, GA, May 1987.

Geertz, C. (1973). *The interpretation of cultures.* New York: Basic Books.

Geertz, C. (1983). *Local knowledge.* New York: Basic Books.

Goodman, N. (1978). *Ways of worldmaking.* Indianapolis, IN: Hackett.

Lanzara, G. F., & Mathiassen, L. (1985). Mapping situations within a systems development project. *Information and Management, 8,* 3–20.

Olafson, F. (1979). *The dialectics of action.* Chicago: University of Chicago Press.

Papert, S. (1980). *Mindstorms.* New York: Basic Books.

Rice, R. R., & Rogers, E. M. (1980). Reinvention in the innovation process. *Knowledge, 1* (4), 499–514.

Salaway, G. (1985). An organizational learning approach to information systems development. Unpublished manuscript, University of California, Los Angeles.

Schön, D. A. (1973). Organizational learning. In G. Morgan (Ed.), *Beyond method*. Beverly Hills, CA: Sage.

Schön, D. A. (1983). *The reflective practitioner*. New York: Basic Books.

Schutz, A. (1973). The problem of social reality. In *Collected Papers* (Vol. 1). The Hague: Martinus Nijhoff.

Unger, R. M. (1987). *False necessity*. Cambridge, England: Cambridge University Press.

Van Maanen, J. (1979). The fact of fiction in organizational ethnography. *Administrative Science Quarterly, 24* (4), 539–550.

Veyne, P. (1984). *On writing history: Essay on epistemology*. Middletown, CT: Wesleyan University Press. (Original work published 1971)

Winnicott, D. W. (1953). Transitional objects and transitional phenomena. *International Journal of Psycho-Analysis, 34* (2).

14

Trying to Understand
What One Is Afraid to Learn About

DAN BAR-ON

EARLY MORNING on August 1, 1985, my wife and I arrived in Wuppertal by night train from Copenhagen. This was my first trip into Germany, four of which followed during the next 3 years. I came to interview children of Holocaust perpetrators, a group no one had studied systematically before. In the present chapter I would like to present my own way of feeling and thinking—how I went about this research. Trying to make a long story short, I will have to rely on thirteen interviews, which appear in full length in *Legacy of Silence* (Bar-On, 1989).

It is difficult for me to define a point in time when this research actually started. In retrospect, it seems that in a way I had prepared myself all my life for this specific study, though I consciously started to think about the research only in the fall of 1983. The language issue can serve as an example of this feeling. I was born in Israel, and Hebrew is my native language. I know German but at that time had not used it since early childhood, when I had spoken it mainly with my grandparents. However, when I started the research my German was suddenly *there*, even with a Hamburg-like accent that made me sound natural to many of my interviewees. This came as a complete surprise to me. I had been ready to carry out the interviews with the help of an English-speaking translator.

WHAT LED ME TO THIS RESEARCH

In retrospect, there are a few milestones that I think had influenced me before I came to think consciously about this research. In 1976, I went with my parents for their annual summer vacation to Switzerland.

It was my first trip to Europe. While walking through the woods in Zermatt, I remember the feeling that once, long ago, I had known these woods. This strange feeling caused me to try to work through some of my own Sabra external layers, to find parts of myself I had tried to dismiss before as belonging only to my parents' generation. Specifically, I remember confronting my fear and helplessness, feelings that I had tended to deny before that period and that had come out in nightmares after the Yom Kippur war.

Later that summer, by coincidence, I met Professor Ulich from the Zurich Institute for the Psychology of Work. He was the first German gentile of my own age with whom I had ever become friendly. He could speak openly about his family's past during World War II. He was empathic toward my own people's fate, but without the signs of guilt so characteristic to other persons of his age group. This special combination helped me confront some of my own stereotypes about the Germans: There must be different people among them, too.

At that time, however, other interests occupied my mind: I was working with kibbutzim on community development, trying to reveal the "untold stories" of the communities' early days, which, I believed, still had an impact on their current decision making due to collective denial. In addition, I was interviewing coronary patients after their first myocardial infarction (MI) for my doctoral dissertation. I was looking for a real-life crisis with which most people cope without necessarily getting psychological help. I wanted to find out how they did it. I asked them to give me their "subjective theories" about their heart attack: Why did it occur, and what would help them cope with it? I sorted out these "theories" in terms of their "effectiveness" vis-à-vis short- and long-range recovery and rehabilitation (Bar-On, 1986b, 1987). Denial also played a role in this study, because it was found to be "helpful" in the short run (for the patients who "used" it) but dysfunctional in the long run (Bar-On, 1985).

During that research I had some of my first encounters with Holocaust survivors. Shlomo was a strong-looking man who did not give much thought to his heart attack. He was the typical "denier." His wife, however, disclosed that he had been screaming in his dreams almost every night for the last 35 years: "Germans," "Nazis," "Arabs." When he screams, she gets up and brings him a glass of water, and they fall asleep again. They never discussed these nightmares. His parents were shot in front of his eyes by the Germans when he was about 7 years old, and only by chance did he escape a similar fate. He had never talked about it with anyone before coming to the intensive care unit after his MI. Shlomo would describe these terrible events to me and then would go back to small talk, smiling as if nothing special had occurred. However, during one of our last conversations, he asked me, with a troubled look in his eyes, if the fact that his 13-year-old son had recently started to scream in his dreams was somehow connected to his own nightmares (Bar-On, 1986a). He had never spoken with his son about his own experiences during the Holocaust, because he "did not want to bother him with it." It was very difficult to convince Shlomo to try to find a way to talk with his son. I myself was not sure to what extent their fears were related or could be alleviated by such a conversation. My conflict and insecurity were no less than his own. Now I occasionally see Shlomo in the hospital unit, where he has been working as a volunteer since his retirement. It is incredible to see the change this man has undergone: He became much more open and seems younger. His example has shown me how people can change at this age; it has also shown me what a burden those early memories, coursing through hidden streams in their minds, have been for them. I could also sense how much more patience was needed when dealing with these well-hidden streams of mind, as compared to other therapeutic situations.

Once I became alert to the impact of these primary traumatic experiences, I became more aware that I was living in a survivors' culture. When I ask my university students at the beginning of the year to identify the source of their first names, I discover that about a third are named after relatives who perished *there*. Students and patients tell how their parents either kept silent or spoke obsessively about their Holocaust experiences. Although they intended to "defend" their children against what had happened *there*, both overreactions created fear and mistrust among their children. I learned from the literature how both the survivors and the society around them did their best to *normalize* these terrible memories so that they could live in the present reality. Still, this normalization did not lift the burden the survivors carried somewhere in them. It was transmitted to their descendants as a kind of double message: They sensed something but had neither the language to talk about it nor parental support and conceptualization to identify what they sensed.

It was during the early 1980s that I started to ask myself: What has happened to *them* (the perpetrators) and *their* children, in terms of psychological aftereffects? Those who carried out the atrocities—what kind of psychology did *they* have? How did the children cope with the knowledge (or lack of knowledge) that their parents had committed such atrocities?

I looked for answers and, to my surprise, except for a few journalistic anecdotes, I could not find any in the psychological literature; nor did any of my colleagues know about such a research. Could it be that there were no aftereffects among the victimizers and their descendants? That was a very disquieting notion. Could it be that we, the researchers, had not tried to learn about them? This was another disquieting thought. These questions increased my curiosity. However, I still felt it was too great a responsibility to undertake myself. In addition, I was living in Israel, and these were questions that were properly in the domain of German or Austrian researchers.

During a conference in Tel Aviv in the summer of 1982, I met Dieter Hartmann from Tübingen, Germany. In our lectures, we both discussed aspects of individual and collective oblivion and denial (Hartmann, 1984). When I asked him my disquieting questions during the intermission, he was fascinated. "You should come and find out because no German researcher will do that, and now is just the right time because we are perhaps mature enough, and distant enough from those events to begin thinking about their effect on us."

In 1983, during my postdoctoral work, I visited some colleagues at the Work Research Institute in Oslo and became acquainted with a Hebrew-speaking member of the Institute. She told me that she came from an Austrian family and that her father had been in the Wermacht during the war. When she learned that her grandmother had been half-Jewish, she changed her name to a Jewish one, went to Israel, and learned Hebrew. When I asked her where her father had been during the war, she said she did not know exactly but she was sure "he was probably involved in terrible things." Did she ever try to talk with him about it? No! There was no point because he would deny it, anyway. That conversation bothered me a lot. This was the first time I had met a person who preferred to attribute atrocities to her father rather than to try to find out what he had really done or avoided doing. After that conversation I began to think seriously about finding the answers myself. Still, it took me 2 more years to work out a plan and to work through my own fears and inhibitions.

What was I so afraid of? In retrospect, I can say today that I was afraid to get close to these terrible murderers and find that their children talk about them as human beings, just like any other person you might meet on the bus or the train; that perhaps, in certain respects, they may not be so different from myself. But in the beginning there were other aspects to this fear: What will they do to me (as if the Nazi regime was still *there*)? How will I find my way in that country, one that I have never before dared to enter? Who will help me find the people I want to talk to? Why should they want to talk with me? Will I be able to control my fear when meeting them, or my anger when they tell me things I do not want to listen to? I remember feeling like the dog in one of Solomon's experiments: Where the food is located, there also awaits the possibility of an electric shock. Shall I try to eat?

FINDING INTERVIEWEES

The process of looking for interviewees helped me control my own fears and inhibitions—that and the realization that others had similar feelings. I will give two examples. The first of these occurred during the first weekend my wife and I stayed with Dieter Hartmann and his wife. One of the initial questions I asked when we arrived was: Whom do you think I could meet here in your small town? They deliberated: There's Manfred (all the names in the book and in this chapter are pseudonyms). His father was a physician both in the euthanasia program and in a death camp—a terrible person. Manfred is such a rigid type; he probably also hates Jews and will throw you out. And there is Friedhelm, he is such a weak person. . . . At that moment I felt that my friends were trying to help but at the same time looking for an "ideal interviewee" for me. I could either agree to that and pack and go home, or start off with whomever they mention.

Manfred

I called Manfred and told him who I was and what I was after ("family memories from the Third Reich"), and we set a meeting for the next morning. When I hung up I had the strange feeling that he has been waiting for this phone call for a long time. Still, I (literally) trembled in front of his house while looking at the family name (his father's name), and I had to take another two turns around the block before entering the house. But then, when I was there in front of him, I knew exactly what I wanted to ask, how to relate to him, and what to expect from the encounter, as if I had been in this situation many times before. We talked for more than 2 hours, and I could not believe that this was the person Dieter's wife had described to me the day before. Though externally he gave a feeling of rigidity, I very easily discovered what a sensitive and open person he could be, a person who was painfully hiding his family's past. Dieter and his wife could not believe it when I tried to tell them about the conversation and how I felt. I now suspected that they themselves related to this man through his father's frightening image. For me, there had been only one moment during which my fears returned. When we separated at the door, he suddenly clicked his heels (in my ears I could almost hear: "Heil Hitler!"). At that moment, I was again paralyzed with fear. All the way home I tried to understand why this little act put me off so completely. Had I been afraid all the time and only toward the end let my fear come out? Or are there small, uncontrolled acts that put me back into the victim's role? Or was it the surprise, since no one in my life had ever clicked his heels to me?

The Psychologist's Brother-in-Law

The second story happened about 2 weeks later. I had interviewed 12 people and was looking desperately for additional interviewees. I was told that a psychologist in Frankfurt would like to see me and help me in my research. I went to see her, and we had a long conversation: She told me all about her family life during the Third Reich (her father was a "follower" of the Nazis, but not a perpetrator). However, in spite of her good intentions, she could not recall a single person who was suitable. I accepted that and was about to leave when she said: "But listen, I suddenly recalled: My sister is married to _____[the son of one of the heads of the euthanasia program and one of Hitler's personal physicians]." I learned a lot from this small incident: The people I am looking for are all around, in your family, around the corner from your house, in your department at the university. Most of the people I met knew what their father had done during the Third Reich. But the fear and "collective denial" were so strong that they just did not recall when I asked them about it, even when they had the best intentions of helping me in my study. Using this story helped me overcome similar inhibitions in subsequent meetings.

Frau Himmler

There were also people who refused to see me, and I was glad; for example, Himmler's daughter. I had had her phone number with me for weeks (usually I called people within days). Finally, I decided to call her from my hotel room. Frau Himmler (she has a different name today) answered the phone, and I told her who I was and what I wanted. There was a long pause and then she said: "I'm sorry, I do not see people on this subject." I tried to convince her for a few more minutes, but, in a way, I felt relief. Later I found out that she is still active in neo-Nazi politics in Germany. Probably those who still believed in their parents' deeds would not be willing to talk with me. To that extent, some of the potentially less cooperative interviewees (9 out of 78) biased the "sample" I was trying to establish in my research-oriented mind: I wanted no preselection by attitudes, personality types, or socioeconomic backgrounds. I should perhaps mention here that I was initially thinking about my encounters in Germany as quasi-formal research. I would see a hundred people from all over Germany, coming from different socioeconomic backgrounds, espousing different religious and political beliefs, and so forth. I was trying to construct a random sample, although neither I nor anyone else could define the boundaries of which this sample should be representative; no one knows much about the population characteristics of the Holocaust perpetrators.

I tried to recruit people through ads in newspapers. I did not really believe that children of perpetrators would respond to such ads, but I was curious to find out who would show up. I assumed that these would be a highly selective group, unlike those I contacted by phone. I decided that they would function as a kind of control group if they and the research sample displayed a similar distribution of the main background variables.

HOW THE RESEARCH DEVELOPED

I thought of the interview as being semi-structured: I would try to create a more relaxed atmosphere by moving away from the "hot" issues. This I could do by neutral information seeking ("When were you born? Where? What did your parents do for a living?") or by being "psychological" ("Were you the first child? How were the relations between the siblings? What are your first memories from home?"). When I felt that the person was "in" his or her memories (away from my own presence), I would start to ask about the external events: the parents and the Third Reich, the Nazi party, and the war. Only at that stage would I ask something about the perpetrating role of the parents, if this issue had not been brought up spontaneously by my interviewee beforehand. I would conclude the interview with some direct questions about the impact of those events on the interviewee's life, according to his or her perceptions.

At some point I even considered using some of the familiar psychological tests. I traveled around during my first stay in Germany with a TAT in my bag. I never used it. The interviews were very demanding, and it became evident that such an external tool would create more disinformation because it would provide a new source of defensiveness. It was difficult enough for me to handle the interviews as such, relating and controlling my own emotions, relating to and leading my interviewees through their thoughts and emotions.

The Son of the *Einsatzgruppen* Commander

There were instances in which I was more successful (such as the interview with Manfred, when I felt at home right away), and there were others in which I was furious or intimidated and barely managed to end the interview in a reasonable way. I remember specifically one such interview in a small town in southern Bavaria. The interviewee, the son of a well-known *Einsatzgruppen* (mobile killing unit) commander, was peeping through the kitchen window when I approached his home. He opened the door with a strange look in his eyes. When I asked (as usual) to taperecord the interview, he said that he had to consult someone. He went out and made a phone call. He returned and said that he would not agree to be taperecorded (he was a lawyer). During the conversation he denied his father's criminal role, though this was not easy, since his father had been condemned to death in the Nuremberg trials (the sentence was commuted to life imprisonment, and he was released after 8 years). What finally alienated me was his conviction that the Nazis had tried to be fair to the German Jews (he knew my origin) and had "handled badly" only the Eastern European Jews. When I left his home and drove off, I was sure I was being followed by someone. It took me a few days to rethink the whole event and understand that his suspicion and secretiveness (which are perfectly legitimate in such a situation) had made me overreact and lose my temper. This, in turn, clogged up the interview. For example, at some point I asked him what he told his 16-year-old daughter about her grandfather's actions during the war. "Nothing!" he responded, "I don't want to spoil her admiration for him. He is very old now, and she likes him very much." "But she might open a history book one day," I intervened, "and read about his trial and criminal activity there." He was surprised: "I never thought about such a possibility before." This might have been a lead to some new opening, which I did not follow up (as I did in the interviews with Manfred and others).

I had developed my research-oriented thinking at the beginning of a difficult, exploratory field study. This was the rationale. But unwittingly, I also thereby tried to distance myself from and control my unpleasant emotions. This became very evident toward the end of my fourth trip to Germany. Due to personal reasons I was not in good shape during that trip, and I decided to conclude my interviewing: I had interviewed by then about 50 children of perpetrators and about 30 "children of war," as I defined my "control group." I now sat up for entire nights in my host's large apartment in Wuppertal, trying to see if my research had yielded any results in terms of background, process, or outcome variables. I could see, for example, that children of perpetrators were significantly less likely to be married and more likely to be childless when compared to the "controls" (a hypothesis that, at an early stage, grew intuitively from my interviews). I mapped out every possible variable I could think of and had enough information about. But all this effort yielded almost nothing: The variability was so great and the sample, so small. And again, I knew nothing about the population, anyway, so there could be no claim to representativeness. For days I walked around very disillusioned, as if all this effort had been for nothing. I had conducted research about which I would be unable to say anything conclusive. For the distancing researcher in me this was the end of the road: I was in total despair.

Thomas

On one of the days that followed, I had to reinterview Thomas, a previous interviewee, this time in front of a videocamera. I had decided to ask some of the interviewees if we could videotape our discussion, so that I could use it for teaching purposes. Thomas and I had a long and difficult interview. It was difficult because we both felt uncomfortable with the video setup; we could not attain the level of openness we had reached in our earlier encounters. When we adjourned immediately after that session to the local cafeteria, Thomas expressed his own feelings, telling me how much he had learned from the interviews with me, even though he had been consciously dealing with his identity problems for many years before he met me (his father had worked under the father's brother, Gestapo chief Reinhard Heydrich).

At that moment it came to me that I had been manipulating all this research data as a way of distancing myself from my interviewees. Through those variables I was trying to look at them from the outside, as if I had not been a part of the encounter. Did this reflect a tendency on my part to solve complex emotional issues by a simplistic methodology? Or was it too difficult for me to confront some of the more sensitive findings? I began looking for a different research methodology. I had earlier experience with more qualitative analysis, but I was not sure whether I was ready to do any kind of analysis yet. I wanted to say something about how these encounters were actually part of the process; about my own role as a participant, not merely an external research agent. I think it was then that I first thought about writing a book in which the interviews themselves would present what I had found. This was a difficult decision, because it meant giving up some of the ability to "objectify" and to generalize. Those who have experienced a more rigid scientific education probably know how difficult it is to give up these expectations.

USING THE INTERVIEWS TO FRAME CONCEPTS

However, when I went back and listened to my interviews, I was overwhelmed by a lot of idiosyncratic details. Each interviewee was unique, and so many things could have affected what was said; so many things could still be asked or dealt with on that very personal level. I felt at a loss again. I was now looking for some intermediate type of conceptualization to mediate between the personal and unique, and the objective kind of generalizations that I had decided to give up. That was the stage at which conceptualizations such as the "double wall" phenomenon, "the dark side of the mind," and "the paradox of morality" started to evolve and I was ready to write some papers about them.

Anfred

Some of these concepts developed quite by coincidence. For example, in one town I was officially invited to visit a German-Israeli friendship association and could not refuse. One of their organizers, Anfred, asked me to come over for tea, and he was extremely nice and polite. At some point, feeling somehow "on duty," I asked him what his father did during the war.

> ANFRED: He was a locomotive driver, but he only drove ammunition trains.
> DAN: (*What a strange reaction, I thought to myself.*) How do you know he only drove ammunition trains?
> ANFRED: Well, he told me. He was stationed in east Prussia, not far away from Bialistock, between 1942 and 1944, and that's what he had to do.
> DAN: There were many transports of Jews during that time. Did he know nothing about them?
> ANFRED: I don't know, but I can ask him when I see him next weekend.

This ended the short conversation. We had tea together, he drove me back to my hotel, and I forgot about the whole matter. However, he came to pick me up a few days later in order to bring me to the group's meeting, where I was supposed to describe my research intentions. When we sat down in his car, he began right away:

> ANFRED: I talked with my father, and he again insisted that he only drove ammunition trains.
> DAN: But did he not know about the transports of Jews?
> ANFRED: No, the people who drove *those* trains were party members, and no one had access to those trains whatsoever.

I raised an eyebrow. Anfred was himself an engineer and knew enough about the setting to test his father's arguments. However, the father denied the whole issue, and there was no point in going on with this conversation. As I was about to step out of the car, Anfred added quietly:

> ANFRED: And this time he also told me how he had to watch when they executed a whole group of prisoners of war at the train station. Everyone else was pushed out, but he was on duty and saw the whole thing.
> DAN: (*I sat back down.*) What a terrible experience for your father. He never spoke about it before with you?
> ANFRED: No, he never mentioned it till this last conversation.

I had the strange feeling that while I was emotionally moved by his father's story, Anfred was not. He was at ease during the whole meeting and invited me and a couple of friends for beer afterwards. We met again in Israel the following spring, and I asked him to come for a video-taping later that summer. There we went through his whole story again in detail, but he could no longer recall that specific story that his father had told him a year ago.

In reconstructing the event, I could see how the son, through my questioning, naively approached his father. The father, his memory awakened by his son's interest (which the son may never have shown before in this way), told him of this devastating experience of his, about which he had kept silent all these years. The son transmitted the information to me but wiped it out immediately for himself: It was gone from his own memory a year later. While reflecting on this, I started to formulate the first two concepts in my mind: the "dark side of the mind" and the "double wall" phenomenon. The dark side of the mind has an active role in one's mind similar to Spence's (1983) notion of the "paradox of denial": One, in a way, knows where not to look in order not to look there. This also implies a certain "leakage" into the memory, from which someone else could reconstruct the denied area by trial and error. With Anfred, as with the Frankfurt psychologist, I elicited the denial area as well as the "leakage" into their memory. The "double wall" phenomenon was related not only to the experience I had with Anfred and his father. Many parents build a wall of silence around their own unpleasant experiences and the emotional turmoil associated with them (pleasure? disgust? indifference?). However, I also found that many children (and, to some extent, society in general) construct a wall of their own around those fearful experiences, which they did not know about directly but could sense. Even when one side tries to open a window in its "wall," it usually comes up against the other's wall (as happened to the father in Anfred's case). Rarely, if ever, will one find an event in which one side tries to open a window and meets a window in the wall of the other side. This is, of course, true regarding many issues between children and parents. It is probably a family construct that was already there, ready to absorb also the experiences of the Holocaust. In the case of the perpetrators, the wall was thicker, perhaps higher and less penetrable. Penetrating such a wall needs careful planning, and this is perhaps what therapy or interviews such as mine could be about.

In earlier years, children's inquiry into the parents' role in the Holocaust was avoided through either identification with or accusation of the parents. In such an atmosphere it was not possible to test more complex feelings or memories. For many of my interviewees, it was too late, since their parents had died long before they were ready to take such an initiative. Anfred's case shows us how the son's need to deny was stronger than both his father's wish, as well as my own, to tell the story of his war experiences. It is reasonable to assume that the father had actually not done anything wrong. He may have had nothing to hide about his actual deeds but may have feared being associated with the events he witnessed, even in retrospect.

After these concepts evolved, I started to ask myself some more difficult questions: Is the opening of windows important for my interviewees or for me? Why not let people like Anfred live with their denial? Is it "dysfunctional" from their perspective, or am I trying to impose my own perspective on them? I started to reexamine my own motives: Why did I come? What did I expect to find? Am I willing to accept what I have found?

I assumed that I had come to Germany to understand and that I had already worked through my own need for revenge or my need to find guilt and regret on their part. I knew I was going to meet people who had themselves done no evil, who had by coincidence been born into this unbelievable situation. I wanted to understand what it was like to grow up in a family where the father (or mother) had been actively involved in atrocities during a substantial part of their childhood. But on the emotional level, I found their active denial more difficult to bear than their acknowledgment. I could not be indifferent to their working through of that part of their family's secrets. It became clear to me that I was not an objective researcher who could observe or describe these phenomena in a detached way. Still, those researchers who might be detached (where were they all these years, anyhow?) might not look for what I was looking for. What was it, exactly, that I was looking for?

Coming back to Anfred. He bothered me not because of his denial as such. I could even see how that denial had been functional for him as he grew up and formed his own life perspective. What bothered me was the combination in one person of such friendliness toward Israelis and the total denial of what had happened in his family a generation earlier. It was his internal inconsistency that put me off, rather than his ongoing need to deny. This new idea was a relief, because I wanted to be able to accept interviewees' different styles of coping before I went on interviewing.

REFINING IDEAS THROUGH FURTHER ENCOUNTERS

The initial interview was often a beginning: Both my interviewee and I needed time to digest what was said, to find the "empty spots" that we tended to disregard but that are important for a deeper understanding. There was Gerda, for example, who agreed to see me the first time only in the company of the person who had referred her to me and who did not agree to disclose her father's identity until our third meeting, a year later. Or there was Renate, who went into therapy after our first interview and before the third interview opened her father's suitcase in the attic, where he had left his letters and papers; according to our earlier conversations, she "was not allowed to touch" this suitcase or its contents.

Peter, Gerda, and Their Fathers

But there were also more subtle issues that could be clarified only through further encounters, and I did not always succeed in doing so. Peter's father is one example. I met the father because this was the only way to reach his children. He was a physician in Auschwitz who had been acquitted by the Poles because of the help he provided to inmates and his refusal to participate in the selections. I therefore had a positive impression of him prior to our meeting. His resemblance to my own father made me feel even more positively toward him at the outset. However, during our interview some of these feelings changed considerably. He used old Nazi expressions ("overload of the gassing capacity"); he expressed his admiration of Mengele, "who was the only person one could talk to in the camp." I came out of the interview torn to pieces, and it took me more than a year before my curiosity surfaced again: How could these two sides of him—the moral, human side and the inhuman side—live together beneath a mask of complete normality with which he deceived everyone, including himself (see Scheffel-Baars, 1988). Still, I could not bring myself to go to see him again. When I did try 2 years later and found that he was away on holiday, I felt relief. I suppose this reflected the upper limit of my ability to try and understand.

Both Peter (the physician's elder son) and Gerda (child of another perpetrator) were very defensive during our initial encounter. Gerda was holding on to the image of the wonderful father whom she still admires, having no insight whatsoever about his role in the Nazi regime, including the criminal aspects that he must at least have known about. Peter was using clichés such as "things like Auschwitz happened before and will always happen," or "it all comes from the genes—there are meat-eaters and plant-eaters. The first could do it again to the Turks today, if the regime would only let them."

I felt terrible, but the interview with the father helped prepare me for worse expressions. I did not criticize him but listened carefully. At some point I could say to Gerda that she must have had difficulty starting a life of her own, with all the public criticism of her father. To Peter I could explain that I wanted to understand: How could people do it, or witness it being done, and go on loving their own wives and children at the same time, going back and forth between these two settings for years? Is this normal?

My approach helped new reactions surface, as if hidden layers unfolded in both of them. Gerda asked for a more "differentiated way" to see the good and bad sides of her father's behavior. During our last conversation she handed me his testament (written before he committed suicide in Nuremberg), in which he wrote mainly about the mistake of anti-Semitism that should now be corrected. She really tried very hard to match the ideal picture of her father with the terrible events that occurred when he was in power. I came to understand that maintaining her love for her father had a positive effect on her own life, allowing her to develop positive feelings toward other people while struggling with a very difficult reality of her own. Gerda taught me an important lesson:

I could get close to these people only if I related to the steps they were willing to take within their own context, not if I judged them by any absolute or external measure.

With Peter things took a different course. In responding to my questions he desisted from his clichés and was able to admit that he had never thought about how his father really managed in Auschwitz. He had never tried to talk with him about it. I could see that myself: Peter could tell me the facts about his father's role during the war, but about the emotional part of his father's reactions to my questions the son could report nothing. He then referred to his early separation from his parents and to the fact that he chose a very different profession because he wanted to prove to them that he could make a decent living without going to the university. However, he made these decisions without consciously connecting them to his father's role in Auschwitz (they may indeed have been independent events). However, toward the end of our conversation, he went back to his earlier clichés. I felt as if he were saying to me, unwittingly: "You've started something, but if you leave me alone now with it, I'd better return to my old defenses." And I could accept that as legitimate.

THE FATHER'S ROLE AND OTHER LIFE EXPERIENCES

This interview brought up another issue that I had to try to untangle. I met people in their 40s, 50s, even 60s. They told me their life stories from their current perspectives. In order to understand the effect—if any—the father's role in the Third Reich had had on them I had to get a feeling about how things were at that time, independent of other intrapersonal or interpersonal processes, especially ongoing family structures. And these events did not happen independently, because they always had occurred within specific family structures. For example, Gerda's parents divorced before the war broke out: How can one establish whether she did not create a family of her own because of her parents' divorce, her father's role in the Third Reich, or other possible reasons? Peter had had no relationship with his father as a child. The father was away for years, and when he returned he went back to work as the village physician. The son rebelled and left home early: Does Auschwitz really play a role in his life story?

Helmuth

Helmuth is another good example. Helmuth's first memory is of lying in his father's arms on the beach. Later, he felt intimidated by his father, who wanted to bring him up as an Aryan, while the son was "afraid of sheep." His sisters used to laugh at his weaknesses, but they did not have to live up to the father's expectations because they were females. When Helmuth was 11 he overheard a conversation between his parents: Should the father kill the whole family, as their friend in Berlin had done, or should he only commit suicide? The father was afraid that the Allies would "now do to [them] what [they] had done to others." He knew what he was talking about, because he was involved in planning and implementing the euthanasia program. A few days later the father asked his son to join him for a walk in the woods. The father carried his son on his shoulders (the son being eleven!), and they sang their favorite children's songs. His father cried. (Helmuth cried himself while telling me this story.) That afternoon the father committed suicide. During the months that followed, Helmuth refused to eat at home because he was sure that his mother was going to poison them all. He was sent to a boarding school, where he stayed until the age of 18. Helmuth later talked about his oldest son, who had committed suicide a few years earlier, and asked "Am I a victimizer too?" He seemed to be suggesting that he and his former wife had not responded to the alarm signals given out by their son.

Helmuth was a victim of his home (his father; his mother, who never stood up for him; his sisters, who mocked him). The victimization outside his home (Buchenwald was a living memory for him) was like an echo of his personal experiences. He recalled his mother saying: "Move away from the stove, your suit will catch fire." He remarked: "The suit was important to her, not me." Now, many of us have been told such things during our childhoods, but not all of us later attributed such expressions in the way that Helmuth did. And one cannot even blame him, because he based his reflections upon a certain reality. And now, regarding his son, there was a feeling of fate: The circle had closed, and there was no way out for him. When the interview was over, he showed me his garden and described the plants in the same detailed way his father used to do, something he had so hated as a child.

Deborah and Her Father

Helmuth's interwoven family and political reflections brought me back to Deborah. Deborah came to me for therapy in Israel while trying to find out when and how her father, a Holocaust victim, had been taken from Paris to Auschwitz. She had seen him for the last time when she was 5 years old. She survived the war with her mother and brother. However, she had never really said good-bye to her father, and throughout all the intervening years she had expected him to ring the doorbell one day. During the 3 years of therapy she had a dream that occurred three times. In the dream she, a 4-year-old girl, sits near the window wearing a white shirt while her father plays the piano. Suddenly the Germans enter and take him away. When the dream came up the first time, Deborah identified with the little girl, feeling helpless as the Germans come and take her father away. This was very much her feeling when she finally mourned his death, after receiving the details from the Red Cross about her father's deportation. When the dream reappeared after about a year, Deborah identified with her father, playing the piano to his little girl until the Germans enter and take him away. At this time she felt more competent in her daily life, and her interpretation of the dream was congruent with her evolving reality. The dream appeared for the last time shortly after she came back from a visit to Paris, where she had met some of her father's friends who told her a few new details about him. This time she identified with the Germans. She now recalled that her parents had divorced shortly before the outbreak of the war. She suddenly felt this terrible anger toward her father for deserting her. She actually lost her father twice: once through the divorce and then through the Holocaust. The first loss was still the most painful, but she had never felt that her anger was legitimate because of what happened during the war.

Living through this dream three times with Deborah helped me comprehend that working-through is a slow process of knowing, understanding, and feeling contradictory feelings within a still very stigmatized context of the Holocaust. Deborah taught me a very important lesson: how the experience of the Holocaust colored previous normal experiences and emotions to such an extent that they could not be legitimately untangled afterwards. She needed me for this legitimation. The rest she achieved by herself. After the third time, the dream disappeared. However, only after a few more years had passed and long after therapy had ended did Deborah call me up and say: "Yesterday it suddenly came back to me, the clear memory of when I saw my father for the last time. He came to visit us, the children, but left shortly afterwards because my mother disliked his coming to the house."

WORKING THROUGH A PARENT'S INVOLVEMENT: THE FIVE-STAGE PROCESS

Monika

Monika had started to become actively interested in her father before she met me. She contacted me through Dieter's wife in order to talk about her father with me. However, the more she found out about her father, the more devastating the picture of his role during the extermination process became. She had not known her father (she was his illegitimate child). Her mother had always portrayed him as a hero and a wonderful, loving husband. Monika constantly looked for information about him until she found a history book in which his part in the execution of the Jews of Riga is described in detail. She tried to confront her mother but quickly learned that this was an almost impossible task. She tried not only to accuse but also to understand: How could this man love and carry out these atrocities at the same time?

Monika worked herself through all these stages:

1. Learning the details about his involvement in the Holocaust
2. Understanding the moral meaning of what he did and how he did it
3. Feeling furious about it (especially how he had deceived her mother)
4. Feeling also the contradictory warm feelings toward her father, whom she had never met
5. Trying to integrate all of this into her own "moral-self."

In a way, over all these years, she unwittingly worked through the five stages that Deborah also went through in therapy.

Until I met Monika, I could not formulate such a five-stage scale of working through because I had no example of its later stages within the German context. Once I met her, the working-through continuum was suddenly there in my mind, and I could group people in clusters around this continuum. This does not mean that one continuum answered all my questions; but it did reflect the ambiguity that is resolved when a certain person fills a hidden gap in your mind—a necessary step in this process of understanding.

Now I could rearrange the people I had met on a hidden scale—name the stage at which they were "stuck" in their working-through process. If Monika had reached the more advanced stage of integration, Anfred and Peter were still at the initial stage of either not knowing or not understanding the full meaning of what they did know about their fathers' roles during the Holocaust: Anfred could not remember what his father had told him only one year earlier, and Peter had never thought about what it means for his father to have been at Auschwitz. Manfred could not "feel" what he rationally understood about his father's involvement in the death camp. Gerda was emotionally still attached to her father, being unable to confront that feeling with her knowledge about what had happened during the years of his leadership. Thomas moved back and forth between his father and uncle, two parts of himself he could not integrate into one whole. Helmuth's situation was similar to Thomas's: He also moved back and forth between his warm emotions toward his father (lying on the beach, walking in the woods) and his anger toward him (trying to make a man out of him, considering killing the whole family). Renate was trying on her own to move forward on this scale (trying to regain some of her more positive feelings toward her father). The interview with me had helped, but she needed more help and went into therapy.

After Renate and Monika, I met Gonda. This was a relief in another way. I was traveling around Germany alone, accumulating all these stories, and many times I felt as if I were in a dream: Am I doing it? Am I unreal (believing what I hear in these interviews) or are my surroundings unreal (not learning about it before)? Then I met Gonda, first in Beer-Sheva and then in Holland. Gonda and a few other Dutch NSB children (children of collaborators with the Nazis) had established a self-help group in 1981 to cope with their common problems. These revolved around both their parents and the Dutch society that condemned them for their parents' deeds (Scheffel-Baars, 1988). Gonda introduced me to some of the other group members. They were different from my German interviewees: The group had helped them legitimize their personal issues. They had learned to untangle their specific family histories from their common NSB fate, to help one another work through these difficult stages.

I began writing articles about the working-through process. I was in the mood for summarizing. But when I had finished the articles and given them to a few of my colleagues, their comments gave me the feeling that again I had missed something. I was still trying to be the researcher, this time looking not for variables that correlate significantly but for patterns that emerge out of the data. It was still too difficult for me to present the interviews as raw data, to let readers crystallize their own concepts or conclusions. Only after going over the interviews for the third time did I finally decide to write a book in which readers would be their own researchers. Even then, my valuable readers still had to edit out my emotionally loaded or analyzing comments again and again. I had to "let go" of the *researcher* in me completely and let the *person* who was part of the encounters speak freely. This was, for me, extremely exposing, tearing away all the previous "coats" I had wanted to put on this material, on myself.

CONCLUSION

One year later I held a conference in Wuppertal. In addition to the scientific program, I invited my interview partners and Gonda, with some of her group members, to take part in the conference. I had to convince each interviewee to come: Helmuth "consulted his father" and decided not to come because he is not of the "groupy type." Manfred was getting married, and Peter did not answer my invitation. Finally, about ten showed up, including Renate, Fritz, Gerda, and Monika. I showed a video-taped interview with another one of my subjects, Rudolf, who was sitting there with his wife. After the session Gerda left the room crying and did not come back.

The other interviewees gathered in the next room with the Dutch people, each acknowledging that he or she was "Dan Bar-On's interview partner." But soon Renate said to Rudolf (crying): "You can be proud of your father, even if he went out of his mind. I could only condemn mine." They had first to sort out their differences before they could relate to their similarities. In the evening, during the intermissions, an unstructured group process began, which they decided to continue. As of this writing, they have just met for the third time. Is it possible that my interviewing and the encounter with the Dutch group was necessary in order for this process to start? In a way it proved to me that these people had been waiting for this to happen but could not start it by themselves. No German psychologist (or priest or minister) had found a way to help them go ahead and do something about it. Maya (Fritz's wife) who hosted the last meeting told me that toward the end they asked "When are we meeting again?"—not "Shall we meet again?"

I have been asked several times about what these interviews did to me. I do not know if I can answer this question, because many other things, some very difficult, have happened to me during these years. I believe that I learned from my interviews that most of my interviewees, and probably most of their parents too, were ordinary human beings. If so, how could their parents have been mass murderers? I do not know for sure, but probably under certain circumstances most of us can become mass murderers. Did I become more pessimistic because of this? I am not sure. I think my ideas about optimism and pessimism have changed. You can be an optimist by denying reality, and this means you are a potential pessimist. You can be a pessimist because you acknowledge and work through what really happened, and thereby you create a quest for hope that was not there before. Perhaps in a few years the gap that exists will not be between children of perpetrators and children of survivors, but between those of both groups who could not work through their parents' past and those who did manage to work it through.

REFERENCES

Bar-On, D. (1985). Different kinds of denial account for short and long term recovery of coronary patients. *The Israeli Journal of Psychiatry and Related Sciences, 22* (3), 155–172.

Bar-On, D. (1986a). *The pantomime's stick: An account of conversations with parents and children.* Tel Aviv: Merav.

Bar-On, D. (1986b). Wisdom of the community. *Quality of Work Life, 3* (3–4), 251–261. Shorter version also in *Kibbutz Studies,* February 1985, pp. 18–23.

Bar-On D. (1987). Causal attributions and the rehabilitation of heart attack victims. *Journal of Clinical and Social Psychology, 5* (1), 114–122.

Bar-On, D. (1988). Children of perpetrators of the Holocaust: Working through one's moral self. In D. Bar-On, F. Beiner, & M. Brusten (Eds.), *Der Holocaust: Familiale und gesellschaftliche Folgen* (pp. 33–55). Wuppertal, Germany: University of Wuppertal Press.

Bar-On, D. (1989). *Legacy of silence: Encounters with children of the Third Reich.* Cambridge, MA: Harvard University Press.

Hartmann, D. D. (1984). Compliance and oblivion: The absence of sympathy in Germany for victims of the Holocaust. In I. W. Charny (Ed.), *Toward the understanding and prevention of genocide* (pp. 199–203). Boulder, CO: Westview.

Scheffel-Baars, G. (1988). Self-help groups for children of collaborators with Nazis in Holland. In D. Bar-On, F. Beiner, & M. Brusten (Eds.), *Der Holocaust: Familiale und gesellschaftliche Folgen* (pp. 80–94). Wuppertal, Germany: University of Wuppertal Press.

Spence, D. P. (1983). The paradox of denial. In S. Breznitz (Ed.), *Denial of stress* (pp. 103–123). New York: International University Press.

Concluding Comments

DONALD A. SCHÖN

IN THE INTRODUCTION to these essays, I described the reflective turn and, in the interest of exploring some of its implications for good studies of practice, I posed four main questions:

1. What is it appropriate to be reflecting on?
2. What are the appropriate ways of observing and reflecting on practice, including ways of representing what practitioners already know?
3. What constitutes appropriate rigor?
4. What does the reflective turn imply for researchers' stance toward their enterprises—toward their "subjects", their research activity, and their own role in it?

I shall focus here on the third question, the one about "appropriate rigor," but this question will lead to the others and to a discussion of the ways in which "giving reason to practitioners" makes the study of practice into a reflective practice in its own right.

WHAT IS SHARED

So long as they lay claim to knowledge, all those who conduct empirical studies are vulnerable to being asked how they know what they claim to know. This global challenge can be broken down into three more specific ones, corresponding to the specific knowledge claims implicit in empirical studies—about phenomena (what is going on here), about causality (what caused it), and about the generality of what is said to be going on and what is said to have caused it. Around these fundamental issues, debates have long swirled. In what sense, if any, are descriptions of phenomena and attributions of their causes *objective*, that is, independent of an inquirer's "think-so" and interpersonally consensual among inquirers? What is the nature of causality, and what are the appropriate forms of valid causal inference? Under what conditions, and under what models of inference, can we make valid generalizations from limited observations?

With perhaps one or two exceptions, the authors of the essays in this volume (henceforth, I shall say simply "the authors") do not directly address such questions; but implicitly they take positions on them, and their positions have several points in common. All of them purport to describe what is *there*, laying claim to a certain kind of objectivity. All of them adopt some form of what has come widely to be known as the ethnographic method, the careful qualitative description and analysis of case studies drawn from actual observation of an individual's or a group's practice. And all of them represent their findings about practice in a distinctive way: They tell stories.

It is true that the essays by Mattingly, Lanzara, and Clandinin and Connelly stand out because they express an intellectual interest in narrative discourse. But all of the authors *employ* narrative discourse, which is not surprising, since they were asked, after all, to present a case study of practice. To present a case *is* to tell a story in the sense first enunciated by Aristotle (as Mattingly reminds us): the imitation of an action, with a recognizable beginning, middle, and end, and with recognizable characters, plot, and setting.

The essays in this volume reveal several different modes of story telling. I shall call these "manifest stories of practice," "metastories of research on practice," "causal stories," and "underlying stories." In some instances, a single story may fall into more than one of these categories. But the categories are nonetheless distinct from one another, and the effort to distinguish them is central, as I shall try to show, to the question of appropriate rigor.

All of the authors tell manifest stories about an individual's or group's practice. Russell and Munby, for example, tell us how two young teachers, Diane and Roger, learn on the job to reframe their ways of thinking and acting as teachers. Clandinin and Connelly tell both a story of Phil's attempts to create a community school and a story about the origins of these attempts in Phil's earlier life. Forester tells the story of the review of a proposed building project and, within it, the role played by a planner.

In several of the essays, a manifest story of practice is embedded within a metastory about the author's own research. So Putnam tells a story about Paul, the organizational consultant, within the framework of a story about Putnam's multiyear interaction with Paul. Greenwood and Newberg tell stories about Mondragón and an urban school system, respectively, within the framework of stories about their participatory action research ventures. Bamberger tells stories about particular teachers and students within the context of a story about her project at the Graham and Parks School, and Bar-On sketches evocative stories of particular individuals, German and Israeli, within the larger story of his quest for truth about the experience of the children of Nazi perpetrators.

Most of the essays contain causal stories. They lay out temporal sequences of events in such a way as to give causal explanations of events. Sometimes these are contained within a larger practice story. So, for example, Colin (in Erickson and MacKinnon's essay) and Bamberger and Briggs (in Bamberger's essay) offer constructions of the spontaneous understandings that lie behind their students' responses. Sometimes, on the other hand, the manifest story of practice is, in its entirety, a causal story. Baum's story of Latham presents a causal account of Latham's career in a state bureaucracy, and Forester's story is a causal account of the planner's actions in a project review. These stories have an inherent dramatic structure. They begin with a puzzle, and they "imitate" the protagonists' actions in such a way as to build toward a causal explanation of behavior that would otherwise remain mysterious. As with Aristotle's classic prototypes, they end with an illumination.

I shall make clear in the following section what I mean by an underlying story.

WHAT IS NOT SHARED, BUT STILL SHARED

All the authors select certain categories of description as privileged, but they differ in their strategies of selection.

Consider the several stories about teachers, students, and schools. In Russell and Munby's account of teachers' on-the-job learning, the categories they emphasize are mainly relationships among teachers, students, and parents. The emphasis is on such problems as maintaining classroom order and getting children to read. The authors have little or nothing to say about subject-matter learning of the sort illustrated by teachers' understandings of the meaning of *variable*, or the different senses of *faster*, which play such a central role in Bamberger's essay. Erickson and MacKinnon describe Colin's analysis of and influence on his students' changing understandings of batteries-and-bulbs. But when the authors turn to Colin's interaction with Rosie, they focus, as Russell and Munby do, on interpersonal relationships.

Newberg's "Bridging the Gap" deals with the massive dropout rate that afflicts a center-city school district, and it refers generally and indirectly to learning and teaching in the schools. Its explicit focus, however, is on categories of interaction among teachers, administrators, and parents as these affect "gaps" Newberg links to the dropout rate. None of the relationships or interactions central to Newberg's essay come to the surface in Bamberger's or Erickson and MacKinnon's work.

For Baum and Hirschhorn, the categories of primary interest have to do with their subjects' unconscious lives—the ways in which the mental life of the individual is reflected in the social world of the organization, as Hirschhorn puts it. Unconscious mental lives are largely absent from all of the stories described above.

Clearly, each author privileges some categories of description and neglects others, fixes attention on one family of practice phenomena and ignores or gives fleeting attention to others. How are we to make sense of such different strategies of selective attention? I might say that they serve the different purposes of the stories the authors have chosen to tell. But here I use *story* in a new sense to mean *underlying* stories. These are the fundamental messages or arguments the various authors seek to communicate through the telling of a manifest story. They have a generic, prototypical character, often linked, more or less explicitly, to the author's favored theoretical perspective. An author tends to carry an underlying story around, embodying it now in one manifest story, now in another.

We storytellers may be unaware, or only partially aware, of the underlying stories that incorporate our deeper purposes. But we can *construct* an underlying story from the data of a manifest one, by asking why the manifest story includes some features and ignores others, why it begins and ends when it does, why it is couched in terms of certain categories and not others, what accounts for its thrust and direction. And, of course, any such construct may be found to be mistaken.

The stories underlying the essays in this volume seem to me to differ considerably from one another, yet they share an interesting structural characteristic: They pivot on certain essential differences in ways of looking at things.

Baum, for example, has an underlying story that contrasts a professional's overt practice with his less visible use of his organizational situation to perform tasks of personal development. Baum's message is that these two practices constrain and shape each other. Hirschhorn's underlying story hinges on unconscious ambivalence toward authority, which yields characteristic dramas of organizational life as an authority figure and her subordinates more or less unconsciously collude with one another.

Mattingly focuses her attention, at one point, on the construction of a cluster of types of stories habitually told by project officers in the World Bank. Each of her story types has its particular origins, its special genre, its characteristic rhetoric, and its distinctive organizational functions. There are stories project officers tell in order to gain board approval for loans, stories they tell each other in the field as they try to figure out what is happening in their projects and what they need to do next, stories that celebrate the heroism of field exploits or affix blame for failure, and stories that provide organizational legitimacy for project activities while masking what is really going on. Mattingly sees these different types of stories as serving different purposes and capturing different features (in some cases interjecting events that never happened at all), but in all cases helping to throw light on the organizational processes of the Bank. Moreover, Mattingly believes that through a sophisticated understanding of the multiple representations of reality promulgated by members of the organization, she is able to identify those that best capture what really happened in the field—she is able, that is, *to establish a discoverable fit between Bank stories and Bank reality.*

A basic tension between two representations of phenomena informs Bamberger's main argument: the formal, explicit, symbolic representations that are privileged in schools and the representations expressed by individuals' effective actions in making things—their "smart hands." Between these modes of representation, she proposes that the computer and the procedural modes of description proper to computer programming can function as an intermediary, a "transitional object." The moral of Bamberger's underlying story is about the importance of moving back and forth across, combining and coordinating, these usually disparate kinds of representations.

TESTS OF VALIDITY

The use of *story* to name the normative conceptual structure that underlies a manifest story of practice—*underlying story* rather than *assumptions* or *framework*—suggests a loosening of the bond between concept and reality. *Story* keeps the story*teller* in the picture, suggesting that different narrators might make very different things out of the "same" reality. *Story* connotes "*just* a story," thereby posing a question of objectivity (is there really anything out there independent of any particular observer's description of it?) and, by the same token, raising the specter of relativism.

A relativistic approach to appropriate rigor might take one of two forms. We might argue that the adequacy of a study of practice should be judged by how sensitive an author is to the underlying story and how well that author marshals evidence to support it. Or, alternatively, its adequacy should be judged by the degree to which any given reader shares the author's purposes and perspective. The judgment would be relative in the first case to the fit between manifest and underlying story and, in the second, to the fit, or agreement, between the underlying stories preferred, respectively, by author and reader.

But we are likely to hunger after a less relativistic approach to the question of appropriate rigor. Is it possible to recognize *both* the observer's role as a constructor of stories of reality *and* the corrigibility of stories in the face of resistances posed by that reality? Is it possible to recognize, in other words, that while every description of a practice is a construction, it need not be an arbitrary one?

So we are led, willy-nilly, to the ancient and vexing question of validity.

Traditionally, three tests have been applied to determine the validity of a proposition: correspondence (does it fit the facts?), coherence (does it hang together in an internally consistent and compelling way?), and pragmatism (does it work?). Traditional discussions of validity also point out how each of these tests may be vulnerable to vicious circularity. "Fitting the facts" may mean nothing more than fitting the facts one chooses to notice, the facts ignored being those least compatible with the proposition in question. "Coherence" may be preferentially applied to the explanation most congenial to one's already accepted theoretical framework. And the inquirer who can derive a more or less effective intervention from any one of several explanations may simply choose to *make* work the one he or she already prefers.

A more rigorous approach to testing the validity of a proposed account of reality, although it provides no guarantee against vicious circularity, is the one for which Karl Popper is best known (Popper, 1968). Popper's argument is that, since we cannot confirm hypotheses and can at best *disconfirm* them, the fundamental test of validity consists in competitive resistance to refutation. One must juxtapose alternate plausible accounts of the phenomenon in question, and one must try to discriminate among these by means of a crucial experiment—that is, by making an observation consistent with only one of the contending hypotheses. Popper's advice is applicable, as well, to the very attempt to *imagine* how a belief might be disconfirmed by experiment. It is very difficult to treat a belief as a disconfirmable hypothesis if one does not have access to alternate beliefs that suggest conditions under which the first may turn out to be false. In the absence of an alternate hypothesis, one is likely to be overwhelmed by the obviousness of what one already believes.

If we follow Popper's line of thought, then, appropriate rigor in the study of practice will depend on the researcher's ability to generate, compare, and discriminate among multiple representations of practice phenomena—that is, to formulate alternate causal stories of the phenomenon in question and test their competitive resistance to refutation. The performance of this task will depend, in turn, on two main factors:

1. The researcher's underlying story, with its implicit or explicit theoretical framework
2. The approach adopted by the researcher

With respect to the first condition, the *ontology,* or fundamental categories, of an underlying story determines the kinds of observations that must be made in order to disconfirm an explanation derived from that story. Categories that underlie the essays in this volume are, for example, "a student's 'aha' experience," "childhood images that shape adult aspirations," "smart hands," "ambivalence toward authority," "democratic pluralism," or "teachers' natural ways of learning on the job." One can then imagine the different kinds of observations that might be pertinent to these categories.

With respect to the second condition, research approach, as I have already mentioned in the Introduction, the 14 essays in this volume can be roughly arrayed along a continuum of distance/closeness, at one pole of which are "pure" studies carried out by a distant observer and at the other, frankly interventionist inquiries that may take the form of participatory action research, consultative research, or collaborative self-studies. Each of these approaches opens up certain ways of testing the validity of the researcher's interpretations and makes other ways difficult or impossible. For example, a "pure" study of practice offers the possibility of gathering data undistorted by the researcher's interventions (except when the researcher's very presence functions as an intervention), but, by the same token, it forecloses the possibility of using intervention as a test of one's interpretations. In contrast, when consultation is used as a research method, the researcher can design interventions that are intended both to help the client and to test hypotheses; but such interventions may yield results whose interpretations are difficult to disconfirm. For example, an intervention may suggest truths the client then mirrors back or may induce the client to comply with the consultant's beliefs. When the researcher engages a subject in collaborative self-study, the subject becomes a co-researcher who can help in formulating questions and puzzles as well as in searching for answers and solutions. But the co-researcher's biases may then find their way into the research process, compounding the difficulty of detecting and correcting error.

The degree of fit, or agreement, of these two factors—research approach, and the fundamental categories of the researcher's underlying story—will be very important to the achievement of appropriate rigor, since *it will determine whether the observations required for the purpose of discriminating among contending hypotheses are ones the researcher is likely to make.*

Let us consider how various combinations of these two factors may work out.

Pure Studies

Baum's underlying story draws on Erik Erikson's stage theory of development to explain Latham's career in a state planning bureaucracy. Using it, Baum suggests that Latham spends years at the margins of the organization, defined (by himself and others) as a social planner who remains peripheral to the agency's dominant physical planning orientation until he builds sufficient confidence in his own identity and competence to take on the role of community planner. At this point, Latham moves to the center of the agency's organizational world.

Baum tells Latham's story in such a way as to render it coherent and convincing, at least to me. An important part of the art by which he does so is that he includes *just the details that fit his Eriksonian interpretation.* But one might advance other interpretations of Latham's case on the basis of very different categories. For example, Latham might be seen as a late bloomer. Perhaps his story might be told in terms of a gradual accumulation of planning skills that eventually equip him for the community planner's role. Or one might tell the story as one of opportunistic exploitation of chance events. Perhaps Latham's move to the center of the organization had to wait until a rare event provided him with a suitable opportunity. For each such alternate story, Baum might have chosen to include as evidence for that story a somewhat different set of relevant details.

In the face of alternate, plausible accounts of the main puzzle, Baum would be able to take his developmental explanation as a serious hypothesis to be tested. But how might he test a hypothesis derived from Eriksonian theory? Presumably, it would be necessary to gather data that would illuminate Latham's unconscious motivations for his actions—the sorts of data accessible to a psychoanalyst who saw the patient regularly over a long period of time. Baum is cut off from this source of data, however, by his decision to remain in the role of a distanced observer. In this sense, I think it is fair to say that his commitments to underlying story and theoretical perspective are in conflict with the research approach he has chosen to adopt. They generate the sorts of hypotheses he is unable to test so long as he remains within his chosen research role.

Consultation as a Research Method

Larry Hirschhorn also draws on psychoanalytic theory—in his case, the theories of the Tavistock school that adapted the views of Melanie Klein and D. W. Winnicott to the study of organizational dynamics. Armed with this theoretical perspective, Hirschhorn constructs coherent, internally consistent stories about the ways in which the mental lives of individuals are reflected in the configurations of their social worlds. He explains, in his case study, how individuals' unconscious ambivalence toward authority conditions the patterns of a group's relations with an authority figure.

Important consequences follow from the fact that Hirschhorn formulates his puzzles and frames his interpretations of them in the context of his role as a consultant. His approach is, in effect, to understand an organizational world by trying to change it. His consulting interventions may function as exploratory experiments that generate hypotheses, or they may serve to test hypotheses. But they must also serve the purpose of *helping* his clients. Thus Hirschhorn must continually try to figure out what is going on in an organization so that he can design useful interventions, which will also function as tests of his conjectures. Because research and intervention are inseparable components of Hirschhorn's practice, he must conduct his exercises in Tavistockian interpretation "on the fly." And, indeed, it seems to me that he demonstrates considerable virtuosity in this process.

How does Hirschhorn deal with the question of the validity of his interpretations? He employs three criteria. Is the explanation plausible and coherent in its own terms? Is it consistent with his preferred theoretical framework? And does it "work"? The first two criteria seem to me to be evident from inspection of the interpretations themselves; the third Hirschhorn discusses explicitly. He notes on several occasions that his interpretations seemed convincing to his listeners, served to relieve the tension, or paved the way for some useful change in practice. But he does not explicitly consider alternate accounts of the phenomena he tries to explain. For, as he argued in our working sessions, a consultant-researcher who tried to entertain alternate causal stories would face the dilemma of testing them in real time, when he is also called upon to act.

This would require an extraordinary ability to manage complexity under stress. Still, some of us countered, it might be possible to meet this challenge if the consultant were prepared to open up alternate causal stories in the client's presence. But this strategy would shift the researcher's approach toward collaborative self-study, an approach Hirschhorn has so far chosen not to adopt.

One might suppose, to compound the problem, that, in any situation, the critical analysis of alternative accounts of behavior based on theories of unconscious inner life would demand understandings and skills that lie beyond the reach of most clients. I do not know whether Hirschhorn would say this or not. In our workshop discussions, however, he did make the following argument: Granted that alternate explanations of organizational behavior might be as plausible as the one adopted by the consultant, the overriding requirement is that the consultant's explanation provide the basis for an intervention that works, which means that it must be invested with *authority*, which means, in turn, that it must be perceived by the clients as internally consistent.

While this argument is certainly an understandable one, it has a circular twist, pivoting, as it does, on the view that a consultant's authority depends on advocacy of a single, self-consistent (presumably correct) causal story. An alternative view would make the consultant's authority dependent on a demonstrated ability to put ideas to the test, learn under fire and, if necessary, undergo a change of mind. And this view would allow a consultant to open up alternate accounts of the situation in the course of an intervention—a move that would change both the research approach and, in all likelihood, the underlying story.

Participatory Action Research

Both Greenwood and Newberg try to construct stories that answer questions about the qualities of organizational settings they have chosen to study. In Fagor, for example, have the members become apathetic? How are we to explain the contrasting behavior and attitudes of members in the general assembly and on the shopfloor? In Newberg's regional school system, what are the causes of the dropout rate? What makes the key transition points between grade levels problematic?

Both of these researchers (in contrast to Hirschhorn) try to answer their questions in concert with their participants. Greenwood, for example, draws Fagor managers into the role of researchers on organizational practice, deliberately abandoning the expert's role in the belief, as he tells us, that "every literate person can do good fieldwork."

Both Greenwood and Newberg deal directly with multiple views of organizational reality, but in their cases it is the participants who propose different causal stories. Greenwood and Newberg deal with contending claims to truth by collecting the storytellers and allowing them to come into mutual confrontation in face-to-face meetings. For example, the "positive" and "negative" snippets quoted at the beginning of Greenwood's chapter convey the members' different perceptions of the state of the Fagor cooperative, all bearing on the question, "Are we really in trouble?" Then, in the roundtable discussions conducted in the second stage of the project, the participants debate their discordant views. Greenwood is not very much interested in determining which of the contending views comes closest to the truth. Instead, he calls attention to the process of debate itself, which he takes as evidence of there being a healthy, pluralistic democracy at work in Fagor. Certainly, he concludes, the workers are not apathetic. Certainly, as well, the cooperative is not in deep trouble if the values of pluralism and democratic debate, so much honored by the founder, are alive in the organization.

In Newberg's study, the various actors in the school system begin by telling different causal stories of the dropout phenomenon according to their parochial, blame-oriented biases. Some high school teachers deplore "social promotions" in the earlier grades. Some elementary school teachers criticize the high school's failure to provide an atmosphere of intimacy and support. In the early stages of his action research project, Newberg brings these stories into collision with each other. Subsequently, as the result of cross-grade visits, exchange of views, and joint inquiry, the participants begin to see their earlier stories as biased or partial accounts. They begin to construct a fuller, more systemic view of the dropout phenomenon in which all parties are seen as playing some causal role, and the dysfunctions of the school system begin to look as though they might be subject to influence by the participants' collective action.

The theoretical constructs adopted by these practitioners of participatory action research lend themselves particularly well to the practitioners' chosen ways of handling conflicting stories of organizational reality. Based as they are on the participants' commonsense ideas, these constructs pose no great obstacle to the participants' collective inquiry. Imagine, by way of contrast, how the psychoanalytic, Piagetian, or Model II perspectives of Hirschhorn, Bamberger, or Putnam, respectively, might fare in Greenwood's roundtables or Newberg's workshops.

Collaborative Self-Studies

In all forms of intervention research, and especially in collaborative self-studies, reflection-in-action is centrally important to the process of bringing to the surface and testing alternate accounts of reality. It may

take the form of an attempt to build a superordinate story that incorporates the multiplicity of conflicting stories and allows you, as Putnam
suggested in our discussions, to empathize with all those who are actors
in the situation. Or reflection-in-action may consist in inventing a new
story that explains a surprising event and derives from it the design of
a new intervention. This happens, for example, in Mattingly's account
of the occupational therapist who invents a way of hooking on to the
fact that her patient wants to comb his hair, and in Erickson and
MacKinnon's essay where Colin seizes on a student's comment to help
her discover what batteries-and-bulbs circuit produces the brightest
light.

These researchers, or researcher/practitioners, discover a mismatch
between the particular story they are telling (or living out) and the surprising reality at hand. The effect is to create an opportunity, and a demand, for *reflection-in-action*. One must make some new sense of the
situation in order to incorporate the surprising event, the backtalk, or
the multiple plausible stories one has discovered. And one must then
test the new sense by an on-the-spot experiment, as Dan Bar-On sometimes at a crucial moment in an interview invents a new and telling
question, or as Bamberger explores with her group of teachers the implicit ideas they bring to their understandings of the hands-on tasks,
how they construct *revolution and rotation* and *variable*. As Bar-On
pointed out in our workshop discussions, proposals Bamberger puts to
the teachers *are ones they can alter*. She offers speculative interpretations
based on their observations so as to stimulate their thinking, and she
presents these as material for the teachers' further examination and
change.

Similarly, when Mattingly joins her occupational therapists in examining their videotapes, she helps them identify the stories they live
out with their patients, noting how they reflect-in-action in response to
surprises they encounter when their stories seem ill matched to the patients' situations, when the stories they thought they were in turn out
not to be the ones they are in after all. She helps the occupational therapists discover, at times, that patients can have stories of their own, just
as Bamberger and Briggs repeatedly discover that their students have
stories of their own.

Of all the authors of collaborative self-studies, Lanzara is perhaps
most explicitly concerned with the problem of validity posed by the existence of multiple and shifting stories, and his research approach reflects this concern. His version of collaborative self-study depends on
the discovery of the *Rashomon* phenomenon, that is, of multiple stories
of reality, each of which is internally compelling in its own terms but

incompatible with all the others. First, Lanzara points out, one builds up the stories as data. Then one discovers discrepancies among them. And finally, one takes these discrepancies as objects of inquiry and puzzles to be explored. When the participants take issue with the researcher's stories, he must remain open to their backtalk, for he thereby gains access to potentially disconfirming data.

In Lanzara's case, the researcher's reflection-in-action consists in *making himself into a subject.* As he puzzles over the Music Faculty's rejection of his first story of the "demo," he asks himself how he came to generate that story. His reflections lead him first to revise it and then, when the whole process repeats itself, to question the wisdom of revision.

In our workshop discussion of this example, Putnam pointed to a danger inherent in accepting a subject's backtalk uncritically. He asked, "What if the faculty member denied his hostility to the new music curriculum in order to cover it up?" Lanzara felt that it would have been out of place for him to challenge the faculty member's motives and that such a confrontation might have disrupted their dialogue.

This exchange led us to question the interpersonal competencies essential to a collaborative self-study. Could a researcher challenge his partner's revision of a story without undermining their collaboration? He would have to be able to explore the understandings that informed his partner's reconstruction of past events while remaining skeptical of it, challenge it without being responsible for making his partner defensive. He would have to be able to "affirm without dogmatism and confront without hostility," as Raymond M. Hainer once put it (1968, p. 36). Capabilities such as these are examples of what Chris Argyris and I have called "Model II competence" (Argyris & Schön, 1974). In a collaborative self-study, in Putnam's view and in my own, the researcher needs not only to exhibit these sorts of competence but also to help his co-researchers acquire them. This is a tall order. But it may be justified when the researcher is also an intervenor, because the competencies essential to reliable research also serve the purposes of intervention.

THE RESEARCHER'S PARADOXICAL STANCE

In a collaborative self-study, a Hall of Mirrors unfolds. The researcher wants to conduct with her partner a collaborative inquiry into the ways of thinking, knowing, and understanding implicit in their patterns of action. She intends, at least in part, to help them learn to conduct this sort of inquiry for themselves; she must therefore be able to live out with them what she wants them to learn to do. So she is personally on the line in a special way.

Collaborative self-study demands what community psychiatrist Leonard Duhl has called an "existential use of the self." Abandoning the expert role of spectator/manipulator, the researcher presents himself to his subjects as a person who seeks to enter into their experience of practice. He says to them, in effect, "I join you, I try to put myself in your shoes, I try to experience what you are experiencing." As Bar-On pointed out in our discussions, this takes time. Many of our cases are the products of researchers who have been willing to stay with social situations long enough, delving into them deeply enough, to get just such a feeling for their subjects' experience. But as the researcher asks his subjects to make themselves vulnerable to him, so he must make himself vulnerable to them. He tries to remain fully present as a person. As Emerson once spoke of farmers as "men farming," so the researcher sees himself as a person inquiring.

At the same time, the researcher must recognize that there are limits to reciprocal empathy and vulnerability, limits rooted in a legitimate demand for a certain kind of objectivity and consistency. He and his readers and co-researchers want to believe that his findings will not consist merely of thoughts and feelings he happens to have experienced or gained through empathy with his subjects. What is demanded of him, in addition, is that he filter these materials through his own critical intelligence, making use of understandings that may go beyond those entertained by his subjects at any particular moment.

The researcher must try to make her own understandings problematic to herself, subjecting them to the test of her collaborators' backtalk, which, on the other hand, she must also challenge. So, for example, Bamberger seems to say to the teachers with whom she works, "I am with you, I am one of you, and I allow myself to be confused when you are confused, which sometimes takes very little effort!" As she pointed out in our discussions, the slightest hint of a superior attitude on her part and her teachers would head for the hills. Yet at the same time, she finds that she has ideas about their shared experience that they have probably not yet entertained, and in another corner of her mind she monitors the process in which she joins them; for example, she watches for moments when seeing a resemblance might trigger the emergence of a not-yet-articulated idea, or when their conversation might serve as a prototype of the sorts of conversations they may learn to conduct with their students. The reflective turn calls for a paradoxical stance toward many things, and especially toward the whole question of objectivity.

The researcher must recognize, as Mattingly pointed out, that there is no given, preobjectified state of affairs waiting to be uncovered through inquiry. All research findings are someone's constructions of reality. And yet the researcher must strive to test her constructions in the situation by bringing to the surface, juxtaposing, and discriminating among alternate accounts of that reality. If there is a problem with the objectivist stance, it does not lie in the striving for objectivity but rather, as Dan Bar-On observed, in the belief that it is possible to establish the validity of a claim to objective truth with finality.

A LAST WORD

I have argued that to take the reflective turn is not only to "give practitioners reason" but to recognize that any particular account of their reasoning is an observer's construction that may be mistaken or radically incomplete. The researcher who would "give reason" has an obligation to turn his thought back on itself, to become aware of his own underlying stories, to search out possible sources of blindness and bias in his own ways of making sense of the reality he has observed. And he cannot do this unless he is prepared to entertain and test other ways of seeing his material.

Moreover, when the researcher is also an interventionist who views her subjects as clients or co-researchers, Popper's test of validity becomes a principle that constrains and guides intervention: The imperative of competitive resistance to refutation does double duty here as a restraint on the researcher's unilateral control of the situation. The sharing of control—a value held, I believe, by all the authors of these essays—demands a willingness to seek out and honor ways of seeing the situation that differ from one's own. At the same time, the value of striving after a never-to-be-finally-attained objectivity requires that the researcher seek to refute these alternate constructions of reality, along with her own, by means of such experiments as are feasible within the practice situation.

I have argued that the applicability of Popper's test of validity depends on a match between a researcher's chosen approach to research and the ontology of her underlying story. In our review of some of the different research approaches adopted by the authors, we have learned some things about the conditions under which such a match may be obtained. We have seen that the categories fundamental to a researcher's underlying story may not lend themselves to test through the conduct of a "pure" and distant study. A consultant/researcher may construe the requirements of workable intervention in such a way as to preclude bringing to the surface and testing alternate causal stories in real time. Where the subjects of research are also co-researchers, the categories of an underlying story must be ones the participants can understand and use in making and testing their own causal inferences. All forms of intervention research require reflection-in-action, at least in the conduct of on-the-spot experiments in the practice situation. And collaborative self-study places special demands on the researcher. It requires her to contribute to the creation of a behavioral world conducive to reciprocal reflection-in-action.

It is important, however, to recognize a limit to the applicability of Popper's test. Each of the case studies in this volume proceeds *from* some fundamental theoretical perspective *to* its instantiation in a causal account of a practice situation. Within the framework of a theoretical perspective, causal accounts of practice phenomena are in some cases considered and put to the test. But the theoretical perspectives themselves are not subjected to the tests of critical analysis or experiment. Putnam, for example, considers alternate accounts of Paul's attempts at "action science" interventions but does not critically examine action science. Greenwood helps the participants in his study to consider and debate alternative views of the predicaments of the Fagor cooperative but does not seek alternatives to the theory of pluralist democracy within which he locates their debates.

Surely it is legitimate in a relatively brief practice study to forgo critical inquiry into one's own framework, to seek truth within a frame rather than about and across frames. Yet the very diversity of stories and perspectives underlying the essays in this volume provokes a further question. Can we say that one underlying story or frame is more adequate—more pertinent, more valid—than another? Or that certain underlying stories *ought* to be combined in order to create fuller, more adequate studies of practice—for example, studies of teaching and learning in schools? These questions are closely bound up with the issue of the generalizability of the findings of practice studies such as these. They seem to me to pertain not so much to individual studies as to families of studies, and to research programs and careers, in the course of which competent inquirers have been known on occasion to change their minds in a fundamental way. I shall not try to address these questions here. I would like to explore them in the context of empirical studies of the processes through which underlying stories and perspectives are sometimes transformed.

REFERENCES

Argyris, C., & Schön, D. A. (1974). *Theory in practice*. San Francisco: Jossey-Bass.
Hainer, R. M. (1968). Rationalism, pragmatism, and existentialism: Perceived but undiscovered multicultural problems. In M. W. Shelly & E. Glatt (Eds.), *The research society*. New York: Gordon & Breach.
Popper, K. (1968). *Conjectures and refutations*. New York: Harper & Row.

About the Contributors

JEANNE BAMBERGER is Professor of Music at the Massachusetts Institute of Technology. In addition to her music text, *The Art of Listening: Developing Musical Perception* (with Howard Brofsky; 1987), which is now in its fifth edition, she has written extensively on music cognition and musical development. Her most recent publication is *The Mind Behind the Musical Ear* (1990).

DAN BAR-ON is currently a senior lecturer in the Department of Behavioral Sciences at Ben-Gurion University of the Negev. He received his Ph.D. in psychology from the Hebrew University in Jerusalem and has worked as a therapist, O.D. consultant, and senior field psychologist for the Israel Defense Forces. He is the author of *Legacy of Silence: Encounters with Children of the Third Reich* (1989), which is based on his pioneering field research in Germany on the psychological and moral after-effects of the Holocaust on the children of the perpetrators.

HOWELL S. BAUM teaches organizational behavior and social planning at the University of Maryland's Institute for Urban Studies. He has a Ph.D. in city and regional planning from the University of California, Berkeley. A founding member of the International Society for the Psychoanalytic Study of Organizations, his writings include *Planners and Public Expectations* (1983), *The Invisible Bureaucracy: The Unconscious in Organizational Problem Solving* (1987), and *Organizational Membership: Personal Development in the Workplace* (1990).

D. JEAN CLANDININ is an associate professor at the University of Alberta in the Department of Elementary Education. She is a former teacher, counselor, and psychologist. She received her B.A. and M.A. from the University of Alberta and her Ph.D. from the University of Toronto. She is the author of *Classroom Practice: Teacher Images in Action* (1986) and (with F. Michael Connelly) *Teachers as Curriculum Planners: Narratives of Experience* (1988). She is currently working on a collaborative study of teacher education as narrative inquiry.

F. MICHAEL CONNELLY was educated at the University of Alberta, Canada; Teachers College, Columbia University; and the University of Chicago. He is also Director of the Joint Centre for Teacher Development at OISE and the Faculty of Education, University of Toronto. He taught secondary school in Alberta and held teaching positions at the Universities of Alberta, Illinois, and Chicago before coming to Toronto, where he is Professor of curriculum and teacher studies at the Ontario Institute for Studies in Education and the University of Toronto. He coordinates the Canadian component of the Second International Science Study, is editor of *Curriculum Review,* and is a member of the board of directors of the John Dewey Society for Education and Culture. He recently co-authored an Ontario government teacher-education policy paper. His research interest is in the study of teaching, and he is co-director, with D. Jean Clandinin, of a long-term study of teachers' personal practical knowledge. Drs. Connelly and Clandinin are co-authors of *Teachers as Curriculum Planners: Narratives of Experience* (1988), as well as numerous articles and chapters in contributed volumes. Dr. Connelly was the recipient of the 1987 Outstanding Canadian Curriculum Scholar Award of the Canadian Society for the Study of Education.

GAALEN ERICKSON's educational background includes a master's degree in chemistry from the University of Alberta and a doctorate in science from the University of British Columbia, where he currently teaches in the Department of Mathematics and Science Education. His writings have focused on identifying and representing students' intuitive reasoning about scientific concepts and examining the educational implications that follow from students' thinking seriously. These interests, combined with a concern for nurturing reflective practice in science educators, have led him to develop a collaborative network of school and university educators working together on action-research projects.

JOHN FORESTER is an associate professor in the Department of City and Regional Planning at Cornell University. He has recently published *Planning in the Face of Power* (1989) and, with Norman Krumhold, *Making Equity Work* (1990). He received his Ph.D. in planning from the University of California, Berkeley.

DAVYDD JAMES GREENWOOD is the John S. Knight Professor of International Studies and Director of the Center for International Studies at Cornell University. A graduate of Grinnell College, he received a Ph.D. in anthropology from the University of Pittsburgh. His work focuses on diverse dimensions of the political economy of development and ethnic conflict in the Spanish Basque Country. Recently, he co-directed a 3-year participatory action research study of the Fagor Cooperative Group in Mondragón. He has also written on biological determinist theories, the history of evolutionism, and medical anthropology. His books include *Unrewarding Wealth: The Commercialization and Collapse of Agriculture in a*

Spanish Basque Town (1976), *Nature, Culture, and Human History: A Bio-Cultural Introduction to Anthropology* (with William A. Stini; 1977), *The Taming of Evolution: The Persistence of Nonevolutionary Views in the Study of Humans* (1985), and *Culturas de FAGOR: Estudio antropológico de las cooperativas de Mondragón* (with José Luis González; 1990).

LARRY HIRSCHHORN conducts his consulting and research practice as a multidisciplinary thinker and practitioner. He has a Ph.D. in economics from the Massachusetts Institute of Technology and has worked intensively in the fields of organizational renewal and development. He is a recognized expert on the problems and prospects of manufacturing plant modernization and has frequently helped executive teams and professional partnerships assess their working relationships. In additional to numerous articles on organizational renewal and economic development, he is the author of *Beyond Mechanization: Work and Technology in a Post-Industrial Age* (1984), *The Workplace Within: Psychodynamics of Organizational Life* (1988), and *Managing in the New Team Environment: Skills, Tools, and Methods* (1990).

GIOVAN FRANCESCO LANZARA is Associate Professor of Organizational Theory at the University of Bologna, Italy. Since receiving a doctorate in civil engineering from the University of Pisa and a master's in urban design from Harvard, he has pursued an "off-the-track" research career, exploring the fields of systems analysis, design theory and practice, organizational behavior, and learning, and is the author or co-author of numerous articles in these areas.

ALLAN M. MacKINNON completed a master's degree in education at the University of Calgary and a doctorate in science education at the University of British Columbia. His research interests have been primarily directed toward identifying the nature of the process whereby beginning teachers are encouraged to reflect upon their practice and toward documenting the conditions that seem to nurture this type of reflection. He is currently teaching at Simon Fraser University.

CHERYL MATTINGLY holds a joint appointment as Assistant Professor in the Department of Occupational Therapy at the University of Illinois at Chicago and Research Fellow in the Department of Social Medicine at Harvard University. Her research over the past ten years has been an investigation of narrative as a vehicle by which professionals make sense of their work experience. She is currently writing a book on the role of narrative in guiding therapeutic interventions, using occupational therapists as case examples. She received her doctorate in anthropology and urban studies from the Massachusetts Institute of Technology.

NORMAN NEWBERG is an adjunct associate professor in the Graduate

School of Education of the University of Pennsylvania and a consultant working in Canada, Israel, Belgium, and throughout the United States. Using an action-research methodology, he works with both public and private schools focusing on ways to restructure their systems of governance, instructional decision making, and the roles of board members, faculty, and administration. A graduate of Temple University, he received his M.A. from the University of Illinois and his Ph.D. from the University of California. He has conducted numerous research studies and is the recipient of an Alfred North Whitehead Fellowship at Harvard, as well as a Ford Foundation Fellowship.

MALCOLM PARLETT is an organizational consultant and Gestalt psychotherapist, with a background in educational program evaluation and psychological research. He received his Ph.D. from Cambridge University. He is the originator of "illuminative evaluation" and has written numerous papers and reports. His current writings are in developing Gestalt theory for applications beyond therapy.

ROBERT PUTNAM is a consultant, educator, and researcher whose work focuses on helping practitioners learn to promote individual and organizational learning and on helping researchers develop skill in combining research with intervention. He has been on the faculty of Harvard University as an instructor on education. He is co-author, with Chris Argyris and Diana McLain Smith, of *Action Science* (1985). He received an A.B. in political science from Syracuse University and an Ed.M. and Ed.D. in counseling and consulting psychology from Harvard University. He is a partner in Action Design Associates, a consulting firm specializing in educating interventionists.

DONALD A. SCHÖN is currently Ford Professor of Urban Studies and Education at the Massachusetts Institute of Technology. He is the author of *The Reflective Practitioner* (1983) and *Educating the Reflective Practitioner* (1987). He received a B.A. from Yale and an M.A. and Ph.D. from Harvard, all in philosophy.

Index

R